THE PLAGUE OF WAR

Ancient Warfare and Civilization

SERIES EDITORS:

RICHARD ALSTON ROBIN WATERFIELD

In this series, leading historians offer compelling new narratives of the armed conflicts that shaped and reshaped the classical world, from the wars of Archaic Greece to the fall of the Roman Empire and the Arab conquests.

Dividing the Spoils
The War for Alexander the Great's Empire
Robin Waterfield

By the Spear
Philip II, Alexander the Great, and the Rise and Fall of the Macedonian Empire
Ian Worthington

Taken at the Flood
The Roman Conquest of Greece
Robin Waterfield

In God's Path
The Arab Conquests and the Creation of an Islamic Empire
Robert G. Hoyland

Mastering the West
Rome and Carthage at War
Dexter Hoyos

Rome's Revolution
Death of the Republic and Birth of the Empire
Richard Alston

The Plague of War
Athens, Sparta, and the Struggle for Ancient Greece
Jennifer T. Roberts

THE PLAGUE OF WAR

Athens, Sparta, and the Struggle for Ancient Greece

Jennifer T. Roberts

OXFORD
UNIVERSITY PRESS

OXFORD
UNIVERSITY PRESS

Oxford University Press is a department of the University of Oxford. It furthers the University's objective of excellence in research, scholarship, and education by publishing worldwide. Oxford is a registered trade mark of Oxford University Press in the UK and certain other countries.

Published in the United States of America by Oxford University Press
198 Madison Avenue, New York, NY 10016, United States of America.

Library of Congress Cataloging-in-Publication Data
Names: Roberts, Jennifer Tolbert, 1947– author.
Title: The plague of war : Athens, Sparta, and the struggle for ancient Greece / Jennifer T. Roberts.
Description: New York, NY : Oxford University Press, [2017] |
Includes bibliographical references and index.
Identifiers: LCCN 2016012098 (print) | LCCN 2016016368 (ebook) |
ISBN 9780199996643 (hardcover) | ISBN 9780199996650 (ebook) | ISBN 9780199996667 (ebook)
Subjects: LCSH: Greece—History—Peloponnesian War, 431–404 B.C. |
Greece—History—Peloponnesian War, 431–404 B.C.—Influence. |
Greece—History—Spartan and Theban Supremacies, 404–362 B.C. |
Athens (Greece)—History, Military. | Sparta (Extinct city)—History, Military. |
City-states—Greece—History. | Greece—History, Military—To 146 B.C.
Classification: LCC DF229.2 .R63 2017 (print) | LCC DF229.2 (ebook) |
DDC 938/.05—dc23
LC record available at https://lccn.loc.gov/2016012098

1 3 5 7 9 8 6 4 2

Printed by Edwards Brothers Malloy, United States of America

for my husband, Robert Lejeune,
who saw war close up as a child in France in the 1940s

and my father, Jack Tolbert,
who was seeing it just as frightfully as a soldier in the Pacific
at the same time

CONTENTS

LIST OF FIGURES AND MAPS

FIGURES

MAPS

PREFACE AND ACKNOWLEDGMENTS

I GREW UP IN a haunted house. The specter of war hung over my sister and me, for our father had been badly damaged by his experiences fighting in the Pacific as a captain in the US Army shortly before we were born. My mother, too, had served in the Pacific, in the Red Cross, and it was in the Pacific that my parents met and married, but my mother had not been in combat, and she had oddly warm associations with the war and the friendships she formed in wartime with people she would otherwise never have encountered. My mother's war was a good war, but my father's war was terrible, so much so that he spoke of it comparatively little, and I came to understand only fairly late in our time together why he had to take pills in the morning to get through the day—to understand that war was, as Thucydides said, a violent teacher. My father was courageous and determined—when he developed the dengue fever that deprived him of all his teeth and half his hearing, he doggedly refused to be sent home—but he was also sensitive. Noticing that he was terrified of choking, my sister, a psychotherapist, asked him toward the end of his life if he had any idea why. He told her how a young Japanese soldier barely out of his teens had come up behind him in the jungle one night and put a rifle across his windpipe. In the scuffle that followed, they both lost their weapons. "What did you do, Pop?" my sister asked. Tears rolling down his cheeks, my father replied, "I did what I had to do," leaving it to her to infer that he had put his hands around the neck of this boy who, as far as he knew, had never done anything wrong in his life, and squeezed until he was dead.

My father discouraged my attempts to broach the subject of war with him, and understandably I grew up afraid of it. It was in attempting to overcome this fear that in college I became fascinated by Thucydides' work, a fascination fostered by studying with the stellar Donald Kagan. It seemed to me to have considerable application to modern times, and it has seemed so to many others as well.

Thucydides tells us in the very first paragraph of his narrative that he undertook his history because he foresaw the magnitude of the war that had just broken out. Indeed, the conflict between Athens and Sparta has lost none of its epic dimension with the passing of time. Classicist Basil Gildersleeve, founder of the *American Journal of Philology*, published a famous essay on the American Civil War in the *Atlantic* in 1897 entitled "A Southerner in the Peloponnesian War."[1] Among later writers, life in the bipolar universe of the Cold War focused much attention on the Peloponnesian War. During the Korean War *Life* magazine ran a series of articles cautioning Americans about the catastrophe that might attend on ignoring the lessons of the Hellenic past. Robert Campbell's series "How a Democracy Died" was designed for high drama, beginning with an account of deadly powers facing one another across the 38th parallel (the border between North and South Korea). The powers in question, however, soon proved to be the superpowers of fifth-century Greece rather than any nations of his own era, for the 38th parallel also passes through Sicily, Euboea, and the northern suburbs of Athens. Despite its democratic pretensions, Campbell lamented, Athens ultimately "failed to grasp the most elemental principles about the free association of nations" and instead substituted the rule of force for the "bond of principle."[2]

The war in Vietnam sparked analogies with ancient imperialism in general and the Sicilian expedition in particular among teachers, scholars, journalists, and many other Americans who had studied classical history. The role of such parallels in the college classroom was underlined by Walter Karp, a contributing editor to *Harper's*, in an essay in the magazine entitled "The Two Thousand Years' War: Thucydides in the Cold

1. *Atlantic* 80 (1897): 330–42.
2. *Life* 30 (1 January 1951): 96.

War" that appeared in March 1981. Reminiscing about his college days in the 1950s, when his Humanities 1 professor proposed to the students an analogy between the Peloponnesian War and the newly named Cold War, Karp reported that parallels immediately leapt to the eye, with authoritarian Sparta evoking the Soviet Union and democratic Athens America. Returning to Thucydides a generation later, Karp was struck by the deepening of the parallel between fifth-century Athens and the United States of his own time, as he perceived analogies with the Athenians' overconfidence after the Spartan surrender at Sphacteria both in Harry Truman's attempt to conquer North Korea after MacArthur's victory at Inchon and in John F. Kennedy's ripeness for a war in Vietnam after his triumph over Khrushchev in the Cuban missile crisis. Now in the twenty-first century some, like strategy consultant Stefan Haid, in search of classical parallels, have their eyes fixed on the Middle East, comparing American intervention there with the Athenians' expedition to Sicily, attributing both to a mixture of greed, fear, and the quest for glory, and warning of the consequences of overstretched resources and ignorance of the faraway land in question.[3] And then there is the newly dubbed menace, the "Thucydides trap." This phrase, coined by Graham Allison of the Kennedy School at Harvard University, refers to Thucydides' claim that the Peloponnesian War was caused by the growth of Athens, a new power, and the fear this inspired in Sparta, an existing power, and is used to justify dire warnings about impending conflict between the United States and China.

In 1995 my friend Barry Strauss from Cornell University, a passionate student of war and peace, invited me to participate in an extraordinary conference at the Woodrow Wilson International Center for Scholars in Washington, DC. This gathering brought together ancient and modern historians to explore the connection between war and democracy by studying the Korean War and the Peloponnesian War in a comparative context.[4] As scholars from Korea spoke of wartime atrocities

3. S. Haid, "Why President Obama Should Read Thucydides," *DIAS-Analysis* 34 (2008): 1–10.

4. The proceedings of this conference appear in D. S. McCann and B. S. Strauss, eds., *War and Democracy: A Comparative Study of the Korean War and the Peloponnesian War* (Armonk, NY: M. E. Sharpe, 2001).

very similar to those recounted by Thucydides and Xenophon, tears fell and silence came over the room. To survive in this world, we seek to numb ourselves to real history, but if we read carefully the surviving accounts of the Peloponnesian War, we find that there is much to weep over in this long-ago war as well, a war in which entire cities were obliterated from the face of the earth. In 2000 my colleague in the Association of Ancient Historians Lawrence Tritle, a Greek historian who served in Vietnam, used that other modern war as a touchstone to explore the nature of war and violence in human life in parallel to the Peloponnesian War in his book *From Melos to My Lai: A Study in Violence, Culture, and Survival.*[5]

American statesmen have also sought guidance in studying the epic conflict between Athens and Sparta. In 1919 Woodrow Wilson himself re-read Thucydides' *History* on his voyage across the Atlantic en route to the Versailles Peace Conference. In 1947 US Secretary of State George Marshall, speaking at Princeton, declared, "I doubt seriously whether a man can think with full wisdom and with deep convictions regarding certain of the basic international issues today who has not at least reviewed in his mind the period of the Peloponnesian War and the fall of Athens."[6] Journalist and political theorist Robert Kaplan carried Marshall's conviction into his own day, writing that "Thucydides is the surest guide to what we are likely to face in the early decades of the twenty-first century."[7]

Such thinkers would do well to read on in the less analytical Xenophon, Diodorus, and Plutarch to learn how the story continued past the death of the great master, and indeed past 404—to read about the bloody Thirty, the persistent Conon, the inexorable Agesilaus, the shifting alliances of the Greek city-states, the brilliant Epaminondas, and the final blow dealt the Spartans on the field of Leuctra. Great thinker that he was, it is time that Thucydides was uncoupled from the history of the Peloponnesian War. The march of folly that was this seemingly unending war has much more

5. London: Routledge.

6. See his speech of February 22 in the *Department of State Bulletin* 16, 391.

7. R. Kaplan, *Warrior Politics: Why Leadership Demands a Pagan Ethos* (New York: Random House, 2002), 22.

to tell us if we study it as it continued to shape the history of the Greek city-states throughout the fourth century.

In the creation of this narrative I have received invaluable assistance from many quarters. Plainly anyone who writes about the Peloponnesian War after studying with Donald Kagan owes him an enormous debt. At Oxford University Press Stefan Vranka provided constant guidance and series editor Robin Waterfield offered frequent challenges to my claims that sometimes drove me to distraction but made this a far better book. Sarah Svendsen at Oxford put up with a great deal from me in the way of technological idiocy, and I deeply appreciate her endless patience. Paul Cartledge, A. G. Leventis Professor of Greek Culture Emeritus at Clare College, University of Cambridge, read the manuscript with painstaking care and provided me with abundant comments at a time when he had much else to do, and I shall be forever grateful for his deep fund of knowledge, boundless energy, and eagle eye (none of which implies endorsement of all the arguments advanced herein). The City College of New York was kind enough to grant me a sabbatical leave in 2013–14 to conduct the research that became the foundation for this book and to provide a grant that covered the cost of some permissions. I am most grateful to Larry Tritle for permission to reproduce his photograph of the remains of the Piraeus walls that appears as Figure 14. I am greatly indebted to my old (but ever young) classmate John Hale, whose keen military mind was the genius behind maps 6, 10, and 11. As always, Nickolas Pappas of the City University of New York gave more than generously of his time in discussing Socrates and Plato with me. Walter Blanco, also of CUNY, read the entire manuscript and uncovered numerous ambiguities and infelicities, not to mention factual errors. Donald Lateiner, John R. Wright Professor Emeritus of Humanities-Classics at Ohio Wesleyan University, offered his customary insight into several of the issues raised by Thucydides' narrative. Carlos Riobò, chair of the Department of Classical and Modern Languages and Literatures at the City College of New York, has always strived to make my life easier while I applied myself to finishing the manuscript, and I am greatly indebted to him for his support. Dee Clayman, Executive Officer of the Department of Classics at the City University of New York Graduate Center, was kind enough to assign me a graduate seminar in Thucydides during the writing of this book during which my students taught me a great deal that expanded my understanding of Greek history. Bryce and Edith M. Bowmar Professor in Humanistic Studies at Cornell University Barry Strauss, a fellow student of war and peace and a friend of many decades, has encouraged my interest in the Peloponnesian War in many ways. Among the co-authors of *Ancient Greece: A Political, Social, and Cultural History,* Stanley Burstein, Professor Emeritus of History at the California State University at Los Angeles, gave guidance in numerous areas of ambiguity, and David Tandy, Distinguished Professor of Humanities Emeritus at the University of Tennessee at Knoxville, shared his opinions about the early period of Athenian democracy in an ongoing email exchange; Sarah Pomeroy, Distinguished Professor of History and Classics Emerita at Hunter College and the City University of New York Graduate Center generously fielded email queries about topics as different as the location of Pythagorean communities and the economic situation of Spartan daughters. All of them kindly gave permission for the adaptation of a few passages from *Ancient Greece.* During much of the time I was writing this book I was also privileged to direct my student Nicholas Cross's dissertation *Interstate Alliances in the Fourth-Century BCE Greek World: A Socio-Cultural Perspective,* and I am most grateful to Nick for enriching my understanding of this time period through his work.

Laura Kogel, Istar Schwager, and Debi Unger offered much-needed support along the way. As always, the insights of my wise sister Page Tolbert have been invaluable. Without the steadying hand and sage advice of Jeff Halpern, it is difficult to see how this manuscript would have been brought to completion. My comrades at arms in the Association of Ancient Historians have always provided a welcome structure for my scholarly life. As always, my students at the City College of New York and City University of New York Graduate Center have been a source of inspiration and renewal. My witty and articulate son Chris Roberts and many enchanting grandchildren scattered around the globe have always kept me aware of the world beyond the study. Above all, I am indebted to my husband, whose warm smile kept me going during the many months it took to get this manuscript off my desk.

Naturally my confidants and partners in crime bear no responsibility for any inanities that remain.

A NOTE ON SOURCES

Our understanding of the ancient past is invariably grounded in a pastiche of written texts and physical remains. Historical writings, literary works, buildings, artifacts, tombs, inscriptions as well as the very soil itself help us form a picture of the world we have lost. In understanding the relations among the Greek states between the Persian Wars and 411 BC, our sources are primarily written, sustained texts backed up by inscriptions, and a unique role is played by the historian Thucydides, whose magisterial history of the Atheno-Peloponnesian War (or, as it has been Athenocentrically known, the Peloponnesian War) and the events leading up to it has left a stamp on our impression of that period that cannot easily be undone by the accounts of any other writer or by the contradictory evidence of inscriptions or physical remains. A rich man born around 458 into the illustrious Philaid clan to which Miltiades, hero of the Battle of Marathon, also belonged, Thucydides lived to see the end of the war and to develop ideas of it as a unit, though he may have written different portions of his work at different times, inserting observations in hindsight at key moments. As an event in world history, the Peloponnesian War is very much Thucydides' war; without him, it would be simply a miserable series of battles, one thing after another, hopes and fears, successes and failures.

Indubitably the many speeches included in Thucydides' narrative pose a problem for the modern historian. Ancient historians both

Greek and Roman sprinkled their works quite liberally with speeches, many of which they could not possibly have known very much about. In some cases, we must be very skeptical indeed—as, for example, when Thucydides' predecessor Herodotus reports conversations that took place in the royal bedchambers of Persian kings and queens. In other cases, it seems reasonable to take a more balanced view. Thucydides was present at many of the speeches given in the Athenian assembly, and he also spoke with many Greeks on both sides of the war after his exile. I have therefore chosen to take his speeches seriously as reasonably accurate accounts of what was said rather than literary compositions of his own designed to make points about the human condition. Plainly it is easier to place some speeches in this category than others: the speeches of the Corcyraeans and the Corinthians before the Athenian assembly, for example, are much more likely to be historically accurate than the conversation ascribed to the Athenians and the Melians on the island of Melos.

Thucydides was not only a participant in the war; he was a hard thinker who saw it through until what looked to most people alive at the time like the end, in 404, though we cannot know if he finished writing up the whole time span from the war's outbreak until that time. If he did, the manuscript does not survive. His account breaks off in 411, from which point we become dependent on Xenophon's *Hellenica*, eked out, of course, by other works such as Diodorus's *Library of History*, Plutarch's various *Lives*, the speeches of Athenian orators, inscriptions, and the relevant portions of the anonymous papyrus found at Oxyrhynchus in Egypt known as the *Hellenica Oxyrhynchia*, composed at some time between 387/6 and 346.

Xenophon was an Athenian soldier and man of letters who extended the tale of warfare among the Greek states down to 362 BC in his *Hellenica* and also wrote up the story of those who fought with Prince Cyrus in Asia in his *Anabasis*. He was not keen on his native Athens. He knew and admired Socrates, but he also knew and admired the Spartan king Agesilaus, whose biography he wrote, and he wound up exiled by the irate Athenians and forced to seek asylum in Sparta. The author of works on many topics, he lacked Thucydides' keen powers of analysis, although many have been charmed by the lively storytelling in the *Anabasis*, on which countless generations of intermediate Greek students have cut their teeth, and his *Constitution of the Lacedaemonians* is our most reliable (or least unreliable) source for Spartan institutions during the fifth and fourth centuries, since Plutarch, who wrote so much about Sparta, followed him by several centuries. (The words "Spartans" and "Lacedaemonians" were often used interchangeably in antiquity, although "Lacedaemonians" sometimes embraced non-Spartan inhabitants of Spartan territory who fought for Sparta but were not Spartan citizens.) Much Attic (Athenian) oratory survives, although a great deal is lost. Most of it is the work of native Athenians, although there are some important speeches by the metic (resident alien) Lysias (c. 445–c. 380), who had immigrated to Athens from Syracuse in Sicily. In his long life Isocrates (436–338) wrote numerous speeches on political topics. The speeches of Andocides (c. 440–c. 390) *On the Mysteries* and *On the Peace* are particularly valuable to our understanding of two important events in Athens.

Quasi-primary sources also survive in the form of authors who derived their material from contemporary sources that are lost to us today. Diodorus of Sicily, for example, composed his *Library of History* between around 60 and 30 BC covering a wide span of history, beginning with the mythological period before the fall of Troy and going down to his own time. Much is lost, but the portions dealing with fifth- and fourth-century Greece survive, although they are not as full as those of Thucydides or Xenophon. His use of the term "library" reflects his awareness that he was drawing on the work of earlier authors who had lived closer to the events he was describing, such as the fourth-century historian Ephorus from Aeolian Cyme, whose work we no longer have, and the Sicilian Timaeus of Tauromenium (Taormina) (c. 345–c. 250 BC), whose work does survive in fragments and was a valuable source for Sicilian history.

The vast output of Plutarch of Chaeronea (c. AD 46—AD 120), who wrote when Greece had come under the domination of Rome, also casts light on Greek history during the fifth and fourth centuries. Among his other writings, Plutarch left behind him biographies of Greek and

Roman politicians and military men now popularly known as the *Parallel Lives*, as he linked them in pairs, one Greek to one Roman. His lives of Themistocles, Cimon, Pericles, Nicias, Alcibiades, Lysander, Pelopidas, and Agesilaus are particularly helpful, as is his biography of the Persian king Artaxerxes II. A large body of his work is also classified as *Moralia*, or "Moral Essays," which includes notable and characteristic sayings of Spartans. Although several centuries divided Plutarch from classical Greece, he had access to many sources we lack today; he also spent time in Athens and observed it as it then was. It is for this reason we are fortunate that his work survives. On the other hand, his interest was primarily in biography and character; he was not an astute political analyst, nor was he always a good judge of the comparative merits of his sources.

Attic drama is valuable as well. While we do not always know the precise relationship between a Greek play and the historical background against which it was composed and produced, we would be much the poorer without the tragedies of Sophocles (c. 496–406) and Euripides (c. 480–406) and, in particular, the comedies of Aristophanes (c. 446–c. 386), whose strong opposition to the Peloponnesian War was evident throughout his work, particularly in his *Acharnians, Peace*, and *Lysistrata* and to a later extent his *Assemblywomen* and *Wealth*. A. W. Gomme includes a close scholarly discussion of the non-Thucydidean sources for the Peloponnesian War in the first volume of his *Historical Commentary on Thucydides* (29–84).

Translations from Herodotus and Thucydides in this work are by Walter Blanco from the Norton Critical Editions cited in the footnotes and bibliography. All other translations from the Greek are my own.

TIMELINE

Slashed dates sometimes appear because Greek calendars did not begin on January 1. The Attic calendar, for example, went from summer to summer.

490	Darius's forces defeated at Battle of Marathon
480–479	Battles of Thermopylae, Artemisium, Salamis, Plataea, Mycale; Xerxes' forces expelled from Greece
477	Foundation of Delian League
c. 467	Cimon victorious at the Battle of the Eurymedon
464	Earthquake in Sparta followed by helot rebellion
461–460	Strain between Athens and Sparta intensifies; Ephialtes proposes democratic reforms in Athens and is assassinated; Pericles takes his place as leader of Athenian democrats; Megara defects from the Peloponnesian League to Athens; construction begins on Athenian Long Walls
458	Outbreak of "First Peloponnesian War"; Aeschylus's *Oresteia* trilogy (*Agamemnon, Libation Bearers, Eumenides*) produced
457	Battle of Tanagra, Battle of Oenophyta
454	Athenians move league treasury from Delos to Athens
447–432	Building of Parthenon at Athens
447	Death of Cleinias, Alcibiades' father, in battle; Alcibiades becomes ward of Pericles
447	Battle of Coronea

446	Revolt and recapture of Euboea
446/45	Thirty Years' Peace ends First Peloponnesian War and results in exile of Spartan king Pleistoanax
c. 441	Sophocles' *Antigone* produced at Athens
c. 440	Revolt and reconquest of Samos, Byzantium by Athens
435	Outbreak of hostilities between Corinth and Corcyra over Epidamnus
433/32?	Last of Megarian decrees enacted by Athenians; Athenians vote to accept Corcyra into their alliance; Battle of Sybota
432	Athenians lay siege to Potidaea; Sparta and its allies vote that the Athenians have broken the Thirty Years' Peace
432–431	Spartans send embassies to Athens seeking negotiations
431	Theban attack on Plataea sparks mobilization for war; Archidamus sends herald Melesippus to Athens in vain effort to avoid war
	First Peloponnesian invasion of Attica begins
	Pericles delivers funeral oration
431–422	Brasidas active on behalf of Sparta
430–426	Plague assails Athens (in two waves)
430	Pericles deposed from generalship and fined; Potidaea surrenders to Athens
429	Peloponnesians besiege Plataea
429	Pericles re-elected but dies of plague a few months later
427	Civil war in Corcyra; Mytilene revolts from Athenian Empire; Cleon already prominent at Athens; Plataeans surrender to Peloponnesians
427	Death of Archidamus, accession of Agis II; recall of Pleistoanax to Sparta;
427	Sojourn of Gorgias in Athens
426	Campaigns of Demosthenes in western Greece
425	Demosthenes and Cleon capture Spartans at Sphacteria off Pylos; Spartans sue for peace; Athenians refuse at urging of Cleon

424	Aristophanes' *Knights* produced; Congress of Gela in Sicily; Athenian generals in Sicily are impeached on return; Boeotian victory at Battle of Delium; Brasidas seizes Amphipolis, resulting in exile of Thucydides
423	One-year truce between Athens and Sparta; Aristophanes' *Clouds* produced
422	Brasidas and Cleon killed fighting at Amphipolis
421	Aristophanes' *Peace* produced; Peace of Nicias signed; Athens and Sparta sign alliance for fifty years; the Athenians obliterate Scione
419	Athens allies with Argos, Mantinea, and Elis; Alcibiades and Nicias are rivals at Athens
418	Peloponnesians defeat new alliance at Battle of Mantinea
416/15	Athenians besiege and destroy Melos
415	Euripides' *Trojan Women* produced; Athenians resolve to invade Sicily; scandals of mutilation of the herms and profanation of Eleusinian Mysteries rock Athens
415/14	Athenian expedition sails for Sicily; Alcibiades is recalled to Athens to stand trial on charges stemming from profanation of Mysteries but defects to Sparta; Spartans reopen war on Athens after the Athenians' Argive allies prompt it to attack Laconia
414	Athenians seize heights of Epipolae outside Syracuse; Gylippus arrives in Sicily
413	Agis occupies Decelea in Attica; Nicias asks for help, Demosthenes goes to his aid; Athenians suffer stunning defeat by Syracusans in Sicily; thousands die or are enslaved; generals Demosthenes and Nicias are executed; board of senior advisers established at Athens; Athens' allies begin to revolt; new phase of conflict in East, the "Ionian War," begins
412/11	Alcibiades defects from Sparta to Tissaphernes
411	Persians become involved in the war; Athenians decide to use the emergency cash reserve on the Acropolis

411	Athenians victorious at Battle of Cynossema; Aristophanes' *Lysistrata* produced; coup of Four Hundred takes place at Athens; Alcibiades abandons Persians, elected general at Samos; Four Hundred overthrown by "Five Thousand," who restore Alcibiades
410	Athens victorious at Battle of Cyzicus; "Five Thousand" overthrown, democracy resumes
409	Work on Erechtheum resumes at Athens
c. 409	Death of Pleistoanax in Sparta, accession of Pausanias
408	Athenians led by Alcibiades capture Chalcedon, Selymbria, Byzantium
407	Alcibiades returns to Athens, elected commander-in-chief; Cyrus allies with Lysander
406	Lysander defeats Antiochus at Notium; Alcibiades deposed and withdraws into exile; Callicratidas's Peloponnesian fleet destroyed at Arginusae; Athenians condemn and execute 6 of their 8 victorious generals; Spartans sue for peace; deaths of Euripides and Sophocles
405	Athenians allow themselves to be bottled up in the Hellespont by Lysander; he catches them unawares at Aegospotami and captures nearly the entire fleet, although Conon escapes
404	Starved into submission with their grain supply gone, Athens surrenders; the Long Walls are pulled down; Athens is forced to join the Peloponnesian League; Spartans refuse request of their allies to exterminate Athens by killing all the men and enslaving all the women and children; Lysander imposes oligarchic "decarchies" of ten men on cities throughout the Aegean but establishes a board of Thirty in Athens, who later establish a board of Ten in Piraeus; Plato's relative Critias is prominent among them; the Thirty commit many murders at Athens, confiscate property; Theramenes killed at Critias's instructions; Artaxerxes II succeeds Darius II as King of Persia

403	Thrasybulus in exile in Thebes mobilizes support to overthrow the Thirty; Critias is killed, the democrats retake the city with the help of the Spartan king Pausanias; an amnesty is arranged between the democratic and oligarchic parties
401–400	Xenophon's march with the mercenaries of Cyrus in Asia Minor that is written up as the *Anabasis*; Cyrus killed at Battle of Cunaxa in 401
c. 400	Death of Agis II, accession of Agesilaus II
399	Trial and death of Socrates
c. 398	Conspiracy of Cinadon at Sparta
396	Agesilaus sets out for Asia
395	Boeotia, Corinth, Athens, and Argos go to war with Sparta in Corinthian War; Lysander killed at Battle of Haliartus; Pausanias flees to Mantinea to avoid trial; succeeded by his son Agesipolis; Agesilaus defeats Tissaphernes at Battle of Sardis; Tissaphernes executed by Artaxerxes
394	Agesilaus is forced to return to Greece; Spartans victorious at the Battles of Nemea, Coronea; Conon leads Persian-Phoenician navy to victory at Battle of Cnidus and returns to Athens; Pharnabazus accompanies Conon to mainland Greece with money
392	Failed peace negotiations
388	Thrasybulus killed at Aspendus
387	Plato founds the Academy
387/86	New negotiations issue in the King's Peace
382	Phoebidas seizes Thebes for Sparta
380	King Agesipolis dies, succeeded by Cleombrotus
379	Pelopidas and other patriots retake Thebes with Athenian aid
378	Failed raid of Sphodrias angers Athenians; Sphodrias is acquitted at Sparta; Athens allies with Thebes against Sparta; Second Athenian Confederacy is launched
375	Common Peace established in Greece

371	Another Common Peace attempted but fails; King Cleombrotus marches against Thebes; Boeotians under Epaminondas and Pelopidas defeat Spartans at Battle of Leuctra, killing Cleombrotus
362	Epaminondas leads Thebans to victory at Mantinea over coalition of Spartans, Athenians, and others but is killed fighting
359	Philip II accedes to the Macedonian throne
338	Philip II of Macedon ends Greek freedom at Battle of Chaeronea

THE PLAGUE OF WAR

INTRODUCTION

In the summer of the year known to us today as 431 BC, thousands of soldiers from Sparta and its allies gathered at the isthmus of Corinth, the narrow strip of land that separated the Peloponnesus from the little state of Megara and the territory of Athens (see Map 1). It was with a heavy heart that the Spartan king surveyed the troops that had gathered there at his command, for his command was out of keeping with his desire. His recommendation to avoid or at least postpone war had been overridden by the majority of Spartan voters, and Sparta's allies in the Peloponnesian League were eager for blood. The king in question was Archidamus, son of Zeuxidamus, son of Leotychidas. Like other Spartan kings, he and his father and grandfather could trace their ancestry all the way back to the god Heracles. Archidamus was about seventy and had reigned for some forty years. But his ability to control foreign policy was circumscribed by the wishes of his fellow citizens and his allies. And so, despite his concern that Sparta did not have the money to fight wealthy Athens and his belief that it was better for the rivals to live in peace, he dutifully exhorted his army to march forward, assuring them that all Greece was counting on them to bring down the hated Athenian empire.

Yet no sooner had he finished his stirring talk than he dispatched an envoy named Melesippus to Athens to discover whether perhaps when the Athenians learned that a Peloponnesian army was already on the move they might be inclined to submit. After the Athenians turned Melesippus back with orders to be across the border by sundown, the

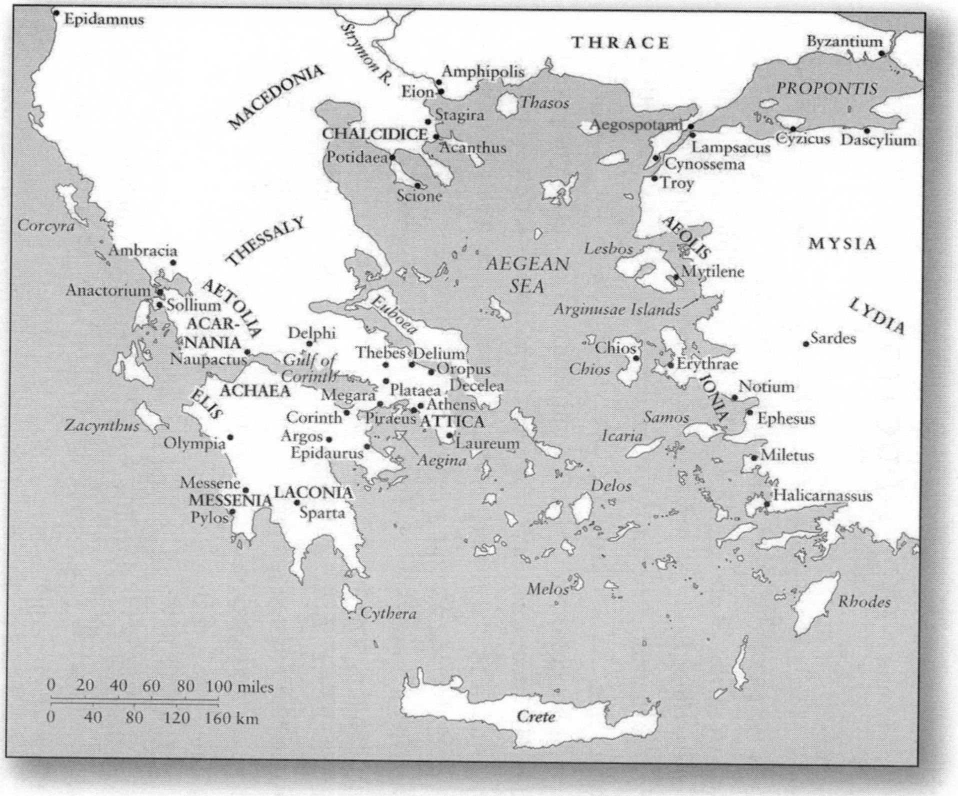

MAP 1

The Greek World, stretching from Epidamnus in the west to Byzantium in the east and including Crete in the south.

envoy proclaimed as he crossed over, "This day will mark the beginning of evils for the Greeks."[1] And so it was.

Still, Archidamus was not without hope of avoiding bloodshed. When he brought his army into Attica, the territory of Athens, he made for the fortress of Oenoe. This was an odd choice, since it took him to the northeast and away from Athens, which lay on the southerly route. The fortress, moreover, posed no threat to anyone, and it was almost impregnable. Hammering away at it was a losing cause, and it is hard not to believe that Archidamus's purpose in attacking it was to give the Athenians time to rethink their response. Only after considerable grumbling in the ranks did the reluctant king finally move his forces toward Athens and begin the war that had been forced upon him.

Meanwhile in Athens, Archidamus's opposite number Pericles, son of Xanthippus and Agariste (thus a member of the illustrious Alcmaeonid family on his mother's side), was having things very much his own way. It was ironic that Pericles should have been able to control policy in Athens more effectively than Archidamus could in Sparta, since not only was he no king, and unable to trace his lineage to any god, but he was not even the chief executive. Athens had no chief executive; rather, ultimate authority lay with its voluble assembly, which, unlike the assembly at Sparta, debated vigorously as well as voting. In terms of individual officers, the highest were the ten generals, and while Pericles had nine colleagues in that office, he was the one who had been held in the greatest esteem during the years leading up to the war, and it was his innovative policy that the Athenians were following while Archidamus and his Peloponnesians were marshalling their forces to invade Athens; it was in accordance with Pericles' novel strategy that they abandoned their beloved farms and huddled inside the so-called Long Walls built around the middle of the fifth century, counting on their imperial navy to bring in food from abroad. This plan, Pericles persuaded the Athenians, would work, and Pericles had

1. Thucydides 2. 12. 3. All quotations from Thucydides in this work are from *The Peloponnesian War: Norton Critical Edition*, edited by Jennifer Tolbert Roberts and Walter Blanco, translated by Walter Blanco. Copyright © 1998 by W. W. Norton & Company. Used by permission of W. W. Norton and Company, Inc. Another good edition, with ample and detailed maps, is R. B. Strassler, ed., *The Landmark Thucydides: A Comprehensive Guide to the Peloponnesian War*, trans. R. Crawley, revised (New York: Free Press [Simon & Schuster], 1996).

no ambivalence about the war whatsoever. Indeed, the war was his baby. Before the Spartans invaded the Attic countryside he took care to turn his own land over to the state, since as luck would have it he and Archidamus were what Greeks called "guest friends"—*xenoi*. This "guest friendship" *(xenia)* was a relationship passed down from one generation to the next between a man of one city and a man of another that placed them under obligations of mutual hospitality that were almost familial in nature, and it was a crucial building block of international relations in the Greek world. This is the relationship that provides a poignant scene in the *Iliad* when the Greek Diomedes and the Trojan ally Glaucus are on the verge of fighting but hold back on realizing that they have inherited a relationship of *xenia* from their ancestors; instead of going for one another's throats they exchange gifts, Glaucus being so excited to discover his guest friend that he gives him golden armor in exchange for bronze, "a hundred oxen's worth for that of nine."[2] Archidamus and Pericles probably inherited their *xenia* from the time when Archidamus's grandfather Leotychidas II and Pericles' father Xanthippus were sharing the command of the Greek fleet in 479 at the end of the Persian Wars. Fearing that Archidamus might feel the need to spare his land because of their *xenia*, Pericles made it public property before his old friend led the mighty army of the Peloponnesians into Attica. The existence of a relationship of *xenia* between the most powerful men in each leading state was symbolic of the full pathos of this war.

Athens and Sparta were each hegemonic states, that is, states that stood at the head of organizations of other states that were compelled to follow their lead in war. The war did not concern Athens and Sparta alone. Sparta and Athens, much as moderns love to contrast them, were by no means the only combatants; the war was not a mere contest between a forward-looking naval democracy and a totalitarian state that moved in lockstep and would brook no departure from tradition. Those who see the war as a template for future conflicts such as World War II or the Cold War of the later twentieth century overemphasize the role played in it by ideology. In fact, it was driven, like many other wars, largely by

2. *Iliad* 6. 235–6.

time-honored considerations of prestige, self-interest, and fear. States other than Athens and Sparta played key roles. Shrill Corinth with its indispensable navy exercised great influence over its landlocked Spartan hegemon. Little Megara, controlling the land bridge that gave access from the Peloponnesus to Attica, was important to the Spartans as well, and its complaints against Athens had to be taken seriously. Corcyra, until 435 a rare neutral in the bipolar world of Athenian and Spartan alliances, was a key player in international diplomacy.

During the fifth century BC, the Greek world consisted of some 1,500 city-states (*poleis*, sing. *polis*), many of them allied with one of the two hegemons. Some had been founded as colonies of other poleis, but unlike, say, the British colonies in North America, a Greek colony was, as a rule, politically independent of its founding state, known as its *metropolis* (mother city), though they generally shared religious and cultural ties. Indeed, the first recorded naval battle in Greek history pitted Corinth against its colony Corcyra. Colonies served to relieve population pressure in their mother cities and open up new trade routes. Some colonies founded colonies of their own, like the colony of Miletus in Asia Minor, which was said to have founded seventy colonies, though the real number was surely far smaller. A polis might contain a few hundred inhabitants or a few hundred thousand. Including colonies and original settlements, some poleis were located as far west as Spain, others as far east as the eastern parts of modern Turkey; some were in North Africa, some on the Black Sea. The focus of the Greek world was the water. Nearly all Greeks lived within a day's walk of the sea and used it to trade with other states for the necessities that their own land did not provide.

Water, of course, also served as a conduit for warships, and the Greek city-states fought almost as often as they traded. Athens, famed for its uplifting tragedies and beautifully proportioned temples, was at war at least two years out of three during the classical period. By far the most famous of the wars of this era is the one that broke out in 431 and has gone down in history as "the Peloponnesian War" because of the Athenian orientation of its chief historian, Thucydides. The Spartans, who led the coalition against which Athens and its allies fought (the Peloponnesian League), no doubt called it the Athenian war. It is conventionally believed to have ended decisively with the Battle of Aegospotami in 405, but in reality the fighting resumed shortly afterward.

The many states of Greece had a variety of constitutions, ranging from democracies of free adult males to ironclad oligarchies of a few; Sparta, as in so many respects, was different, having two kings concurrently, one from each of two royal houses, the Agiads and the Eurypontids. During our time period, the Agiads were Leonidas I (who died defending the Thermopylae pass), Pleistarchus, Pleistoanax, Pausanias, Agesipolis I, and Cleombrotus (who died at the Battle of Leuctra); the Eurypontids were Leotychidas II, Archidamus II, Agis II, and Agesilaus II. At least from the time of the Persian Wars (490–479 BC), there was a strong sense of a shared culture, even in the absence of any political unity among the poleis. Thucydides' predecessor Herodotus, historian of the Persian Wars, portrayed the Athenians as explaining what held them back from going over to the Persians: "what we as Greeks all share—our blood, our language; our temples and sacrifices to our gods; our Greekness."[3] Our Greekness; *to hellenikon*; "the Greek thing."

Nice speech, but "the Greek thing" never prevented Greek states from warring with one another. During the period between the Persian Wars and the Peloponnesian War known as the *pentecontaetia* (the "fifty years," really more like forty-eight), the Greeks fought each other frequently. Feeling the need for protection against the Persians should they attack again, many Greek poleis sought a powerful state to lead them in a new alliance. The obvious choice was Sparta, long considered the mightiest power in Greece. When the Spartan regent Pausanias alienated his fellow Hellenes by his high-handed behavior, however, they turned to Athens. The Athenians were happy to take over, but since the alliance would have to be of a naval nature, money or ships would be required of the allies. Some chose to give money, some ships. When the league had been successful in its operations, and particularly after a stunning victory over the Persians at the hands of Cimon, a relative of the historian Thucydides, a number of league members began to feel "joiner's remorse," questioning whether protection against Persia was still necessary, but there was no secession to be had: the Athenians clamped down on rebels with the full force of their powerful navy.

3. Herodotus 8. 144. 2.

There was not always war in fifth-century Greece. Though the development of the Athenian alliance—the Athenian empire, as it became—entailed a major shift in the balance of power in Greece, where Sparta had previously been held in higher regard than any other state, most Spartans bowed to the inevitable and acceded to the shift graciously. For most of the period between the end of the Persian Wars and the beginning of the Peloponnesian War, the two leagues were at peace. Yet they fought intermittently from 460 to 446/5 in what is called the "First Peloponnesian War," as opposed to the war that began in 431, "the" Peloponnesian War. When Samos, off the coast of modern Turkey, rebelled from the Athenian empire in 440 and Sparta summoned its allies to discuss sending aid, the plan was quashed by the opposition of Sparta's ally Corinth, despite the Corinthians' long-standing trade rivalry with Athens. It is telling, however, that the Spartans should have called a meeting of their allies to discuss the matter of aid to Samos in the first place.

The balance between war and peace was plainly delicate, but it would be a mistake to assume that the Athenians and the Spartans were by nature so mired in rivalry, so wedded to status, so skittish about the slenderest slight to honor that they were compelled to enter on the bloodbath that erupted in 431 and continued (with some interruption) for decades. But enter on it they did, and we have Thucydides' detailed narrative to lead us through most of it—and, in some cases, mislead us. The survival of Thucydides' long and detailed text is primarily a great blessing, but it has its downside. Seductively persuasive, Thucydides was not always correct in his interpretations. He did not like Athenian democracy, and within a few years of the war's outbreak, a rift developed between him and government that had exiled him, probably at the behest of the populist politician Cleon, whom he excoriated at every turn. This orientation sometimes led him to make judgments different from those that more detached observers have formed. (On the other hand, his absence from Athens after his exile gave him opportunities to talk with Athens' enemies and gain valuable information from them.) But in one respect he was absolutely correct. "Never before," he wrote, "had so many cities been captured and depopulated, either by barbarians or by Greeks at war with each other, and then, in some cases, resettled by new inhabitants.

Never before had there been so many exiles and so much killing, some brought about by the war itself and some by civil strife."[4]

Just as there was nothing inevitable about the outbreak of the war, so there was nothing predestined about the course it took. Every decision, every near miss and narrow escape, contributed to its outcome. Nor, for all the misery it engendered, was Lysander's victory decisive. After twenty-seven years of butchery on land and at sea previously unparalleled in Greece, nothing had really been gained by either side, not even by the Spartan "victors." Spartans seemed to be constitutionally incapable of winning wars in any meaningful sense; as events of the subsequent decades were to show, it was their habit to win a war and then lose the peace. The Spartans never seemed to learn. Unlike, say, the Romans' genuine victories in the Punic Wars, which marked only one step in the inexorable march of Roman power across the Mediterranean, the Spartan triumph at Aegospotami in 405 was only a blip on the screen of history. In reality, the fighting went on for years and years. Thucydides and Xenophon were wedded to the notion of a twenty-seven-year war, but we need not be.[5]

For one thing, the Athenian admiral Conon had eluded Lysander's grasp at Aegospotami, fleeing to Cyprus, where the local dynast offered him refuge. Several years later he found himself in command of a formidable fleet fighting on behalf of Persia against Sparta. Scoring a stunning victory at Cnidus in 394, he was able to sail back to Athens along with the Persian governor of Phrygia, bringing considerable funds to aid in the rebuilding of the Athenians' walls, which Lysander had demolished. Two ancient historians whose work survives only in fragments, Theopompus of Chios (c. 380–c. 315 BC) and Cratippus of Athens (fl. c. 375 BC), dated the end of the Peloponnesian War to the Battle of Cnidus, robbing Lysander of a clear victory, and they were right to do so.[6] This is really where the

4. Thucydides 1. 23. 2.

5. Thucydides was wedded to a twenty-seven-year war: Thucydides 5. 26. 1.

6. I subscribe to the belief that these men wrote the relevant fragments of the *Hellenica Oxyrhynchia*. Victor Hanson calls attention to their argument about Cnidus in *A War Like No Other: How the Athenians and Spartans Fought the Peloponnesian War* (New York: Random House, 2005), 291.

war ends, and not with Sparta triumphant; in fact, the outcome was more of a stalemate.

The fighting in Greece, moreover, would go on and on: within less than ten years of the Spartan victory at Aegospotami, Sparta's old allies Corinth and Thebes were sufficiently disaffected that they chose to ally with Athens and Argos in fighting their old hegemon in what is known as the Corinthian War (395–387). Although the principal victor in that war was in fact Persia, as the Greek states were forced to abide by principles of autonomy and make substantial concessions to King Artaxerxes II, the Spartans emerged from it in a favorable position as the guarantors of the peace; but they immediately set about angering their fellow Greeks on that occasion as well. In 382 they installed a pro-Spartan government in Thebes. These puppets were expelled in 379 with Athenian help, however, and shortly afterward the Thebans allied with the Athenians for mutual protection against Sparta. Soon the Athenians were strong enough to establish a new league. Thebes, moreover, went from strength to strength until in 371 its crack infantry shattered the myth of Spartan military supremacy forever on the battlefield of Leuctra. The Spartans' seeming victory at Aegospotami had in fact won them nothing but enemies.

The consequences of these decades of warfare were devastating, but our sources for the war are so Athenocentric that we know far less about other poleis. Many inscriptions date from this time period, but no sustained prose—or poetry—survives from Megara, Thebes, Corinth, or Sparta, though one pro-Spartan Athenian, Xenophon, wrote quite a bit about fourth-century Sparta, and Athenian comedy is somewhat helpful; Aristophanes in his *Lysistrata* highlighted the sufferings of women across Greece brought on by the dearth of husbands, and his *Acharnians* featured a starving Megarian prepared (in farce, but deadly serious farce) to trade his children for garlic and salt.[7]

Out of these decades of fighting, one good came: shortly after the Battle of Leuctra in 371, Epaminondas of Thebes liberated the tens of thousands of state serfs that the Spartan elite had held in bondage in Messenia in

7. Aristophanes *Acharnians* ll. 729–835.

the Peloponnesus for as long as anyone alive could remember. But this action had been preceded by several generations of struggle and was certainly the furthest thing from the Spartans' minds when they joined the Thebans in going to war with Athens in 431. In all other respects, Greece simply devoured itself for one generation after another. Yet despite the biting sorrows the fighting occasioned, it remains a gripping saga of plots and counter-plots, murders and lies, thrilling chases at sea and desperate marches overland, missed opportunities and last-minute reprieves, and, as Thucydides had hoped, lessons for the future—though there is considerable disagreement as to just what those lessons might be.

1

SETTING THE STAGE

We Greeks, Plato said, live around the shores of the Mediterranean and the Black Sea like ants or frogs around a pond.[1] Hundreds of miles separated the easternmost from the westernmost poleis, the southernmost from northernmost; some were colonies of others, and some were even colonies of colonies. All were agrarian to some degree, but they traded extensively with one another, since it was hard for any individual polis to be completely self-sufficient. Most trade went by sea, since travel overland was time-consuming, difficult, and often more expensive in terms of transportation costs. Throughout Greece, religion was an important part of civic life. Greeks all worshipped the temperamental Olympian gods and sought to garner favor with them by gifts, vows, and prayers. An individual Greek might be devoted to a particular divinity, but it was important to cover oneself by showing proper respect to other gods as well, participating in the religious festivals that dotted the calendar of each city. Greeks did not find it difficult to work up enthusiasm for attending these since a key aspect of such events was the sacrifice of animals, and for most Greeks animal sacrifices offered their only opportunity for the consumption of meat. Some Greeks were more religious, others less; for some, participation in festivals offered a profound sense of communion with a deity while others simply welcomed the opportunity to share food and drink and music with friends. Shrines were also maintained in private homes.[2]

1. Plato *Phaedo* 109b.

2. In the scrutiny Athenian men faced before being qualified for office, they were asked to show that they had shrines for the worship of Apollo and Zeus in their homes (Pseudo-Aristotle *Constitution of the Athenians* 55. 3).

Athena, of course, was the patron deity of Athens, but Poseidon, god of the sea, had a cult there as well, and Athena also had a temple at Sparta. Of course, all Greeks spoke Greek, and though there were several different Greek dialects, it was unusual that Greeks had trouble understanding speakers of another dialect. Greeks also belonged to different ethnic groups. Chief among these were the Dorians and the Ionians. The Dorians lived mostly in the Peloponnesus, but there were some elsewhere (Crete, in particular) as well. Athenians were Ionian, as were many cities on the coast of Asia Minor. Dorians and Ionians were held to be ancestral enemies, although they often got along perfectly well. Stereotypes of these can be extracted from Thucydides' history: Dorians were austere in habit, courageous on the battlefield, blunt in speech; Ionians (Athenians in particular) were elegant in manner, tricky of tongue, and adventurous of spirit. Some distinctions in religious practice divided the two groups; it was the Dorians alone, for example, who celebrated the festival of the Carnea in honor of Apollo, whereas the Ionians celebrated a wide variety of other festivals, and representatives from all over Greece came together at Olympia to participate in (or watch) the games held there in honor of Zeus every four years. Greeks from all over—and non-Greeks as well—came to Delphi to consult the revered oracle of Apollo there. Despite their ethnic differences, the Greeks shared a commonality of culture, and this commonality was solidified, as so often in history, by an attack on the part of a foreign power: the wealthy and powerful Persian Empire.

THE IONIAN REBELLION

Shortly after 500 a curious artifact made its way across the Aegean to Sparta. It was a bronze tablet onto which had been inscribed a map of the whole known world, complete with seas and rivers. Aristagoras of Miletus in Ionia had come to Sparta bearing the map in the hope of securing support for a rebellion against the Persian king Darius I.[3]

3. The Ionian rebellion is the subject of Book 5 and part of Book 6 in the *Histories* of Herodotus. The *Histories* are available in many English editions. All quotations from Herodotus in this work are from *Herodotus: the Histories*: Norton Critical Edition, edited by Jennifer T. Roberts and

The Greek cities under Darius's rule on the west coast of Asia Minor and the offshore islands were heavily taxed and frequently found themselves ruled by puppets imposed by the Persians. In 500, the oppressed cities revolted, and at that point their leader Aristagoras set off for the Greek mainland in search of backing for the rebellion.

The handy map backfired. The Spartan king Cleomenes was horrified at the idea of going three months' journey from home, and Aristagoras was sent on his way.[4] The Athenians, however, were more receptive, offering to contribute twenty ships to the effort, and even little Eretria on the island of Euboea to the north sent five.[5] The revolt failed, but it triggered a series of events that would bring the states of mainland Greece, Athens and Sparta among them, together in war against Persia several years afterward—and decades later would create divisions rather than union among those same poleis.

In the course of the rebellion, Darius's capital city of Sardis in his western province of Lydia caught fire, and the Persian king was furious. He had probably been contemplating an invasion of mainland Greece for a long time, and the revolt was the last straw. The Persians under Darius's generals Datis and Artaphernes—the king saw no need to go in person—easily gobbled up Eretria, which was betrayed from within after only a week's siege.[6] From Eretria it was only a short distance to Marathon in northeastern Attica. The 600 or so Persian ships arrived at Marathon in 490 with a large number of troops—perhaps as many as 16,000 infantry plus some cavalry and archers—and a great deal of confidence.[7] This confidence proved misplaced, for the Athenian polis had been evolving for over a century into a well-oiled machine that was quite prepared to fight for its freedom.

4. Herodotus 5. 51. 3.

5. Herodotus 5. 97, 5. 99.

6. Herodotus 6. 101.

7. We really have no idea how many men the Persians had with them.

THE ATHENIAN DEMOCRACY

In many ways Athens was no different from other Greek states. Everyone belonged to an *oikos* (pl., *oikoi*), or household, whether as father, mother, child, or slave. Most oikoi could afford at least one slave, and those that couldn't yet do so were generally saving up for one. Some households were desperately poor and in debt, while others prospered. Farming one's own land was the preferred way of feeding the family and perhaps producing extra crops to sell. Farming someone else's land, or working in a shield-making shop or tannery—what we would call having a job—was considered déclassé.

In one respect, however, Athens was different from other Greek poleis. Over several generations it had evolved into the most democratic state in Greece, and it was as a democracy that it would meet the challenges first of the Persian and then of the Peloponnesian War.

At a time of unrest, its early sixth-century lawgiver Solon had devised a system for Athens whereby officeholding was allotted entirely in accordance with income and not at all with birth (although of course in Athens, as in all societies, life was not lived on a level playing field, and for all Solon's efforts, birth would continue to play a considerable role in determining income). This may not sound very democratic, but it was a radical change from what had gone before, when power lay in the hands of a small group of men in rich, prominent families known as "Eupatrids"—literally, men with good fathers—who were chosen to serve as administrators called archons, first a total of three, and then a total of nine. One, the *archon basileus* (king archon) was particularly concerned with the religious life of the state. Another, the polemarch (warlord), served as the senior military commander. (Other states had polemarchs as well.) A third, the "eponymous" archon, gave his name to the year; his office carried the most prestige. In time six additional archons were added, the "legislators," and the number of archons in Athens remained at nine even when the archons had lost a great deal of their power. The archons governed along with a body that met on a hill (*pagus*) sacred to the war god Ares and thus was called the Council of the Areopagus. This body, however, was not really different from the archons, as it consisted of all the former archons, and its members served for life. There was also an assembly of adult citizens over the age of eighteen.[8]

Solon's reforms dealt a severe blow to the power of the Eupatrids. According to Solon's new system, men whose land produced at least 500 measures of grain, oil, and wine in any combination, known as the *pentakosiomedimnoi* (500-measure men), were eligible for the office of state treasurer and other high offices. Next came the *hippeis*—horsemen, since these were the men who could afford to maintain a horse for the cavalry, with an income of 300–499 measures. Along with the *pentakosiomedimnoi*, the *hippeis* could stand for the archonships and other higher magistracies. After the *hippeis* came the *zeugitai,* who with incomes of 200 to 299 measures could afford a team of oxen. Like their richer compatriots, the *zeugitai* could run for the lower offices. Finally came the *thetes*, the poor farmers who could not run for office but could participate in the assembly—and serve on juries. (When Athens developed its world-class navy, the thetes became indispensable as rowers.) No offices, of course, were open to slaves or women, but by working hard, poorer men might become richer; for male citizens, the door to social mobility was open, although not very wide. The body known as the *heliaea* represented an even more radical innovation than discarding birth as the criterion for political privilege, for it was from the *heliaea*, for which all adult male citizens from each of the four income groups were eligible, that Solon's newly conceived popular juries would be selected. To prevent bribery, juries were large, traditionally hundreds of men. At first these juries were courts of appeal only, but in time they came to serve as courts of first resort.

One of the Athenians' goals in setting up Solon as a lawgiver had been to prevent power from falling into the hands of a *tyrannos*, loosely translated "tyrant," although the men so identified who had come to power in other mainland Greek states (Megara, Sicyon, Corinth, for example)

8. On Greece in the Archaic Period, see A. Snodgrass, *Archaic Greece: The Age of Experiment* (Berkeley: University of California Press, 1980); J. M. Hall, *A History of the Archaic Greek World: ca. 1200–479 BCE*, 2nd ed. (Malden, MA: Blackwell, 2013); H. A. Shapiro, ed., *The Cambridge Companion to Archaic Greece* (Cambridge: Cambridge University Press, 2007) and K. A. Raaflaub and H. van Wees, eds., *A Companion to Archaic Greece* (Malden, MA: Wiley Blackwell, 2009).

around the seventh century were not necessarily tyrannical by modern standards. Rather, they were strongmen who seized power at times of civil discord and governed independently of constitutional restraints—something most Athenians did not want. Although Solon accomplished a great deal, his reforms did not prevent a tyranny from springing up in Athens. Ironically, the tyrant in question, Peisistratus, was a distant relative of Solon himself.[9]

He had distinguished himself in fighting against Athens' neighbor Megara, and he came to power in a coup around 561. He had mixed support both from the populace and from the aristocracy; in fact, he was twice expelled from the city and twice needed to plot his return. Once entrenched, he ruled until his death from natural causes in 527. In addition to safeguarding his own position, Peisistratus was very concerned about Athens' economy, both agricultural and commercial. Under his rule, fine painted pottery from Athens spread far and wide, and it was under Peisistratus's son Hippias that the first of Athens' famous "owls" were issued—silver coins with an image of Athena on one side and her symbol the wise owl on the other. These coins soon became the most reliable currency in Greece.

In the city of Athens Peisistratus developed a variety of building projects that served many purposes: self-aggrandizement, the attraction of more visitors to Athens, and the provision of jobs to the poor. State cults were celebrated with more fanfare than previously, and the festival of the Great or City Dionysia saw the birth of the tragic drama that eventually led to the great tragedies of Aeschylus, Sophocles, and Euripides. With more construction jobs available in the city, Athens' population grew.

Peisistratus was succeeded by his son Hippias; another son, Hipparchus, may have ruled along with Hippias, although Thucydides claims that Hippias ruled alone. When Hipparchus was assassinated in 514 as the result of a personal quarrel, the previously genial Hippias became predictably paranoid and dictatorial, and in 510 he was driven out with Spartan help.

9. On the Peisistratids in Athens, Herodotus 1. 59–64; Thucydides 1. 20. 2, 6. 53–9; Pseudo-Aristotle *Constitution of the Athenians* 13–19.

Progress on the road to democracy did not follow on the expulsion of the tyrants. Indeed, shortly after the expulsion of Hippias, the conservative Isagoras was elected archon, evidently on a platform of shrinking the citizen body by disfranchising all those whose ancestors had received citizenship under Peisistratus and Solon. His opponents gathered around Cleisthenes, a member of the Alcmaeonid clan. Cleisthenes promised to restore civic rights to the disfranchised, upon which Isagoras suddenly remembered an ancestral curse on the Alcmaeonids arising from some sacrilegious act performed by one of their members while holding the archonship in the seventh century. Cleisthenes and many others were banished, and at Isagoras's behest the Spartan king Cleomenes arrived and also exiled a significant number of households identified by Isagoras, though probably not the full 700 claimed by the author of the pseudo-Aristotelian *Constitution of the Athenians* (probably the work of one of Aristotle's students).[10]

The Athenians, however, would have none of this and rose up en masse, recalling Cleisthenes. Feeling the need to return to settle matters, Cleomenes found himself in the midst of an embryonic constitutional crisis. By ancient tradition, Sparta was ruled by two kings concurrently, one from each of two royal houses. Since liberating Athens entailed a major expedition, the Spartans had marched in 506 with both their kings, Demaratus and Cleomenes, as well as their allies. Just as the fighting was about to begin, not only did the Spartans' allies the Corinthians have a change of heart, but Cleomenes' co-king Demaratus did as well, and then, when the other allies saw the two kings at odds with one another, they too departed. The Spartans shortly passed a law forbidding both kings from accompanying the army at the same time.

Cleisthenes, returning with the exiled families, then set in motion the ingenious reforms he had worked out before his exile—the very reforms that had provoked the Spartan intervention. Previously Athenians had been divided into four tribes known as *phylai*, kinship groups in which aristocratic families wielded considerable power. (These four groups had nothing to do with the four wealth classes Solon had established.) To

10. Pseudo-Aristotle *Constitution of the Athenians* 20. 3.

break down the power of the aristocracy, Cleisthenes decided to create ten new artificial tribes formed on a partially natural, partially artificial basis. He divided Attica into thirty units known as *trittyes* (thirds). Each *trittys* (singular) consisted of a varying number of neighborhoods known as demes; some demes were of long standing, whereas others were new creations. The number of demes in each *trittys* could not be fixed since some demes were much bigger than others. Cleisthenes then took one *trittys* from each of three sections of Attica—the city, the coast, and the inland—and made them into one tribe. To reinforce tribal identity at the expense of family ties, men were henceforth to be known not as so-and-so, son of so-and-so but rather as so-and-so from the deme such-and-such (though in reality many people clung to the old nomenclature). The new tribal system meant that the old aristocratic families saw much of their land divided among different tribes.

Each tribe would send fifty men, chosen by lot, to a new Council of Five Hundred, which would prepare business for the assembly and manage financial and some foreign affairs. The year was divided into ten prytanies, and each tribe would serve for one prytany. Since members of the Council could originally serve one-year terms (though they could serve one additional term at a later date), the total percentage of Athenian male citizens who served on the Council was very large, a key democratic element in the government. The fact that these men were chosen by lottery was another democratic element that would soon turn up elsewhere in Athenian government as well. The tribes also elected important officials. Chief among these were the generals, one from each tribe.[11]

It was probably Cleisthenes too who invented the fascinating institution of ostracism.[12] In accordance with the rules of this odd procedure, the Athenians would vote each spring as to whether they wished to hold

11. On the civil strife at Athens at this time and the reforms of Cleisthenes, Herodotus 5. 66, 5. 69. 2, 5. 72. 1–73. 2; Pseudo-Aristotle *Constitution of the Athenians* 20–1; on Cleisthenes and the evolution of democracy in fifth-century Athens, see M. Ostwald, *From Popular Sovereignty to the Sovereignty of Law: Law, Society and Politics in Fifth-Century Athens* (Berkeley: University of California Press, 1986); P. Cartledge, *Democracy: A Life* (New York: Oxford University Press, 2016).

12. A nuanced treatment of ostracism appears in S. Forsdyke, *Exile, Ostracism and Democracy: The Politics of Expulsion in Ancient Greece* (Princeton, NJ: Princeton University Press, 2005).

an ostracism. If they decided to go ahead, and if the required quorum of 6,000 votes was obtained, on the due day each voter would hand in a piece of broken pottery (*ostrakon*) with the name of the person he would most like to see go into exile for ten years scratched or painted on it. No charge needed to be laid against anyone, no crime proven (though ostraka that have been found show allegations of everything from adultery to collusion with Persia). The illiterate could corral friends or neighbors into inscribing a name on their behalf (although they risked being tricked by their "helpers"), and archaeologists have found collections of pre-inscribed ostraka ready for use by those unable to engrave their own. The winner of this bizarre inverse popularity contest could return after his ten years were over, move back into his home, and resume activity in Athenian political life. This unusual device seems to have been designed to avoid civil war in the event that two powerful leaders were deadlocked in seeking the backing of the people, or to prevent any one man from becoming too powerful, perhaps even establishing another tyranny. Though used on only a few occasions, ostracism and the threat of ostracism would serve as an important tool in Athenian politics throughout the fifth century.

FACE-OFF AT MARATHON

It was this democratic state under its assembly and ten elected generals that confronted the full wrath of Darius on the plain of Marathon in 490. It was also an Athens filled with the same brand of trained soldiers to be found elsewhere in Greece: the hoplite. Starting with the rise of the polis, the Greeks—not just the Athenians—developed a fighting formation known as the hoplite phalanx. The fully evolved phalanx was customarily eight rows deep and ideally contained soldiers fitted out with the full hoplite panoply, each standing several feet from the next; of course, some less affluent soldiers could not afford a full panoply and were not as well armed offensively or defensively as their comrades. Customarily a hoplite soldier would carry a spear, usually about seven to nine feet long—maybe as much as ten—and a short slashing sword with a blade of some two feet, encased in a wooden scabbard covered in leather. He was well protected against the sharp points aimed at him by unfriendly soldiers on the opposing side. His name came from his *hoplon*, a round concave shield about three feet in diameter made of wood faced with bronze and frequently emblazoned with vivid designs, sometimes from myth—though Spartans had their shields marked with the letter lambda, the first letter in Lacedaemon (the official name for the Spartan state). Because of its size, the *hoplon* was often quite heavy, sometimes nearly twenty pounds, and some soldiers even added a leather flap to the bottom to protect their legs, increasing the weight of the panoply still further. Additional weight was added by a cuirass, greaves, and helmet, all designed to be strong and to cover large areas of the body. (See figure 1.)

Helmets varied widely in design and often had horsehair plumes, which made the soldier look not only more imposing but literally taller;

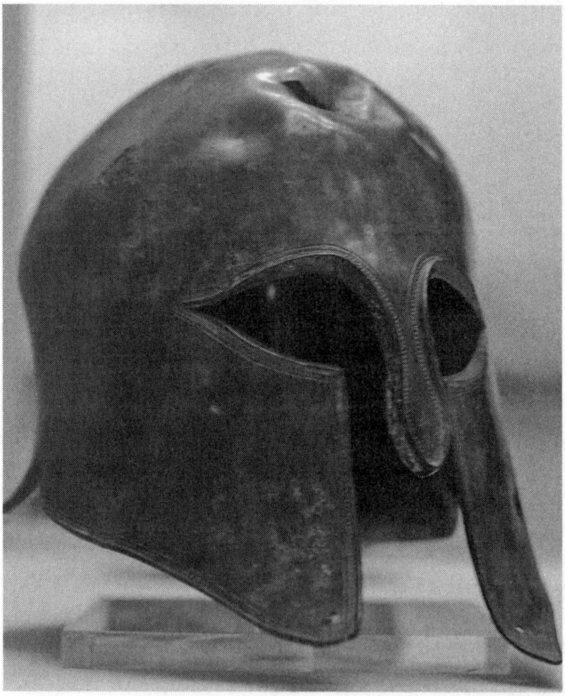

FIGURE 1
Bronze helmet used by Spartan warriors.
Credit: Photograph by John Antoni; location: British Museum.

both Greeks and Romans, neither of them a tall race, regularly wore headgear in battle to compensate for their shortness of stature (not that the plumes made them any taller than their enemies, who were generally short men in tall plumes as well). As the armor was not customarily government issue, however, quality of defensive armor varied in proportion to the financial circumstances of the individual soldier; some cuirasses were made not of metal but of various layers of linen or canvas, and for many men a horsehair helmet was out of the question. The full panoply in all its glory probably cost as much as a mid-price automobile today.

Most important to this style of fighting was the *hoplon*, for since the soldier gripped it with his left arm only, each hoplite would have every incentive to stick close by the soldier to his right and not cut and run. It was the design of the hoplite shield that made the phalanx, and in many ways the phalanx shaped the evolving middle class in the many city-states of Greece: it required solidarity, and it was open only to those who could afford the weaponry. Though Sparta, with its unique social structure, did not have a middle class, it certainly had hoplites in abundance, and to these men the state probably provided arms and armor. With the Persians bearing down on them, the Athenians indeed sent to the Spartans for aid. But the Spartans, an exceptionally religious people, were celebrating the festival of the Carnea in honor of Apollo and responded that their army could not march until the full moon. So the Athenians faced the Persians at Marathon with only a small contingent from their nearby ally Plataea to back them up. While the Persian force was more versatile, with its cavalry and archers, the Greek hoplites fought in heavy armor and disciplined formation in defense of their own land. According to Herodotus, of their ten generals it was Miltiades who convinced the Athenians after several days of waiting in a strong position on a hill, looking down at the Persians who outnumbered them mightily, that they had best not wait any longer, since there was disaffection in the city and any further delay might induce many back in Athens to go over to the Persians.[13] A relative of Thucydides, the persuasive Miltiades went down in history as the hero of this great battle.

13. Herodotus 6. 109. 5.

Hoplite battle was terrifying under the best of circumstances—the difficulty of seeing through the helmet, the insufferable heat inside the armor (quite possibly complicated by the hot urine and excrement of the petrified soldier), the clanging of weapons, the slippery ground soaked with blood, the choking dust everywhere, the groans of the dead and the dying. And with such a slim chance of victory. . . . Yet in the end, those Greeks who were convinced that they were literally throwing themselves into the valley of death were mistaken. Knowing they were outnumbered, their commanders had intentionally left their center thin, concentrating all their strength on the wings. Their heavier armor and longer spears stood them in good stead, and though the Persians broke through their center as expected, the Greeks succeeded in routing them on their wings. Fleeing to their ships, many of the Persians drowned flailing about in the marshes. It would be hard to say who was more surprised by the Greek triumph, the Greeks or the Persians.

The Spartans arrived in time to survey the battlefield but too late to participate in the fighting, as the Persians had sailed off. The names of those Greek citizens who had died were recorded: 192 Athenians and 11 Plataeans. No doubt slaves died fighting too, but their names and numbers are unknown to us: Greeks were not very generous about acknowledging the contribution of slaves to military victories (or slave losses in defeats). Herodotus reports that 6,400 Persians died.[14] (We are free to disbelieve this suspiciously large and round number.) Any plans the enraged Darius might have had for a rematch were foiled by his death in 486.

Their experience at Marathon taught the Athenians about the supreme importance of military command, and beginning in 487 they began selecting the archons by lot, thus clearly signaling a decline not only in the prestige of the archons but in that of the Council of the Areopagus, which consisted entirely of former archons. From then on, all men of ambition would stand for the generalship, not the archonship, and the prestige of the ten generals rose accordingly. These were the highest officials in the Athenian government—other than the Assembly, which was really coming to be sovereign. The generals had the power to summon

14. Herodotus 6. 117. 1.

the Assembly and the privilege of speaking first, in order of age. Each tribe elected one general, creating a board of ten—with equal power, although, as was the case with Pericles for quite some time, one general might exercise more authority by virtue of the esteem in which he was held. Like the members of the Council, the generals served one-year terms, though they could be re-elected again and again. When Pericles became so popular in the fifth century that he was elected to the generalship year after year, Thucydides, who did not like democracy but did like Pericles, explained that Athens at this time was a democracy in name but in reality government by its first citizen.[15] He was quite wrong; in 430, when the Peloponnesian War that had just broken out was going badly, the assembly deposed Pericles from office and fined him heavily.[16] The fact that it was the assembly and the people's courts to which generals in the field had to answer for their actions would play a significant role in military decisions.

THEMISTOCLES SEES THE FUTURE

The Athenians soon made two important discoveries. First, Darius's son and successor Xerxes was building ships frenetically throughout his extensive empire and was planning his own, much bigger invasion of Greece. Second, the silver mines at Laurium in southeastern Attica worked by slaves had thrown up not their usual humble yield but more than two tons. The populace was of two minds as to what to do with the windfall. Aristides, a politician of distinguished descent, led those who wanted to parcel it out among the citizens—predictably a popular course. Themistocles, on the other hand, who had no lineage of which to boast, had a talent for thinking outside the box. Like many populist politicians, he saw Athens' future in its navy, and he envisioned the Persians coming over the horizon imminently. Knowing that the Athenians did not want to think about Persia, however, he reminded

15. Thucydides 2. 65. 9.

16. Plutarch *Pericles* 35. 4; Diodorus 12. 45. 4; Thucydides 2. 65. 3–4; Plato *Gorgias* 516a.

them of the constant threat posed by their neighbor Aegina, an island that had just inflicted a major setback on their trade by a naval defeat. The opinion of Themistocles carried the day in the assembly, and soon shipwrights were busy bringing their fleet of trireme warships up to a strength of 200 seaworthy vessels.[17] The rivalry between Themistocles and Aristides meanwhile continued and soon issued in an ostracism; Aristides "won" and was instructed to leave Athens for ten years. (He was recalled almost immediately when the Persian threat materialized and he was needed at home.)

Athens' navy would play a key role not only in the war to come but in the entire future of the city. Indeed, two generations later the Spartan king Archidamus hesitated to enter on war with Athens precisely because of the formidable Athenian navy, and he had to be pressured into it by his people and his allies. The ships the Athenians built at Themistocles' instigation were triremes—sleek, fast, and easy to maneuver in both defense and offense. Triremes not only sailed; they rammed enemy vessels and sent them to the bottom. Triremes were about 120 feet by 15 feet, powered by 170 rowers operating in 3 rows and carrying 10 to 20 soldiers on board. These would be the ships with which Athens won and lost its vast fifth-century empire and imposed on its allies, some more willing than others, the tribute that helped it build the imposing structures that stood on the Acropolis, pay its jurors, and put on the great tragedies and comedies that survive today (and the many more that are lost) and are still frequently performed. The triremes were manned by a variety of rowers, including Athens' poorest citizens, the thetes, who thereby greatly improved their situation; they received daily pay, and their role in the Athenian armed forces also made them a powerful force in the burgeoning democracy. Inevitably, resident aliens and slaves would fill out the complement of rowers in the huge Athenian navy, for there were not enough citizens to do the job.

Many kinds of timber went into making a trireme (see Figure 2). As the strength of the ship depended on its keel, oak was needed for this. But a variety of other woods was used for the remainder of the vessel: ash,

17. Herodotus 7. 144. 1.

FIGURE 2
The reconstructed Greek trireme *Olympias* at sea.
Credit: © The Trireme Trust.

mulberry and elm, fir and pine.[18] On top of the sleek hull sat a wide outrigger, from which a canvas could be hung to shade rowers from the sun or a screen to ward off enemy projectiles; it also bore the tholepins that held the top tier of oars in place and served as a fulcrum for their motion. Ropes, cables, a mast, sails laboriously woven of linen, two anchors per ship—this was an elaborate operation. Once a ship had been built, a coating of pitch had to be applied to keep it watertight. Finally, the bronze ram: wax, clay, marble as well as metal all went into its careful formation. Thin slabs of white marble were placed on either side of the ship to serve as its "eyes" to guide it safely across the seas, their irises indicated by circles painted in red ochre. Some really believed the wooden vessel had life;

18. For the construction and operation of a trireme, see L. Casson, *The Ancient Mariners: Seafarers and Sea Fighters of the Mediterranean in Ancient Times*, 2e (Princeton, NJ: Princeton University Press, 1991), J. S. Morrison, J. F. Coates, and N. B. Rankov, *The Athenian Trireme: The History and Reconstruction of an Ancient Greek Warship* (Cambridge: Cambridge University Press, 2000), and J. R. Hale, *Lords of the Sea: The Epic Story of the Athenian Navy and the Birth of Democracy* (New York: Viking, 2008), 15–28.

others considered the notion hogwash but appreciated the decoration for its esthetic value, and the dramatic adornment probably had the added advantage of looking intimidating to opposing ships. Finally, goldsmiths were called on to gild the ram's figurehead of Athena that would leave no doubt in the onlooker's mind as to the vessel's port of origin.

But hoplites too would play a key part in pushing back any Persian invasion, and the hoplite phalanx was well developed throughout Greece. In a war with Persia, Athens would need the cooperation of Sparta. Fortunately, this time it would be forthcoming. For if the Spartan way of life prepared its citizens for anything, it was war.

A UNIQUE WAY OF LIFE

Sparta was not like any other Greek polis.[19] Early in their history the Spartans resolved to address their food shortage not by sending out colonies, like other states, but by expanding into Laconia to the south and Messenia to the west. Defeated in war, some of the inhabitants of those areas were turned into *perioeci*, "dwellers round about," who were free to live their lives as before but subject to service in war if called up, though they had no political rights in Sparta. Spartan manpower declined throughout the fifth and fourth centuries, and so the military service of the perioeci became increasingly central to the survival of the state. The less fortunate of the defeated became helots, slave/serfs bound to the land that had once been theirs.[20] Living off the produce of this

19. On this unusual state of ancient Greece, see W. G. Forrest, *A History of Sparta, 950–192 BC* (New York: W. W. Norton: 1968); P. Cartledge, *Sparta and Lakonia: A Regional History 1300 to 362 BC*, 2e (Oxford: Routledge, 2002); and N. Kennell, *Spartans: A New History* (Malden, MA: Wiley-Blackwell, 2010). Spartan exceptionalism has recently been called into question by Stephen Hodkinson and other scholars. For a discussion of this topic, see, for example, the debate between Hodkinson and M. H. Hansen in S. Hodkinson, ed., *Sparta: Comparative Approaches* (Swansea: Classical Press of Wales, 2009), 385–498. A recent and very detailed account of Sparta by Josiah Ober portrays Sparta as an exceptional state indeed: *The Rise and Fall of Classical Greece (The Princeton History of the Ancient World)* (Princeton, NJ: Princeton University Press, 2015), although Ober shows awareness of Hodkinson's work.

20. On perioeci and helots, N. Luraghi and S. Alcock, eds., *Helots and Their Masters in Laconia and Messenia: Histories, Ideologies, Structures* (Trustees for Harvard University, Cambridge, MA: Center for Hellenic Studies, 2004).

land, the Spartans did not work at trades but rather devoted themselves full-time to military preparedness. The land apportioned to free Spartan citizens—Spartiates, as they were called—was attributed to a mysterious reformer named Lycurgus. Whether such a person ever lived is uncertain; according to Herodotus, the priestess at the oracle of Apollo at Delphi addressed him as a god, but we are under no obligation to share either her perception or her diplomacy.[21] The Spartan ethos taught that all Spartiates were equal to one another, or at least close to equal: they were *homoioi*, or "similars/peers." Although some Spartans were richer than others—in some cases, a good deal richer—they were all expected to live frugally, in modest homes, wearing ordinary clothing that did not distinguish richer from poorer. No Spartiate was likely to be truly poor, for a key element in the Spartiate way of life was participation in the *syssition*, the dining club that was attached to the military unit to which each male Spartan belonged. Though richer men were encouraged to make larger contributions to the *syssition*—better bread, meat from the hunt—a minimum contribution was required of everyone, and anybody who failed to produce it was dropped from the citizen rolls. Helot families were assigned to individual Spartan families. "Burdened like donkeys," in the words of the Spartan national poet Tyrtaeus, they could not be sold abroad, and they were required to bring a fixed amount of what the land would yield to their masters. Still, this left them a good deal for themselves. Helots did not go hungry, but they lacked something more important than material sustenance; they lacked dignity, honor, and, of course, freedom. Helots outnumbered the Spartiates substantially—more and more as Spartiate numbers dropped—plainly creating a precarious situation. Particularly promising Spartan youths might hope to be selected for the *krypteia*, a secret service of sorts whose purpose was to seek out and kill any helots who seemed especially high-spirited—and to give the young Spartans a taste for violence. Those selected for the *krypteia* were assigned to hide out in the countryside at night and keep watch for particularly troublesome helots, staking out helot villages in this chilling rite of passage from adolescence to full adult warrior manhood. Yet history

21. Herodotus 1. 65. 3.

shows that the dividing line between Spartan and helot was not as binary as one might imagine. During the Peloponnesian War, helots might fight for their Spartan masters or serve on garrison duty. Sometimes it was the well-being of their families at home that guaranteed their good behavior, but beginning in the 420s they sometimes had the hope of being freed as a reward for military service (though they could never become Spartiates, and in the end the Spartan state paid dearly for its unwillingness to expand its citizen body).

In all Greek states, the purpose of education was to socialize young people and to inculcate in them the values of their elders—particularly their fathers—and of the community. This persisted until teachers like the sophists ("intellectuals") came along toward the latter part of the fifth century, urging the young to question authority—and provoking considerable outrage for doing so. In most states, however, this education was in the hands of the family. In Sparta, things were different. There Spartan boys were taken at a young age from their parents and sisters and younger brothers—their older brothers were gone already—and placed in military academy. The education they received there, later known as the "upbringing," was harsh. The youths slept outdoors on mats made of reeds they themselves had pulled by hand from the Eurotas River. To further toughen them up and prepare them for what military endeavors might demand of them, they were made to go barefoot and given insufficient clothing to keep them warm. They also were given so little food that they were often hungry; stealing food was encouraged to train them in stealth, but punishments for getting caught were severe. Plutarch in his *Life of Lycurgus* recounts the story of the hungry boy who had managed to steal a fox to eat and, needing to conceal it, shoved it under his cloak, whereupon he suffered in silence until, the animal having torn out his bowels with its teeth and claws, he fell down dead.[22] Combat between boys prepared them for the contests they would face on the battlefield, and staged battles could be bloody; the fact that stiff punishment awaited any combatant who actually killed another boy attests to this. Boys were assigned to groups according to age until they reached eighteen, at which

22. Plutarch *Lycurgus* 18. 1.

point a cadre would be chosen to serve in the *krypteia*. Then around the age of twenty each boy would be assigned to a *syssition*—a dining mess—or not. Failure to be chosen for any mess at all was disastrous and might mean a young man's exclusion from the army for which his entire education had been preparation. For Spartan education was not only the upbringing of citizens but the upbringing of future hoplites.[23] Growing young Spartan women, who had much more freedom than women in Athens, were educated by the state in music and poetry as well as dance and gymnastics, and they also played a role in the education of males by watching their exercises and humiliating them publicly if they were not up to snuff. It was not just helotry and the peculiar dual kingship, then, that set Sparta apart from the rest of the Greek states.

Sparta also had a council of thirty elders, the *gerousia*: twenty-eight elected men over the age of sixty who served for the rest of their lives and were usually rich men of high status, although technically any man could be elected to this body, plus the two kings. Bills passed by the assembly required the approval of the gerousia; this body also functioned as a criminal court of first resort for serious cases such as those concerning homicide or treason. A board of five ephors (overseers) was elected annually for terms of one year from candidates over thirty years old. One of their important functions was to oversee the kings on behalf of the people, and they had the power to impeach and depose them. Two ephors accompanied a king on campaign; they also dealt with foreign embassies. As was the case with the archons in Athens, one of the ephors gave his name to the year.

While Sparta's mixed government was intriguing, particularly with respect to the closely supervised dual kingship, what most Greeks, and most moderns, found noteworthy about Sparta was that it was an armed camp, always alert to the danger of keeping a large and restive population enslaved. The Spartan *homoioi* felt the need to live in a state of perpetual

23. On Spartan education, see N. Kennell, *The Gymnasium of Virtue: Education & Culture in Ancient Sparta* (Chapel Hill: University of North Carolina Press, 1995) and J. Ducat, *Spartan Education: Youth and Society in the Classical Period*, trans. E. Stafford, P. J. Shaw, and A. Powell (Swansea: Classical Press of Wales, 2006).

military readiness. For this reason Sparta thus had the only professionally trained army in Greece; all the other poleis relied on citizen militias. This was lucky for the combined defenders against the Persians, for in 480 Xerxes bore down on the Greeks with a truly remarkable force gathered from throughout his multiethnic and variously weaponed empire.

UNITING AGAINST XERXES

A congress of delegates from various Greek states met at Corinth in 481 to plan the defense of Greece. To be sure, a league of Greek states already existed, the Peloponnesian League—a group of poleis that Sparta had gradually gathered around itself as allies since the middle of the sixth century. That league—the league that would eventually go to war against the Athenians and the allies Athens was yet to acquire—consisted of most of the states of the Peloponnesus (excluding Achaea and powerful Argos), as well as some key states outside it, such as Thebes, the most powerful city in Boeotia, north of Attica. Because it did not contain all the states in the Peloponnesus and did contain some states outside it, it was not strictly Peloponnesian, and since its members owed allegiance to Sparta rather than to one another, it was not strictly a league. Still, it was a formidable organization. Sparta could request that any state send a third of its military in time of war, or two thirds for a campaign far from home. The Peloponnesian League, however, was based too far to the southwest to be suitable for fighting the Persians on its own. To repel Xerxes' invasion, therefore, a new league was formed that modern historians call the Hellenic League consisting of a little more than thirty states—not a very large number when we bear in mind how many Greek poleis there were.

The first operation of the new league in 480 was amphibious—a naval battle off Artemisium that ended in a draw, and the famous defense of the Thermopylae Pass up in Phocis just south of Thessaly. The Spartans already had a fearsome reputation, but ironically it was their actions at Thermopylae, where they did not in fact succeed in defeating the Persians, that won them undying fame. Aided by a band from loyal little

Thespiae, the Spartans and those under their leadership held the pass as long as they could, buying time for the Greeks to the south, until they were betrayed to a jubilant Xerxes by a traitor; many reverses in Greek history were due to treachery rather than skill or courage.[24] But the bravery of the Spartan king Leonidas and the picked 300, nearly every one of whom remained with him until the end, all but two dying at the hands of the Persians, became legendary.[25] Their courage in the face of certain death gave heart to the Greeks to the south awaiting Xerxes' next assault and was embodied in an epitaph composed for the Spartan dead attributed to the poet Simonides:

> Go, tell the Spartans, stranger passing by,
> That here, obeying their commands, we lie.

The Greeks next met the Persians in the straits that divided the mainland of Attica from the island of Salamis, where the trickery of the Athenian Themistocles helped bring victory over Xerxes' forces in a decisive naval battle that sent the king back to his home in Persia, leaving the war in the hands of his cousin Mardonius. The following summer, backed by the perfidious Thebans, the Persian general encountered the largest Greek army ever to have taken the field. At Plataea, Pausanias, regent for the underage son of the dead Leonidas, finally led the Greeks to victory after a long and hard-fought battle in which Mardonius died at the hands of an indomitable Spartan who bashed his skull in with a boulder. Following the battle, Pausanias performed sacrifices to Zeus and led the allies in confirming the autonomy of Plataea as the site of this great victory; henceforth, if anyone attacked it, all present would rise up and defend it.[26] These words would ring hollow half a century later when the Thebans triggered the actual fighting of the Peloponnesian War, after months of negotiations, by attacking, of all places, Plataea—and received backing for this move from, of all

24. The traitor from Malis: Herodotus 7. 213. 1.
25. Events at Thermopylae: Herodotus 7. 200–39.
26. Thucydides 2. 71. 2.

people, the Spartans. For now, however, things were peaceful among the Greeks. On or about the same day, the Greeks defeated the Persians in a final contest at Mycale in Asia Minor, the Athenians led by Xanthippus (father of Pericles) and the Spartans led by Leotychidas (grandfather of Archidamus). The war was over.

2

THE GREEK CITY-STATES AT WAR AND PEACE

THEIR VICTORY OVER PERSIA had changed the balance of power among the Greek states, and there was no telling how this development would play out. Before the invasions of Darius and Xerxes, the city-states of Greece had accorded the most respect to Sparta with its professional army. Now, however, it was plain that the Athenians had contributed an enormous amount to defeating the Persians, first at Marathon, where no Spartan hoplites had participated, and then at Salamis, where the Athenian navy played a key role. Now, in the wake of the Persians' departure from the Greek homeland, it was unclear what the relationship would be among the various states of Greece.

THE BEGINNINGS OF THE DELIAN LEAGUE

When the Greeks decided that a new naval league would need to be formed for the purpose of defense against any future Persian attacks (and in order to take reprisals against the Persians for past wrongdoing, gathering booty where possible), it seemed at first that the league leadership would indeed fall to the Spartans. After all, the regent Pausanias, victor of Plataea, was on the spot in postwar Byzantium in his role as commander-in-chief of the Hellenic League. But Pausanias promptly alienated the Greeks in the area by his arrogance, wearing Persian garb and going about with an eastern bodyguard, and the Greeks chose the Athenians to lead the new league instead. This development most Lacedaemonians accepted readily at the time, though many came to have regrets later on.[1] After all, Spartans were not at heart a seafaring people, and their own alliance, the Peloponnesian League, consisted of mainland Greek states that, except for Corinth, were not naval powers either.

Called by modern historians the Delian League because of the original location of its treasury on the island of Delos, the new alliance consisted ultimately of about 150 states.[2] Members of the League, many of them island states or states on the coast of Asia Minor or in Thrace or the Hellespont, signaled their fealty by sinking iron weights into the sea, swearing to remain loyal until those weights should rise to the surface—in other words, forever. Some of the members of the Hellenic League chose to join, but many, particularly those that were members of the Peloponnesian League, did not: the most powerful of the ones who remained outside the League were the Thebans and the other Boeotians; the Corinthians; the Megarians; and of course the Spartans themselves. In time it would become clear that Greece was divided into two blocs, the Delian League and the Peloponnesian League; and of course there were some neutrals. Naval operations do not come cheaply, and substantial tribute needed to be paid annually to the League treasury. Widely admired for his probity, the Athenian Aristides was chosen to assess each member state of the Delian League in money or ships. By the time the treasury was moved to Athens in 454, the one sixtieth of each contribution dedicated to the goddess Athena was inscribed on marble pillars known (and published) today as the *Athenian Tribute Lists*, with the result that, so far as they are preserved, we can reconstruct who paid what, although of course some states were periodically delinquent in whole or in part. *ATL*, as it is known, is a valuable tool for assessing the popularity of the Athenians' league and the Athenians' success in

1. Thucydides 1. 95.

2. On the Delian League in its context, R. Meiggs, *The Athenian Empire* (Oxford: Oxford University Press, 1972) and P. Low, ed., *The Athenian Empire* (Edinburgh: Edinburgh University Press, 2008).

imposing their will on their "allies," who were eventually converted into subjects.[3]

The League extended over a wide area indeed—from Rhodes off the southwest coast of Asia Minor to Potidaea (ironically, a Corinthian colony) in northern Greece.[4] As it happened, two of the great commanders of the Persian Wars, Miltiades and Themistocles, came to grief at the hands of their countrymen and were no longer on the scene. Miltiades was impeached after an unsuccessful military expedition, and the brilliant but arrogant Themistocles, accused of pro-Persian sympathies by the Spartans and the object of considerable resentment at home (he had never been known for his modesty), suffered both ostracism (around 470) and exile, finding refuge, of all places, in the Persian empire, at the court of Xerxes' son and successor Artaxerxes I.[5] League operations therefore were led by Miltiades' son Cimon, and they tended to be successful. Two actions of the Athenians made clear how they perceived their League. When the people of Carystus in southwestern Euboea (off the coast of Attica) declined to join, the Athenians used force to compel them, and when the island of Naxos in the Cyclades decided it wanted to leave the League, the Athenians used the full might of their fleet to prevent this.[6] The Naxians were forced to pull down their walls and convert their tribute to money payment, yielding control of their ships. A decisive moment in the history of the League came when Cimon's forces defeated the Persians at the mouth of the Eurymedon River in southern Asia Minor around 467.[7] Now that the Persian threat seemed to be receding, the Athenians might have trouble holding their alliance together, and indeed it seems likely that the unsuccessful revolt of the

3. B. D. Meritt, H. T. Wade-Gery, and M. F. MacGregor, *Athenian Tribute Lists* (Cambridge, MA: Harvard University Press, and Princeton, NJ: Princeton University Press, 4 vols., 1939–53).

4. This geographical extent is aptly pinpointed in R. Sealey, *A History of the Greek City States, ca. 700–338 B. C.* (Berkeley: University of California Press, 1976), 246.

5. On Miltiades, Herodotus 6. 132-6; Nepos *Miltiades* 7–8; on Themistocles, Plutarch *Themistocles* 22–32; Thucydides 1. 136–8; Diodorus 11. 55–9. Suspicions of Themistocles were tied up with suspicions of the regent Pausanias, who was believed to be engaged in treasonous correspondence with the Persian king. The suspicions about Pausanias led to his death at Sparta and became an issue in the negotiations leading up to the Peloponnesian War (see Chapter 3, this volume).

6. Carystus and Naxos: Thucydides 1. 98. 3–4.

7. Thucydides 1. 100. 1.

important island of Thasos just off Thrace in the north was a response to that victory: the Thasians were not happy that the Athenians, by having them in the League, gained access to the gold mines they possessed on the opposite shore. (By chance Thucydides had family connections up there and would soon inherit the right to work some of those mines.) The Lacedaemonians, it was rumored, had promised to help the Thasians against the Athenians but were distracted by a devastating earthquake that hit Sparta in 464, killing thousands and triggering a revolt on the part of the Laconian and especially Messenian helots. When the Spartans found themselves unable to dislodge the rebels from their stronghold on Mt. Ithome, they sought aid from Athens and other states to which they were allied by the terms of the Hellenic League, which had never been dissolved.

The traditionalist Cimon, who like many fifth-century generals was also an important politician, had always championed a pro-Spartan policy and an Athens where no further democratizing changes were made in the government. His son Lacedaemonius could not have been more aptly named. Predictably, Cimon sought to persuade the Athenian assembly that, as Athens and Sparta were time-honored allies and Greece would benefit from their dual hegemony, his countrymen needed to march to the Spartans' assistance. The democratic leader Ephialtes, however, who had different ideas about Athens' future, argued that "the pride of Sparta should be trodden underfoot." Cimon carried the day and was sent off to Sparta at the head of a substantial force of Athenian hoplites.[8]

Cimon's expedition proved the end of his pro-Spartan party, for when he and his Athenian hoplites arrived in the Peloponnesus, the Spartans dismissed them, though they did not send their other Hellenic League allies away. Long known to be xenophobic by nature, they found something alarming about the presence of Athenian troops in such large numbers; they feared that the Athenians, being of a revolutionary cast as well as "of a different race from themselves" (i.e., Ionian rather than Dorian) would change sides and support the helots, and perhaps they were right.[9] (Years later, when the Spartans finally managed to overcome

8. Plutarch *Cimon* 16.8.

9. Rebellion of Thasos: Thucydides 1. 100. 2. The Thasians obtain a promise of Spartan assistance but the Spartans are prevented from doing anything by an earthquake in Sparta that triggers

the helots' resistance, they permitted the Athenians to give them safe conduct to a new home in the port of Naupactus, which guarded the western approaches to the Corinthian Gulf—something that inevitably made the Spartans' Corinthian allies apprehensive of Athens, of which Naupactus became an ally.)[10] The Spartans had no doubt heard about the debate in the Athenian assembly, which, like all such meetings, had been held in the open air, and knew there was an anti-Spartan grouping in Athens that meant them no good. The conservative Cimon was rewarded for his miscalculation with ostracism, and Ephialtes pushed through radical reforms in the Athenian government, persuading the assembly to transfer many of the functions of the Council of the Areopagus to the Council, the assembly, and the juries. These developments plainly met with some strong opposition: Ephialtes was assassinated in 461 by those who disagreed with his policies. An assassin from Tanagra up in Boeotia was engaged to do the deed, so the story went.[11] But Ephialtes' place in Athenian politics was promptly taken over by his associate Pericles, son of the Persian War general Xanthippus and his wife the Alcmaeonid Agariste (Figure 3). Pericles would remain the most prominent politician in Athens until his death in 429, and the notion of "dual hegemony" in Greece espoused by Cimon and no doubt by many in Sparta was now on life support.

THE "FIRST PELOPONNESIAN WAR" (460–446/45)

As would be the case with what we call "*the* Peloponnesian War," the one that broke out in 431, the "First" Peloponnesian War did not begin with conflict between the hegemons Athens and Sparta. Rather, shortly after Ephialtes' death, trouble broke out when Megara, at odds with Corinth over the border they shared, defected from the Peloponnesian League

a helot rebellion: Thucydides 1. 101. 1–2; the Spartans obtain Athenian assistance against the helots but offend them by sending Athenian soldiers home after they have arrived: Thucydides 1. 102. 1–4, Plutarch *Cimon* 16–17.

10. Thucydides 1. 103. 3.

11. Pseudo-Aristotle *Constitution of the Athenians* 25; Boeotian assassin, 25. 4.

FIGURE 3
Pericles: Roman copy of a bust by Cresilas originally made c. 430 BC.
Credit: Photograph by Jastrow, location Museo Pio-Clementino, Muses Hall, public domain.

and was welcomed into the Delian League instead. By gaining Megara as an ally, Athens secured control of its two ports, Pegae on the Corinthian Gulf and Nisaea on the Saronic Gulf; and indeed, Athens built for the Megarians walls that linked Megara to Nisaea. In the fighting that ensued, each side suffered, but one episode stands out: a contingent of Corinthians got lost and wound up in a trench, and when the Athenians saw them there, they blocked off the area and stoned them to death.[12]

When Corinth combined with the offshore island of Aegina against Athens, the Athenians built the fortifications known as the Long Walls linking Athens to its principal port of the Piraeus and also to its other port, Phalerum[13] (see Map 2). These were the walls that would effectively

12. Thucydides 1. 106.
13. Thucydides 1. 107. 1.

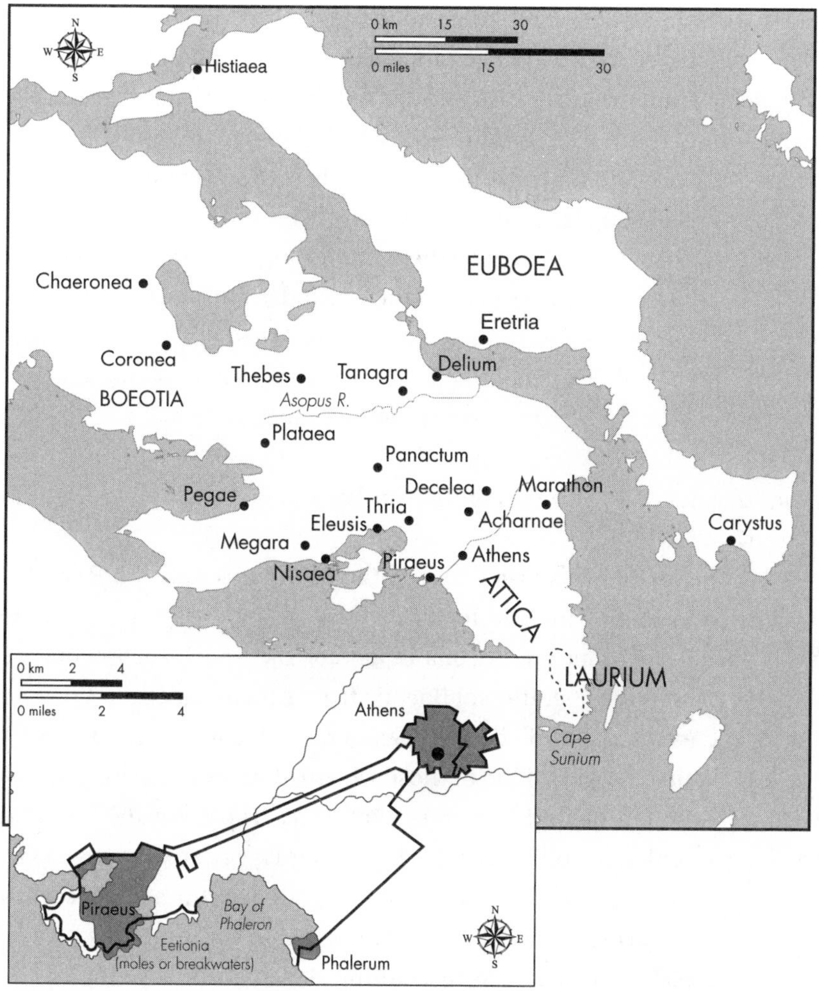

MAP 2
The Greek Mainland: Attica, Boeotia, and Euboea, with inset map of Long Walls.

turn Athens into an island, a fortress into which foodstuffs could be imported by the navy. The Long Walls would be central to Pericles' strategy during the Peloponnesian War. This was an important turning point in the city's security; without the walls, the Athenians never would have been able to contemplate going to war with Sparta in 431.

In 457, the Spartans joined in the war their allies were fighting, though despite their victory at Tanagra they accomplished nothing lasting or decisive. Soon Athens had come to control all of Boeotia except for Thebes, which had recently been fortified with Spartan aid. Still at war with Persia, the Athenians also decided to back the Egyptians when they rebelled from the Persian Empire, into which they had been incorporated by the Persian king Cambyses II in 525, but their efforts ended in disaster, with the loss of some 200 allied ships and their crews—40,000 men. At this point it seemed good to the Athenians, feeling vulnerable, to transfer the league treasury from Delos to Athens. Modern historians traditionally use this date, 454, to stop referring to the Athenians' alliance as the Delian League and begin calling it the Athenian Empire. Finally in 450, shortly after Cimon's term of ostracism was up and he had returned to Athens and then died, fighting with Persia ceased, either after a formal peace negotiated by Cimon's brother-in-law Callias or simply by mutual agreement.

After the fortunes of war between the Athenians and the Peloponnesians had swung back and forth for some years, the Athenians were badly beaten at Coronea in Boeotia in 447/46. The principal consequence of the battle was the liberation of Boeotia from Athenian domination and the attendant creation of the anti-democratic Boeotian League under the leadership of Thebes. One of those who died fighting for Athens was Cleinias, who left behind him two small sons. These boys would find their home with none other than Pericles, Cleinias's relative by marriage, and they were apparently hell-raisers. The younger child, Alcibiades, a rogue and a charmer, made a deep impression on the Athenian people. He would play a critical role in framing Athenian policy during the Peloponnesian War and continued to have avid supporters even after he had made so bold as to defect to Sparta.

Meanwhile trouble—serious trouble—was brewing in the Athenians' empire. Seeing Athens weakened by its defeat at Coronea, its allies on the nearby island of Euboea took the occasion to rebel. As Euboea paid considerable tribute and was located on the route to the Hellespont, the possibility that it should fall into Spartan hands was considered by the Athenians to be potentially catastrophic, and Pericles went in person to put down the revolt. No sooner had he arrived, however, than he received alarming news: Megara had rebelled as well and slaughtered its Athenian garrison.[14] Bad as this was for the Athenians, the return of Megara to the Peloponnesian League was particularly opportune for the Lacedaemonians, opening up as it did the land bridge from the Peloponnesus into Attica. And indeed a Spartan king promptly headed for Athens—the young Agiad Pleistoanax, with his adviser Cleandridas. Pericles rushed back to deal with the invasion, and deal with it he did. Just as it appeared that combat was impending, something odd happened. Pleistoanax took his men back to Sparta.[15]

Not surprisingly, the king's contemporaries both at home and abroad were astonished. In Sparta, Pleistoanax was prosecuted and fined, and being unable to pay he was forced into exile. This development gives us some sense of the limited clout of Spartan kings, who did not run around shouting "off with his head" if one of their countrymen displeased them. The power dynamic ran very much the other way, just as it did in Athens, where the people exercised power over the generals and regularly called them to account for their actions. Greeks were suspicious of too much power at the top. The Agiad king found a new home on Wolf Mountain in Arcadia in the Peloponnesus. There he made his house halfway inside a sanctuary of Zeus in case he had to flee a posse of unforgiving Spartans. He was replaced in office by his son Pausanias (a common name in Sparta), who was only a child. Cleandridas, for his part, went into voluntary exile and was condemned to death in absentia.[16] Plutarch in his *Life of Pericles* offers a simple explanation for the Spartans' withdrawal from Attica: Pericles bribed Cleandridas. This was certainly a rumor in Athens at the time. The biographer also cites other authors—though Aristotle's pupil Theophrastus is the only one he mentions by name—who claim that Pericles gave a large sum to the Spartans each year thereafter for several years, thus buying time to prepare for a more substantial war. Pericles did not suffer the immediate wrath of the Athenians as Pleistoanax and Cleandridas did of the Spartans, but irregularities in his accounts seem

14. Rebellions of Euboea and Megara: Thucydides 1. 114. 1.

15. Pleistoanax returns home: Thucydides 1. 114. 2.

16. Exile of Pleistoanax: Thucydides 2. 21. 1; fate of Cleandridas: Plutarch *Pericles* 22. 3. On the vulnerability of Spartan kings to punishment, E. David, "The Trial of Spartan Kings," *Revue internationale des Droits de l'Antiquité* 32 (1985): 131–40.

to have given his enemies an opening for an abortive impeachment that never got off the ground in 438, and these may well have had to do with monies funneled to the Spartan king and his adviser at that impromptu conference that avoided a battle years before.[17]

Whether or not money changed hands before Pleistoanax's withdrawal from Attica, the absence of a battle at that juncture is easy to understand. The two sides had been evenly matched in the war. The Spartans and Boeotians had defeated the Athenians at Tanagra in 457, but shortly afterward the Athenians defeated the Boeotians at Oenophyta. Pleistoanax may well have realized that there was no advantage in continuing to throw the forces of the Peloponnesian League at the Athenians when Athens' real strength lay in its naval empire.

The Athenians and the Spartans therefore came to a formal understanding that they would fight no longer. The peace on which the two sides agreed in 446/45 is known at the Thirty Years' Peace, though it did not in fact last half that long. The principal terms of the peace were five:

1. neither hegemon was to interfere with the allies of the other
2. neutrals were free to join either side
3. disagreements were to be settled by arbitration
4. no ally was permitted to switch sides
5. each hegemon was permitted to use force to resolve conflicts within its own alliance

Athens thus acknowledged the loss of its land empire in central Greece—a loss that was a fait accompli after Coronea anyhow. The state of Argos in the Peloponnesus, an old rival of Sparta that had made its own Thirty Years' Peace with Sparta in 451, was permitted to make a treaty with Athens if it so wished, although it could not, of course, take any action against Sparta until its treaty with Sparta expired in 421. On the whole, the peace involved a pragmatic assessment of the strengths and wishes of both sides, and it was not unreasonable to imagine that it would endure for the full thirty years its framers imagined.

17. Plutarch *Pericles* 22. 2.–23. 1.

THE PEACE IS TESTED

The treaty's first test came only a few years later. Ironically, it arose from discord within the Delian League itself. Around 440, conflict erupted in Asia Minor between Athens' subject allies Samos and Miletus concerning control over the town of Priene, which lay between them.[18] After some deliberation, the Athenians decided to throw their support to Miletus, taking fifty Samian boys and fifty men as hostages. The Samians were by no means cowed. Soon the revolt there was in full flood, aided by Pissuthnes, the satrap (governor) of Lydia in the Persian Empire. The rebellion spread to Byzantium as well, sparking considerable fear among the Athenians for the safety of their grain supply, for which they counted on the area around the Black Sea. Mytilene, the most important city on the island of Lesbos, also seems to have sent feelers to Sparta about aid should they revolt, and was waiting for an answer.[19] The Samians themselves also approached Sparta for assistance.

The Athenians were petrified. Everything that had seemed so secure a few months before was now on the verge of collapse, and it all hinged on the attitude of Sparta and its allies. The Spartans, it seems, gave thought to helping the Samians, for they called a meeting of their allies. Speaking at Athens on the eve of the Peloponnesian War some years later, the Corinthians insisted that it was they who turned the vote of the Peloponnesian League against aiding Samos, invoking the terms of the Thirty Years' Peace that permitted each hegemon to resolve conflicts within its own league.[20] (Unlike the Athenians, who had converted their allies into subjects and could act autocratically, the Lacedaemonians required the approval of their allies before taking military action.) The very fact that the Spartans had seen fit to summon a congress of their allies to consider the matter and that the Corinthians had played a key

18. Thucydides 1. 115. 2.

19. Samos and Byzantium rebel: Thucydides 1. 115. 5–6. Mytilene seeks aid from Sparta: the Mytileneans make reference to such a request in 428, and it is almost certain that it was at this time: Thucydides 3. 2. 1.

20. Thucydides 1. 40. 5–6.

role in a tight vote shows that this was a close run negotiation, but the favor shown to Athens by Corinth was a promising sign for peace.

Without aid from the Peloponnesian League, the widespread revolutions could not succeed. Still, putting them down was work. All ten Athenian generals went on the expedition, including the playwright Sophocles, who had been elected general for that year. The Samians lay under siege for nine months, but in the end the Athenians prevailed. Samos was charged with a war indemnity, and Byzantium had its tribute raised.

Pericles would undergo some harassment in the years that followed in the form of attacks on his associates—the sculptor Pheidias, who was busying himself creating the striking gold and ivory statue of Athena on the Acropolis; the natural philosopher Anaxagoras; and the cultivated courtesan Aspasia of Miletus, who since Pericles' divorce had lived with him as his common-law wife. Already before the Samian War, the trouble had begun when a relative of Thucydides, also called Thucydides, had attacked Pericles for using League funds for beautifying the Acropolis with such structures as the Parthenon (Figure 4) (though in reality

FIGURE 4
The most recognizable building in classical Greece, the Parthenon, a temple built in honor of the goddess Athena "Parthenos," the Virgin.
Credit: Photograph by Serendigity.

Thucydides' aim was probably to undermine the democracy and restore the more restricted franchise of earlier days supported by his relative Cimon).

At first, Plutarch reports, the assembly was persuaded by his arguments, but when Pericles rose to the occasion and offered to pay for the entire building program—providing that the dedication be made in his name alone—they cried out that he should spend whatever he thought necessary from the public funds; and an ostracism held in 443 soon sent Thucydides into exile.[21] Glorious buildings rose on the Acropolis, and the position of Pericles in Athens, and that of Athens in Greece, remained secure along with the treaty the Athenians enjoyed with the Peloponnesian League—until, as is so often the case, trouble broke out in the most unlikely of places.

21. Plutarch *Pericles* 14.

3

SPARTA PROVOKED, ATHENS INTRANSIGENT

THUCYDIDES THOUGHT HE KNEW the cause of the war: "the growth of Athenian power, and the alarm it occasioned in the Spartans, forced Sparta into it."[1] In reality, though, Athenian power was no greater when the war broke out than it had been years before. Rather, the war was the product of a perfect storm of coincidences that combined with Athens' proclivity for provoking Sparta's allies—allies on which Sparta was dependent first for support against its helot population and second for naval forces to complement its own infantry in the event that war did come.

Just as the Thirty Years' Peace had been tested in 440 by tensions in the east when war broke out between Samos and Miletus, so it became strained again in 435 when trouble developed in the town of Epidamnus in the far northwest in what is now Albania—so far did the Greek world extend. This time, however, the challenge to the peace would not dissipate, and within three years the Peloponnesian League had declared war on Athens.

CORCYRA BETWEEN MOTHER AND DAUGHTER

Technically Epidamnus was a colony of Corcyra, the modern resort island of Corfu; Corcyra itself was a colony of Corinth. Thus Corinth,

1. Thucydides 1. 23. 6. This particular "cause and effect" construction of the outbreak of the war has now been dubbed "the Thucydides trap" and extrapolated to possible modern wars: see Preface.

mother city of Corcyra, was in effect grandmother to Epidamnus, and in fact by tradition the man chosen to fill the role of founder of Epidamnus had come from Corinth. Corinth and Corcyra, however, hated each other and in 664 had fought the first recorded naval battle in Greek history. Corinth, moreover, was a key member of the Peloponnesian League, whereas Corcyra and Epidamnus were neutrals.

In 435, civil strife that had been brewing for some time in Epidamnus came to a head when the oligarchs who had been expelled by the masses returned with some local non-Greek peoples to plunder the city. This kind of conflict was endemic to the polis and would haunt the Greek states throughout their existence. The Epidamnian *demos*—the populace, who supported a democratic government—decided to seek aid from their mother city Corcyra, but the Corcyraeans saw no profit in becoming involved in their plight.[2] In desperation, the Epidamnians then turned to grandmother Corinth, where they received an entirely different response. The Corinthians, it proved, were absolutely delighted to send help. Their eagerness may have been due in part to concern about developing a power base in the northwest and securing ports on useful commercial routes—Corinth was a major trading state—but the primary reason seems to have been sheer orneriness. For years they had bewailed the disrespect, indeed, hubris, with which they had been treated by the Corcyraeans, their own colonists. Although Greek colonies were politically independent of their founding cities, it was customary for them to treat their founding states with warmth and deference. This the Corcyraeans did not do. At intercity festivals they did not offer the Corinthian representatives the choicest cuts from the sacrificial animals, as did the other colonists. They also had a navy superior to that of Corinth—hardly anything to apologize for, but it rankled that the Corcyraeans were evidently wont to boast about it. For all these reasons, the Corinthians, whose own government was oligarchic, nonetheless chose to favor the democrats of Epidamnus against the Epidamnian oligarchs.[3]

The discovery that the Epidamnian populace had entrusted itself to Corinth completely changed the Corcyraeans' attitude to their colony.

2. Thucydides 1. 24. 6–7.

3. Thucydides 1. 25. 3–26. 1.

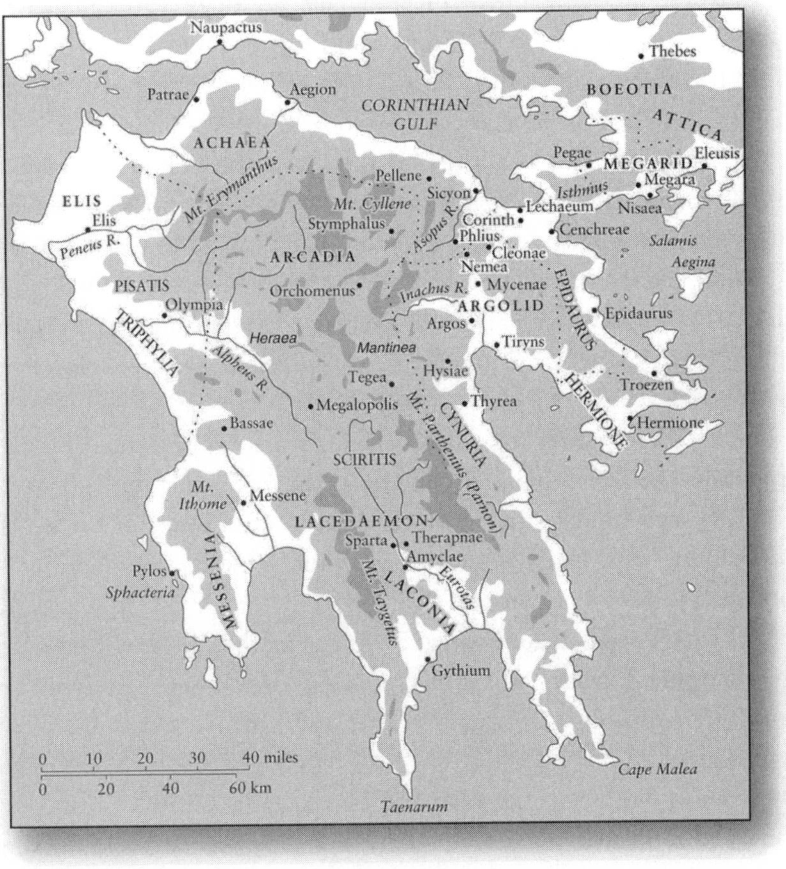

MAP 3
The Peloponnesus, Megara, Corinth, the Corinthian Gulf, and Naupactus.

Now they set sail with twenty-five ships and ordered the Epidamnians to expel the soldiers the Corinthians had sent and restore their oligarchic exiles. When the Epidamnian demos refused, the Corcyraeans besieged them. Learning of the siege, the Corinthians mustered a fleet that included allied ships from several states, receiving aid from such Peloponnesian allies as Megara and Thebes[4] (see Map 3).

At this point, the Corcyraeans took a step back and began to reflect on what they were doing. What, really, was the sense in all this? Their navy

4. Thucydides 1. 27.

was stronger than Corinth's, but they had no allies, whereas Corinth was a key member of the Peloponnesian League. Why, the Corcyraeans asked themselves, stake their fleet on protecting Epidamnus? Deciding that issues of honor and status in a competition with their disagreeable mother state were not worth risking their fleet, the Corcyraeans offered to submit the matter to arbitration by Peloponnesian cities agreeable to both sides. Alternatively, they were also happy to go to Apollo's oracle at Delphi and let the god decide. Both of these proposals seemed on the surface to be good offers: arbitration had been specified under the terms of the Thirty Years' Peace, and the oracle at Delphi was highly esteemed by all Greek states.

But the Corcyraeans' offers fell on deaf ears. Unimpressed by their proposals, the Corinthians declared war on them, and the two navies (Corinth supported again by Megara) faced each other in battle. The Corinthians were badly beaten, and on the same day Epidamnus fell to Corcyra. To commemorate their naval victory, the Corcyraeans in accord with Greek custom set up a victory marker on the promontory of Leucimme, toward the south end of Corcyra. They also kept their Corinthian prisoners of war in chains and killed the prisoners from other states.[5]

Driven by both burning rage and cold calculation, the Corinthians spent the next two years assembling a great armada, building ships and hiring rowers from throughout Greece. Alarmed at this news, the Corcyraeans realized they could no longer pursue their previous practice of isolationism. They needed to ally with one of the great powers. Because of the inevitable opposition of Corinth at Sparta—and because they were a democracy—they chose the Athenians over the Lacedaemonians, and learning of the impending arrival of Corcyraean ambassadors at Athens, the Corinthians sent envoys of their own to run interference.

The ambassadors from both states addressed the Athenians at a meeting of their assembly, outdoors on the hill of the Pnyx and attended by thousands of male citizens. The Corcyraeans took the position that war with the Spartan alliance was coming and that if the Athenians did not

5. Thucydides 1. 29. 5–30. 1.

ally with them, there was serious danger that before that war broke out, Sparta's chief naval ally, Corinth, would have swallowed up Corcyra's navy; conversely, if Athens allied with Corcyra, it would have Corcyra's ships as well as its own with which to fight the Peloponnesians. They also pointed out that allying with them was no violation of the Thirty Years' Peace, which stipulated that neutrals were free to join either side.

The Corinthians replied with a clever piece of rhetoric that included a general character assassination of the Corcyraeans, a list of favors performed for Athens by the Corinthians, and some Athenian sins. Most particularly, they reminded the Athenians of the role Corinth had played in dissuading the Spartans from intervening to help the Samians in their recent rebellion. The chief burden of their speech, however, was to point out that war with the Peloponnesian League was far from guaranteed. This they threw in almost as an aside in the hope of frightening the Athenians into thinking that by allying with Corcyra they would only bring on themselves a war that they might well otherwise have been spared, but it is crucial to their argument.[6]

The Corinthians' strategy presented the Athenians with an agonizing dilemma. What the men of Athens had to decide at this pivotal juncture in their history was whether to risk making themselves vulnerable in the event of a war or to risk bringing on a war with the entire Peloponnesian League by angering the Corinthians. For many present at the meeting it was the most important decision they had taken in their lifetimes. At first, most were inclined to steer clear of an alliance with Corcyra for fear of breaking the oaths taken at the time of the Thirty Years' Peace, but at the second meeting of the assembly, after talking it over again among themselves and perhaps also with wives, mothers, and sisters, at the urging of Pericles they settled on a compromise. Instead of turning the Corcyraeans down flat or making a full offensive and defensive alliance with them, they would make a defensive alliance only: each state would come to the aid of the other only if it were attacked by a third party.[7] This, of course, was a subterfuge, one that foreshadowed the Romans' habit of

6. Corcyraeans and Corinthians at the Athenian assembly: Thucydides 1. 32. 1–43. 4.

7. Thucydides 1. 44. 1.

making alliances with states that they had every reason to know were about to be attacked; it was in precisely this way that Rome would later manage to build an empire without appearing to violate its principle that all Rome's wars were defensive ones.

The Corcyraeans had promised undying gratitude if the Athenians would take them into their alliance, but their gratitude cannot have been great when they saw that the Athenians were sending them only ten ships.[8] Ten was just enough to cause an international incident but not enough to turn the tide of battle. Worse still, the assembly had instructed the Athenians not to become involved in the battle unless the Corinthians were actually on the point of landing on Corcyra. Events, however, did not go as planned. At the battle off the Sybota Islands, near the southeastern tip of Corcyra, when the Athenians saw the Corcyraeans really hard-pressed, they disobeyed the assembly's orders and jumped into the fray.[9] The Corinthians were still winning—the best of all possible worlds, some of the more bellicose of them must have thought, since they had also gotten the Athenians to break the Thirty Years' Peace. Regrouping after rowing through the wrecks and killing as many men as they could (in the confusion, some of their own allies), the Corinthians had set out to attack once more when the astonished Corcyraeans observed something very strange happening.

The Corinthians had suddenly begun to back water.[10]

Why?

They had seen something on the horizon. Ships. Squinting, they made out the Athenian insignia. The approaching vessels were indeed Athenian reinforcements. Coming under attack for the paltry contingent he had dispatched to Corcyra, Pericles had sent out twice as many ships to join them.[11] The Corinthians, however, had no way of knowing that they now had only twenty new ships to deal with. What they conjured up in their minds—particularly as it was getting dark—was the full force of the Athenian navy.

8. Thucydides 1. 45. 1-2.

9. Thucydides 1. 49. 7.

10. Thucydides 1. 50. 5–51. 2.

11. Plutarch *Pericles* 29. 3.

Daylight brought the realization that the Athenians had not, in fact, sent their entire fleet, but still the Corinthians were disinclined to fight again. Instead, they sent several men out in a boat to accuse the Athenians of breaking the treaty. If this was the Athenians' intention, they announced, they should just go ahead and take them as their first prisoners.

"Take them," shouted the Corcyraeans, "and kill them!"[12] The Athenians, however, remained calm and told the Corinthians they were free to sail anywhere they wanted except Corcyra. The Corinthians promptly headed for home, selling most of the Corcyraean prisoners as slaves but keeping 250 as hostages and treating them exceptionally well. These tended to be of the upper class, and the Corinthians held on to them with the idea in mind that they might be useful in winning Corcyra over to them in the future.[13] In fact, the Corinthians' return of these oligarchs to Corcyra would set off one of the bloodiest civil wars in Greek history.

POTIDAEA, THE DUTIFUL DAUGHTER

One victim of the escalating tension between Athens and Corinth was the town of Potidaea that sat on the entrance to Pallene, the westernmost of the three narrow "fingers" of the Chalcidic peninsula in northeastern Greece (see Map 4). Its position in the Greek world had always been peculiar, and now it became untenable: it was both a member of the Delian League and a Corinthian colony—but not just any Corinthian colony. Whereas Corcyra was aloof to the point of disrespect, Potidaea was so deferential as to take its magistrates from its mother city. Bearing in mind the festering resentment of Corinth and knowing that there was unrest in the region, in part sparked by the wily Perdiccas II, who had acceded to the Macedonian throne around 448 and was stirring up other northerners against Athens, the Athenians ordered the Potidaeans to pull

12. Thucydides 1. 53. 3.
13. Thucydides 1. 55.

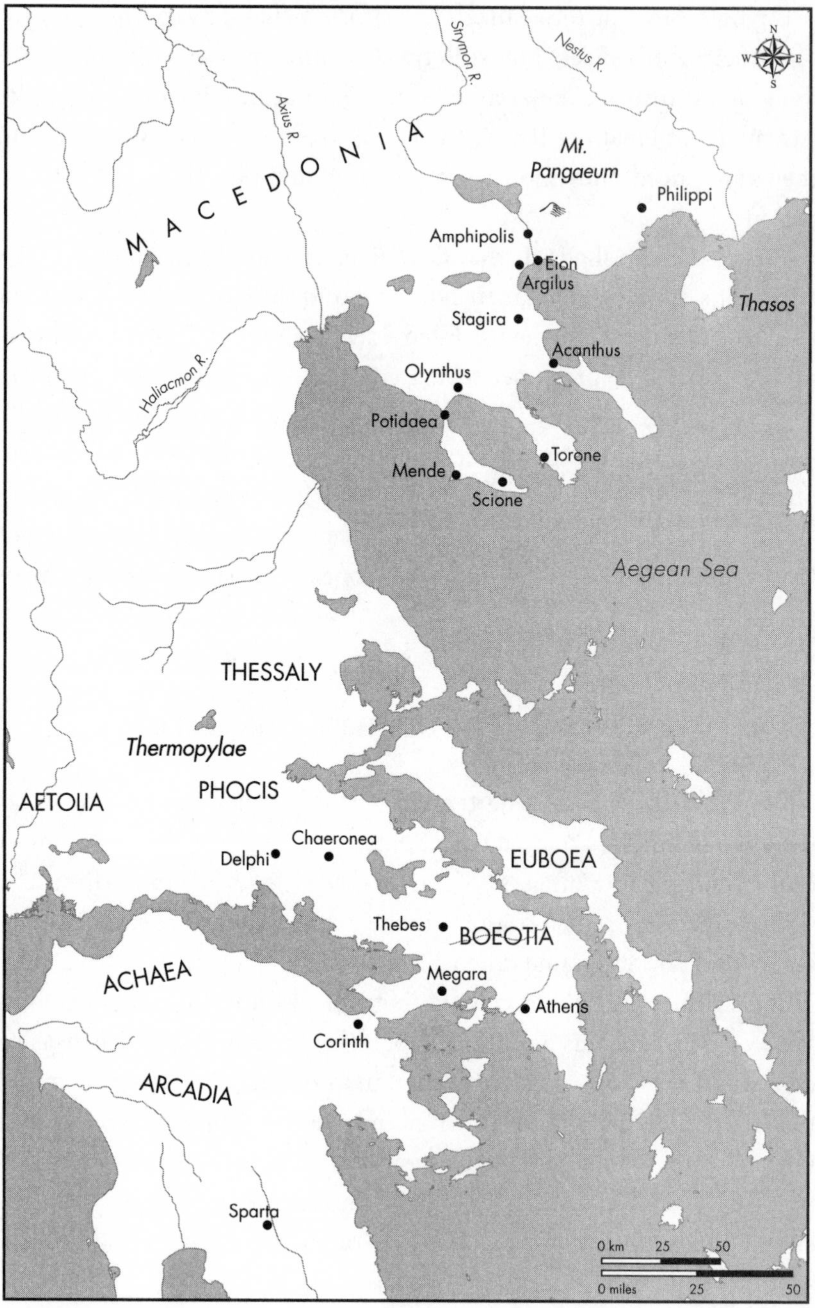

MAP 4
Chalcidice.

down the walls that protected them on the Pallene side, to dismiss their Corinthian magistrates, and to give hostages for future good behavior.

The Potidaeans' attempts at negotiating with Athens failed, and with Corinthian backing they received secret Spartan assurances that Sparta would invade Athens if Potidaea rebelled from the empire.[14] Secret, but false: Potidaea did rebel, along with other cities in Chalcidice, but Sparta did not invade, at least not in time to help Potidaea. Evidently there was both a war party and a peace party in Sparta, as is natural in times of international tension; the war party promised to invade Athens, but when the peace party prevailed, the Spartans failed to deliver. In their rebellion, the Potidaeans also surely received encouragement from Perdiccas, who had been none too pleased at the arrival of an Athenian colony practically on his doorstep: Amphipolis, which Pericles' associate Hagnon had founded in 437 in a bend on the Strymon River. The Athenians soon blockaded Potidaea, and the siege would be a long and painful one. It further angered the Corinthians, moreover, not only because Potidaea was their colony but because they had sent some troops to assist it, and many Corinthian soldiers were trapped inside when the siege began. Technically, of course, the Athenians' treatment of Potidaea did not violate the Thirty Years' Peace; it was not the Athenians' fault that some Corinthians were stuck inside the city—theoretically, they were volunteers, in any case—and the treaty allowed each hegemon to discipline its own members. But in the eyes of the Corinthians, the Athenians were bullying their "child" (no matter that they themselves had gone to war with their other child, Corcyra).

THE LAST STRAW

Around the same time, the Athenians passed a decree against Megara, probably the last of several issued during the 430s.[15] The decree was

14. Thucydides 1. 58. 1.

15. On the decree, D. Kagan, *The Outbreak of the Peloponnesian War* (Ithaca, NY: Cornell University Press, 1969), 254–72; G. de Ste. Croix, *The Origins of the Peloponnesian War* (Ithaca, NY: Cornell University Press, 1972), *passim*; as well as C. Fornara, "Plutarch and the Megarian Decree," *Yale Classical Studies* 24 (1975): 213–23; B. MacDonald, "The Megarian Decree," *Historia* 32 (1983): 385–410; P. Stadter, *A Commentary on Plutarch's Pericles* (Chapel Hill: University of North Carolina Press, 1979), 272–83.

of a nature unprecedented in history: a peacetime embargo, barring the Megarians from trading in the Athenian city center and marketplace known as the *agora* or in the ports of the Athenian empire. The Thirty Years' Peace had specified that each hegemon could make rules regarding its own sphere of influence, and the Athenians argued that this was all they were doing, billing the decree as retaliation for the Megarians' cultivation of sacred borderland that did not belong to them and for harboring some runaway slaves. Retaliation for contributing ships to the Corinthian fleet at the battles of Leucimme and Sybota would be closer to the truth; it could be a "proportionate response" to Megarian involvement there, a middle ground between doing nothing and taking military action. Bitterness over the Megarians' slaughter of the Athenian garrison in 446? Too late. A warning shot across the bow to discourage other Peloponnesian states that might be thinking of aiding Corinth in another encounter with Athens? Possibly. Pressure on the Megarians to rejoin the Delian League? Though at first this might seem farfetched, not only had Megara defected from the Spartan to the Athenian alliance once before, but it would in fact swallow its pride and move to do so again within ten years, in 424. Megarian membership in the Delian League brought priceless advantages to Athens, bringing as it did control of the land bridge from the Peloponnesus. Was it unthinkable that the Megarians might approach the Athenians, tell them they had been considering their options, comparing their time in the Peloponnesian League with their time in the Delian League, and offer alliance once again?

Some years later the comic dramatist Aristophanes put forward a degrading and implausible explanation for Pericles' actions toward Megara in his play *The Acharnians*, produced in 425 when the sufferings of the war had been going on for six years. Dicaeopolis, the play's protagonist and an advocate for peace, has his own interpretation of the war's outbreak. It all began, he says, when some drunken young Athenians stole a prostitute from Megara, and the Megarians, enraged by the insult, stole two whores from an establishment run by Aspasia of Miletus,

Pericles' common-law wife after his divorce. Not very believable, but it seems to have gotten a good laugh.[16]

Whatever its purpose—and it is not likely to have had anything to do with purloined prostitutes—the decree against Megara fanned the flames of the ill will already simmering in Greece against Athens, and at the instigation of (naturally) Corinth, the Spartans announced that any state that wished to do so might address the meeting of the Spartan assembly that would be held in 432. This was most unprecedented.

A STAB IN THE DARK

A number of speeches were delivered at this gathering, not counting private conversations and heckling, but Thucydides' narrative presents only four. This quartet may or may not accurately record the substance of what was said, and the Eurypontid king Archidamus's forecast of a long war is suspiciously prescient, but they are all we have to work with, and they do seem accurately to reflect the concerns of those present. The first speech, by the Corinthian ambassadors, by no means seeks to capture the Spartans' goodwill. Rather, its aim is to shame them into taking

16. Aristophanes parodies the cause of the war in *Acharnians*, ll. 515–39. The ancient sources on Aspasia are collected and analyzed in M. Henry, *Prisoner of History: Aspasia of Miletus and Her Biographical Tradition* (New York: Oxford University Press, 1995); see also Stadter, *Commentary*, 233–42. Plutarch also introduces a self-serving and disreputable motive for Pericles' intransigence about yielding to any of the Spartan embassies. His associate Pheidias the sculptor had been the contractor for the great gold and ivory statue of Athena on the acropolis and had been accused of helping himself to some of the materials; at the same time Aspasia was accused of impiety. So much anger, moreover, was directed at his friend the unconventional philosopher Anaxagoras that he felt the need to arrange his safe departure from Athens. Feeling that the people's wrath would next descend on him, he brought on the war to create a distraction. It now seems clear, however, that the trial of Pheidias (and thus the other attacks on Pericles' friends as well) took place in 438/37 and thus could not have played this role in sparking the war; see F. J. Frost, "Pericles and Dracontides," *Journal of Hellenic Studies* 84 (1964): 69–72, for the evidence for Pheidias's trial and for a nuanced discussion of the attacks, Stadter, *Commentary*, 283–305. Plutarch, whose evidence seems to come from Ephorus via Diodorus, does not vouch for the theory but claims that it was widely believed.

action by comparing their national character unfavorably with that of the Athenians:

> They are impetuous where you procrastinate and they are explorers where you are homebodies, because they think they might get something out of going abroad whereas you think that moving will threaten what you already have. . . . They are the only people on earth for whom achieving what they have in mind and hoping for it are virtually the same because of the speed with which they attempt whatever they decide to do. . . . In brief, the truth is that Athenians were born not to have peace and not to let anyone else have it, either.[17]

Your ways, they say, are outmoded. In politics as in all areas of life, it is important to keep pace with new developments. Do not let the world leave you behind but rather set aside your natural sluggishness. Come to the aid of your allies, and invade Attica at once. Otherwise, we may be forced to seek some other alliance. (Argos, Sparta's great rival in the Peloponnesus? Or, could it be . . . Athens? Not likely, but the very idea must have struck terror in the Spartans.)

Before the Spartans had time to absorb this onslaught of "constructive criticism," an Athenian rose to speak, one of several men of Athens who claimed to be in the area on "other business" rather than as part of an official delegation. As it is impossible to imagine what other business they might have had in Sparta, they were plainly an official delegation that called itself something else. In the speech they stress the fact that they defeated the Persians at Marathon single-handed (not true—they were backed up by their allies the Plataeans) and the prominent role of their navy and their commander Themistocles in the decisive sea battle at Salamis—Themistocles whom the Spartans themselves had greatly honored for his role in the defeat of Persia. The postwar naval alliance, they argue, was handed to them only after the Spartans turned it down, and it was only natural that they did not let

17. Thucydides 1. 70. 4–9.

it go. "It is an eternal law," after all, "that the strong should rule the weak."[18] If you were to rule after defeating us in war, they say, you might very well lose all the goodwill you now have from those who fear us. (And in fact Sparta for all its military victories never did gain the slightest goodwill.) Deliberate slowly, they warn,

> and do not, persuaded by the opinions of others, bring trouble on your own house. Assess before you are actually in it how great is the incalculable element of war, how it tends to degenerate into a gamble the longer it lasts. We are only at the start, but which way it will go is a stab in the dark.[19]

Most of all, they say, let us submit these differences to arbitration according to the terms of our treaty.

At this juncture the foreigners are dismissed so that the Spartans may deliberate by themselves. Although most are inclined to go to war at once, the Eurypontid king Archidamus (the only one in Sparta, the Agiad Pleistoanax still being in exile) is clearly alarmed by what he sees as a surging tide of war fever consuming the assembly, particularly the young who have limited experience of war. The proposed war, he points out, will not be easy or quick. The Athenians have resources that the Spartans do not: enormous wealth and a huge navy. Yes, he says, of course we can go to war with them, but not yet. We need to build up our strength; the Athenians cannot be defeated except at sea, and we do not yet have the ships to do that. Given their conduct, nobody could blame us if we cultivated non-Greek allies (i.e., Persia). And we should certainly send ambassadors to Athens to negotiate with them, particularly about Potidaea, in case the war can be avoided altogether.

The next speaker is Sthenelaidas, one of the five ephors. The Athenians, he maintains, patted themselves on the back a lot but nowhere denied that they had wronged Sparta's allies. Besides, if they

18. Thucydides 1. 76. 2
19. Thucydides 1. 78. 1–2.

were good in the past and are bad in the present, they deserved to be punished twice over. They may have money and ships and horses, but the Spartans have allies who must not be betrayed to the Athenians—an ironic proclamation indeed, since time would soon make clear that betraying its allies was what Sparta did best. And none of this deliberation! (Not for nothing do we derive the word "laconic" from Laconia.) The Spartans must vote for the war that Spartan honor demands.[20]

Spartans voted by shouting, but Sthenelaidas asked those who believed the Athenians had broken the treaty and those who did not to separate into two groups, claiming that he could not tell which side was louder. No doubt he wanted to use peer pressure to shame any who were wavering (or who were supporters of Archidamus) into voting for war. It worked. The group supporting the belief that the treaty had been broken was significantly larger than the other group. Still not entirely certain of their best course of action, however, the Spartans sent envoys to Delphi to ask if they should indeed go to war. As so often in interactions with the tricky oracles of Greece, no yes or no answer was forthcoming. Rather, the god replied that if they fought with might and main then victory would be theirs—and that he would aid them, whether they called on him or not.[21] If the Spartans lost, the oracle could always displace the blame onto them, claiming that they had not tried hard enough. But the response was certainly more encouraging than not, so the Spartans then summoned a congress of their allies. Not surprisingly, the Corinthians canvassed the individual cities before the meeting, urging them each to vote for war, and in fact a majority did—though some did not.[22] Thucydides was mistaken about the growth of Athenian power, but he was not mistaken about Spartan fear. What the Spartans feared was not that the Athenians were about to invade the Peloponnesus, however, or even pick off the Spartans' allies one by one, but rather that their own alliance would disintegrate from within if they did not meet their allies' demands.

20. Thucydides 1. 86.
21. Thucydides 1. 118. 3.
22. Thucydides 1. 119. 2, 1. 125. 1.

WILL THERE BE WAR?

Yet no war broke out. The Spartans began sending embassies to Athens. Were these simply designed to garner favor in the eyes of gods and Greeks—so that, as Thucydides put it, the Spartans "would have the strongest grounds for war should the Athenians refuse to listen," or was there a genuine opportunity for negotiation here?[23] After all, the Athenian "non-envoys" had spoken of arbitration. The first embassy demanded that the Athenians drive out "the curse of the goddess," a curse that had been incurred some 200 years previously by an archon who belonged to the Alcmaeonid family, to which, of course, Pericles belonged on his mother's side. The Spartans' intent is not clear. Surely they knew that the Athenians would not exile Pericles. The Spartan demand was met with a clever riposte: theAthenians for their part insisted that the Spartans expel not one but two curses—the curse of Taenarum and the curse of Athena of the Bronze House. The first referred to the murder of some helot suppliants, the second to the murder by starvation of the regent Pausanias, who had taken over for Leonidas after the king's death at Thermopylae. Many charges had been made against Pausanias in the years following the Persian Wars—that he was conspiring to marry Xerxes' daughter, to stir up the helots in revolt, and so forth. When he saw the ephors coming for him, so Thucydides reports, he sought refuge in the temple of Athena of the Bronze House. The ephors walled him up there until he was about to expire of hunger; then they dragged him out to die in the open air, to avoid the pollution that would attend on his dying in the temple.[24] But what person or persons did the Athenians want expelled to expiate this curse? A case has been made for Archidamus, who might have been involved as a young man with both of those episodes, but the answer is unclear.[25] The next embassies had some real meat in them.[26] Plainly not

23. Thucydides 1. 126. 1.

24. Thucydides 1. 134.

25. Logically, of course, the last Spartan any peace-seeking Athenians would want to see expelled would be the dovish Spartan king, but this portion of the negotiations was not a serious dialogue, merely a game of tit for tat. See J. Marr, "What Did the Athenians Demand in 432 B. C.?" *Phoenix* 52 (1998): 120–4.

26. Thucydides 1. 139. 1–3.

all Lacedaemonians were eager for war. The envoys asked that the siege of Potidaea be lifted and that, most of all, the Megarian decree should be rescinded. When Pericles was shielding himself behind the technicality that a particular law prevented him from taking down the tablet on which the decree was written, the Spartan ambassador Polyalces cried, "Well then, just turn it around to the wall; surely there's no law against that!"[27] Pericles declined to comply with this request, and the law remained in its original position.

The Spartans' final embassy was indeed designed merely to put the Athenians in a bad light: the Spartans want peace, their three ambassadors said, but only on the condition that the Athenians grant the Greeks their independence, that is, lay down their empire.[28] But of course the Athenians were no more likely to do that than the Spartans were to dissolve the Peloponnesian League.

Let us return to the middle embassies. When the Athenian assembly met to consider these demands, many men, Thucydides reports, said many things, some arguing in favor of the necessity of war, others advocating the revocation of the Megarian decree and pointing out the foolishness of letting it stand in the way of peace.[29] All that remains in the way of evidence for these deliberations, however, is an unyielding, indeed bellicose, speech in the text of Thucydides' history, given by Pericles. In it Pericles presents a threefold argument, maintaining, first, that the Spartans are at fault for refusing arbitration; second, that going to war over the Megarian degree is hardly going to war over a trifle, because if the Athenians concede on a small point, they will soon be asked to concede on a larger one; and third, that the war is winnable.[30] After hearing this speech, the majority of the Athenians voted as Pericles wished, although they were still open to arbitration.[31]

27. Plutarch *Pericles* 30.1.

28. Thucydides 1. 139. 3.

29. Thucydides 1. 139. 4.

30. Pericles offers to rescind the Megarian decree if the Spartans abandoned their longstanding practice of the expulsion of non-Spartans from their land (Thucydides 1. 144. 2), but this is obviously a non-starter. The Spartans had sound reason for their policy, namely, the fear that foreigners would stir up the helots.

31. Thucydides 1. 145.

This was a war that might well not have happened. The king of Sparta had no stomach for it, and his countrymen were anxious enough that they sent to Delphi throughout for reassurance even after they had voted for it. Even with the pressure relentlessly applied by Corinth, not all the Peloponnesian League members voted for it, though Thucydides does not tell us which ones voted against it, or on what grounds. Many in Athens were averse to fighting. The assemblymen there had at first been persuaded by the arguments of the Corinthians and were loath to make the provocative alliance with Corcyra. Later on, when debating whether to rescind the Megarian decree or accede to other Spartan requests, some spoke out in favor of conceding to the Spartans before the final vote was taken—and even then, they were open to arbitration. Believing that the war had at some point become inevitable, however, Thucydides gives short shrift to the possibility that it could have been avoided and does not share with us the names of those at Athens who spoke out in opposition or record their speeches, though he surely knew them. This gives us a very distorted view of the thinking of the Athenians. The frequency of war in human history can easily blind us to the fact that war disrupts farming, trading, and the breeding and raising of the next generation, but people contemplating entering on a war are sometimes aware of these things. The Athenians in particular had much to protect at this time in their history. They had just finished work on the glorious temple to Athena that sat atop their Acropolis, the Parthenon, and other building projects in their civic space were still in progress. Ultimately, however, the sentiments of those Athenians who preferred peace were overcome by those of the war party that Pericles led so intractably, and the Spartans acceded to the pressure of their allies, on whose goodwill they depended to maintain preeminence in the Peloponnesus and their security against the helots.

The first decade of the war that ensued is known as the Archidamian War, after King Archidamus, but this is a misnomer. This was very much Pericles' war; Archidamus did not want it and, like Pericles, died soon after it began, in 427. When Pericles lay dying of plague in 429, his friends, thinking he was unconscious, sat commenting on his many outstanding achievements as a general. Being, in fact, conscious, he interrupted and pointed out that such achievements were often due to fortune and expressed surprise that they had not commented on his greatest claim to admiration—"that no living Athenian had ever put on mourning clothes because of me."[32] This delusion would have been compounded exponentially had he lived a few more years.

At this point there were three principals in the war: Athens, Sparta, and Corinth. The squawky Corinthians bear much of the blame for goading the Spartans into war. The Spartans were not completely under the thumb of Corinth, as witness their evident willingness to call off the war if only the Athenians would rescind the Megarian decree. But the Spartans had much to lose by ignoring the concerns of their allies. Tragically, they found themselves gripped in the coils of an entangling alliance. Even more than the Athenians, moreover, they were tormented by real or perceived slights to their status. They had done their best to tolerate the shift in the balance of power in Greece that followed the Persian Wars, but ultimately they failed. The Athenians for their part neglected to recognize that some restraint in dealing with Peloponnesian allies would be prudent, and that engaging in brinksmanship with such actions as the Megarian decree might not be in their own interest. Each hegemon, concerned about its own status and honor, might have given some consideration to the fact that the other had similar concerns, but that would have been most un-Greek. Agamemnon had not taken care to avoid stepping on Achilles' toes, nor Achilles on Agamemnon's. The mythical Trojan War hung on the kidnapping of the Greek Helen by the Trojan Paris, but the plot of the very real *Iliad* hung on a trading of insults between the Greek commander-in-chief Agamemnon and the best of the Greek fighters, Achilles, that led Achilles to withdraw from the action.[33]

It is important to remember that neither the Athenians nor the Spartans who voted for war (some, of course, did not) were voting for the Peloponnesian War as we know it. Such a thing was unimaginable in

32. Plutarch *Pericles* 38. 4.

33. The notion that questions of honor and status underlay the Archidamian War just as they had undergirded earlier Greek conflicts forms the premise of J. E. Lendon's *Song of Wrath: The Peloponnesian War Begins* (New York: Basic Books, 2010). His point is well taken, although he sometimes carries it to extremes.

classical Greece. What they anticipated was something on a much smaller scale; Pericles himself told the Athenians that they had the resources to hold out for perhaps three years. Archidamus (if we may believe the eerily prophetic speech that appears in the pages of Thucydides) had warned the Spartans that this was a war they would leave to their children, but this seemed so improbable that his gloomy prognostications were discounted. Greek wars were generally very short—indeed, many lasted only a few hours. The Persian Wars, as Thucydides himself pointed out, were decided in just a few battles.[34] The so-called First Peloponnesian War had been an on-and-off affair, not a steady hammering. Had the Athenian assembly or the Peloponnesian League known what it was getting into, serious negotiations might very well have stopped hostilities in their tracks.

34. Thucydides 1. 23. 1.

4

WAR BEGINS

THOUGH SEVERAL MONTHS PASSED between the Peloponnesian vote to go to war with Athens and the actual outbreak of hostilities, the attack when it did come issued once again from a rather unexpected quarter. Despairing of any action from their hegemon, the Thebans sprang into action, triggering the long and brutal war that would change the course of Greek history, introduce new ways of fighting, blur social distinctions, multiply civil strife within poleis, and eradicate the time-honored tradition of fighting only in the spring and summer. Soon the farmer-hoplites and sailors would be unable to return home every year to harvest their land: the capture of Amphipolis in 424, which led to the exile of the historian Thucydides while he was serving as general, took place in the snows of December. For the first time in Greek history, war became an all-consuming, year-round way of life.

THEBES POUNCES

Conspicuously absent from the complainants in the Peloponnesian League on the eve of war were the Thebans, head of the Boeotian League. Less than eight tantalizing miles (thirteen kilometers) to the south of Thebes, Plataea, though in Boeotian territory, was allied with hated Athens. The Thebans resented it bitterly, but they could not bend it to their will and force it into the Boeotian League.

The Thebans' desire to gain possession of Plataea was not merely a matter of taming its stubbornness. Though a small polis, Plataea lay on the one route that connected Thebes with the Peloponnesus via Megara, bypassing Attica. Control of Plataea would be extraordinarily useful for attacks on Athens. And so it was that on a cloudy March night in 431 more than 300 Thebans crossed the Asopus River that marked the border of Plataea and were admitted to the town by the oligarch Nauclides and his partisans, men who aimed to destroy the democracy then in power there and rule the city under the aegis of the Boeotian League.

The Thebans imagined that the panic-stricken Plataeans would accept their offer of membership in the Boeotian League; it was nighttime, and the invaders were armed, but as the Plataeans mulled things over, they began to notice that the number of Thebans in the city was actually rather small. Digging through the walls that connected their houses so they would not be conspicuous passing through the streets, they made barricades out of unhitched wagons. In a turnabout, the Thebans soon found themselves under attack in the dark in an unfamiliar place—in a downpour, to boot, for it had begun to rain heavily—with women and slaves screaming and throwing stones and tiles down on them from the rooftops. Few of the Thebans knew what roads they needed to follow to save their lives, and there was no moon, so most of them were killed, and they were trapped in the city when a Plataean locked the gate by jamming a spear butt into the sliding bar where the locking pin would have gone. Of those who climbed the wall and jumped, most died. Some did find an unguarded gate and smashed the lock with an axe a woman had given them, but only a few, for the opening was quickly discovered.[1] Finally, the 180 Thebans trapped inside the city were rounded up and captured.

This was not at all what the Thebans had expected, but their backup plan had already been set in motion. The rest of the Theban army was on standby in full strength in case the projected betrayal by Nauclides was unsuccessful. But the rainfall had swollen the Asopus to full flood, and it was not easily crossed. By the time the reinforcements arrived, it was too late. Fearing for the folk in the country, the Plataeans sent a herald to the Thebans warning them not to harm the people or property outside

1. Thucydides 2. 2. 2.–4. 4.

the city, lest they kill those men they had taken alive. The Thebans then withdrew. Having brought their people and property in from the fields, the Plataeans proceeded to kill their 180 prisoners, among whom was Eurymachus, one of the leaders of the attempted takeover.[2]

The Athenians had been told of events in Plataea and had immediately arrested any Boeotians found in Attica, expressly instructing the Plataeans to do nothing about the Theban prisoners until the Athenians could participate in the deliberations about them. Their hearts sank when they learned that the men were already dead. War had not yet broken out, and it might still have been prevented, something some Athenians seemed to want. Eurymachus was a prominent man in Thebes. He and the other 179 prisoners could have made excellent hostages, either in the event of war or to prevent it from happening. However much they may have regretted the Thebans' rash behavior, the Athenians behaved like a loyal ally and sent food and a garrison to protect the city against the next wave of attack and removed the women and children and the men unfit for military service, though 110 women remained, evidently as cooks.[3]

The Spartan war party—not to mention the Corinthians and the Megarians—was no doubt thrilled that after all those months of nothing but talk, someone had finally done something. But those who had sent the embassies to Athens seeking peace could not have been happy that their Theban allies had taken advantage of the volatile situation in Greece to strike at little Plataea, hallowed site of the final victory over Xerxes—Plataea, which the Spartans in 479 had sworn would forever remain inviolate in honor of its special place in Greek hearts.[4] After all the Spartans' efforts to couch the war in fair-sounding slogans like "give the Greeks their freedom," the Thebans had launched a sneak attack on, of all places, Plataea. Many Spartans, surely, were horrified. But it was done.

Yet Archidamus still had hopes of avoiding a Greek world war. When the events in Plataea became known, the Spartan king duly sent word to all Spartan allies to send two thirds of their troops to muster at the

2. Thucydides 2. 5. 1–7.
3. Thucydides 2. 6, 2. 78. 3
4. Thucydides 2. 71. 2–4.

isthmus at Corinth, the required contribution specified by the terms of membership in the Peloponnesian League for an expedition far from home. Nonetheless, before moving his troops into Attica he made one final push for peace; it was at this juncture that he sent the envoy Melesippus to Athens to see whether the Athenians would make concessions in light of the fact that the Peloponnesians were already on the march. But this embassy bore no fruit, and the war was really on.

PLANS AND GOALS

The Spartans sought to undo the Athenians' empire, if at all possible, by pouring infantry into Attica. If that did not work, they would have to build a substantial navy. But whatever the method involved, they aimed to break up the far-flung empire of the Athenians and liberate the oppressed Greeks from Athenian tyranny. Other members of the Peloponnesian League had auxiliary goals. Megara, of course, wanted the decree compromising its commerce lifted and to see the Athenians punished for having imposed it. The Potidaeans (not, of course, a member of the Peloponnesian League, but a close associate of their mother-state Corinth) wanted to be freed from their newly unpleasant hegemon. The Corinthians wanted their commercial rival Athens knocked out as a trading power. The Athenians' goal was much simpler: not to let any of this happen. They might grab Peloponnesian territory in the course of the conflict, but that was only as a means to push the Spartans toward surrender. What they chiefly wanted, as at the time of the Thirty Years' Peace, was for the enemy to concede Athenian parity with them. Stalemate would be fine as long as the Peloponnesians recognized it for what it was.

In the broadest strokes, each side had a clear strategy at the outset of the war, but of course circumstances change strategies, and war changes circumstances. Archidamus, capitalizing on the Peloponnesian League's superiority in infantry, planned to hit the Athenians by marching into Attica and devastating its crops. Either the Athenians would march out and fight, in which case they would surely lose, or they would surrender to prevent further ravaging of their land. If the first attempt did not work, it could be repeated the following year, and, if absolutely necessary, the year after that. He also aspired to expand the Peloponnesian navy in hopes of making it viable in contests with Athens and its allies.

The strategy that Pericles sold to the Athenians was to accept their inferiority to the Peloponnesians in hoplite strength and to wait them out inside the city walls, refusing to be provoked to battle: their 13,000 or so hoplites of suitable age (twenty to forty-five) and fitness would be no match for the dazzling combined infantry of the Spartans and the Boeotians, the best hoplites in the world. Huddling inside the city as if it were an island, the Athenians could not be starved out, for the Long Walls meant that food would flow in readily through the Piraeus. Along with the 13,000 hoplites on active duty, 16,000 others were available for service, boys too young for the draft and the resident aliens known as "metics" who could defend the city walls, the Piraeus, and the Long Walls, and there were 1,200 cavalry, including mounted archers and 1,600 bowmen who went on foot. Most of all, the Athenians had their splendid navy. When the war broke out there were 300 seaworthy ships in the dockyards, and another 100 or so were available from Corcyra, Chios, and Lesbos. In a pinch, some older ships could be refurbished as needed.

Money, of course, would be needed to maintain the vessels and pay their crews (as well as land forces), but Athens was a very rich state, as Archidamus had warned the Spartans. Four hundred talents came in annually from internal sources such as customs duties, market taxes, rents, and court fees, but this provided no surplus; the surplus came from the 600 talents of imperial revenue. (A talent was a large sum of money—say, the amount that it cost to pay the crew of a trireme for a month, over half a million US dollars. A man who had a talent was wealthy.) That would not be sufficient for the costs of the war, but the Athenians held on the Acropolis 6,000 talents of coined silver as well as at least 500 talents' worth of uncoined silver and gold, in addition to sums in other temples. And if they found themselves in truly dire straits, there was the gold plate that covered the great statue of Athena on the Acropolis, removable and worth 40 talents, though melting it down for the war effort was certainly a horrid prospect. With these resources, both income and reserve, the Athenians could hold out for three years—not more; but Pericles calculated that the Spartans, who disliked leaving the Peloponnesus and had been ambivalent about the war to begin with, would abandon their fruitless efforts to break the Athenians' will after a campaigning season or two.

Against the Athenians and their allies, what the Peloponnesians had to offer was about a hundred ships (not all in good repair) manned by inferior sailors—and crack infantry: the hoplites of Boeotia were famous, and the Spartans had lived in barracks since boyhood, drilling together while leaving the matter of food production to helots. Athenians, on the other hand, spent their lives as farmers (or, sometimes, craftsmen) doing their military service on a hit-or-miss basis when called up. The Athenians, the Peloponnesians believed, would be no match for the hoplite force that was threatening to cover Attica like a tsunami.

And yet. To watch one's land being ravaged and do nothing; to decline a challenge to battle; to see the enemy getting closer and closer and stand fast; all these were challenges to one's manhood that no Greek could take lightly. Since the days of Achilles, bravery in warfare had been the supreme virtue of a Greek man. In Sparta, the only men commemorated in death with a named tombstone were those who died in battle, just as the only women so commemorated were those who had died in childbirth. The epitaph of the Athenian poet Aeschylus, the father of Greek tragedy who won a remarkable thirteen first prizes for his plays before dying in Sicily, commemorated only his military service at Marathon:

> This monument in wheatbearing Gela
> Hides a dead Athenian, Aeschylus, son of Euphorion.
> Of his illustrious courage the field of Marathon could tell
> And the longhaired Persian, who had cause to know it well.

Now Pericles was asking Athenian men to tie themselves instead to the mast like the more evolved Odysseus and not be lured onto the rocks of the battlefield by the siren song of taunting—and marauding—Peloponnesians. It is a testament to Pericles' skills as a statesman and orator that he was able to persuade the Athenians of the wisdom of the "island strategy"—though he did not persuade all the Athenians all the time.

It was by no means an entirely defensive strategy. Cavalry and archers would harass the invaders and make their time in Attica unpleasant, and at the same time the navy would hit the coast of the Peloponnesus with more than casual intensity. These forays on land and sea might keep hands busy and distract minds from feelings of helplessness and frustration, but more important, they might even wear the Spartans down enough to lead to peace. If Thucydides reported correctly, Greeks of the day hoped not: all of Greece, he said, was lining up on the side of Sparta, some fearing that they would fall under Athenian domination and others hoping to get free of it.[5]

Would Brawn, then, march against Brain, Achilles against Odysseus? Not quite, for this war involved not only Athens and Sparta but their many allies. In addition to the Boeotians and the Corinthians, all the states of the Peloponnesus were lined up with Sparta except Argos and Achaea, which remained neutral (though Pellene in Achaea did fight for Sparta); the Spartans could also count on Megara, Phocis, Eastern Locris, and the island of Leucas off the coast of Anactorium in northwestern Greece and Ambracia to its north. Allied with Athens were Corcyra with its formidable navy, Zacynthus off the west coast of the Peloponnesus, Euboea, Thrace, the Hellespont, the coastal cities of Ionia and Caria in Asia Minor and the offshore islands there, particularly Chios and Lesbos, the Messenians who had been settled in Naupactus, the Zacynthians, most of the Acarnanians, most of the Aegean islands except Melos and Thera, and of course Plataea[6] (see Map 5). The whole world was watching to see how it would turn out—not only the poleis of Greece, but states farther afield as well, most particularly Persia, which had kept a vigilant eye on activity in Greece ever since its misadventures there earlier in the century.

5. Thucydides 2. 8. 4–5.

6. Thucydides 2. 9, 2. 78. 3.

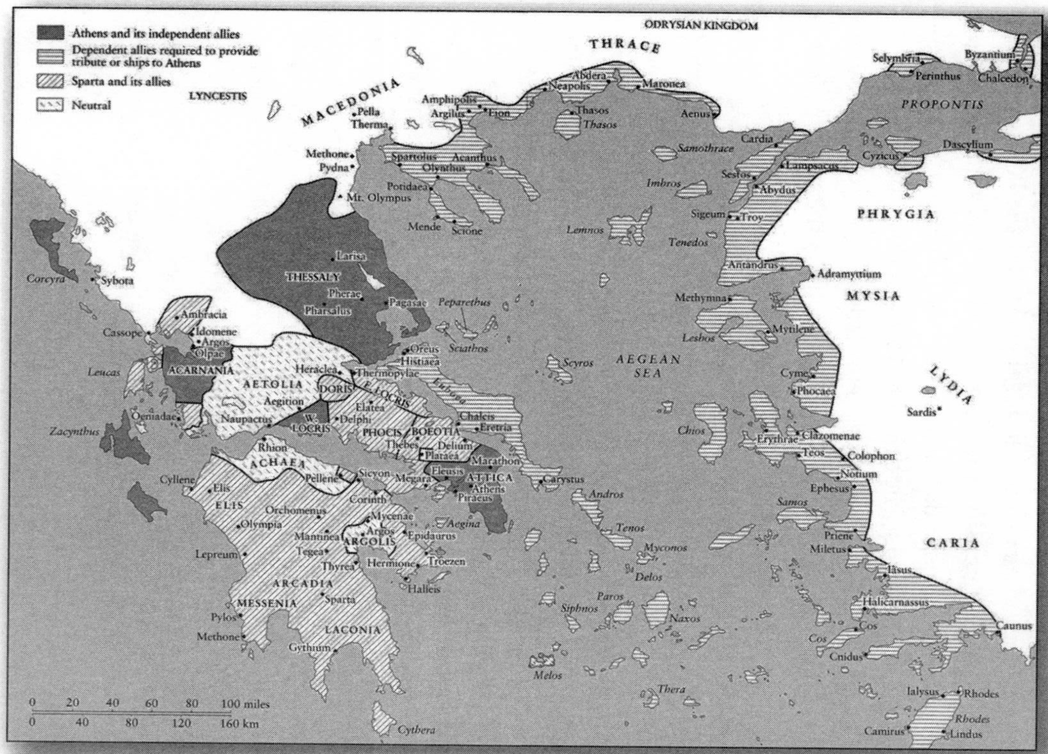

MAP 5

Allies of Athens and Sparta at the outbreak of the war.

SPARTA AND ATHENS TAKE ACTION

It was with regret that the Spartan king at last advanced on Attica in what would be the first of several invasions. There he was joined by a Boeotian contingent that included cavalry; an additional Boeotian force was detailed to devastate the area around Plataea. The Lacedaemonians also sent embassies to Persia seeking assistance and to the Dorian settlements in Sicily and Italy requesting that they send money and step up shipbuilding, hoping in time to amass a fleet of some 500 ships: as Archidamus had pointed out in trying to persuade the Spartans to allow some time to build up their resources for war, Athens could not be defeated except by undermining its naval empire, and for that the Spartans would need many more ships than they had.[7] These missions proved unproductive, and the Spartans' inability to build a navy early in the war would cost them dearly. The Persians would not give help without promises that the Spartans yield to them the Greek cities on the west coast of Anatolia, something embarrassingly incompatible with their war slogan of "freeing the Greeks"; it would be years before the Spartans would make this disgraceful bargain with Persia. And the western Greeks were indifferent to the squabbles of the mainlanders.

In accordance with Pericles' strategy, however, the many Athenians who lived outside the walls duly abandoned their homes during the invasions for an unfamiliar life in a city some of them had never before seen. Household goods they could take with them, and even the wood frames of their houses. Their sheep and oxen were conducted to Euboea and other coastal islands. Though some had relatives and friends who were

7. Thucydides 1. 81. 4. On Spartan strategy during the Archidamian War, P. A. Brunt, "Spartan Policy and Strategy in the Archidamian War," *Phoenix* 19 (1965): 255–80, and T. Kelly, "Thucydides and Spartan Strategy in the Archidamian War," *American Historical Review* 87 (1982): 25–54. On Pericles' strategy, H. D. Westlake, "Seaborne Raids in Periclean Strategy," *Classical Quarterly* 39 (1945): 75–84; D. W. Knight, "Thucydides and the War Strategy of Perikles," *Mnemosyne* 4th series 23 (1970): 150–61; A. J. Holladay, "Athenian Strategy in the Archidamian War," *Historia* 27 (1978): 399–427; I. G. Spence, "Perikles and the Defence of Attika during the Peloponnesian War," *Journal of Hellenic Studies* 110 (1990): 91–109; and J. H. Hunter, " Pericles' Cavalry Strategy," *Quaderni Urbinati di Cultura Classica* n. s. 81 (2005): 101–8.

happy (or at least willing) to take them in, most did not. Some shrines were open for habitation, but others were off limits on religious grounds, including the Acropolis. Some families were compelled to erect shelters on whatever open ground they could find. In time, housing was found in Piraeus and along the fortifications, but it was hardly luxurious.[8]

For a family accustomed to its ancestral farm and family shrine, surrounded by friends and cousins going back many generations, living in a small face-to-face community, suddenly to find itself in a huge city of perhaps as many as 300,000 people was profoundly disorienting. The pain was particularly great since some had just finished restoring their property after the destruction of the Persian Wars.[9] Some of the men had been to the city before, of course, to attend the assembly or even the meetings of the Council; others had not. The women might have come to the city for festivals, but the country festivals were very lively, and since travel over bumpy land was not always agreeable, many women had probably contented themselves with participating in the rural festivals near their homes and may not have come to Athens often, if at all. Were these women traumatized by the hustle and bustle of life in Athens, or before the misery hit in full force, did they for a short time welcome the unaccustomed stimulation? It must have been quite an experience looking up at the splendid new buildings on the Acropolis—the Parthenon most of all, glistening in the sun, reminding them of all they were fighting for: the empire with whose revenues it was in part built, and their patron goddess Athena. Measuring 228 by 101 feet (8 by 17 simple Doric columns), the majestic building was brightly colored in the fifth century, presenting a very different image to the eye from the austere white marble we see today. Around it relief sculptures depicted striking scenes such as the Olympian gods battling giants, Athenians battling Amazons, and the legendary Athenian king Theseus leading a battle against the half-man, half-horse Centaurs.

As the Athenians gathered behind their walls, the Peloponnesian army prepared for an assault on Oenoe, a walled fortress near the

8. Thucydides 2. 14.

9. Thucydides 2. 16. 1.

Attic–Boeotian border, and Archidamus took no little abuse for what some of his men considered a delaying tactic that betrayed his continuing lack of commitment to the war; the road to Athens lay to the south. There was much talk in the camp. Why had they marched all this way if the Spartan king himself was not keen on the war and was just going through the motions? Others, more sympathetic, however, thought Archidamus was holding off in the hope that the Athenians would give way while their land was as yet unharmed.[10] They were right, but Archidamus's hopes were disappointed, and in the end, eighty days after the Theban attack on Plataea, in late May when the Attic grain was ripe, the Peloponnesian army began its southward march, ravaging as it went. They finally settled in the region of Acharnae. The choice of Acharnae was a wise one, for it was the largest and most bellicose of all the Attic demes, and Archidamus was optimistic that the large Acharnian contingent shut up in the city—the Acharnians alone accounted for 3,000 of the Athenians' hoplites—would be unable to endure the destruction of their land and would incite all the others to battle.[11]

The Athenian response to the devastation of their land was predictable: many, and not only the Acharnians, insisted on going forth from the walls and fighting the invaders. What kind of a general was Pericles, people wanted to know, if he did not lead his people into battle? Wasn't that what generals were supposed to do? Somehow Pericles managed to hold the people together and persuade the officials who had the power to do so not to call an assembly—an assembly that might well have voted his island strategy out of existence. But tempers were short, anxiety was pervasive, and oracle-mongers were everywhere in evidence.

Though he had no intention of sending Athenian hoplites to face certain death at the hands of the formidable enemy force encamped in Attica, Pericles did keep up a steady dispatch of men on horseback to harass the Peloponnesian cavalry.[12] Finally, after about five weeks, when their provisions ran out (for they had mysteriously neglected to arrange for a supply

10. Thucydides 2. 18.
11. Thucydides 2. 20.
12. Thucydides 22. 2.

train), the Peloponnesians returned home and disbanded, each contingent to its own city. The Athenians were busy at home, voting to set aside a reserve fund of 1,000 talents from the funds in the Acropolis that was not to be spent unless there was an enemy actually making a naval attack on the city—the worst nightmare of the queen of the sea. So anxious were they that they also voted a penalty of death to be imposed on anyone who so much as put a motion that this fund be used for anything else.[13]

When the Peloponnesians were still in Attica, the Athenians had already initiated their strategy of naval reprisals, making clear to the Peloponnesians that there was a price to be paid for ravaging their land and the wretchedness imposed on the populace. The naval reprisals also offered Pericles an outlet for the energies of the men in the city, mostly young, who were spoiling to take action against the enemy. A hundred ships were sent out carrying 1,000 hoplites and 400 archers. These were joined in time by 50 more from Corcyra and other western allies. The fleet made a number of landings on the Peloponnesian coast, most memorably at the perioecic town of Methone in Messenia, which might well have been taken had it not been for the alert and energetic Spartan officer Brasidas, son of Tellis, who happened to be in the area with a small mobile force. Dashing through the Athenian line, he lost a few men but saved the town. For his daring, the Spartans rewarded him with a vote of gratitude, but this was just the beginning: Brasidas went on to become one of the greatest Spartans in history and one of Athens' most formidable adversaries.[14]

A voyage northward to Acarnania placed the Athenians in the Corinthian sphere of interest. There they captured the towns of Sollium and Astacus as well as the substantial island of Cephallenia. Sailing back to Aegina, they also expelled the populace there, as the island's proximity to the Piraeus gave them pause in wartime; Pericles had famously labeled it the "eyesore" of the Athenian port.[15] At the same time they

13. Thucydides 2. 24. 1–2.

14. Thucydides 2. 25. 1–2.

15. Sollium, Astacus, Cephallenia: Thucydides 2. 30; expulsion of Aeginetans: 2. 27. 1; eyesore of the Piraeus, Plutarch *Pericles* 8. 5.

shored up security to the north by making an alliance with the Thracian king Sitalces and reconciling with Perdiccas of Macedon, who, still smarting from the Athenians' foundation of Amphipolis in 437, had been lending support to their enemies. Perdiccas then joined the Athenian forces who were attacking the Potidaeans' local allies. The climax of the summer, however, was the invasion of Megarian territory by a substantial Athenian force of citizens and metics led by none other than Pericles himself: 10,000 Athenian hoplites and 3,000 metics, backed by a good number of light-armed troops, the largest Athenian army ever assembled in the field. When the Athenians in the fleet learned of the expedition, they sailed that way and joined forces with them to make an amphibious operation. This was Pericles' chief response to the invasion of Attica, and it was repeated again and again, bringing much misery to the Megarians.[16]

Despite the ravaging of Megara, the balance sheet at the end of the first campaigning season showed the Spartans well ahead. The Athenians' vines had been trampled, their crops burned, their houses destroyed. The siege of Potidaea was draining money from their treasury. And there was no reason to think the Peloponnesian infantry would not be back in full force the following spring.

PERICLES SPEAKS

Although the number of men who died in this initial year of fighting was not large, it was the custom at Athens to choose a distinguished man to deliver a speech over the dead in any time of war. That Pericles was selected indicates that he had not entirely lost his popularity even at this dark hour. The speech that appears in Thucydides' work—and it is all that we have—amounts to a praise of the Athenian way of life interspersed with invidious comparisons with the Spartan.[17] It begins with a tribute to the ancestors who handed down the land of Attica

16. Thucydides 2. 29. 6–31. 3.
17. Pericles' funeral oration: Thucydides 2. 35–46.

from one generation to the next as a free state and to the immediately previous generation that acquired the empire Athens now possessed. (Subtext: you owe it to these men to hold on to that empire.) Pericles then praises the entire Athenian way of living, what Greeks called a *politeia*, a concept that embraced not only laws and government but also values and daily life. Athenians, he says, are relaxed in their manner of conducting their affairs, yet would be very frightened to break the law, whether a written one or an unwritten one that carries with it the penalty of shame. In addition, they enjoy many luxuries. We do not, he says, like the Spartans, keep foreigners from our city lest some enemy profit by learning what is open to view, nor do we feel any need to pack children off to barracks in boyhood. Yet we are in no way inferior in courage. The proof of this is that the Spartans do not dare to march into our land on their own but only accompanied by their allies, whereas we will gladly send our own citizens, unaccompanied, on expeditions abroad—and defeat men who are defending their homes.

We cultivate refinement, yes, but without ostentation, and we love knowledge but without effeminacy. For us wealth is something to make use of, not something to brag about. And the life of the city is primary with us; we are the only people who consider a man who takes no interest in politics to be leading a life that is not quiet but rather useless. We alone frame political decisions properly, for we do not believe that public discourse hampers action. Rather, we consider that failure to apprise oneself about the issues through discourse will hinder good decision making.[18] To sum up, he concludes, "I tell you that this city, taken all in all, is the school of Greece, and as far as I am concerned, any man among us will exhibit a more fully developed personality than men elsewhere and will be able to take care of himself more gracefully and with the quickest of wit."[19]

Yet this soaring speech now turns oddly chilly as Pericles seeks to console the bereaved with helpful suggestions like having more children to take the place of those they have lost—and prevent underpopulation.

18. Contrast Cleon on Mytilene below, Thucydides 3. 37.

19. Thucydides 2. 41. 1.

Those too old to reproduce should look back on their happier years as profit. As for the women, of whom he says he feels compelled to make some mention, he suggests that they should be "no worse than [their] natures and strive for the least possible reputation among men for good or ill."[20] This peculiar ending was not his finest hour; it is hard to know exactly what he meant, and it has not endeared him to modern readers. Much of Pericles' gripping rhetoric, however, has stood the test of time.[21] Snippets from the funeral oration were placed strategically in advertising slots on London buses in 1915 to fortify passengers for the war that had broken out the year before.[22]

The line stands proudly inscribed in a part of the world Pericles could scarcely have imagined—over the entrance to the Auckland War Memorial Museum in New Zealand, generally considered one of the finest Greco-Roman buildings in the Southern Hemisphere. The whole world indeed. Despite the lack of evidence, some admirers of Abraham Lincoln's Gettysburg address cling to the belief that Lincoln had read Pericles' oration and based his speech on it. Certainly Harvard president Edward Everett, the primary speaker at Gettysburg in November of 1863 (Lincoln had been added to the program as an afterthought), peppered his two-hour speech with paraphrases of Thucydides and ended with a line from the funeral oration: "'The whole earth,' said Pericles, as he stood over the remains of his fellow citizens, who had fallen in the first year of the Peloponnesian War, 'the whole earth is the sepulcher of illustrious men.'"[23]

Predictably, the next summer saw a second Peloponnesian invasion of the same size as the first, and the territory the dogged soldiers ravaged

20. Thucydides 2. 44. 3–45. 2.

21. For the enormous bibliography on the funeral oration, see pp. 41–2 in J. Grethlein, "Gefahren des *logos*: Thukydides' 'Historien' und die Grabrede des Perikles," *Klio* 87 (2005): 41–71. Funeral orations played an enormous role in shaping the identity of the city; see N. Loraux's classic *The Invention of Athens: The Funeral Oration in the Classical City*, trans. A. Sheridan (Cambridge, MA: Harvard University Press, 1986).

22. Cited in F. M. Turner, *The Greek Heritage in Victorian Britain* (New Haven, CT: Yale University Press, 1981), 187.

23. Everett's speech is reproduced and analyzed at length in G. Wills, *Lincoln at Gettysburg: The Words that Remade America* (New York: Simon & Schuster, 1992).

and scorched was far more extensive than the previous year. Archidamus had deliberately left the elegant homes close to the city untouched during the first invasion hoping to motivate their wealthy owners to agitate for peace, but this time these fine houses were burned to the ground. Then all of Attica became the Spartans' playground, all the way down to its southern tip where the holy temple of Poseidon could be seen by approaching sailors, for the Athenians claimed not only Athena but Poseidon as a patron deity. Indeed, there was a story set in mythical times about the rivalry between the two divinities for the role of the city's guardian spirit, a rivalry depicted on the west pediment of the Parthenon. (Athena won, but eventually the two gods found a way to work together—a rare example of Olympian cooperation.) To Poseidon the Athenians had built the glorious temple at the very tip of Cape Sunium around 440. The Spartans smugly made their way there and ruined the land nearby, although they would not risk the wrath of the god by desecrating the magnificent temple itself. Similarly they came right up to the important sanctuary of Artemis at Brauron but would not violate it. Brauron was associated with the most vulnerable of Athens' citizens: its littlest girls. The lucky ones among them were chosen to "be a bear for Artemis," going to the goddess's sanctuary there before they reached puberty to perform ritual dances in yellowish costumes, mimicking the distinctive gait of bears. At one time they evidently wore real bearskins, but by the late fifth century bears were hard to come by in Greece.

But when the Spartans were only a few days into this rampage, doing all the damage they could with fire and metal and hands and feet, something much more sinister befell the Athenians: a horrific plague the likes of which they had never seen. It wrought havoc on the city for two years, then left for a year only to return the following year for another assault. Both the Athenians and the Spartans had spoken of the importance of expecting the unexpected, but this exceeded their worst nightmares.

5

THE PLAGUE OF WAR

THE ATHENIANS COULD FORTIFY the Piraeus against ships but not against germs; they could protect the city from soldiers but not from noxious winds. Doctors, gods, oracles—all were powerless. The disaster was made worse by the overcrowding in the city and the attendant decrease in sanitation. Thucydides was eager to report the symptoms and course of the illness so that it would be recognized if it should occur again, but there has never been a consensus either among physicians or among historians as to what the plague actually was. Theories have included typhus, toxic shock, tularemia, smallpox, measles, Ebola, scarlet fever, viral hemorrhagic fever, dengue fever, acute influenza, a combination of diseases, or something else entirely; right now it seems probable that it was typhoid fever.[1] Whatever it was, it had a devastating impact on Athens. Not only did it cause indescribable misery while it ran its course; it drastically reduced the number of available fighting men. Among the hoplites 4,400 died and of the cavalry 300. An expeditionary force sent to Potidaea also became infected; 1,050 of the 4,000 men sent there died from the disease.[2] Many were young men who had yet to father children—or older men who would have fathered more children

1. Various candidates for the plague are discussed in R. Sallares, *The Ecology of the Ancient Greek World* (Ithaca, NY: Cornell University Press, 1991), 244–62. The typhoid fever hypothesis put forward by Manolis Papagrigorakis outlined in the January 25, 2006, issue of *Scientific American* magazine is accepted by many today, but see R. J. Littman, "The Plague of Athens: Epidemiology and Palaeopathology," *Mount Sinai Journal of Medicine* 76 (2009): 456–67.

2. Thucydides 2. 58. 3.

had they lived. A large number of women and children, too, died before reproducing. In total, the city's population was reduced by about a third, though exact figures are lacking.

THE WORLD TURNED UPSIDE DOWN

Typically the disease came on suddenly, attacking the head and the eyes, swelling the throat and tongue blood-red; breathing was irregular and breath smelled foul; then came sneezing, hoarseness, and coughing before the illness took hold in the stomach, causing the vomiting of every sort of bile, as well as ineffectual retching producing ghastly convulsions. The internal heat of the body was so intolerable that people could not endure the weight of even the lightest of linen coverings, and most of all they wanted to throw themselves into cold water. In fact, many of those who were not looked after did cast themselves into cisterns. Their thirst was unquenchable, nor could they sleep. Many people died after several days. Of those who made it through this interval, most still died from a terrible diarrhea that was the next stage. Survivors were often maimed by the loss of genitals, fingers, toes, and sometimes eyes—and memories.[3]

The trauma was so great that those left alive simply could not get their heads around it. A quarter to a third of the populace was suddenly gone: mothers, fathers, children, brothers, sisters, cherished friends. Bodies were lying around unburied, and this in a society in which proper burial was so important that Sophocles some years before had written a play based on it, probably in 441: *Antigone*, in which the title character faces execution rather than leaving her brother unburied. Appropriate disposal of the dead, and honoring the deceased once they were gone, was integral to the functioning of the polis, where a decorous passage from this world to the next was considered essential. Once an Athenian had died, women would generally wash the body and anoint it with oil—women over the age of sixty, ideally, and only those closely related to the deceased. Then the body was dressed in garments specially chosen

3. Thucydides 2. 48. 1–50. 1.

for the occasion and adorned with flowers and ribbons, and placed on a high bed under a cloth with pillows under the head and sometimes also chin straps to guard against the off-putting gaping of the jaws. The family would hold a vigil during which laments were sung. The burial itself would take place before dawn two days later, allowing time not only for the entertaining of visitors who dropped by to offer condolences but to make sure the "deceased" was truly dead and not merely unconscious. Then the body was carried to its final resting place to the music of the *aulos*—the same oboe-like instrument whose music accompanied the Spartans as they marched into battle. By law, the procession made its way through quiet side streets, cutting off the possibility of an ostentatious public spectacle.[4]

Following a death, family members were expected to visit the tombs of the deceased on a regular basis. *The Libation Bearers* by Aeschylus portrayed the encounter of Agamemnon's children Orestes and Electra at Agamemnon's grave, where both have come bringing offerings. Athenian men seeking public office needed to show that they maintained family tombs.[5] This was the world as the Athenians had known it. But all cherished proprieties went by the wayside in the chaos induced by the pestilence. With the city in the grip of the plague, some Athenians even resorted to such sacrilegious methods of disposal as throwing their own dead on the funeral pyres of others. Construction to prepare Athens for the 2004 Olympics turned up a fascinating "city beneath the city." Among the finds was a mass grave dating to the age of the plague with 150 skeletons lying helter skelter, attesting to the desperation of the survivors.[6]

According to Thucydides, who caught the plague but survived to record the symptoms, the pestilence introduced a general lawlessness in the city. "Fear of the gods? The laws of man? No one held back, concluding

4. On funeral rites (largely Athenian), see D. Kurtz and J. Boardman, *Greek Burial Customs* (London: Thames and Hudson, 1971), 143–8, and R. Garland, *The Greek Way of Death* (Ithaca, NY: Cornell University Press, 1985), *passim*.

5. Pseudo-Aristotle *Constitution of the Athenians* 55. 3.

6. See E. Baziotopoloulou-Valavani, "A Mass Burial from the Cemetery of Kerameikos," in *Excavating Classical Culture: Recent Archaeological Discoveries in Greece. Studies in Classical Archaeology* I, ed. M. Stamatopoulou and M. Yeroulanou (Oxford: Archaeopress, 2002), 187–201.

that as to the gods, it made no difference whether you worshipped or not since they saw that all alike were dying; and as to breaking the law, no one expected to live long enough to go to court and pay his penalty. The far more terrible verdict that had already been delivered against them was hanging over their heads—so it was only natural to enjoy life a little before it came down."[7]

Most Greeks were confident about where plagues came from. The *Iliad* had made this quite clear. Plagues came from Apollo. Slighted by Agamemnon, the priest Chryses, who was devoted to Apollo in particular, had asked the god to punish the Greeks. Down from Olympus strode Apollo, Homer says, and let fly arrows in his anger: "And the fires of the corpses burned thickly."[8] Had not the envoys whom the Spartans sent to Delphi before sounding out their allies about an Athenian war been told that Apollo would help them?[9] To Thucydides, the plague seemed to have begun in Ethiopia and then moved through Egypt and Libya, but most Greeks thought it came straight from the god of Delphi and carried with it a strong suggestion that Apollo was playing for Sparta.

PERICLES IMPEACHED; POTIDAEA TAKEN; PLATAEA BESIEGED

Pericles led a seaborne raid on Epidaurus on the northeastern coast of the Peloponnesus with ships, men, and even horses as the plague was taking hold. He thus kept many safe from its clutches; he had with him 100 vessels, 4,000 hoplites, and 300 cavalry. In Epidaurus stood the shrine of Apollo's son the healer god Asklepios. If the Athenians could capture it, perhaps the son might undo what the father had wrought. But the Athenians' assault on Epidaurus failed, and it would be a decade before Asklepios would come to Athens.

7. Thucydides 2. 53. 4.
8. *Iliad* 1. 52.
9. Thucydides 1. 118. 3.

When the Athenian forces returned home, Pericles sent some of them north to hammer at the still obdurate Potidaea (where the plague got them, even outside Athens), while he remained in the city to keep spirits up. So great was the demoralization, however, that he was unable to dissuade his countrymen from seeking peace from the Spartans (on what terms we do not know); but the negotiations came to nothing.[10] Briefly he restored the Athenians' confidence by a rousing speech, but in the end he could not contain their discontent. Who put the motion we do not know, but there were enough voters who wanted to fight and enough who wanted to seek peace at pretty much any price that when they combined forces against Pericles, he was deposed and slapped with a heavy fine to boot.[11]

Typically, Thucydides does not tell us which particular individuals were behind Pericles' downfall, though he surely knew. Plutarch mentions Cleon, Simmias, and Lacratides as possibilities. Cleon, as his later career showed, would have been one who wanted to fight; for the inclinations of Simmias and Lacratides, there is no evidence.

The deposition of Pericles under the strains of war is not surprising. Ample machinery existed at Athens to depose unpopular politicians, and it was used frequently; the fourth-century orator Demosthenes complained that every Athenian general stood trial for his life two or three times in the courts.[12] During the Peloponnesian War alone, about 11 percent of the known generalships culminated in the prosecution of the general holding the office.[13] The charge against Pericles was evidently embezzlement or the vague "deceiving the people," not uncommon accusations in Athens.[14] This means little. The Athenians threw charges like these around liberally when they wished to visit their wrath

10. Thucydides 2. 59. 2.

11. Thucydides 2. 65. 3; Plutarch *Pericles* 35. 4; Plato *Gorgias* 515e–516d; Diodorus 12. 45. 4; Demosthenes 26. 6; M. Hansen, *Eisangelia: The Sovereignty of the People's Court in Athens in the Fourth Century B.C. and the Impeachment of Generals and Politicians. Odense University Classical Studies Vol 6* (Odense, Denmark: Odense University Press, 1975), 71–3; J. T. Roberts, *Accountability in Athenian Government* (Madison: University of Wisconsin Press, 1982), 30–4.

12. Demosthenes 4. 47.

13. D. Hamel, *Athenian Generals, Military Authority in the Classical Period* (Leiden: Brill, 1998), 131.

14. Plato *Gorgias* 515e–516a.

on officials with whom they were dissatisfied. But when it came time for the annual elections and no new leader had materialized to resolve their predicament—no plan for fighting the Peloponnesian infantry or workable peace plan had been put forward—Pericles was returned to office, his fine having been paid, perhaps with the aid of friends.[15]

While Pericles was out of office, the two sides collided in Thrace, where a couple of Athenian envoys observed a Peloponnesian embassy of six seeking the assistance of the Thracian king Sitalces as it made its way to the Persian court. There the ambassadors hoped to negotiate an alliance with King Artaxerxes I. This was a chancy move, as Sitalces was an Athenian ally—indeed, to cement his loyalty the Athenians had made his son Sadocus an honorary citizen, an extraordinary step for a state that guarded its citizenship jealously. It was Sadocus whom the Athenian envoys persuaded to have the six envoys arrested. We can only imagine their terror when they found themselves being transferred to Athenian custody just as they were about to board a ship that would carry them across the Hellespont. The Athenians put them to death without trial on the very day they arrived in Athens. They justified their actions on the grounds that this was how the Spartans had treated the crews of any Athenian, allied, or neutral trading vessels captured sailing near the Peloponnesus, but it also had something to do with the fact that one of the six was none other than the Corinthian Aristeus, a key player in the rebellion at Potidaea.[16]

The following winter, in 430/29, the Athenians finally scored a victory in their battle of wills with their rebellious subject in the north: the Potidaeans saw that they could no longer hold out against their besiegers. What siege engines and battering rams had not accomplished, starvation did. Provisions were no more, and in their desperation to fill their stomachs some had been reduced to cannibalism.

The Athenians had already spent 2,000 talents on the siege, what with the soldiers' pay and the siege equipment. This was a huge sum—about two years' total income. Many men had also been lost through death and

15. Thucydides 2. 65. 4; Plutarch *Pericles* 36. 1; Pseudo-Demosthenes 26. 6.
16. Thucydides 2. 67. 1–4.

others wounded, including Alcibiades, who was saved by the intervention of his friend and mentor Socrates.[17] The generals in charge, Xenophon (not the future historian), Hestiodorus, and Phanomachus, wanted the siege to end and treated the Potidaeans with remarkable leniency. Later in the war the cost and bother of the siege would no doubt have led them to kill the men and sell the women into slavery, but this was early days. Instead, they granted the Potidaeans free passage out of the city with one garment for each man and two for each woman and a fixed sum of money for the journey. The Athenian assembly was not pleased, thinking that the generals could have taken the city without any concessions, and it blamed them for coming to terms without authorization from home.[18]

Despite their rancor, however, the assembly evidently did not impeach the generals, for the following summer, in 429, we find them still campaigning in Chalcidice, where the rebellion had persisted even after the surrender of Potidaea. Counting on aid from a treasonous democratic faction in Spartolus, they attacked the town—with disastrous results. Just as the democrats there received aid from Athens, the oligarchs brought in a garrison from neighboring Olynthus. Although the Athenians were strong in hoplites, the Olynthians were superior in cavalry and light-armed troops. The Athenians lost 430 men and all their generals.[19] If they had not realized before the damage that could be done to hoplites by non-hoplite forces, they knew it now.

In May, rather than invading Attica once again, Archidamus took vengeance on Plataea once and for all. He was not happy about this, but the Thebans would wait no longer. When the Plataeans reminded him of the oaths the Spartans themselves had administered many years before, after the Persian wars guaranteeing the independence of Plataea, Archidamus invited them to abandon their long-standing alliance with Athens and join in the fight to liberate Greece from Athenian tyranny.[20] He made them an extraordinary offer: they could leave their city and go wherever

17. Plutarch *Alcibiades* 7. 3.
18. Thucydides 2. 70. 1–4.
19. Thucydides 2. 79. 1–7.
20. Thucydides 2. 71. 2–72. 1.

they wished (presumably Athens) and the Spartans would pay them a fair rent for their land for the duration of the war, restoring it to them when peace returned. He also permitted them to send to Athens to consult about these matters. The Athenians encouraged them to remain in their alliance, promising to support them to the best of their abilities.[21]

Yet Athens apparently had no ability to help Plataea, or at least no intention of doing so. The Athenians had not left their walls to help themselves, and at no point did they leave their walls to help the Plataeans. Still, their proximity did prove useful to Plataea shortly afterward.

Archidamus, anxiously having taken care to call the local gods to witness that he had made the Plataeans every reasonable offer, then directed his men to throw up a ramp around the city. It was no small operation. They began by tossing into it any useful thing that came to hand—earth, stones, brushwood. The Plataeans for their part extended the height of their city walls and slowed the construction of the ramp by opening a hole at the bottom of their wall and hauling dirt from the ramp through the hole as fast as the Spartans and Thebans could pile it up. They later repeated this on a larger scale, digging a tunnel; the Spartans and Thebans did not notice this for quite a while, so they wondered why they weren't making more progress. All this activity would have made a great comic skit had not so many lives been at stake. The Spartans also had with them battering rams. The first attack by ram was quite successful: it knocked down a large part of the extended wall the Plataeans had built. But the terror this misfortune occasioned inspired new strategies. From then on, every time the Spartans shoved a ram toward the wall, the Plataeans would lasso it before it hit, jerking it aside or shattering it with large wooden beams they had prepared for the purpose.[22]

The Spartans had one more trick up their sleeves. The city was small. Why not burn it down? That would save the expense of a siege. First they threw bundles of brushwood over the ramp, and then more bundles, and then they tossed lighted torches along with sulfur and pitch on top of the bundles to set them on fire. The wood blazed up into the largest

21. Thucydides 2. 72. 3–73. 3.
22. Thucydides 2. 75. 1–76. 4.

man-made fire, Thucydides says, that anyone had ever seen. Done! But, no. The wind for which they were hoping never came. Instead, so the story goes, rain began to pour, and the flames were extinguished. Foiled again; there would have to be a siege.[23]

PHORMIO, HERO OF THE WESTERN SEAS

Meanwhile in the west a new conflict arose between the Athenians and the Peloponnesians. Allies in the north, the Ambraciots and Chaonians, approached the Spartans, hoping that they would send ships and hoplites to attack Acarnania as the beginning of a larger strategy to keep the Athenians from sailing around and attacking the Peloponnesus. If Acarnania fell, so might the islands of Zacynthus and Cephallenia, and even the key Athenian stronghold of Naupactus that guarded the northwest entrance to the Corinthian Gulf. Not incidentally, more power would fall to the Ambraciots and Chaonians. It looked like a good strategy, and had it worked, the balance of power would probably have tilted toward the Peloponnesians.

There was only one problem. The Athenians' commander in the west was Phormio, a man already known for his cunning at sea. Not long afterward he would appear in Eupolis's comedy *The Officers*, providing military training to the god Dionysus, who manages to flee the persecution of Hera by enrolling in the navy. Though the Athenians had only twenty ships in the region, at Naupactus, the presence of Phormio changed everything. To no avail did the navarch (high admiral) of the Spartan navy, Cnemus, attack Stratus, the largest city in Acarnania; the Stratians' skill as slingers served them well. But the Peloponnesians were not ready to abandon their efforts in the west. Reinforcements were on the way, and soon they had forty-seven ships with which to fight Phormio's twenty. A Peloponnesian victory seemed certain. The Peloponnesian and the Athenian ships, however, were of different kinds. Because the Peloponnesians were ferrying many hoplites to Acarnania,

23. Thucydides 2. 77. 1–6.

their ships were heavier and less maneuverable than those of the Athenians. (On Athenian triremes, see Chapter 1.)

For some reason the Peloponnesians disregarded their superiority in numbers and adopted a defensive formation. Several hours before the sun was to rise Phormio led his fleet south across the Gulf of Patrae (see Map 6). There he found the Peloponnesians drawn up in the *kyklos*, or "wheel" formation. The troop transports formed a wide circle, prows outward, with just enough distance between them not to bump against each other but not enough for enemy ships to sail between them. The small craft and five fast ships were stationed inside the circle, ready to dash out speedily to wherever the enemy might attack. It was a recognized military tactic—the Greeks had used it at Artemisium during the Persian Wars. Phormio led the twenty lighter Athenian triremes in a single line in a gradually tightening circle. Periodically a single ship would break from the line to feint a charge at a Peloponnesian ship, only to pull back—but not before the startled vessel would instinctively pull back, thus dangerously narrowing the Spartan circle, which slowly contracted. But all this was foreplay. Phormio, the experienced seaman, was waiting for the dawn and the easterly wind that he knew came with it, blowing out of the Corinthian Gulf. (It still blows today.) And then he felt the wind, and saw the Peloponnesian ships thrown into chaos. Sailors, cursing, sought to push the colliding ships apart with boat hooks, but it was no use, and the lack of experience among the oarsmen compounded the situation. At that point the seasoned Athenian commander gave the signal for attack. Every Athenian trireme sprang into action, and twelve Peloponnesian ships were captured with most of their crews, adding up to some 2,000 men. One of the captured ships was hauled onto land and dedicated to Poseidon and the legendary Athenian hero-king Theseus (whose father was rumored to be none other than Poseidon himself). The Athenians had not lost a single ship.[24]

The Spartans were livid when they learned that their fleet had been routed by one less than half its size, and they sent out Brasidas and two others to serve as advisers to Cnemus, whom they blamed in particular,

24. Thucydides 2. 83-84.

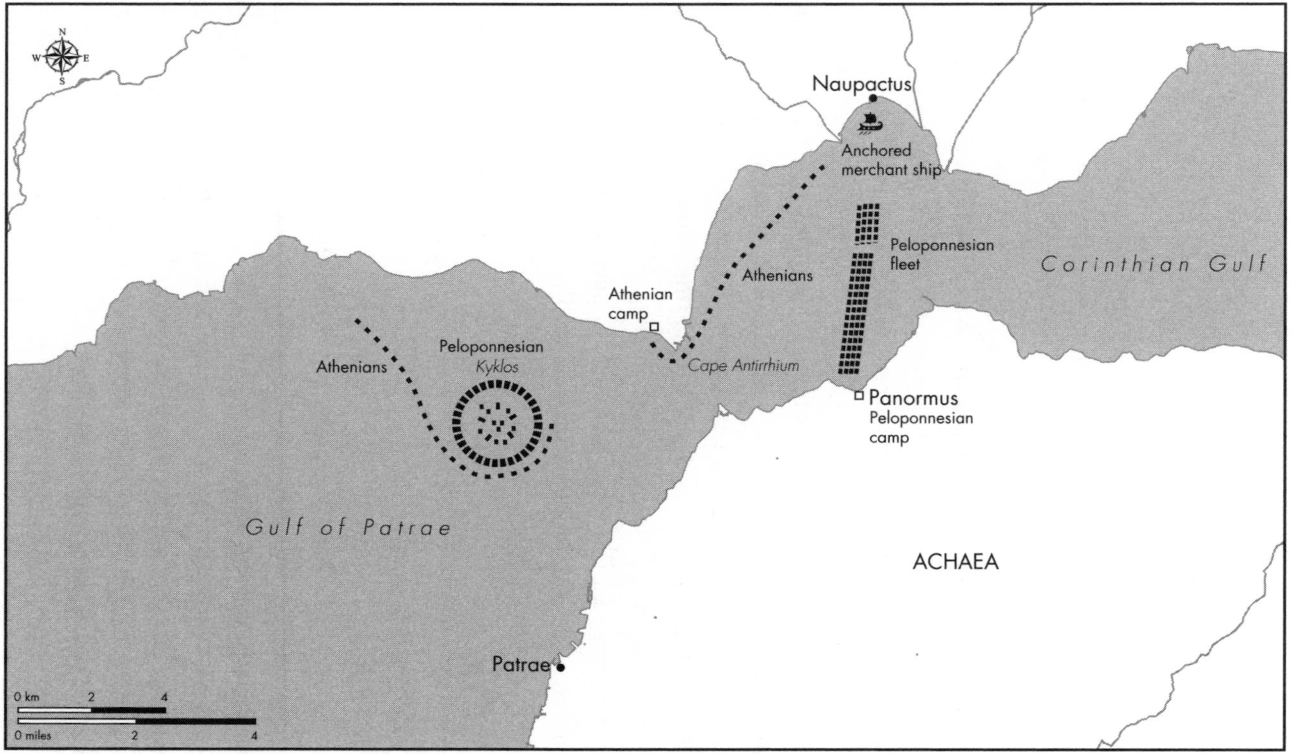

MAP 6
The Corinthian Gulf.

since as navarch he was ultimately responsible for the entire campaign.[25] These men would be in charge of an allied fleet that totaled seventy-seven ships. The Athenians meanwhile promised Phormio an additional twenty ships but diverted them first to deal with an emergency in Crete, where they had been summoned by one of their allies—surely an odd choice.[26] By the time Phormio faced the Peloponnesian fleet, he still had only the initial twenty that had conducted themselves so well at the Battle of Patrae, and this time the Peloponnesian ships were not carrying heavily armored soldiers. He stationed his ships at Cape Antirrhium, just outside the narrows that separated the Gulf of Corinth on the east from the Gulf of Patrae to the west. Things were not looking good for the Athenians. There was no sign of the promised twenty triremes. Daily the Peloponnesians drilled, and as they did so they molded ships from eight different states into a coherent fighting unit. Brasidas, Cnemus, and Lycophron each led one line of battle, and Timocrates of Sparta led a special flying squadron posted beyond the right wing, commanding a trireme from the island of Leucas as his flagship. The day after Phormio had delivered a pep talk to his men promising to do everything possible to ensure that the battle would be fought in open water allowing plenty of room for classic Athenian maneuvers, the Peloponnesians' daily exercise turned out to be an attack—in the narrow waters of the Corinthian Gulf. Their fleet was moving in a quadruple column, making not for the Athenians at Antirrhium but for Naupactus, which the Athenians were charged with protecting.

It would be unconscionable for Phormio to abandon his Messenian allies at Naupactus to the Peloponnesians. With a heavy heart he ordered his slender fleet to sea; meanwhile the Messenians who were with him scurried home overland to their families. Although the Peloponnesians had a head start and had been training for days, the Athenians had been training all their lives, and in time the leading Athenian ship pulled ahead of the leading Peloponnesian ships. As it proved, however, the purported Peloponnesian assault on Naupactus was a feint aimed at drawing

25. Thucydides 2. 85. 1-2.
26. Thucydides 2. 85. 4-6.

out Phormio's fleet. On a signal, the entire Peloponnesian fleet made a sharp left, their rams pointing directly at the Athenians. Their timing was less than perfect—the leading Athenian ships escaped—but nine Athenian vessels were pushed onto the land. Some of the sailors were overcome by boarding Peloponnesians, others scrambled safely to shore. The remaining eleven Athenian ships were still making for Naupactus as fast as they could, with Timocrates' flying squadron in hot pursuit of one of Athens' two official state triremes, the *Paralus*. One after the other the surviving Athenian triremes arrived safely at Naupactus and turned to face the pursuing Peloponnesians. Commanding the *Paralus*, Phormio learned from a lookout that a merchant vessel was lying at anchor off Naupactus.[27] This, he realized instantly, could be a godsend. There was not a minute to lose; at once he commanded the oarsmen to execute a sharp turn around the merchantman, making his ship temporarily invisible. Then they swung around rapidly in a U-turn and reappeared, heading straight for Timocrates' own vessel, the flagship. Stunned, there was nothing Timocrates could do to avoid taking the hit, and soon the bronze ram of the *Paralus* sank deep into his hull, filling the shattered ship with water.

The sight of the flagship sinking below the surface threw the Peloponnesians into a panic. So certain had they been of their success that they had actually begun singing the victory hymn. In their overconfidence they had fallen out of order, and some slowed down to wait for the others—a big mistake, given the proximity of their attackers. Some, from inexperience, ran their ships aground in shallow water. The Athenian ships in Naupactus dashed out and attacked, killing some of the crews and holding others for ransom. Timocrates availed himself of a sharp blade he had ready to hand and so ended his life; his body washed ashore at Naupactus. The surviving Peloponnesians fled, fearing the arrival of Athenian reinforcements; things had gone badly enough without them. Phormio had scored a great victory. Had his fleet been defeated, Athens would have lost its key foothold in the west. His two consecutive successes sent a strong message about the invincibility of the Athenian fleet.

27. Polyaenus 3. 4. 3.

He seems to have died soon after his exploits in the west, but his efforts did not go unappreciated by the Athenians, who buried him in the state cemetery near the grave of Pericles himself and placed his statue on the Acropolis just west of the Parthenon, a rare honor.[28] Still today one of the streets leading to the harbor in Naupactus bears Phormio's name.[29]

The strategy of the Peloponnesian commanders had been well formulated indeed, and they had abundant strength in numbers. But they were foiled by several mistakes—an error in timing, and overconfidence toward the end—and one wild, unlucky chance: the presence of that merchant vessel in the Naupactus harbor. Yet it was not just chance that undid them. It was chance combined with the cunning of Phormio and the Peloponnesian sailors' loss of nerve under pressure. Democratic Athenians did not panic at the loss of a commander, but other states did not hold up as well.

Knowing they would not be receiving a warm welcome in Sparta, Cnemus, Brasidas, and the other commanders allowed themselves to be persuaded to risk a raid on the Piraeus. The persuaders were the Megarians, who had been suffering terribly in the war—first from the economic sanctions of the Athenians, and then from the regular ravaging of their land. The raid was not a crazy idea. Because the sailing season was past—it was just about November—and because of their known naval superiority, it had not occurred to the Athenians to fortify their port against attack. There were ships there, but not poised for combat. The Peloponnesians launched their vessels at night from the Megarian port of Nisaea, but wound up making not for the Piraeus but for the offshore Athenian island of Salamis. There was talk of "adverse winds" prompting their decision, but it was pretty clear that they simply thought better of what they were about to do. The people of Salamis, as the island was being plundered, lit warning fires. When the

28. Phormio in the west: Thucydides 2. 80. 1–92. 7; Diodorus 12. 48; D. Kagan, *The Archidamian War* (Ithaca, NY: Cornell University Press, 1974), 107–15; J. R. Hale, *Lords of the Sea: The Epic Story of the Athenian Navy and the Birth of Democracy* (New York: Viking, 2009) 151–70; J. E. Lendon, *Song of Wrath: The Peloponnesian War Begins* (New York: Basic Books, 2010), 154–63. I owe much of my reconstruction to Hale.

29. J. F. Lazenby, *The Peloponnesian War: A Military Study* (London: Routledge, 2004), 47.

Athenians saw the fires, they were petrified, believing that the enemy was already in the Piraeus. At once they were on the move, and by daybreak they had reached the port. Ships now manned and infantry standing guard, an attack would have been impossible, but as it was, the Peloponnesians had already decided to sail quickly home from Salamis with their booty.[30] The decision to hit Salamis rather than the Piraeus may have greatly prolonged the war, which could well have been brought to a swift and dramatic conclusion by a surprise attack on the Athenian port.

Meanwhile the Athenians were about to face new problems. Pericles was back in office, having been returned to the *strategia* at the spring elections, but he was not the same man he had been—the plague seemed to have taken hold of him and lingered—and he died in September of 429, having lost his two legitimate sons to the disease, first Xanthippus, named after his grandfather the Persian War general, and then Paralus. The Athenians granted their leader's dying wish and conferred legitimacy on his son by Aspasia, Pericles the younger. But the young man was not of an age (or a temperament) to succeed his father, and indeed neither was anyone else. Pericles' steady hand had guided Athens for three decades, freeing it from the kind of civil strife that plagued many other city-states. His leadership had built the Athenian empire (not without considerable bloodshed) and entrenched democracy in the city. Without the stability provided by Pericles' popularity, the democratic edifice built over generations by Solon and Cleisthenes might well have given way to the forces of oligarchy. By his eloquence, he had persuaded the citizenry to make considerable sacrifices, abandoning their homes and relocating within the city walls to carry out his novel war strategy. But the same powers of persuasion had enabled him to talk the Athenians into undertaking a deadly war that in the end they lost, and not just because of the unforeseeable plague.

With Pericles gone, it was unclear what policies Athens would follow. Though the government was democratic, for decades one man had played a prominent role in shaping its policies. Now a multiplicity of ambitious

30. Thucydides 2. 93. 1–94. 4.

men less talented than he would compete for power, and political life would be very different. Rudderless, the Athenians faced a future yet more uncertain than before, and their first crisis was very serious indeed. The Spartans had always hoped for rebellion in the empire, and now in 428 it was happening.

6

NEW CHALLENGES AND NEW LEADERS

JUST WHEN THE ATHENIANS had been weakened and demoralized by the plague, they were faced by the first of many revolts in their empire. Despite their huge navy with its experienced rowers, this was where they were vulnerable, for most of their subject allies were some distance away (unlike Sparta's, who tended to cluster nearby in mainland Greece). Many members of the empire were in Asia Minor or just off its coast, and if those allies became unhappy—and, worse still, gained the aid of Sparta or Persia—it might be difficult for Athens to keep them in line. No doubt their understanding of this situation had been an important factor in the Spartans' thinking as they made the decision to go to war. Then again, aiding these faraway allies would pose no small challenge for Sparta with its limited naval resources.

MYTILENE REBELS

In 428, Mytilene, the largest city on the island of Lesbos off the coast of Asia Minor, revolted, taking three of the other towns on the island with it. (Methymna, a democracy, remained loyal.) As Lesbos was one of the two islands in the empire that had been permitted to remain autonomous, paying its tribute in ships rather than money (Chios to its south was the other), the Athenians were particularly outraged. Unlike most cities in the empire, Mytilene was governed by an oligarchy, not a democracy, and its elite did not enjoy taking orders from the imperial democrats. The loss of Lesbos could easily set off a chain reaction throughout the east, and the revolt alarmed the Athenians. The ships Athens promptly sent to deal with the rebellion were not sufficient to put it down, and an armistice was granted during which the Mytileneans could send envoys to Athens.[1] In addition, Mytilene dispatched ambassadors to seek aid from the Peloponnesians. Their efforts were successful, and the Spartans ordered the allies to gather at the Isthmus for an invasion of Attica while forty ships would sail for Mytilene.[2]

The Athenians manned 100 ships to harass the coast of the Peloponnesus and, seeing that they would need additional funds if a siege of Mytilene would be required, for the first time in their history they levied a property tax on their wealthiest citizens, thereby raising 200 talents. The general Lysicles was also sent out with four others to collect additional moneys from the allies. The allies manifested their displeasure by killing him and many of his men.[3] The new levy did not go over well at home either. In addition to various indirect taxes (sales, import/export, etc.), the customary personal tax system in Athens was the liturgy. This involved harnessing the wealth of the elite in such a way that both rich and poor benefited: the rich could take pride in their civic-mindedness, the poor would be spared having to pay for certain things themselves, and everybody was happy. (The rich also profited from all the liturgies they had performed; it helped no end to recite them should they find themselves haled into court for one reason or another.) Liturgies included major expenditures such as maintaining a trireme and training its crew (the trierarchy—the most expensive liturgy), preparing a chorus for performances at festivals of Athena or Dionysus, or leading and financing a delegation to a religious festival in another Greek state (see Figure 5). Both the Athenian military and the cultural life of Athens were dependent on this system of voluntary taxation. But this new tax seemed crippling on top of everything else the rich had been doing, and the well-to-do resented it.

1. Thucydides 3. 2. 1–3. 4.
2. Thucydides 3. 8. 1, 3. 15. 1; 3. 29. 1.
3. Thucydides 3. 19.

FIGURE 5
Grave stele of Chairedemos and the trierarch Lykeas, two men from Salamis whose names appeared on casualty lists during the Peloponnesian War.
Credit: Gianni Dagli Orti/The Art Archive at Art Resource, NY.

THE PLATAEAN BREAKOUT

Around the same time as the revolt at Mytilene, the Plataeans, still under siege and with food running out, decided to make a break for it. Later, about half of them had second thoughts, but 220 went ahead with the plan, which was well thought out and had many stages: the escape route was a regular obstacle course. The first stage of the undertaking involved a careful measurement of the Peloponnesians' wall, done by many men counting the number of bricks separately and comparing notes so as to be sure they had the right number. In this way they could build ladders that would be precisely the correct height. Too short and they would not reach; too long and they would be visible. The Plataeans made sure to choose a moonless and stormy night, with a howling wind that would muffle sound. Going up the ladders, they made sure to keep a good distance between one another so as not to bang into each other's armor, although they were fairly lightly armed to begin with. When most of them had gotten to the top of the wall, the sentries were alerted by a falling tile, but this contingency had been foreseen; immediately the Plataeans inside the city made a sortie on the other side of the wall, so that the Peloponnesian garrison was unable to determine what was going on and where. Warning flares were thrown up toward Thebes, but again the Plataeans were prepared; they threw their own signals up on the walls, thoroughly confusing the Thebans as to what was happening. When the escape party was entirely over the wall, the Peloponnesians went after them with torches, but this was to the Plataeans' advantage, for in the mixture of rain and snow, they could see the Peloponnesians but the Peloponnesians could not see them, and the escapees had come equipped with plenty of arrows, which easily found their marks.

The next obstacle was the ditch, and that would be unpleasant, for it was filled with icy water, but the Plataeans' motivation was great: food and freedom. The water was neck deep, but they made it across and put it behind them with the greatest relief. As they left, they breathed thanks to the gods to see the Peloponnesians marching swiftly down the road after them—the road to Athens. But they were not on the road to Athens; that would be idiocy. They had cut off onto the road to Thebes, which they followed for less than a mile before turning into the mountains and from there back to Athens. Safe![4]

CRIME AND PUNISHMENT: DOES DETERRENCE WORK?

Meanwhile the Spartans were making plans for their amphibious operation in aid of Mytilene, invading Attica and sailing to Lesbos. The Mytileneans hoped reasonably enough for the promised Spartan fleet, but what they got was a total of one Spartan, Salaethus, who sought to encourage the townspeople by assuring them that a Spartan rescue force

4. Thucydides 3. 20. 1–24. 3.

would indeed be coming.[5] Time passed and the Spartans had not come. Hoping to break through the Athenian blockade, Salaethus decided to supply the lower classes with hoplite arms. At that point, the new "hoplites" demanded an equal distribution of food and threatened to hand the city over to the Athenians if that was not done. Greatly fearing that the others would make a peace that excluded them, the Mytilenean oligarchs then surrendered to the Athenian general Paches. Paches sent Salaethus off to Athens along with a number of Mytileneans whom he considered most responsible for the revolt, promising that he would not imprison, enslave, or kill any Mytilenean until the return of the embassy that he would permit to go from Mytilene to Athens to negotiate a permanent settlement. Still, some fearful Mytileneans fled to the altars of the gods for sanctuary. Subsequent events proved that they knew what they were doing.[6]

The Spartan fleet arrived only a week after the fall of Mytilene, and it is all too easy to blame its commander Alcidas for its late arrival. The lateness, however, may have been due not to a slow crossing but rather to a bumpy start leaving the Peloponnesus. Just as Sparta's allies were tiring of the land war, some were beginning to have second thoughts about the projected trans-Aegean operation. The Aegean, after all, was patrolled by the mighty Athenian fleet. Alcidas, then, may have lost quite some time rounding up reluctant allies for the voyage before he finally departed with his force of some forty ships.[7] The Peloponnesians were not far away when they learned that Mytilene had fallen, and Alcidas assumed he would be taking his fleet home. Teutiaplus of Elis had a more daring plan. Rubbish! he said. We have the advantage of surprise, and we should use it. The Athenians have no idea we're here, and the last thing they're expecting is an attack at sea, where, for a change, we have particular strength. Their infantry too has probably scattered to their quarters, having let down their guard after their victory. I bet we can

5. Thucydides 3.25.1.

6. Thucydides 3. 27. 1–28. 2.

7. Possible reasons for Alcidas's lateness are explored in J. Roisman, "Alkidas in Thucydides," *Historia* 36 (1987): 385–421.

take the city if we fall on them suddenly at night, especially if we still have allies there.[8]

It may or may not have been a good plan. A weak link was that the Peloponnesians did not in reality have allies in the city; Paches had rounded up the pro-Spartans there and sent them up north to the island of Tenedos in preparation for transfer to Athens. Still, it might have worked and was probably worth a try. Alcidas, however (who might have known that Paches had gotten the pro-Spartans out of town), was not persuaded. Others suggested to Alcidas that he seize one of the cities in Asia Minor in order to foment revolt there, but this too seemed risky: getting blockaded there would be disastrous. And so Alcidas, outrunning Paches' ships in hot pursuit, returned home.[9]

Upon Salaethus's arrival in Athens with the other prisoners from Mytilene, the terrified Spartan offered the Athenians a deal: if they would spare his life, he would persuade his countrymen to lift the siege of Plataea. But the Athenians were too angry about the rebellion of a privileged state, too frightened by the precedent of revolt in the empire, too alarmed that the Spartans had, for the first time in the war, crossed *their* sea, to think of negotiating with Salaethus, and they wasted no time in putting the troublemaker to death.

Next up for discussion was the fate of the Mytileneans. It is in the debate over what to do with them that Thucydides introduces Cleon, a politician who had evidently been on the scene for some time but had probably come to prominence only after Pericles' death. Unlike men such as Pericles and Cimon (and Thucydides), Cleon belonged not to the landed aristocracy but to the trading class. His family owned a slave-staffed tannery. It offended snobbish sensibilities that he was not only in business but in a smelly one at that. Though he himself did no tanning, jokes about his literally malodorous family trade were rife; Aristophanes, who hated him, put his tanning connections front and center in his *Knights* of 424, which savaged Cleon mercilessly. He was, Thucydides

8. Paraphrase of Thucydides 3. 30.

9. Thucydides 3. 30. 1–33. 3.

says, the most "violent" man in the city in terms of his personal style—loud-mouthed and vulgar—but the most trusted by the populace.[10]

It was at Cleon's urging that after some debate the men of Athens, gathered in assembly, voted the execution of all the Mytilenean prisoners present in the city—and indeed all the males in Mytilene above the age of puberty. The women and children were to be sold into slavery. A trireme was promptly dispatched to Paches with orders to wipe Mytilene off the face of the earth. The next day many had second thoughts. Learning of this, the Mytilenean ambassadors present in the city found cooperative Athenians to persuade the authorities to call a special second assembly to reconsider the matter. There, in a speech probably heard by Thucydides himself, Cleon reiterated the harsh measures he had proposed so successfully the day before. Like the Corinthians at Sparta on the eve of the war, he suggested that the Athenians needed him to explain reality to them. Where Pericles had praised democracy, Cleon began by condemning it. I have frequently noticed, he says, that democracies cannot rule others. You trot along casually from day to day, not suspecting one another, and that's fine; but when you extend the same nonchalance to your allies, it is most decidedly not fine.

> You don't understand that you hold your empire as a tyranny and that your subjects are schemers who are governed unwillingly. They won't obey you because of the good you do them to your own hurt; you will prevail because of your strength and not because of their high opinion of you. Worst of all would be not making your decisions stick and not knowing that it is better for a state to enforce bad laws which are always obeyed than to have good ones which go unenforced. . . .
>
> Ordinary people run their cities far better than intelligent ones, for these want to seem wiser than the laws and to top whatever nonsense is said in public assemblies, as though they couldn't possibly be talking about anything more important. They are the downfall of cities because of this sort of thing.[11]

10. Thucydides 3. 36. 6.
11. Thucydides 3.37. 2–4.

Pericles had earlier acknowledged that the Athenian empire was rather like a tyranny, but he had never said that it actually was one, nor made the crass argument that bad laws and ignorance could ever trump good laws and intelligence.[12] As was his wont, Thucydides presented only one other speaker, although he acknowledges that other speeches were made. Diodotus, son of Eucrates, had also spoken in the earlier assembly. He may have been an officeholder, or simply a member of the assembly; we do not know. He appears nowhere else in the historical record. Like Cleon, Diodotus concerns himself with which course of action is most likely to discourage further revolts. If he was motivated by compassion, he was clever enough not to let on. His argument is more sophisticated than Cleon's. The issue, he maintains, is not justice, but rather what is best for Athens—not right versus wrong, but expediency. Now, nobody has ever committed a crime, he says, unless he thought he could get away with it. People are led on by poverty, greed, desire, hope; and when it comes to a whole city, each man, led on by the others, unreasonably imagines himself to be more powerful than he is: "Simply put, when human nature itself is eagerly rushing forward to do something, only a fool would think that it is possible for the force of the law or any other bugbear to stop it."[13]

Think about it, he says. As things are now, a rebellious city has a motive to surrender—to come back into the Athenian fold on lenient terms, and become once again a tribute-paying member of our empire. But if we adopt Cleon's proposal, cities will hold out until the bitter end, subjecting us to costly sieges. And consider this: so far, the common people in all the cities are well-disposed to you (a dubious argument, but useful to Diodotus). If you follow Cleon's plan, you will lose their goodwill, a loss that will be a great detriment to you.[14]

So spoke Diodotus. The show of hands was nearly equal, but the view of Diodotus prevailed, and instantly the Athenians dispatched another trireme, hoping against hope that it might overtake the first ship, which, after all, had a head start of nearly a day and a half. The ambassadors

12. Pericles comparing the Athenian empire to a tyranny: Thucydides 2. 63. 2.

13. Thucydides 3. 45. 7.

14. Thucydides 3. 46. 2–47. 5.

from Mytilene supplied provisions, and the crew ate and drank as they rowed, not stopping, and sleeping only in turns. The winds were favorable, and the first ship had been in no great hurry to bring its ghastly news. But when the Athenians drew near to Mytilene, a fearful spectacle awaited in the harbor. For there lay the first trireme, safely at anchor. And in fact Paches had received his orders and had announced their fate to the Mytileneans.

Frantically the Athenians scrambled out of their own ship, shouted him down and announced that it was all a mistake. But we can only imagine the terror of the Mytileneans in the interval. "This is how close Mytilene came to extinction," wrote Thucydides.[15] Still, the historian reports that the thousand 'ringleaders' Paches had sent to Athens were put to death, probably about a tenth of the adult male population of Mytilene and of the neighboring cities that had been involved in the rebellion.[16] The Athenians' action here would prove a harbinger of far bloodier conduct to come: as the war continued, it was the ideology of Cleon and not that of Diodotus that would reign supreme.

Around the same time as the execution of the Mytilenean prisoners, the Plataeans who remained in their city surrendered to the Spartans. This was a nasty piece of business indeed; had the Spartans simply stormed

15. Thucydides 3. 49. 1–4.

16. Hornblower in vol. 1 of his *Commentary on Thucydides* (Oxford: Clarendon, 1991), 440, accepts the number; Gomme in his *Historical Commentary on Thucydides*, vol. 2 (Oxford: Clarendon Press, 1956), 325–6 leans toward accepting it, but is open to other possibilities. As for Paches, Plutarch claimed that he committed suicide publicly when called to account for misdeeds committed during his generalship, but the details are shadowy and confused: Diodorus reported that he was happy about the Athenians' change of heart regarding the Mytileneans, which would have provoked Cleon; perhaps he was accused of not pursuing Alcidas long enough as he fled Asia Minor; and perhaps the suicide never happened at all: Plutarch *Nicias* 6. 1–2 and *Aristides* 26. 3; Diodorus 12. 55. 10. D. Kagan, *The Archidamian War* (Ithaca, NY: Cornell University Press, 1974), 167–70 believes in a trial of Paches and connects it with party strife in Athens; Tritle also credits the story (L. A. Tritle, *A New History of the Peloponnesian War* [Walden, MA: Wiley-Blackwell, 2010], 70). Hornblower and Tritle call attention to the alternative interpretation in C. Tuplin, "Fathers and Sons: *Ecclesiazusae* 644–45," *Greek, Roman, and Byzantine Studies* 23 (1982): 325–30, esp. 329. I lean to the skepticism of H. D. Westlake in "Paches," *Phoenix* 29 (1975): 107–16. Suicide was a most un-Athenian act, and Thucydides, who was always eager to call attention to instances of Athenian ingratitude to their leaders, does not mention this episode.

the town, they might have had to give it back at the end of the war, but by making the Plataeans so miserable that they surrendered "voluntarily" they created a situation in which Sparta could later claim that the strategically located city now belonged to them. The wrath of Thebes could be appeased only by their deaths. As each of the men was asked one by one if he had done any service to the Peloponnesians during the war and could only answer no, he was taken away for immediate execution. The women were sold into slavery. In time the Spartans handed the land over to the Thebans. "Practically everything the Spartans did in utterly turning their backs on Plataea," Thucydides wrote, "was done on account of Thebes, which the Spartans considered to be useful at that point in the war."[17] A year later, in 426, Plataea was razed to the ground.

CIVIL WAR IN CORCYRA

Off in the west, a new kind of trouble was brewing, the legacy of the Battle of Sybota in 433 during the run-up to the war. The Corinthians had taken 250 prisoners there to keep as hostages, and now, having treated them very well indeed, they decided the time had come to spring the trap. Letting them loose in Corcyra under the pretext that they had finally been ransomed, they sat back to watch civil war work its mischief. As they had hoped, their new friends began to stir things up, seeking to persuade the Corcyraeans to abandon their alliance with Athens. Peithias, leader of the pro-Athenian faction in Corcyra, was murdered along with sixty of his associates. In the fighting that followed the murder of Peithias and his colleagues, each party appealed to the slaves to join them; most joined the democrats, but the oligarchs brought in 800 mercenaries from the mainland. Following the example of the women of Thebes on the very first night of the war, the Corcyraean women threw down tiles on the oligarchs. Soon the Athenian general Nicostratus arrived with twelve ships seeking to make peace between the parties, but his efforts were ultimately unsuccessful. Fifty-three Peloponnesian vessels also turned up

17. Thucydides 3. 68. 4.

under Alcidas and Brasidas: as was so often to happen during the years to come, the great powers in this bipolar world would be intervening, Athens on the side of the democrats and the Peloponnesians on the side of the oligarchs. Events, Thucydides, wrote, "struck these strife-torn cities as they always do and always will for so long as human nature remains the same."[18] The first sea battle, with the Corcyraeans and the Athenians lined up against the Peloponnesians, was chaotic; the Corcyraeans were so desperate to save their city from Peloponnesian control that they set to sea unprepared and against Athenian advice, and even the Athenians' seamanship could not save the day when they joined in the fighting. Afterward Brasidas apparently suggested to Alcidas that they attack the city. As earlier at Mytilene, however, Alcidas could not be persuaded, and since he outranked Brasidas, there was no attack. Then the Spartans got bad news: signal fires from the nearby island of Leucas warned them of a fleet approaching from Athens. Sixty Athenian ships were en route to Corcyra, commanded by Eurymedon. The Peloponnesians promptly headed for home.[19]

Once the Peloponnesian ships were gone, and right before the arrival of the Athenian flotilla, the democrats on Corcyra set about a veritable orgy of killing. While it was the attempt to subvert their democracy that triggered the bloodbath, every existing grudge, personal or political, recent or long-standing, now came to the fore. No grounds were too trivial to justify murder in this ghastly free-for-all. The oligarchs were understandably terrified when they realized what was afoot. They killed themselves any way they could to avoid being slain by the democrats. Some ended their lives in sanctuaries, a great sacrilege, or hanged themselves from trees. Slaughter of every kind took place. Fathers killed their sons, and people were even walled up in the temple of Dionysus and left there to die—again, a sacrilege beyond words: when the Spartans, many years before, suspecting their regent Pausanias of treason, had walled him up in a temple, they had made sure to drag him out just before he

18. Thucydides 3. 82. 1–2.
19. Thucydides 3. 79. 2–81. 1.

expired, so as to avoid divine wrath. The democrats felt secure in what they were doing, as in an emergency they had installed a backup force just offshore. For during the seven days of indiscriminate butchery in Corcyra, Eurymedon with his sixty ships looked on and did nothing.

Like the debate over the fate of the Mytileneans, the civil war at Corcyra plainly made a deep impression on Thucydides. He may well have served with Eurymedon in western waters and witnessed both the bloodshed and Eurymedon's conduct firsthand. In their democratic society, Athenians tended to be on comfortable terms with their superior officers, and we can well imagine him asking his commander to reconsider his callous indifference. But a new ruthlessness was setting in at Athens, one that echoed Pericles' harsher imperial sentiments rather than the lofty democratic ideals expressed in the funeral oration. As Thucydides himself pointed out in contemplating the widespread civil strife of which the carnage at Corcyra was just the first example, war is a violent teacher.[20]

TAKING STOCK

The optimists on each side had anticipated that two, perhaps three, years of fighting would wear their enemies out and induce them to seek peace. Inevitably, not all on either side were so sanguine, and in fact, the pessimists were right. After four years of fighting, there was no sign of surrender in sight. The failure of the Peloponnesians to raise revolts in the empire was made plain when defection in Mytilene and Corcyra fell through, both of them cities that would have afforded them a substantial gain in naval power. The Athenians, following Pericles' "island strategy," had not marched out to fight on land except for the punitive raids on the territory of Megara every time Archidamus led his troops into Attica, and at the end of each summer. They did, as threatened, patrol the seas and hit Sparta's allies with the fleet. The Spartans followed through with their promised invasions of Attica and sought to assemble a mighty flotilla, but were able to raise nowhere near the 500 ships to which they

20. Thucydides 3. 82. 2.

aspired. Each side detached some allies from the other or even destroyed them, as in the cases of Thebes' dramatic, and humiliating, annihilation of the Athenians' long-standing ally Plataea and Athens' capture of Sollium, a town in the west belonging to Corinth, and the western island of Cephallenia. But nobody was in any sense winning, and it was hard to predict what would happen next.

NEW SCHOOLS OF THOUGHT

It was now, in 427, that the Athenians received a visit from a famous man. His name was Gorgias, and his reputation preceded him.[21] He came as part of a delegation from Leontini, a Greek settlement in Sicily with which Athens had been allied since before the war. The envoys sought Athenian help against the encroachments of Dorian Syracuse, by far the most powerful city on the island. A Corinthian colony, it was also allied to Sparta. But Gorgias was not just any envoy. He was a distinguished rhetorician, and the Athenians, who valued fine speaking, were eager to hear him. He was part of a broad movement in Greece that involved both education and philosophy. The practitioners of his art were the men we know as the sophists, and they filled a vacuum in Greek education. Most Greek children, of course, were too poor to go to school at all, and except for Sparta, Greek states did not provide public schooling. But the more affluent boys, and the occasional girl, were sent by their parents to private teachers, and by the fifth century many upper-class children could read and write as well as recite the poetry of Homer from memory. Still, they were receiving no education in the sorts of analytical skills in which many young people are trained today, and teenagers were raised to respect rather than challenge the values of the society in which they had been brought up. Those who imbued them with these traditional values, moreover, were primarily their fathers, who provided role models in the home.

21. Diodorus 12. 53. 2–5.

In the course of the fifth century, this attitude began to change. Tragic drama, which in the hands of Aeschylus (525–456) seemed to affirm the traditional values of the polis, evolved in the hands of Sophocles (c. 496–406) and Euripides (c. 485–406) into a vehicle for raising questions about such things as the rule of men over women and even the very existence of the gods. The sophist Protagoras (c. 490–c. 420) from Abdera in northern Greece came to Athens, where he became a friend of Pericles. He became famous for his proclamation that each individual person (not any god) was the measure of all things; more shocking still, he also claimed that he had no way of knowing whether the gods even existed. Two obstacles, he said, stood in the way: the difficulty of the subject matter and the brevity of human life.

Even historians could be infected with a new cultural relativism, or at least pluralism. Around the same time, Herodotus in his *Histories* presented his readers with a multiplicity of non-Greek customs that he had encountered in his research and his travels—customs he greeted not with horror but with delight. In Egypt, he reported, women urinate standing up, but men squat.[22] The Gyzantes eat monkeys![23] The Greek word for custom was *nomos*; it was also their word for law. To drive home to his readers (or listeners; he gave recitations of portions of his work) the importance of *nomos*, he recounted the following story:

> When Darius was king he summoned the Greeks who were in his court and asked them how much money it would take to get them to eat their dead fathers. They answered that they would never do it for any amount of money. Next, Darius summoned some Indians known as the Callatians, who eat their dead parents, and asked them in the presence of the Greeks, who understood what was said through a translator, how much money it would take for them to permit their parents to be cremated on a funeral pyre. The Indians made a loud commotion and begged Darius not to so much as speak of such a thing.[24]

Each people, Herodotus concludes, believes its own *nomoi* are best.

22. Herodotus 2. 35. 3.
23. Herodotus 4. 194.
24. Herodotus 3. 38. 3–4.

Some, like Herodotus, were intrigued by the notion that customs varied across societies; others believed they should be fixed by nature—*physis*—and the gods. The question of a flexible *nomos* versus an unchanging *physis* could plainly be the object of contention, and the sophists were just the people to teach young men to make a case on either side of this, or any, question. Particularly in a litigious society like Athens, skill in argumentation would come in handy in court, and young men whose parents could afford their fees flocked to the sophists for instruction.

While the sophists were popular with many of those who could buy their instruction, some resented them for taking fees at all—what was this mysterious skill they were teaching, anyhow?—and others found their moral relativism repugnant. Consider the anonymous treatise known as the *Double Arguments*. Is it possible, the author asked, for sickness to be good? By all means, if you are a doctor. And death too? Death is good for undertakers and gravediggers. The author goes on to argue that no act is intrinsically good or bad by citing the many examples of cultural difference collected by Herodotus. For all these reasons, the sophists drew to themselves a considerable amount of odium. Even some of the men who had paid to have their sons schooled in argumentation repented of the consequences.

Of course, in many ways the sophists were simply an expression of the Zeitgeist. The power of persuasion was also evident in the works of the dramatists and the historians (Thucydides included), and they had not necessarily studied with sophists, although it's quite possible some of the money from Cleon's family tannery made its way into a sophist's pocket. Thucydides evidently came to hear Gorgias perform in Athens. Gorgias was a scintillating speaker who held controversial views. He believed, for example, that nothing existed, an idea that he communicated in his treatise *On Non-existence* (a work which, however, existed). A conspicuous example of sophistic reasoning in Greek tragedy—and there are many—is found in a speech in Euripides' *Medea*, produced in 431 just as the war was breaking out. In it the cherished Greek hero Jason, of Argonaut fame, having abandoned Medea to marry the local princess despite everything Medea has done for him in betraying her family to help him obtain the

Golden Fleece, justifies his action on the grounds that by having children with his new wife, he will improve the situation of the sons he has had with Medea by providing them with royal step-siblings. Some hero; he adds to this the argument that Medea is upset only because her sex life is being disturbed—a stereotypical female characteristic, he claims.

Thus the Athenians' excitement at hearing Gorgias was not due to their unfamiliarity with clever argumentation; they were already very much at home with it and eager for more. Nor was it his dazzling rhetorical figures that persuaded them to send twenty ships to Sicily under Laches and Charoeades. The expedition had three very concrete purposes. At the outset of the war Sparta had sought ships from Sicily, but they had not been forthcoming; if Dorian Syracuse became more powerful, however, it might indeed send ships to Sparta. Cutting off the grain supply from Sicily to the Peloponnesus would also be useful. Finally, Thucydides reports, the Athenians viewed this mission as a scouting expedition to explore the prospects for bringing Sicily under their control. Certainly the last element in this plan was a dramatic departure from the strategy of Pericles, who had heartened the Athenians by the assurance that they would win the war if and only if they took no risks and refrained from attempting any new conquests for its duration. But Pericles' island strategy was plainly not succeeding.[25]

At first the Athenians did poorly in Sicily. Charoeades was killed. Things turned around, however, when Laches, having established a naval base across the straits at friendly Rhegium in Italy, captured Messina on the tip of the island, thus placing the strait that divided Sicily from Italy under Athenian control. Many of the Sicilian non-Greek natives, the Sicels, came over to the Athenians. Seeing that Athens indeed had some prospects in Sicily, Laches requested reinforcements, and the assembly voted a new fleet twice the size of the original one. Pythodorus was sent out to replace Laches at the end of his term, with Eurymedon and Sophocles to follow later on with the forty ships. (This is Sophocles, son of Sostratides, not Sophocles the playwright, although of course the

25. Sicily: Thucydides 3. 86. 4. Pericles' caution: Thucydides 2. 65. 7.

playwright had also served as general, during the Samos campaign, in 440.) Athens now had a serious commitment to Sicily.[26]

ARCHIDAMUS DIES; DEMOSTHENES IS CAUGHT OUT BUT REDEEMS HIMSELF

Around the same time that Laches and Charoeades were in Sicily, there was a dramatic development in Sparta: after a half century's rule, the Eurypontid Archidamus died. He was succeeded by his son Agis. And another king would rule in Sparta as well, for Pleistoanax had finally been recalled after nineteen years of exile, and his return was attended with all the dances and sacrifices that normally accompanied the accession of a Spartan king.[27] Just as the Athenians had received a request for aid from an ally in the west and realized that new strategies would be necessary to break the stalemate, so the Spartans on receiving a parallel request were open to a new line of approach. The people of Trachis to the north and their southern neighbor Doris, legendary home of all the Dorian peoples, were being harried by a local tribe and sought Sparta's help. The Spartans consulted Apollo, and on the god's advice they set about planting a colony in the area, to be named Heraclea after Heracles, the legendary hero and founder of the Dorian race. Their motive was not entirely altruistic. The settlement—one of only a handful of colonies ever founded by the Spartans in all their history—was ideally situated to facilitate land marches to the north and seaborne raids on the island of Euboea, where the Athenians had sent their livestock for safekeeping at the outbreak of the war.[28]

On the Athenian side, Demosthenes devised a novel strategy as well. Off the west coast ravaging the island of Leucas, he was being pressured by the Acarnanians opposite on the mainland to go beyond ravaging

26. Thucydides 3. 86. 1–90. 4; 3. 115. 5.

27. There were rumors that Pleistoanax and his brother had bribed the priestess at Delphi to command Pleistoanax's restoration (Thucydides 5. 16. 2).

28. Thucydides 3. 92. 1–93. 2.

and besiege their old enemy, knocking it out as a power entirely.[29] But then a more alluring prospect presented itself. The Messenians proposed that instead Demosthenes should attack the Aetolians, who had designs on Naupactus. They should be easy to defeat, they claimed; they lived in villages that were unwalled and widely scattered. They were also lightly armed. Why, it was said that the largest of the Aetolian tribes spoke a Greek dialect that could be understood by nobody else—and they ate their meat raw.[30]

Demosthenes' decision to go with the Messenians rather than the Acarnanians was not based on his concern with the safety of Naupactus, at least not much. The Messenians also argued that if he defeated the Aetolians he could defeat the other mainlanders in the area, consolidating Athenian rule there. That sounded very good indeed, because it offered an overland route into Boeotia. From Western Locris into Dorian Cytinium into Phocis: Demosthenes was oddly optimistic that the Phocians would join with him without protest because of their longstanding friendship with Athens but conjectured that he could persuade them by force if necessary, a more likely contingency. From Phocis—straight into Boeotia. To the north, the Spartans' precious Heraclea wouldn't stand a chance. So he established his base in Oeneon in Western Locris, as the Western Locrians were familiar with the Aetolian mode of warfare and the terrain.[31]

Everything that could go wrong did. Irate at his abandonment of the Leucas campaign, the Acarnanian allies refused to accompany Demosthenes against the Aetolians.[32] The Western Locrians did not arrive at the appointed time, and Demosthenes wound up attacking without the benefit of their expertise. He took the town of Aegitium by storm, not realizing that this victory was made possible only because the inhabitants had moved away from the town and positioned themselves in the hills above: he had walked into an ambush. The men he lost,

29. Thucydides 3. 94. 2.
30. Thucydides 3. 94. 3–5.
31. Thucydides 3. 95. 1–3.
32. Thucydides 3. 95. 2.

Thucydides reported, included more than 120 Athenian hoplites, all in the prime of life and the best men Athens lost in the war. Perhaps some class-consciousness is evident here, or perhaps Thucydides lost someone close to him in this disaster.[33] Having retrieved their dead under a truce, Demosthenes' men returned home, but the general remained at Naupactus, afraid for his safety before the Athenian assembly after the catastrophe.[34]

Demosthenes had learned much from this debacle, and it would stand him in good stead when the Spartans, on receiving word of his humiliation in Aetolia, decided to make a grab for Naupactus. Amazingly, when he went on his knees to those very Acarnanians whom he had rejected only a short time before in the matter of Leucas, they put the past behind them and sent 1,000 hoplites.[35] The Spartan general Eurylochus, having realized that Naupactus was a lost cause, then was approached by the Ambraciots and joined them in a campaign against Amphilochian Argos—not the powerful Argos in the Peloponnesus, but a much smaller state bordering on Ambracia. If he could conquer Argos, indeed all Amphilochia and Acarnania, the Ambraciots suggested, he could bring the whole region into the Spartan alliance. Like Demosthenes earlier, Eurylochus persuaded himself that the prospects for his impending campaign were favorable, and he decided to join forces with the Ambraciots when they seized the hill fortress of Olpae just a few miles from Argos. Demosthenes soon materialized at Olpae with twenty ships, 200 Messenians, and sixty Athenian archers. The Acarnanians had come as well, along with the few Amphilochians who were not trapped by the Ambraciots.[36]

The two armies faced each other for five days. Eurylochus was in a tight spot; his expected Ambraciot reinforcements had not appeared. How long to wait? Finally he decided he could delay no longer, and in the event he made the wrong decision. Although the Peloponnesians had

33. Thucydides 3. 98. 4.
34. Thucydides 3. 98. 5.
35. Thucydides 3. 102. 3–4.
36. Thucydides 3. 102. 5–7, 3.105.1–106.3.

the advantage in numbers, Demosthenes had given more thought to tactics. Fearing encirclement, he had stationed some 400 lightly and heavily armed troops in a bushy hollow on the road to ambush the enemy as they performed the predictable flanking maneuver, and Amphilochian javelin men were on hand as well. When the Peloponnesians outflanked Demosthenes' right wing as expected, the Acarnanians emerged from their hiding place and fell on them from behind. Eurylochus was killed, and so his co-commander Menedaius took over the command on the next day under very difficult circumstances. Defeated on land and with the port of Olpae blockaded by Athenian ships, he had no way to get himself and his men home. But Demosthenes had a diabolical plan: he and fellow generals from Acarnania agreed in secret, Thucydides says,

> to allow the Mantineans, Menedaius, the other Peloponnesian commanders and notables among them to quickly withdraw. They wanted to isolate the Ambraciots and their troops of mercenaries, but most of all they wanted to vilify the Spartans and Peloponnesians among the Greeks in that region as ready to leave them in the lurch if it served their own interests.[37]

Much confusion reigned as some men were seen leaving the camp, and outrage followed as the terms of the agreement became known. Outrage was soon followed by carnage as it began to be uncertain who was who, and some 200 people were killed by those who realized that they were being left behind.[38]

Knowing nothing except that Eurylochus had seized Olpae, the Ambraciots had proceeded to the area and encamped on one of the ridges of Idomene. What they did not realize was that Demosthenes had thoroughly scouted out the territory and sent his advance forces to bivouac on the still higher ridge above them—and he had positioned a large contingent of his forces throughout the mountains below. He himself

37. Thucydides 3. 109. 2.
38. Thucydides 3. 111. 3–4.

settled in on the pass between the ridges. Trapped there, a good number of the Ambraciots were killed on the spot in a dawn attack; those who survived to run down the mountain were weighed down by their hoplite armor and did not know where they were going, whereas the pursuing Amphilochians were lightly armed and familiar with the terrain. Most important, many of the fleeing Ambraciots fell into the ambushes that Demosthenes had strategically placed throughout the area. Few escaped, and the Acarnanians, having set up a victory marker, stripped the corpses naked.[39] Demosthenes for his part was now able to return to Athens in triumph, and he would serve Athens well for many more years throughout the war.

39. Thucydides 3. 112. 1–8.

7

THE FORTUNES OF WAR

DEMOSTHENES WAS ELECTED GENERAL for the year 425/24. As general-elect he easily persuaded the Athenians to send him west along with the expedition that sailed for Sicily at the beginning of the summer of 425 commanded by Sophocles, son of Sostratides, and Eurymedon. But the expedition, it proved, would also be charged with aiding the democrats of Corcyra, who were being harried by oligarchs who had escaped to the mainland during the bloodbath Eurymedon had watched so passively two years before and who had now enlisted mercenaries to help them in their plan to recover their homeland. Demosthenes had also been empowered to raid the coast of the Peloponnesus as the fleet passed by.[1] As it turned out, it was this last element, seemingly a throwaway, that would shape the course of the war over the next years. For this coast included Messenia, and Demosthenes had a special relationship with the Messenians.

HOSTAGES TO FORTUNE, AND TO ATHENS

On southwestern Messenia stood the promontory of Pylos. Demosthenes sought to persuade the generals to put in there and launch a raid, but he could not spark any interest in his plan. By chance, however, a storm blew up and forced the fleet into Pylos despite the generals' wishes.[2] This meteorological accident played a greater role in the outcome of the first

1. Thucydides 4. 2. 2–4.
2. Thucydides 4. 3. 1.

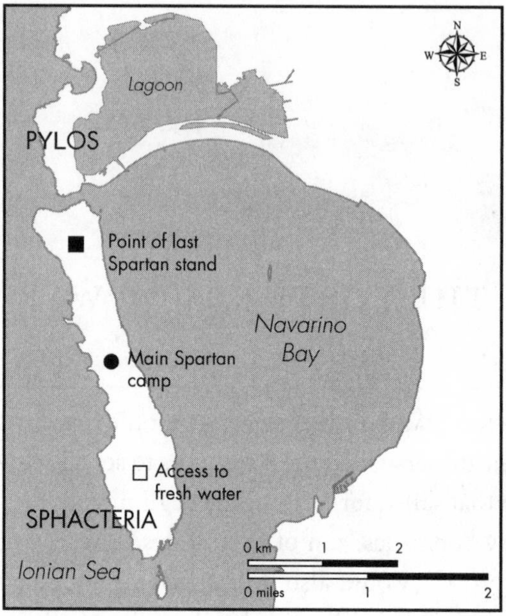

MAP 7
Pylos and Sphacteria Island.

ten years of the war than any act of strategy or tactics. Off Pylos, the narrow island of Sphacteria protected the harbor known today as the Bay of Navarino (see Map 7). To the south a broad strait of around 4,000 feet separates the island from the mainland; to the north, the strait of some 450 feet that separates Sphacteria from Pylos is narrow, but navigable.

What Demosthenes really wanted to do, it seems, was not to launch a raid but to build a fort that would serve as a beachhead in Spartan territory. Pylos was fortified by nature already, and it would not take that much effort, he thought, to make it impregnable. At first both the generals and the men were dead set against the plan, but when the winds had ceased to blow and it became clear that they were becalmed, the men became restless and undertook the task of fortifying the promontory albeit under the most adverse circumstances:

> Though they had no stonemason's tools, they set their hands to work, bringing stones as they picked them out and placing them wherever they

> happened to fit. When they needed mortar, they carried it on their backs for want of pots, bent over so the mortar would lie still and wreathing their hands behind them to keep it from falling.[3]

This was the arduous and uncomfortable work of very determined men. It sounds unpleasant in the extreme, but once the men became committed to it, nothing would stop them. No doubt they sang ribald sailors' songs with what breath the labor left in them. Plainly Demosthenes had not felt safe telling the assembly at home what he was planning, or he would have arranged to bring tools along that would have made this project a great deal less strenuous.

After six days, Eurymedon and Sophocles left Demosthenes at Pylos with five ships and moved on to Corcyra and Sicily. There must have been much cursing when shortly afterward two ships arrived at Zacynthus, where they were resting en route to Corcyra, instructing them to return to Pylos at once to rescue Demosthenes, who was in danger. The Peloponnesian fleet, which had been helping the Corcyraeans, had slipped by the Athenians at Zacynthus and was upon him, as was the Spartan infantry; Agis had terminated his invasion of Attica on hearing of the fortification of Pylos (although bad weather and inadequate provisions also discouraged him from staying on).[4] Knowing the Athenian fleet was nearby, the Spartans made plans to attack at once by land and by sea. Their intention was to land soldiers on Sphacteria Island and to block both channels with ships, but it is hard to see how they could have blocked the southern channel; their sixty triremes were in no way sufficient to block it and still leave them enough ships with which to fight off an Athenian attack on Sphacteria.[5] They seem to have had some awareness of the danger in which they were putting the men on the island

3. Thucydides 4. 4. 2.

4. Thucydides 4. 5. 2–6. 2.

5. Thucydides was in error about the topography of the area. See, e.g., A. W. Gomme, A. Andrewes, and K. J. Dover, *A Historical Commentary on Thucydides*, 5 vols. (Oxford: Oxford University Press, 1945–81), vol. 3, 443–63; R. Strassler, ed., Thucydides, and R. Crawley, trans., *The Landmark Thucydides: A Comprehensive Guide to the Peloponnesian War* (New York: Free Press, 1996), 227–8 nn.; J. F. Lazenby, *The Peloponnesian War: A Military Study* (London: Routledge,

with the bay unblocked. According to Thucydides, the soldiers were sent in relays, chosen by lot from all the battalions of the Spartan army.[6] If this was done by choosing one of the further subdivisions of platoons of thirty-five men in turn from each of twelve battalions, that would explain the number of Spartans eventually trapped on the island: 420.[7] And with all, or most, of these men was an attendant. These attendants would have been either full-blooded helots or possibly helot-born foster-brothers of Spartiates who had been raised alongside them in the "upbringing." Demosthenes for his part received wicker shields and forty hoplites from two Messenian ships that arrived, not by coincidence.[8] They also brought some offensive weapons; Demosthenes had with him some all-important archers, and as the Athenians would be fighting from the heights, even stones would be useful.

When it was clear that the Spartans were going for Pylos, the Athenians took up their positions on the beach. Thucydides identifies the most conspicuous of the Spartans as Brasidas (whom he is always quick to praise). Being the captain of a trireme and seeing other captains hanging back, afraid of harming their ships, Brasidas

> shouted out that it didn't make sense to worry about their ships' timber when their enemies had built walls on their soil. He told them to break their ships to pieces and force a landing, and he called on the allies not to pull back, but to donate their ships to Sparta in return for all her favors, to run aground and land any way they could and take the point and the men on it.[9]

Brasidas indeed made his own pilot run his ship aground, but as he tried to disembark he was beaten back by the Athenians, and as a result of his

2004), 71 with notes; J. E. Lendon, *Song of Wrath: The Peloponnesian War Begins* (New York: Basic Books, 2010), 481, n.7; and most recently W. Shepherd, *Pylos and Sphacteria 425 BC: Sparta's Island of Disaster* (London: Osprey, 2013).

6. Thucydides 4. 8. 9.

7. Lazenby, *Peloponnesian War*, 71.

8. Thucydides 4. 9. 1.

9. Thucydides 4. 11. 4.

wounds he lost consciousness. His shield slipped off his arm into the sea, and when the Athenians joyfully recovered it, they set it aside to use in the trophy they set up to commemorate their victory in the battle—a battle in which, as Thucydides remarked, the Athenians ironically were defending themselves on land from a Spartan attack by sea, reversing the normal course of events.

The Athenian fleet arrived shortly. Sailing easily into the Bay of Navarino, it caught the Peloponnesians unprepared—some of their ships were not yet crewed—and defeated them handily. The Athenians then commenced victory laps around Sphacteria, not only as a security measure but to drive home to the men positioned there that they were now marooned, with no one to come to their rescue. From then on the Athenian fleet would patrol the island twenty-four hours a day.[10]

The Spartans had been thoroughly outfoxed by Demosthenes. He had drawn them to a remote desert promontory where they decided of their own free will to place their ships in a protected bay awaiting a famously skilled navy and recklessly to station their men on an island where they would be hostages to fortune. And that fortune proved to be very bad indeed. When the Spartan authorities learned of the situation at Pylos, they were panic-stricken, for the 420 men on the island constituted a full tenth of the Spartan army. Herodotus reports that the Spartiates numbered 8,000 men in 480, but the population had dropped significantly since then. The Spartans consequently sought a local armistice, and the Athenians had no reason to refuse; indeed, they would have done well to press for more land and security. It was agreed that the Athenians would take temporary possession of the Spartan ships in the bay, and while talks were ongoing at Athens, the Spartans were not to attack Pylos, and the Athenians were to allow food to be brought to the men on the island. The attendants would receive only half the rations of their masters—though they were presumably every bit as hungry.[11]

10. Thucydides 4. 14. 1–5.
11. Thucydides 4.15. 2–16. 2.

The carefully crafted speech of the Spartan envoys, reported in Thucydides, is memorable for its eloquence. You run the risk, they tell the Athenians, of suffering the customary fate of those who have an unexpected piece of good luck: they reach out in hopes of more. You would do better, though, to take a lesson from our present misfortunes. We made a reasonable decision based on the facts available to us, and things turned out badly. The same might well happen to you. We offer peace and alliance in return for the men on the island. Now, if ever, is the right time to make peace, "before some incurable wound is inflicted in the meanwhile which keeps us both from doing so, and forces us to hate you, privately and publicly, forever, or which strips you of the advantage which has brought us to make this offer."[12] These were powerful words. Much pride had been swallowed, and remembering the Athenian eagerness for a truce earlier in the war, the Spartans were optimistic that their offer would be accepted. This, however, was very peculiar thinking. To be sure, there was a peace party in Athens, but circumstances had changed. Now that the Athenians had the men pinned down on the island, they thought they could have peace any time and under any terms they wished, and most of them were in no hurry to come to an agreement. Those opposed to the Spartan offer were egged on chiefly by Cleon, who persuaded the assembly to reject the Spartan terms pending not only the surrender of the men on the island but also the return of the Megarian ports of Nisaea and Pegae as well as Troezen and Achaea in the Peloponnesus, all of which the Athenians had been forced to give up in the Thirty Years' Peace of 446/45. The Spartan envoys did not reject these conditions outright but requested that a commission be established to discuss them, as they could hardly give away the territory of their allies publicly (although they as much as did so in the peace treaty of 421, borrowing much trouble for themselves). When Cleon then declared that their desire for a secret meeting only confirmed his suspicions that their intentions were not honorable, the Spartans did the only thing they could: they went home.[13]

12. Thucydides 4. 20. 1.
13. Thucydides 4. 21. 1–22. 3.

It is easy to see why Cleon did not want the Spartan envoys to meet privately with a group of influential Athenians, for the many citizens of Athens were of different minds about persisting in the war. Most of all, Cleon's rival, the seasoned general Nicias, who probably would have served on the projected commission in 425, almost certainly wanted peace; when peace finally did come four years later in 421, Nicias was the lead negotiator on the Athenian side. And Nicias had powerful followers who might well have either served on the commission or helped sell a peace plan to the assembly.

There was no right or wrong answer to the Spartans' offer. It could be argued that Pericles' aims had been achieved, and the Spartans had learned how much it cost to fight Athens. Peace might be worth a try. Then again, once they had their men back, nothing was to stop the Spartans from resuming the war at a later date. The division among the Athenians, many of whom had lost fathers, brothers, or sons, in the war is easy to understand.

Cleon's popularity declined sharply when bad news arrived from Pylos. The Athenians had not doubted that their 14,000 men camped there could do the job, but they had failed to take into consideration the ratio of men to potable water; Pylos offered only one small spring and what little water could be scraped up from under the pebbles on the beach. Time dragged by, and the men on the island did not surrender, for although they were blockaded by Athenian ships, the Spartans had offered rewards to anyone who would risk running the blockade to bring food in little boats—or by swimming underwater: for the helots, the reward was freedom. Ironically, the marooned Spartans were better fed than the Athenians. Worst of all, winter would soon be upon them. No supply ships could provision them; would they have to abandon their position, leaving the Spartans to escape the island, and let their whole enterprise go for nothing? When news of the situation at Pylos reached Athens, many regretted having refused the Spartan peace offer.[14] Cleon, sensing that he was in trouble for having led the charge in sending the

14. Thucydides 4. 26. 1–27. 2.

envoys away, tried to shift the blame onto Nicias, one of the generals for the year, saying that "if the generals were real men" they could easily capture the soldiers on the island. If he were in command, he continued, that was what he would do—he would either bring the Spartans back alive within twenty days, or kill them on the spot![15] "The bombast of the man," Thucydides wrote,

> struck the Athenians as funny, but the most prudent people were quite pleased with it. They figured this was a no-lose situation. They would either be rid of Cleon—which is what they expected to happen—or, if they were mistaken in their opinion, he would defeat the Spartans for them.[16]

Having received his commission, Cleon set off for Pylos, choosing Demosthenes to join him in the command. At Pylos Demosthenes had been heartened by a brush fire that had sprung up suddenly on Sphacteria, clearing away a great deal of the wood that interfered with visibility and had reminded him of the difficulties the thick forestation had caused him in Aetolia: now he and his men were eager to try a landing. On Sphacteria, a small guard of thirty men protected the south end while another protected the north, which was harder to attack because there happened to be an ancient stone wall there. In the middle of the island the land was flat and there was a well, and it was there that the Spartan commander Epitadas stationed most of his men. The Spartan hoplites were most vulnerable on flat ground, for with the lightly armed troops and archers brought by Cleon, Demosthenes planned to fight the sort of hill warfare in which he had become experienced in the west. After a pre-dawn raid that wiped out the guard on the southern tip, the assault began. Demosthenes had divided the men into companies of about 200, placing them on the highest ground so as to expose the Spartans to attack from all sides. If the Spartans attacked in front, they were shot at from behind; if they moved against the Athenians on one

15. Thucydides 4. 28. 4.
16. Thucydides 4. 28. 5.

side, those placed on the other would move against them. Cleon's lightly armed troops were ever on their backs.

Constantly thrown off balance by the unrelenting bombardment from right and left, the Spartans were thunderstruck by the idea that they, Spartans, were having arrows, stones, and spears rained down on them from above. Finally they began to retreat to the stone wall to the north. When the Athenians found that they could not encircle them, the Messenian commander Comon came to Cleon and Demosthenes and offered to break the Spartans' position if only they would give him some lightly armed troops. Making his way along cliffs so steep that the Spartans had not even bothered to post guards, he and his men suddenly appeared behind them, striking terror in the astonished Lacedaemonians.

The exhausted Spartans at the wall did not want to fight, and it seemed to Cleon and Demosthenes that they should not. What the Athenian generals wanted was prisoners, not corpses. At first hesitant to surrender, their commander Stryphon—for Epitadas was now dead and his second-in-command lay wounded under a heap of corpses—requested instructions from Spartans on the mainland. Finally he was told that he and his men should make their own decisions provided they did nothing dishonorable (Figures 6a and b).

They surrendered.[17]

To the Greeks, Thucydides said, the surrender of the Spartans on Sphacteria "was the most unexpected of all the things that had happened in the war."[18] But unexpected things do happen in war—indeed, with remarkable frequency. Demosthenes evidently remained to secure Pylos, while Cleon brought the captives back to Athens—and within the promised twenty days, yet. Receiving by a vote of the assembly the honors customarily accorded an Olympic victor—meals at the state's expense, front seats in the theater—he was the man of the hour.[19] At least in some quarters. But Aristophanes had no trouble getting a chorus to put on a play that winter at the festival of the Lenaea that painted Cleon in the most unflattering terms.

17. Thucydides 4. 31. 1–38. 3.

18. Thucydides 4. 40. 1.

19. Aristophanes *Knights* ll. 280, 702, 709, 766, 1403–5.

(a)

(b)

FIGURES 6A AND 6B
Spartan shield identified in an inscription as booty from Pylos.
Credit: The American School of Classical Studies at Athens, The Agora Excavations, 2008.01.0128.

CLEON AND PAPHLAGON

The great dramatic competitions at Athens, both tragic and comic, took place at the festivals honoring the god Dionysus known as the City Dionysia in spring and the Lenaea in winter. The festivals were grand events, and they brought together an even greater number of Athenians than meetings of the assembly. Well in advance of each festival, poets who hoped to put on plays—Greek drama was composed in verse—would apply to the magistrate in charge for a chorus. The magistrate might know a great deal about the play's script, or he might make his decision based largely on the playwright's reputation. Only a limited number of plays were performed on each occasion (five comedies, as a rule, though possibly fewer during the Peloponnesian War, to save time and money) so there was competition for gaining a chorus. The expense of training a chorus was one of the several liturgies that wealthy Athenians might undertake to garner goodwill; it was a major investment in time and money. How familiar the magistrate for 425/24 was with the script of the *Knights* we do not know. Aristophanes probably did not need to work hard for the right to compete at the festival after his *Acharnians* had won first prize the year before. Such prizes were eagerly sought after and were awarded by a panel of judges randomly selected from a group of citizens put forward by the Council. But the judges, well fortified as always with food and drink, had most certainly seen and applauded the play along with its competitors at the Lenaea along with the audience of thousands when they voted to award it the first prize in 424, giving Aristophanes two consecutive Lenaean wins. And the butt of the play was unmistakably Cleon.

The play fell into the category known as Old Comedy, a boisterous, frequently obscene, often highly political genre so rife with topical references that ancient editors sometimes supplied footnotes to elucidate the text, creating an entire industry—and where they did not, modern readers are often left puzzled as to the dramatist's meaning. Aristophanes was far from the only practitioner of Old Comedy, but his are the only plays to have survived intact. (After Old Comedy came Middle and New Comedy; neither packed the political punch of Old Comedy or was as specifically intended to send a didactic message to the audience.) The subject matter of the play arose from an ongoing feud between Aristophanes and Cleon. In his lost *Babylonians*, produced at the festival of the City Dionysia in 426, Aristophanes had evidently criticized Athens' imperial policies. Now, the City Dionysia was the occasion for the bringing in of tribute by the allies. Thus they were present in the audience to hear the poet's strictures on his country's conduct as well as his personal attack on Cleon. Cleon had promptly brought charges against Aristophanes for slandering the magistrates, members of the Council, and people of Athens in front of the allies. To his chagrin, the Council had dismissed the charges, and in the following year Aristophanes' *Acharnians* was awarded first prize at the Lenaea. In it the poet took the occasion to respond to Cleon's charges. Even comedy, he says, knows what is just—a belief he frequently reiterates in his self-appointed role as guardian of the city's morals. This time, he says, Cleon won't accuse me of slandering the city in front of foreigners, for this is the Lenaea, not the Dionysia; it's just us Athenians.[20] And much worse was to come in the *Knights* (i.e., men who rode horses).

As in all Greek dramas, tragic or comic, the cast of the *Knights* consisted of a very small number of actors and a chorus—in this case, a chorus of horsemen, men from the Athenian upper classes who served as cavalry in the armed forces. The other characters were Demos, a doddering old Athenian householder who represents the democracy itself; two of his long-standing slaves; a recently acquired slave, Paphlagon, who has made the others miserable by catering to Demos's every whim and gaining his favor; and a sausage seller, whom the ousted slaves put forward as a counterweight to Paphlagon. Typically, a couple of non-speaking actors also appear. The play is an allegory enacting the enchantment of the Athenian people—the "demos"—by the crude and crafty Paphlagon, a slave with a background in (of all things) tanning whose success at Pylos is mentioned repeatedly—in other words, by Cleon, known, of course, as the owner of a successful tannery. The slaves of Demos, then, who put themselves forward as lovers courting his favor, are to their easily manipulated master as its politicians are to the Athenian people.

As the play opens, the two slaves (whom some manuscripts flat out label "Demosthenes" and "Nicias") are lamenting the way they have been sidelined by the newcomer Paphlagon, recently purchased by their master "Demos." In case the profession of tanning was insufficient to clue the audience in as to Paphlagon's identity, one of the slaves immediately

20. *Acharnians* ll. 497–503.

complains of a typical Paphlagonian outrage: why, he says, just the other day I baked a "Laconian cake" at Pylos—but that dirty rat outmaneuvered me and presented it to the master as if he'd baked it himself![21] The word "Pylos" is mentioned at least ten times in the play, often by Paphlagon himself, as he boasts of his exploits there: I do right by Demos, he tells his rival the Sausage Seller:

> I beat the general from Pylos to the punch,
> Sailed right down there, and brought the Spartans back.[22]

Thus in a double plot Paphlagon is represented sometimes as a slave but sometimes as a citizen who is free to travel. The playwright also mentions things he has done before the Council and the Assembly, acts impossible for a slave.

The household plot of the play is simple. Two slaves of Demos have been upstaged by a new arrival Paphlagon, who will stop at nothing to curry favor with the boss—and get the rest of the staff in hot water. What to do? Paphlagon, it seems, has some oracles, and while he is sleeping the slaves steal them. From the oracles they learn about others who will manage the affairs of the city. Some of these correspond to actual Athenian politicians: a hemp seller (Eucrates), a sheep seller (Lysicles), but then comes a new and comical figure: the Sausage Seller. (Whether the Sausage Seller is meant to represent a historical person is unclear: some have suggested Alcibiades, who belonged to the social class of the Knights but lacked their dignity, but this view is not universally shared.[23]) Aha! This Sausage Seller, the slaves decide, will be Paphlagon's downfall. And indeed precisely just such a man is seen approaching. After vetting him, they are delighted to discover that he in fact rivals Paphlagon in baseness and

21. *Knights* ll. 54–7.

22. *Knights* ll. 741, 743–4.

23. A. Solomos, in *The Living Aristophanes* (Ann Arbor: University of Michigan Press, 1974), 97–8, argues that there is no evidence at all for any historical figure's being associated with the Sausage Seller; for the opposite view, see M. Vickers, *Pericles on Stage: Political Comedy in Aristophanes' Early Plays* (Austin: University of Texas Press), 100–101 and K. Sidwell, *Aristophanes the Democrat: The Politics of Satirical Comedy during the Peloponnesian War* (Cambridge: Cambridge University Press, 2009), 155–62.

is ideally suited to be his foil. Putting their plan into action, they push the Sausage Seller as a rival to Paphlagon, and by play's end the Sausage Seller has replaced Paphlagon in the graces of Demos—another hit at the assembly's lack of taste and judgment. Once again Paphlagon tries to offer up a tasty treat to Demos, a sweet made of grain from . . . Pylos, of course, but the Sausage Seller has treats too, and when Paphlagon retaliates by offering the master a wild hare, the Sausage Seller distracts him, grabs the hare, and offers it to Demos himself. To Paphlagon's accusations that he is not playing fair, the Sausage Seller replies that he is simply replicating Paphlagon's conduct with the men at Pylos (that is, the generals for whose victory he had taken credit).[24]

Seeing the light at last, Demos announces that he is commending himself to the stewardship of the Sausage Seller. Using some of the same techniques he has employed in making sausage, the Sausage Seller "boils" Demos down to his handsome—and intelligent—youth of yore.[25] A change of scenery reveals the Athens of an earlier day. Now mortified to learn from the Sausage Seller of his previous susceptibility to fawning, Demos hangs his head in shame. The Sausage Seller is quick to assure him that all the responsibility lies with the unscrupulous men who took advantage of him:

> Don't even think that these things were your fault!
> The tricksters who deceived you are to blame.[26]

It now proves that Paphlagon has been hoarding a couple of Peace Treaties, which are brought out in the form of young girls—girls played by males, of course, since men acted all the parts in Greek dramas. Demos is thrilled to see them: Golly, he says, they're gorgeous! Could I, er, "ratify" 'em up right this minute? As for Paphlagon, he's going to get the Sausage Seller's old job and work a sausage shop at the town gates. The last to exit the stage, he is prodded along by two slaves and dressed haplessly in the costume of his new trade. How the mighty have fallen.

24. *Knights* ll. 1166–7, 1192–1201.
25. *Knights* l. 1321.
26. *Knights* ll. 1355–7.

As if all the assorted allegations that Aristophanes hurls against Cleon in his incarnation as Paphlagon were not sufficient condemnation, Cleon is denounced in his own name in a passage sung by the chorus of Knights. The origin of the quarrel between Cleon and the Athenian knights is uncertain, but some conflict had broken out that had led Aristophanes to choose the horsemen of Athens for his chorus in this play. About two thirds of the way through the play, just after Paphlagon and the Sausage Seller have left the stage, quarreling, the Knights burst into song:

> What a sweet day, what a bright day,
> What a filled-with-all-delight day,
> What a treat for those who live here,
> Also people passing through,
> The day that Cleon meets his doom![27]

Even Cleon's schooldays are grist for the poet's mill, as the chorus sings about how his music teacher had him expelled for his intransigence:

> His classmates tell, this boy said, "No!"
> To learning modes from different tribes,
> The music teacher kicked him out—
> He'd only learn the mode of bribes![28]

Aristophanes and Cleon had a feud going back some time, and the comic poet certainly scored a hit in the *Knights*. Stung by the poet's attack, once more Cleon brought charges against him, but in the end he settled out of court, and Aristophanes' invective did not ruin Cleon any more than such topical humor destroys politicians today; shortly after the Lenaea, Cleon was elected to the generalship for 424/23.

27. *Knights* ll. 973–6.
28. *Knights* ll. 989–96.

8

WAR THROUGHOUT THE MAINLAND AND THE CALL OF THE WEST

THE NEW DEVELOPMENTS AT Pylos changed the dynamic of the war in several ways. First, the Athenians made clear that the POWs would be killed the instant Peloponnesian hoplites set foot in Attica; there were to be no more invasions. Second, feeling confident in Athens' position in the Greek world, its assembly passed a decree substantially raising the tribute throughout the empire. Third, Athens would be following a daring and aggressive war policy—and holding its commanders to exacting standards. Finally, the Spartans, fearful of a helot revolt after their weakness had been exposed and with a joint Athenian/Messenian garrison at Pylos, were at first hesitant to come out and fight the Athenians, but in time they did open up a new front in the northeast at the instigation of Brasidas. Brasidas's campaigns had two dramatic results: in 424/3, Thucydides, while serving as general, was forced into exile for losing Amphipolis, and in 423 Athens and Sparta signed a peace treaty to last for a year while the details of a more long-lasting peace could be fine-tuned.

Under the leadership of Nicias, moreover, the newly buoyant Athenians made numerous assaults on the territory of Corinth and the coast of the Peloponnesus. In Thyrea, where the Spartans had established the Aeginetans after the Athenians had expelled them from their native island at the outset of the war, the Athenians finally settled the score with their old enemy: they put the men to death and, presumably, sold the women and children into slavery in accord with the new brutal practice the war had inspired.[1]

During the years that followed, the war would be fought in unexpected quarters. A replay of the civil war would bring new bloodshed to Corcyra, and a failed attempt at a coordinated attack on Delium would cost the Athenians dearly at the hands of the Boeotian League in the first hoplite battle of the war.

BACK TO CORCYRA

To the west, in Corcyra, lay unfinished business. When Eurymedon and Sophocles, after their delay at Pylos, finally arrived to bring aid to the beleaguered democrats, a ghostly replay of the events of 427 ensued. Overcome by combined Athenian and Corcyraean democratic forces, the oligarchs finally agreed to a truce whereby they would be judged by the Athenian people. Under the protection of this truce, they were conducted by the generals to the nearby island of Ptychia until they could be sent to Athens, on the condition that the truce would be considered void if any one of them were caught trying to escape. The democrats, however, tricked some of the men on Ptychia into trying to flee on the grounds that the Athenian generals were about to turn them all over to the Corcyraean mob. The truce having been broken, the Corcyraeans locked the men in a large building. They led them out twenty at a time, tied them together, and drove them through two lines of hoplites each of whom beat and stabbed anyone he caught sight of who was his enemy. After a while the men still inside the building realized that the men who had been taken out were not just being transferred to some other location, and they refused to leave the building. They also told the Athenians that if they wanted them killed, they would have to do it themselves.

The democrats, after tearing through the roof of the building, started throwing tiles and shooting arrows down onto the oligarchs, who then

1. Thucydides 4. 57. 4.

began to commit suicide much as they had two years before. Thucydides captures the horrific scene:

> They took the arrows the Corcyraeans had shot and shoved them down into their own throats and strangled each other with ropes from beds which happened to be inside and with strips of cloth torn from their own clothes. Night had fallen on their sufferings, and they spent most of it killing themselves any way they could and being killed by objects striking them from above until they were all dead.[2]

Such was the grisly coda to the first episode of civil war on Corcyra. As before, the Athenian generals sat by and watched. Eurymedon had become very skilled indeed in letting others do his killing for him.

SICILY AND AN IMPEACHMENT

When there was nothing left to do—or not do—on Corcyra, Eurymedon and Sophocles moved on to Sicily, their original destination before they had changed course for Pylos to rescue Demosthenes (see Map 8).

The news there was all bad: the Syracusans had captured both Messina and Rhegium. The Athenians had managed to retake Rhegium, but Messina was lost. Inter-city warfare had continued with much loss of life, and Athens' allies were no more in the mood to continue fighting than the other Sicilians. At a conference held at Gela, Hermocrates of Syracuse made a passionate plea for setting differences aside, not so much in the interests of putting a stop to bloodshed as to present a solid front against Athenian aggression. When it was clear that Hermocrates' proposal for peace and solidarity would be ratified, the Athenians' allies sent for the generals and offered them the chance to participate in this agreement. Having done so, they then returned to Athens.[3]

Not surprisingly, their countrymen were not happy to see them. It was ingrained in the Athenian mindset not to take disappointment in their officials lightly, least of all in military men in time of war. All three

2. Thucydides 4. 46. 1–48. 3.

3. Thucydides 4. 24. 1–25.12, 4. 58. 1–65. 3.

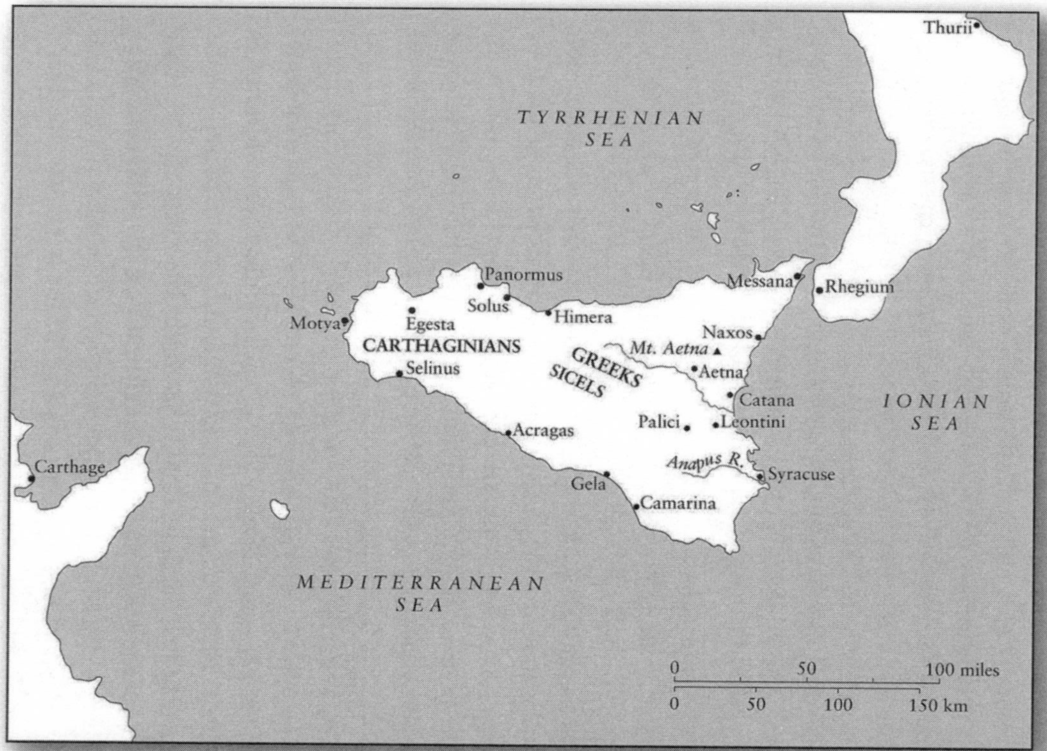

MAP 8
Sicily, the toe of Italy, and Carthage.

generals were accused of accepting bribes. Sophocles and Pythodorus wound up in exile; Eurymedon was fined and went on to serve later in the war. Since the Athenians did not practice extradition, we have no way of knowing whether Sophocles and Pythodorus, sensing which way the wind was blowing, simply skipped town before their trial or were actually exiled by a formal procedure.[4]

Did the generals accept bribes? The taking of bribes was a common accusation against Athenian officials with whom the assembly was displeased or who had political enemies. Accepting gifts abroad, moreover, was not necessarily illegal under Athenian law unless the gifts constituted some form of undue influence.[5] In this case, though, one wonders. Unless Thucydides has grossly misrepresented Hermocrates' exhortation to his fellow Sicilians, it is odd that the generals assented to this provocatively anti-Athenian agreement. Thucydides believed that the Athenians attacked the generals because they were so buoyed up by their recent string of successes that they believed they could do anything they set their mind to, whatever the resources and no matter how impossible.[6] We are free to take this passage at face value, but the impeachment of Thucydides the following year raises questions about the historian's objectivity here.

A VICTORY FOR THE BOEOTIANS AT DELIUM

Both sides now decided to open new fronts to the north. Pericles' strategy clearly dead, the Athenians determined on a two-pronged attack on Boeotia, while Brasidas persuaded the Spartans to let him take 1,700 men, including 700 helots armed, for the first time, as hoplites and 1,000 mercenaries whom he had recruited in the Peloponnesus up toward Thrace.[7]

4. Thucydides 4. 65. 3.

5. See B. Strauss, "The Cultural Significance of Bribery and Embezzlement in Athenian Politics: The Evidence of the Period of 403–383 B. C.," *The Ancient World* 11 (1985): 67–74, and F. D. Harvey, "Dona ferentes: Some Aspects of Bribery in Greek Politics," 76-177 in *Crux, Essays Presented to G. E. M. de Sainte Croix on his 75th Birthday*, ed. P. A. Cartledge and F. D. Harvey (London: Duckworth, 1985).

6. Thucydides 4. 65. 4.

7. Thucydides 4. 80. 5.

Fearing helot restiveness with the Athenians established on bases in the Peloponnesus to which they could flee, the Spartans were happy to see them go. (The 500-odd helots who survived the campaign would go on to become *neodamodeis*, "new citizens"—free men but without any political rights—in exchange for their service, beginning a new pattern in Sparta, and would later serve in a garrison in Lepreum, on the border of Laconia and Elis.)[8] En route, however, the two sides clashed in Megara, where civil strife was brewing. The conflict was so intense that the frightened democrats actually invited the Athenians in to protect them from their own oligarchic exiles. What a bitter pill that must have been to swallow after the Megarian decree and years of relentless pillaging of Megarian land by Athenian troops. So bitter was it, indeed, that the democrats could only conspire with the Athenians to hand over the city in secret and in darkness; an open vote in the assembly to go over to Athens would have been too risky. But one of the Megarians betrayed the plot. And worse, Brasidas was in the vicinity, preparing for the Thracian campaign, and he immediately summoned the Boeotians to send troops to prevent Megara from slipping away from the Peloponnesian League once again. The Athenians soon withdrew, and the Megarians declared an amnesty, swearing solemn oaths that the evils of the past would be forgotten; but when the oligarchs returned to power, they executed a hundred of those who had seemed to be working most closely with the Athenians.[9]

Although the Megarian coup had not been their idea, the Athenian generals involved were more than a little glum at their failure to bring it to fruition. Bigger opportunities, however, seemed to be evolving farther north, where rumors suggested that the moment was right to strike at Boeotia: several cities were said to house democratic pro-Athenian factions that could provide centers for anti-Theban activity. The most promising bases seemed to be Siphae and Chaeronea to the west and Delium to the east, the site of a seaside temple of Apollo. (Ideally, religious precincts were off limits to military operations, but this was wartime, and many

8. Thucydides 5. 34. 1.
9. Thucydides 4. 74. 3.

rules had gone by the wayside.) Siphae was to be betrayed to Demosthenes, and Chaeronea would be betrayed by a pro-Athenian party in nearby Orchomenus, a powerful city that hoped to be to a democratic Boeotia what Thebes had been to the oligarchic one. Demosthenes and his fellow general Hippocrates, nephew of Pericles, formed a plan, one that depended on both secrecy and timing. Demosthenes, having rounded up allies in the northwest, would appear with his troops at Siphae on the very day in early November on which Hippocrates would seize and fortify Delium. Not expecting any of this, the Boeotians would be caught off guard; Demosthenes would easily take Siphae, local traitors would deliver nearby Chaeronea, and the Athenians would have scored points with disaffected Boeotians by establishing for them a base at Delium.[10]

Demosthenes, however, accidentally arrived at Siphae too early, before Hippocrates had set out, and in any event, the plot was betrayed to the Spartans, who told the Boeotians, who in turn secured both Siphae and Chaeronea. Throughout the cities of Boeotia, the would-be rebels now abandoned their brave plans. As Demosthenes evidently had no way to get a message to Hippocrates in time, cautioning him that no western front would divide the efforts of the Boeotian army as planned, Hippocrates merrily marched his troops up to Delium, fortified the place, and sent the army home, remaining with a small garrison to administer the finishing touches. One wonders why he did not find puzzling the absence of either eager democratic refugees or suspicious Boeotian investigators.[11]

The truth, once he discovered it, was chilling. Twelve miles (nineteen kilometers) away at Tanagra, the Boeotian army was mustering in full force, consisting of some 7,000 hoplites, more than 10,000 lightly armed troops, and 1,000 cavalry.[12] To these were added 500 of the semi-lightly armed troops known as peltasts. Originating in Thrace but later appearing throughout the Greek world, these warriors traditionally carried small crescent-shaped wicker shields and a bundle of javelins three to five feet in length, making these fighters more mobile than the hoplites

10. Thucydides 4. 76. 1–77. 2.
11. Thucydides 4. 89. 1–90. 4.
12. Thucydides 4. 93. 3.

with their heavy shields and long spears. Hippocrates had the same number of hoplites and a number of unarmed workers whom he had brought to help with the fortifications, but no huge number of backup men such as the Boeotians had—no lightly armed men, no peltasts, no substantial cavalry. A hill concealed the Boeotian forces from the Athenians, but informants might well have told Hippocrates how many there were.[13] With the Boeotians were the eleven officials of the Boeotian League known as Boeotarchs, however, and we know from Thucydides that ten of them opposed fighting.[14] While it was important to recapture Delium, this could be done without a knock-down, drag-out fight with the entire Athenian army. The Athenians in arms were in fact back at the border, posing no threat—unless they defeated the Boeotians, in which case the festering resentment of which the Thebans had heard might actually come to the fore and bring down oligarchic, Theban-led Boeotia. Hippocrates had reason to question the merits of fighting as well. It was in considerable part to avoid the mighty Boeotian infantry that the Periclean strategy had been developed at the outset of the war. Especially with political unrest at home, would the Boeotians really follow him if he withdrew over the border back into Attica?

They might. And it would be quite a coup for them to defeat the Athenians on their own turf. Then again, for Hippocrates to stand his ground and knock Boeotia out of the war would be an even greater triumph. Plainly there was much to ponder here. Among the Boeotarchs, meanwhile, Pagondas of Thebes, who held the command on that day, disagreed with his colleagues and argued in the strongest terms in favor of attacking.[15] In the end, both sides decided to fight, and there ensued the first hoplite battle of the war.

Pagondas proved to be a remarkable tactician. He drew up his right wing not to the traditional depth of eight men but to the unprecedented depth of twenty-five. These men were Thebans and their neighbors. The other Boeotians were drawn up at assorted but more customary depths.

13. Thucydides 4. 93. 1.
14. Thucydides 4. 91.
15. Thucydides 4. 91-2.

As Hippocrates drew up his men in the standard Greek formation (eight deep), the Athenians would have had a longer line, but the greater length was probably of little use to them, since streams hemmed in the battlefield on each side, limiting prospects for encirclement. When the two sides fell on one another, shoving with their shields, the din was enormous: the pressure, and the noise, built up as the rear ranks pressed on those in front.[16] The Boeotian left gave way almost at once.[17] Only the noble Thespians, whose loyalty to Greece had kept them fighting by the Spartans' side at Thermopylae, held out until the very end, suffering enormous casualties; they were defending themselves in hand-to-hand combat when they were finally surrounded and butchered. It was here on the Boeotian left too that some Athenians became confused and killed their countrymen by mistake. The Athenian left, meanwhile, was holding up remarkably well, and despite the huge mass bearing down on Hippocrates' men, the battle was still in doubt. But Pagondas had another trick up his sleeve, whether envisaged before the fighting began or conceived on the spur of the moment. From behind the hill that had concealed his forces from the Athenians he let loose two squadrons of cavalry. When they saw the horses, the Athenians thought a whole new army had come to attack them. Panicking, they ran in all directions. The Boeotians, particularly the cavalry, pursued them eagerly, and killed many, but dark comes early in a Greek November, so a large number escaped, including the philosopher Socrates, accompanied by his friend

16. I follow here the traditional view of what happened in hoplite warfare: that hoplites in the rear pressed their shields against the backs of the comrades in front of them and pushed, one row after the other. There is considerable disagreement among historians as to the viability of this view. Would not the front rank soldiers lose their balance in the crush? What about stamina, as battles often went on for some hours, as did the battle at Delium? Would not the middle ranks be turned into pabulum in the crush? I believe the balance of the ancient evidence suggests that the hoplite *othismos*, the "push," was doable and that the hoplites did it. A good detailed explanation, with refutation of the opposing view, appears in J. E. Lendon, *Song of Wrath: The Peloponnesian War Begins* (New York: Basic Books, 2010), 307–13. See also on the other side P. Krentz, "The Nature of Hoplite Battle," *Classical Antiquity* 4 (1985): 50–61; a traditional view is reasserted in A. Schwartz, *Reinstating the Hoplite: Arms, Armour and Phalanx Fighting in Archaic and Classical Greece* (Stuttgart: F. Steiner, 2009), and D. Kagan and G. Viggiano, eds., *Men of Bronze: Hoplite Warfare in Ancient Greece* (Princeton, NJ: Princeton University Press, 2013).

17. The battle is described at Thucydides 4. 96.

Alcibiades and the general Laches. Still, Delium saw the highest casualties of any battle in the war to date—about 500 on the Boeotian side and 1,000 on the Athenian, in addition to an unknown but significant number of lightly armed troops and camp followers.[18]

As was customary after a Greek battle, the Athenians sent a herald to request the return of their dead. Under ordinary circumstances, the return of the dead after battle was a routine matter: by requesting their dead back, the vanquished acknowledged their defeat, and by honoring the request, the victors showed that they played by the rules, respecting men and gods. In this case, however, the Athenians had given the Boeotians an opening for denying their request by having used the temple of a god for military purposes.[19] There ensued a battle for the fortress, which the Boeotians finally captured by means of an elaborately constructed flame-thrower. By the time the fortress had been taken and 200 defenders captured, the bodies of the men killed at Delium had been rotting for seventeen days. As they had been stripped naked, it must in many cases have been difficult for their relatives to identify them once they were returned, assuming they could bring themselves to look.

Hippocrates was not impeached for this disaster. For one of the black and bloated bodies returned to the Athenians was his.

BRASIDAS IN CHALCIDICE

The Peloponnesians' fortunes seemed to have turned, and not only in central Greece. In the north (see Map 4), Brasidas proceeded to use a blend of threats and promises (threats about the grape harvest ripening in the fields, promises about autonomy if Acanthus would rebel from Athens) to break down resistance in that city: his speech as Thucydides reports it comes close to comedy, as he first portrays his army as positive martyrs to the cause of Greek freedom, having marched so long and hard

18. Thucydides 4. 101. 2.

19. P. Low, *Interstate Relations in Classical Greece: Morality and Power* (Cambridge: Cambridge University Press, 2007), 224–6, questions whether this was in fact illegal.

to liberate the oppressed Acanthians, and then drops into his honey-tongued rhetoric the threat that if they are not up for liberation he will feel quite comfortable laying waste their fields.[20] For all Brasidas's threats and promises, the Acanthians were plainly ambivalent about abandoning their connection with Athens; they took several votes, on secret ballots. In the end, however, influenced both by Brasidas's oratory and fear for their vineyards, they decided to revolt. North of Acanthus, Stagira, future birthplace of Aristotle, followed suit.

Then came the wonderful news from Boeotia: the Athenians had been dealt a devastating blow at Delium. This, combined with the recent developments in his current campaign, gave Brasidas hope of realizing what had been his ultimate goal in the north all along: seizing the Athenians' cherished colony of Amphipolis, the jewel in their Thracian crown. Well situated in a bend in the Strymon River that came down to the sea at Eion some three miles to the south, the city that came to be known as Amphipolis had been the object of several attempted settlements. Finally in 437 a successful colony was planted under the leadership of Pericles' friend Hagnon, who gave it the name Amphipolis, as the river went around (*amphi*) the city (*polis*) on both sides. The location of Amphipolis was ideal in many respects: it functioned as a source of timber for shipbuilding, it was near the heart of the mining district (Thucydides himself, a wealthy man, had inherited the right to work the local mines, both silver and gold), and it yielded revenue from tolls on the bridge over the river. Perhaps most of all, it blocked the passage over the Strymon east to the Hellespont and the Black Sea, on which the Athenians were dependent for grain.

Knowing what was at stake, Brasidas led his men with astonishing rapidity up the coast. Stopping only to eat, he pushed on through the night despite vile weather until he appeared with his soaked troops at the gates of Argilus, where they were welcomed as liberators and promptly guided to the bridge that led over the Strymon to the territory of Amphipolis. First step accomplished: get there fast, faster than anyone could have

20. Thucydides 4. 85. 1–87. 6.

imagined. The bridge then had to be taken. As it developed, the general in the city had not posted an adequate guard, perhaps because the Athenian general in Amphipolis, Eucles, did not know which citizens in the town were loyal, for the residents of the city were a mixed lot; in addition to the original Athenian settlers, there were many others of various stripes, and by no means all meant the Athenians well. The small fleet of seven ships under the command of Eucles' colleague, moreover, was absent, and not at the port of Eion, either, where it might have been expected to be stationed. It was offshore at the island of Thasos, a half-day's sail away. And so, falling upon the surprised and not perhaps entirely loyal bridge guard in the snow and the dark, Brasidas's men took the bridge and began to overrun the area around the city.

From within the walls, Eucles and those loyal to Athens somehow got word of their plight to the other Athenian general in the region, a man who made Brasidas rather nervous because of his connections in the area—Thucydides, son of Olorus (Olorus being a royal Thracian name), the historian of the Peloponnesian war. Once Thucydides arrived with the fleet and any additional forces he could raise in the neighborhood, the pro-Athenian popular party in Amphipolis would be buoyed up. Consequently, Thucydides tells us, Brasidas offered very moderate terms to the Amphipolitans. (In reading Thucydides' interpretation, we must bear in mind that Brasidas had offered similar terms to the Acanthians, when he had no reason to be apprehensive about the arrival of Thucydides with his ships and his friends; we are free to question just how great a role the fear of Thucydides played in Brasidas's decision making.) Brasidas offered the residents of Amphipolis the opportunity to remain in possession of their property and their citizenship, whatever that might be; alternatively, anyone who wished to depart could do so within five days, taking his possessions with him. Considering the fates that overcame many captured cities during the war—execution of the men, enslavement of the women and children—this offer seemed palatable to most. Besides, there were men inside the city on Brasidas's side arguing in favor of accepting it; and many of those inside the city were related to people who had been captured outside it. Evidently Eucles was losing credit by the hour, and the gates were shortly opened to Brasidas. That evening, when the Spartan was on the point of capturing Eion, Thucydides arrived there with the fleet, having left Thasos posthaste on receiving Eucles' message. There he found refugees from Amphipolis who must have filled him in on what had gone on there.[21]

The loss of Amphipolis was devastating for the Athenians. In addition to losing revenue and timber for shipbuilding, they were no longer able to prevent the Spartans from crossing the Strymon River and heading east. They worried about their control over their northern subject allies, and they were right to do so. In their outrage at this catastrophe they impeached Thucydides. He was either exiled or, more likely, went into exile to avoid a sentence of death passed upon him. Thucydides does not reveal the charge against him or the name of his accuser, although an unreliable ancient biographer says it was Cleon—quite possibly a guess based on Thucydides' obvious dislike of the man.[22]

The Athenians' fears that the defection of Amphipolis would trigger a ripple effect of revolt throughout the region were justified. Several cities went over to Brasidas of their own accord, and others were brought over to Sparta by force. Brasidas started to build boats; it began to look as if he would indeed solidify the Spartans' hold on the north and from there move east to the Hellespont, cutting off the Athenians' supply of timber for their ships and grain for their mouths. But things were not so simple. The Athenians rose to the challenge, sending garrisons northward, while the Spartans declined Brasidas's request for reinforcements. Like Hannibal's two centuries in the future, his accomplishments occasioned envy among the elite at home; besides, a substantial peace party at Sparta had enough of his deeds of valor, preferring the return of the men taken at Pylos to displays of courage in the distant north.

In the spring of 423, consequently, at the instigation of Sparta, the Spartans and the Athenians agreed on a truce, to last for one year while

21. The fall of Amphipolis: Thucydides 4. 103. 4–107. 2.

22. On the impeachment of Thucydides and his responsibility for the fall of Amphipolis, see, e.g., H. D. Westlake, "Thucydides and the Fall of Amphipolis," *Hermes* 90 (1962): 276–87, and J. Roberts, *Accountability in Athenian Government* (Madison: University of Wisconsin Press, 1982), 117–120. The literature on the topic is substantial; see also Thucydides 5. 26. 5.

the details of a lasting peace could be hammered out. It was based on the fundamental premise that each state should keep what it had at the time of the truce, that Athens should accept no runaway helots at Pylos, and that neither side should commit acts of war. Not all Sparta's allies signed; riding high after Delium, the Boeotians saw no need to call a halt to the hostilities, and both the Megarians and the Corinthians were bitter that territories taken from them by the Athenians were to remain in Athenian hands. The Phocians, moreover, were unhappy that the first clause of the truce guaranteed each side access to the oracle at Delphi, as this meant passing through their territory. But the real threat to peace came from the troublemaker in the north, for Brasidas was not the kind of man to proceed as if his accomplishments counted for nothing.

9

MOVING TOWARD PEACE

THERE WAS NOW A most peculiar situation in Greece. The Spartans had become afraid to use their most powerful weapon. War-weariness and discomfort with his enterprising individualism had turned the elite against Brasidas, yet it was unclear how the firebrand could be reined in, and one could not deny that his conquests were doing Sparta some good. The Athenians, for their part, had become at least as nervous about Brasidas as the Spartans. Nor did all of them back the bull-headed bellicosity of Cleon. It was all very well to relish their captive men from the island, but what good did it do to hold on to them forever? Perhaps it was time to stop risking their lives on the battlefield and negotiate.

REMATCH AT AMPHIPOLIS

When the city of Scione on the southwest tip of the peninsula of Pallene in Chalcidice revolted from Athens in response to his rousing rhetoric, Brasidas joyfully accepted Scione into the Spartan alliance. The Scionaeans crowned him with a wreath of gold, proclaiming him the liberator of Greece.[1] The revolt, it seems, took place two days after the truce was announced but before either Brasidas or the people of Scione had gotten word of it. This left Brasidas in something of a quandary: he could hardly "un-accept" the Scionaeans and leave them to the wrath of

1. Thucydides 4. 121. 1.

the Athenians, so he hung on to them. Next to revolt was Mende, just a few miles up the coast from Scione. There no case could be made that either Brasidas or the rebels were unaware of the truce. Everyone was playing with fire. Brasidas transferred as many of the women and children as he could from Scione and Mende to Olynthus and braced for an Athenian attack.[2]

To deal with the situation, the Athenians sent out, under the command of Nicias and Nicostratus, an amphibious expedition consisting of 50 ships, 1,000 hoplites, 600 archers, and 1,000 Thracian mercenaries. To these were added some local peltasts. Their aim was quite limited: to retake Mende and Scione. Nicias above all wanted a lasting peace and was determined to do nothing that would stand in its way. The recapture of Mende, though not accomplished without bloodshed, was not a difficult matter, except of course for those who died in the brief fighting that preceded the return of the city to the hegemony of Athens. The Athenians then moved on to Scione—some with heavy hearts, for the assembly, at the instigation of Cleon, had voted to put all the men there to death and enslave all the women and children.

The Spartans did not remain inactive while the Athenians were busy in Chalcidice. The commanders they sent out under Ischagoras—significantly, another man eager for peace—included Clearidas, who would govern Amphipolis, and Pasitelidas, who would do the same for Torone, a key stronghold on the tip of the Sithonia peninsula (the central prong of the three narrow peninsulas of Chalcidice), for the possession of which Brasidas had fought hard. These new Spartan governors signaled an ominous change of policy, a clear slap in the face to Brasidas, who had promised the cities autonomy. Now Sparta would simply replace Athenian hegemony with its own, and Brasidas would be made to look like a fool.[3] The mission of Ischagoras should not be construed as warlike in intent, for holding on to Chalcidice and, in particular, Amphipolis was crucial to peace negotiations. The Spartans

2. Thucydides 4. 120. 1–123. 4.

3. Thucydides 4. 132.

needed vital pieces to put on the board in exchange for their prisoners from Pylos.[4]

A coalition of peace forces on each side led to an extension of the truce for a few months when it expired in the spring of 422, but finally in August the Athenians had had enough of the Spartans' failure to rein in Brasidas and force him to abide by the provisions of the truce. At Cleon's urging they voted an expedition of 30 ships, 1,200 Athenian hoplites, 300 cavalry, and a large force of allies to be sent to Chalcidice under Cleon himself and other commanders whose names we do not know. Letting Scione lie under siege to be attended to later on and joining with some of the forces already on the scene, Cleon and his colleagues skillfully retook Torone, enslaved the women and children there, and sent 700 men back to Athens as prisoners along with the Spartan governor, the luckless Pasitelidas.[5]

Cleon then prepared to face Brasidas at Amphipolis. Could he wrench this trophy from the wily Spartan's grasp? Still glorying in his stunning victory at Sphacteria and riding on his recent success at Torone, the ambitious Athenian commander thought he could.[6] The Athenians awaited reinforcements in the form of mercenaries from the north; Brasidas meanwhile seized the high ground, prudently concentrating his forces on the hill of Cerdylium to the southwest of the city, in the territory of his friends the Argilians. From this vantage point he could easily observe Cleon's every move. In the meantime, Clearidas would manage the troops in Amphipolis itself. Brasidas had called up 1,500 Thracian mercenaries along with his Edonian peltasts and cavalry forces, and beside the forces he had in Amphipolis he had 1,000 peltasts

4. See the differing interpretations of A. W. Gomme, A. Andrewes, and K. J. Dover, *A Historical Commentary on Thucydides*, 5 vols. (Oxford: Oxford University Press, 1945–81), 3, 623–4, and D. Kagan, *The Archidamian War* (Ithaca, NY: Cornell University Press, 1974), 315–16.

5. Thucydides 5. 2. 1–3.4.

6. On the Battle of Amphipolis, N. Jones, "The Topography and Strategy of the Battle of Amphipolis in 422 BC," *Classical Antiquity* 10 (1977): 71–104, with drawings, and B. M. Mitchell, "Kleon's Amphipolitan Campaign: Aims and Results," *Historia* 40 (1991): 170–92, as well as the classic studies of W. K. Pritchett, "Amphipolis," in *Studies in Ancient Greek Topography*, 1 (Berkeley: University of California Press, 1965), 30–48, and "Amphipolis Restudied" in *Studies in Ancient Greek Topography*, 3 (Berkeley: University of California Press, 1980), 298–347.

from Myrcinus and Chalcidice. In addition to 300 Greek cavalry, he had with him 2,000 hoplites. Of these he kept 1,500 at Cerdylium, leaving the rest in Amphipolis under Clearidas.[7]

When the Athenians' northern reinforcements failed to materialize, Brasidas determined to launch a surprise attack. Already Cleon had more men than he did, and he did not want the imbalance to grow. The city of Amphipolis had two major gates. Brasidas's intention was to make a sudden sortie with 150 hoplites from one gate and then, when the Athenians had their hands full dealing with that attack, have Clearidas fall upon them from the other with the remainder of the army.

Cleon meanwhile was weighing his own options. It had been reported to him that Brasidas had been seen descending from Cerdylium into the city and that he had performed some sort of sacrifices at the altar of Athena. Were these the customary pre-battle sacrifices? He didn't like the smell of things. His excursion north of the city had been intended as merely exploratory, and withdrawal would not bring disgrace. When he learned from scouts that the Spartans' army with "the feet and hooves of many men and horses ready to rush out" was gathered at one of the gates, north of nearly all his men, he saw no reason not to call for a retreat, especially since he had never planned to fight without reinforcements.[8]

Cleon's strategy for the return to Eion entailed wheeling the army's right wing around so as to march left. This not only left its unshielded right side vulnerable but caused considerable confusion as a result of the failure to coordinate with the left wing. In the ensuing chaos, Brasidas burst out from the city and attacked the disoriented Athenian center. When Clearidas and his men then ran through the gate and charged as instructed, the Athenian left retreated. Brasidas went after the Athenian right, where he was wounded and carried off the battlefield by his comrades—almost certainly unnoticed by the Athenians, as Spartan generals wore no special insignia that would distinguish them from common

7. Thucydides 5. 6. 3–5.

8. J. E. Lendon, *Song of Wrath: The Peloponnesian War Begins* (New York: Basic Books, 2010), 358–9, presents an entirely different interpretation of Cleon's strategy, arguing that Cleon had deliberately provoked Brasidas to battle and paid for it with his life.

soldiers. The right wing held up for quite some time, even after Cleon had been killed by a Myrcinian peltast; it maintained formation and held off two or three of Clearidas's assaults, giving up only when the Myrcinian and Chalcidian cavalry and peltasts had finally bombarded them and put them to flight.

The Spartans lost seven men, the Athenians some 600. We know the name of one of the few Spartan dead:

> The men who picked up Brasidas and got him safely out of the battle and into the city brought him in while he still had breath in him. Much later, he lost consciousness and died, but he knew his men had won.[9]

So perished the eloquent and daring Brasidas, death bringing a premature end to an extraordinary career. One of Sparta's finest leaders and certainly its most gifted diplomat, he had never received the recognition he deserved at home; he was probably more admired by Thucydides, whose exile his tactics brought about, than by most of his countrymen. All the allies followed Brasidas's corpse and gave him a public burial in Amphipolis. The Amphipolitans honored him with the rituals appropriate to a hero, instituting annual sacrifices and athletic contests in his name. They tore down any traces of their original founder Hagnon and instead honored Brasidas as the founder of their city.[10]

Thucydides' account leaves Cleon to a coward's death, struck down by a peltast as he ran for his life. This is not the only possible interpretation of events—indeed, not even the only interpretation of Thucydides' own text. The fact that Cleon was running when he was cut down need not damn him; he had stayed with his retreating right wing and may well have been racing to catch up with them as they withdrew.[11] And he had stood his ground after Brasidas's first attack; it was a Myrcinian peltast who killed him, and the Myrcinians came only in the second wave, with Clearidas.

9. Thucydides 5. 10. 11.
10. Thucydides 5. 10. 11–11. 1.
11. Thucydides 5. 10. 9.

Whatever the circumstances of Cleon's demise, the lopsided casualty figures confirm that Brasidas had planned well, Cleon poorly. Even with fewer men than Cleon, Brasidas had used the element of surprise to his advantage. Cleon, for his part, had not organized the Athenian retreat properly. And so October of 422 witnessed the deaths of the men Aristophanes called the twin pestles of the mortar in which the dread God of War ground down the cities of Greece, and by early April of 421 the Spartans and the Athenians had signed a peace treaty to last for fifty years. Both states harbored many who wished to carry on with the war, but the peacefully inclined prevailed. It is easy to understand the Spartans' desire to end the war. Their reinstated king Pleistoanax was deeply disturbed by the ongoing fighting, since many of his countrymen (albeit unreasonably so) blamed their recent misfortunes in the war on his recall.[12] Not everyone had looked with pleasure on Brasidas's string of successes in the north, since these only prolonged the fighting and called for a greater commitment of men than Sparta was inclined to make; and of course, they lent him a stature that made many of the elite uncomfortable. Helot desertions were increasing exponentially, and the Spartans were terrified of another great rebellion. The Thirty Years' Treaty with Argos, moreover, was due to expire. If that were to happen before a Spartan–Athenian treaty was in place, there was nothing to prevent the Argives and Athenians from joining against the Spartans in an alliance that might well prove fatal to them. And of course their POWs continued to languish in an Athenian prison.

It is less easy to understand the Athenians' motivation to end the war. The most rational decision would probably have been to sit back and let events take their course. Once the treaty between Argos and Sparta had expired, it was likely that an Athenian–Argive treaty could be set in place, and alienated democratic allies of Sparta—both Elis and Mantinea had fallen out with the Spartans—would quite possibly join, a truly terrifying prospect for the Lacedaemonians. Encouraged by this shift in power relations, helot disaffection would probably spread, and the Peloponnesian

12. Thucydides 5. 16. 1.

League might well become a thing of the past. Various theories have been put forward to explain the Athenians' willingness to make peace when their position seemed so far superior to Sparta's: plain war-weariness, that they were running out of money, that they were running out of men, fear of revolts in the empire, the sheer shame of the crushing defeat at Amphipolis. But not all were willing to make peace, and toward the beginning of spring, the Spartans, seeing this hesitance, sent word to all the cities in their alliance demanding that they prepare to build a fort on Athens' frontier. That did the trick: the Athenians promptly agreed to sit down with the Spartans and set to work hammering out a treaty.[13]

RIDING A DUNG BEETLE TO THE HEAVENS

With the peace not yet concluded but looking like a good possibility, Aristophanes composed his hopeful *Peace*. By the time the play was actually produced, the treaty was days away from being signed. In this celebratory offering at the festival of the City Dionysia, Aristophanes introduced his protagonist Trygaeus, who, frustrated with the long years of war, is determined to visit Zeus and inquire as to his plans for the suffering Greeks. This he accomplishes by ascending on the back of an enormous dung beetle, an act realized (in a parody of tragic practice) by a huge *mechane*, a sort of crane customarily used to mimic flying or to indicate the presence of a deity. Only after his slaves have gotten belly laughs from the audience by beefing up the creature with a huge meal of excrement is it ready to "fly." Trygaeus adds to the comic element by calling to the machinist offstage in mock terror as he is lifted off the stage,

> Oh, no! I'm terrified. I'm not kidding around.
> Machinist, listen up! Already wind is churning
> All around my guts. If you're not careful, I'll . . .
> You know . . . be . . . feeding the beetle![14]

13. Thucydides 5. 17.
14. *Peace*, ll. 173–6.

When Trygaeus arrives in heaven, he discovers that Zeus and the other gods are away; only Hermes remains to answer his questions. The gods have decamped, Hermes explains, because of the Greeks' persistence in carrying on the war despite the Olympians' preference for peace. The Athenians in Aristophanes' audience cannot have been entirely comfortable with Hermes' even-handed allotment of blame. The gods, he explains,

> were frequently for peace,
> But you guys wanted war. Laconians,
> when once they got a little piece of luck,
> would say, "By God, those Atticans will pay!"
> Or if it seemed that luck was on your side,
> and when the Spartans came about a peace,
> at once you'd cry: "We're being taken in!"
> Athena! Zeus! We can't agree to this!
> If we hang on to Pylos, they'll come back."[15]

The god War, it seems, has imprisoned the goddess Peace in a cave. Having obtained an enormous mortar in which to grind down all the cities of Greece into a popular dish known as *myttotos*, he has sent his slave Tumult in search of pestles. Each ingredient proves to be a Greek place associated with a particular delicacy—Prasiae, noted for its leeks, Megara known for garlic, Sicily famous for its cheese, and Attica long renowned for its honey. Athens and Sparta, however, have recently lost their pestles—Cleon and Brasidas. Without them, there may be some hope of setting Peace free.

Trygaeus is ultimately successful in his attempt to enlist Hermes in the project of liberating Peace. This is no mean task, as it entails getting all the squabbling Greeks to pull together on the necessary ropes. The Argives have no interest in the project and laugh at the participants; the Boeotians are obstructionist. Some Megarians pull, but with little result

15. *Peace*, ll. 211–19.

because they are so weak from the hunger induced by the war. Finally the sturdy farmers—often the object of Aristophanes' praise—manage the task and Peace is brought up into the light. Her anticipated blessings are celebrated in terms that reflect the concerns of the fictional Trygaeus's real-life counterparts in the audience:

> Trygaeus: Fellow farmers! Stop and listen! Can you hear these
> wondrous words?
> No more spears, men, no more javelins, no more fighting with our
> swords!
> We've got peace with all its gifts now, we can trade in all that arming
> For a happy, happy song as we go home to do some FARMING![16]

THE PEACE OF NICIAS

Oaths and libations swearing to the treaty were poured out by seventeen Spartans, including both kings, and seventeen Athenians, including Nicias, whose name the Peace bore. It was probably Cleon's chief rival in Athenian politics, Nicias, who breathed the most audible sigh of relief when hostilities ceased—audible and unbecoming as well, since he had a signal horror of breaking his record of success in battle, and his fear of losing his reputation as a winner played a large part in his desire for peace.[17]

The terms of the peace, sworn for a period of fifty years, were similar to those of the armistice that had gone before. Each side was free to consult common shrines without impediment, prisoners who had not died in confinement were to be returned, and with some exceptions each side was to give back what it had acquired by force during the war. Athens would retain the Megarian port of Nisaea and the former Corinthian territories of Anactorium and Sollium in the west. As for the cities in

16. *Peace*, ll. 551–5.
17. Thucydides 5. 16. 1.

Thrace, the Spartans abandoned them, and the Athenians dealt with them in different ways. Amphipolis and some others were to return to the fold; Acanthus, Argilus, Stagira, Stolus, Spartolus, and Olynthus, whose revolts had been encouraged by Sparta, were to be neutrals, although the Athenians were permitted to use persuasion (whatever that might mean) in an attempt to win them back. The Chalcidians were allowed to live in their own cities, and Athens agreed to abandon its bases on (and just off) the Peloponnesus at Pylos, Methana, and Cythera. An ominous clause, moreover, added, "If either side shall have left anything unmentioned, the Athenians and the Spartans may alter the treaty with due process in accordance with their oaths in such wise as shall seem best to them both"[18]—to them both, but not necessarily to their allies. This rider was not going to win the superpowers any popularity contests in Greece.

So after ten years of bloodshed and marauding, was the slate simply to be wiped clean, and was everyone to pretend their sons, fathers, brothers had never died, their honor remained unblemished, their homes were still intact, their trees yet stood?

Athens and Sparta, each for its own reasons, were willing to swallow their pride and accede to this agreement, acting as if all this had been worth dying for, and most of Sparta's allies signed as well. Most, but not all: Megara, Corinth, Boeotia, and Elis stood aloof. The Megarians, of course, were enraged about Nisaea. Corinth was angry that there was nothing in the truce about Potidaea and about the loss of Sollium and Anactorium. The Boeotians had recently captured Panactum, a fortress on their border with Attica, and they did not want to give it back (although more broadly speaking, they simply did not think peace was in their interest; they well remembered their resounding victory at Delium). The Eleians had no specific objection to the peace terms, but they had a private quarrel with the Spartans regarding Lepreum near the Cyparissian Gulf on the west coast of the Peloponnesus and saw no reason to cooperate with them in foreign affairs. The cities in Thrace, moreover, were unwilling to abide by the terms of the peace, and Clearidas refused to

18. Thucydides 5. 18. 11.

surrender Amphipolis, claiming that he was not strong enough to compel the residents to abandon their loyalty to the Spartans. This was a major blow to the peace, since the recapture of Amphipolis was one of Athens' chief motivations in ending the war.

With the fragility of the peace increasingly evident and the Argives' intentions still uncertain, Sparta and Athens took the Greek world aback by signing a mutual defensive alliance.[19] Designed to last fifty years, it committed each state to defend the other in the event of attack and Athens to come to the aid of Sparta in the event of a helot uprising. After the Peace of Nicias, the Spartans returned their Athenian prisoners; after the signing of the alliance, the Athenians finally returned the prisoners from Sphacteria and Pylos (which they were actually bound to do by the terms of the Peace of Nicias). In effect, then, the Peace of Nicias came in two stages—the original peace, and then the Spartan–Athenian alliance to shore it up. This alliance was the first of many that would follow during the chaotic years subsequent to a peace that did not bring peace. Superficially, the Athenians had prevailed in this long and bloody war. Pericles' goal had been realized: the Spartans had been made to recognize that they could not destroy the Athenians' empire. But the war had not been fought between Athens and Sparta alone, and tensions within the Peloponnesian League would guarantee continuing strains among the Greek states.

19. Thucydides 5. 23.

10

AN UNPEACEABLE PEACE

BECAUSE OF HIS ROLE in negotiating the peace, Plutarch reported, Nicias was the object of boundless gratitude throughout Greece.[1] His name indeed sounded like the Greek word for victory—*nike*. But enthusiasm for the peace was not in fact as universal as Plutarch maintained, for even in Nicias's native Athens, a strong war party remained. Cleon's spirit lived on: the streets of Scione soon ran red with blood as the Athenians made good on their threat to kill all the men and enslave all the women and children.[2] Nor did goodwill reign elsewhere. Although Athens and Sparta refrained from actually attacking one another for nearly seven years, new alliances and new hostilities sprang up at once to take the place of old ones as fear and anger drove the Greek states constantly to seek partners for both defense and offense. Corinth in particular was bitter about its losses and at Sparta's acquiescence in them. Flailing about in frustration brought on by simultaneous rage at both Athens and Sparta, the Corinthians encouraged the Argives to take the lead in a new league designed to save the Peloponnesus from "enslavement" by Sparta. Since their treaty with the Spartans was expiring and they saw war on the horizon, the Argives were quite receptive. Mantinea and Elis were both interested in the alliance; Boeotia, Megara, and Tegea demurred.[3]

1. Plutarch *Nicias* 9. 6–7.
2. Thucydides 5. 32. 1.
3. Thucydides 5. 27. 1–32. 4.

PROMISES, PROMISES

In Athens, the peace facilitated new buildings on the Acropolis. Around 420 the delicate Ionic temple of Athena Nike was finally finished at the southwest corner. At the same time a testament to an entirely different divinity was constructed, as Telemachus, a citizen of either Athens or Epidaurus (perhaps an Epidaurian living at Athens), welcomed the healing god Asklepios to Athens with a monument on the south slope of the Acropolis that became the center of a temple and a cult. Telemachus had evidently brought the sacred snake that was the god incarnate with him from Epidaurus; the holy creature seems to have lived at first with the playwright Sophocles before moving into its sacred space. (The Athenians found nothing peculiar in needing the snake itself to certify the presence and favor of the god.) The manifestation of the healing god was a long time in coming, but clearly his arrival was due to the painful awareness of illness and suffering the Athenians had gained first from the plague and then from the wounds of war, and it was only the Peace of Nicias that cleared the way for negotiations between Athens and Epidaurus about the god's relocation and the establishment of a cult in Athens.[4]

The Spartans meanwhile kept promising the Athenians that they would compel their allies to comply with the terms of the peace, but their promises were not fulfilled; and the Athenians came to regret having returned the prisoners they had captured at Pylos and Sphacteria when important Peloponnesian allies still would not sign the treaty, Amphipolis and the other cities in the north had not agreed to the terms of the peace, the Boeotians still held Athenian prisoners, and Panactum remained in Boeotian hands. Only after protracted negotiations in the summer of 421 were the Athenians persuaded to withdraw the Messenians and other helots from Pylos.[5] But a change of ephors at Sparta brought two men

4. There was also a cult of Asklepios at Zea in the Piraeus established around the same time; it seems impossible to determine which of the two Attic cults was established first. See R. Parker, *Athenian Religion: A History* (Oxford: Clarendon Press, 1996), 175–85.

5. Thucydides 5. 35. 7.

into office who were not favorable to peace, and this plainly would have a profound effect on future relations among the Greek states.[6]

Still determined to regain Pylos, the Spartans sent ambassadors to Boeotia begging them to hand over Panactum and the Athenian prisoners they held. The Athenians were given the prisoners, but Panactum they received only in a rather attenuated form: the Boeotians turned it into a pile of rubble first. In addition, the Boeotians demanded in exchange that the Spartans make an alliance with them. With heavy hearts, the Spartans agreed to the Boeotians' demand, knowing as they did so that they were violating the terms of their treaty with Athens.[7] Now the Spartans were embarrassed and the Athenians livid. Just as a warlike faction had taken shape in Sparta with the entry of Cleobulus and Xenares into the ephorate, so the Athenians began to look for leadership not to the conservative Nicias but to men like Hyperbolus and Alcibiades, who had not been sympathetic to the treaty. Alcibiades in fact saw his future in denouncing Nicias and replacing him as the leader of the Athenians, accusing him of being "soft on Sparta." About Hyperbolus we know less: Aristophanes in the *Knights* attributed to him imperial aims that extended as far as Carthage (something evidently not unusual among his countrymen).[8]

Athens' war party soon had its chance when Argos began to feel needy. On hearing about the destruction of Panactum and the treaty between Sparta and Boeotia, the Argives, thinking the Spartans had been complicit in the razing of the fortress, inferred that by allying with the Spartans the Boeotians had come over into the Athenian alliance as well. Sensing that they had been left out in the cold, they panicked and at first took steps to protect themselves by joining the alliance with Sparta. But before their assembly had approved the alliance they received a message from Athens that inclined them in a different direction entirely.[9]

6. Thucydides 5. 36. 1.
7. Thucydides 5. 39.
8. *Knights* ll. 1303–4.
9. Thucydides 5. 40. 1–3, 43. 3.

ENTER ALCIBIADES

This message came from Alcibiades, recently elected to the board of generals for 420/19. Previously kept by his youth from holding high commands in the war, a veteran of Potidaea and Delium, this flashy young friend of Socrates now planted his feet firmly in the midst of things and would not be removed from center stage. Not even by exiling him could the Athenians rid themselves of Alcibiades and his dogged determination to play a key role in the war.[10]

About no other Athenian politician has such a collection of colorful anecdotes accumulated as Alcibiades (Figure 7). Plutarch in writing his biography had a vast assortment from which to choose. Some were merely "cute," like his speech defect, which for some reason the Athenians found charming, or the day he brought a quail into the assembly which caused a ruckus when it escaped—or the way, as a boy, he refused to step aside for a cart when he was playing knucklebones in the street and instead lay down in front of it, bringing it to a sharp stop. Other tales, however, involved violence, like the time he punched a teacher who confessed that he had no copy of Homer, or, on a bet, subjected his future father-in-law to the same treatment. Most serious was the allegation that he had killed one of his slaves with a stick in the wrestling grounds.[11] Seemingly a perpetual adolescent, Alcibiades made a striking contrast with his sober guardian Pericles, who gave the impression of having been born a full-fledged adult.

Alcibiades was barely out of toddlerhood when his father Cleinias died, and family connections placed him in Pericles' home. The raising of this hellion proved no mean task, and Pericles was either unwilling or unable to engage with the incorrigible youth. But as Alcibiades contemplated Pericles and the regard in which he was held, a question began to form in his mind: "Could I be like that some day?"

10. A tremendous amount of secondary literature has accumulated around Alcibiades to be added to the ancient accounts. See J. Hatzfeld, *Alcibiade: Etude sur l'histoire d'Athènes à la fin du Ve siècle* (Paris: Presses Universitaires de France, 1940, 2e, 1951); E. Bloedow, *Alcibiades Reexamined* (Wiesbaden: F. Steiner, 1973); W. Ellis, *Alcibiades* (London: Routledge, 1989); D. Gribble, *Alcibiades and Athens: A Study in Literary Presentation* (Oxford: Clarendon Press, 1999); P. J. Rhodes, *Alcibiades: Athenian Playboy, General and Traitor* (Barnsley: Pen & Sword, 2011).

11. Plutarch *Alcibiades* 2–10; for the speech defect, also Aristophanes' *Wasps* ll. 44–6.

FIGURE 7
Bust of the young Alcibiades.
© Vanni Archive/ Art Resource, NY.

No, he couldn't, for it would have taken a self-discipline for which charm was no substitute. Still, he was determined to try. Alcibiades had long-standing family connections with Sparta; indeed, his very name was Spartan. For several generations his ancestors were the official representatives of Spartan interests at Athens, but by the time of the Peloponnesian War this connection had lapsed. Alcibiades wished to reinstate it, and so when the Spartans captured at Sphacteria and Pylos had been sent to Athens he had gone out of his way to look after the prisoners.[12] He felt therefore that he should be rewarded with a key role in negotiating the peace in 421. But Nicias too had cultivated the prisoners, and as the older, more prominent man, he was the one the Spartans chose. Resentful and humiliated, Alcibiades now decided that there was

12. Thucydides 5. 43. 2.

no future for him in an Athens at peace with Sparta, and he devoted himself full-time to ensuring that the two states would be at war instead.

It was in this spirit that he contacted the Argives, privately urging them to send envoys to Athens along with ambassadors from Elis and Mantinea as soon as they could to discuss the prospects of an alliance. Pleased with this opportunity, the Argives and their allies did indeed turn up at Athens. At the same time, the Spartans, learning what was afoot, sent ambassadors to Athens as well, among whom was Endius, who had a long-standing family connection with Alcibiades. Appearing before the Council, the Spartan envoys asked for Pylos in exchange for Panactum and insisted that they had meant no harm to the Athenians by their alliance with the Boeotians, explaining that they had come with full powers to resolve the differences between the two states. At this juncture, negotiations took a turn for the bizarre. Fearing that the Spartan envoys' evident goodwill would lead the assembly to reject the projected alliance with Argos, Alcibiades devised the following stratagem. He gave the envoys his personal assurance that he would see to it that Pylos was returned to them and everything else would work out if only they did not repeat before the assembly that they had come with full powers; he himself would address the assembly on their behalf. But when the Spartans appeared before the assembly and denied that they had come with full powers, the Athenians lost faith in them and were more favorably disposed than ever to the Argives.[13] Persuaded by Alcibiades, the Athenians signed an alliance with Argos, Mantinea, and Elis, this pact to last for not fifty years, like the one between Athens and Sparta, but a hundred years.[14] Fortuitously, the terms of the alliance appear not only in the text of Thucydides' history but also in fragmentary form on a piece of marble found in 1876 on the southern slope of the Athenian acropolis.[15] The Corinthians remained allied to Argos but did not join the new coalition; probably some were anxious about Spartan retribution and others were moved by implacable hatred of Athens. The new alliance thus became a coalition of democratic states only.

13. Thucydides 5. 45. 3–4.

14. Thucydides 5. 47. 1–12.

15. A drawing is reproduced in S. Hornblower, *A Commentary on Thucydides*, 3 vols. (Oxford: Oxford University Press, 1991–2008), 3, 110.

SPARTA VERSUS THE QUADRUPLE ALLIANCE

While some no doubt saw the purpose of the alliance as chiefly defensive, others thought differently. Early in the summer of 419 Alcibiades led a campaign to persuade Patrae on the northern coast of Achaea to ally with Athens and build walls right up to the shore. He then lent his support to an Argive attack on neighboring Epidaurus. Rationalized by the Epidaurians' purported failure to supply some required sacrificial victims to a temple over which Argos had authority, this assault in reality had as its goal the creation of an easier route by which the Athenians could send aid to Argos. In response to this activity, Agis led out the Spartans in full strength as far as their border. By tradition, however, border crossings were accompanied by special sacrifices, many of which are depicted in art (see Figure 8). Greeks had established cults for a variety of river gods, and the archaic poet Hesiod had cautioned against crossing a river without praying.[16] The narrative of Herodotus is filled with examples of rituals accompanying border crossings. Xenophon in his *Constitution of the Lacedaemonians* outlines the progression of the religious procedures followed by the Spartan state in time of war:

> First the king and his staff sacrifice at home to Zeus the Leader and the gods associated with him. If the sacrificial omens are favorable, the Fire-bearer takes fire from the altar and leads the way to the frontier. Here once more the king sacrifices to Zeus and Athena. Only when the omens attending on the sacrifices prove acceptable to these two gods does he cross the frontier. The fire taken from the sacrifices leads the way and is never quenched, and animals for sacrifice of all sorts follow. Whenever the king sacrifices, he sets about the work in the morning while it is still dark, as he wishes to secure divine favor before the enemy can do so.[17]

16. *Works and Days*, 737–8.

17. *Constitution of the Lacedaemonians* 13. 2-3. On military sacrifice in Greece in general, see W. K. Pritchett, *The Greek State at War, Part III* (Berkeley: University of California Press, 1979), 47–90.

FIGURE 8
Fragment of an early fifth-century drinking-cup showing battle sacrifice.
Credit: Cleveland Museum of Art, Dudley P. Allen Fund 1926.

The omen produced by the sacrifice was generally determined by examining the lobe of the liver of the slain animal, an art studied and taught by experienced seers throughout Greece, and on this occasion, the omens produced by Agis's frontier sacrifice were not good, and the king took his troops home.

The Dorian festival of the Carnea then intervening, he declined to move again until it had concluded, and he sent word to Sparta's allies to prepare to march afterward.[18] The Spartans were known for their piety, as shown by their anxiety about sending troops to Marathon during this

18. Thucydides 5. 54. 2.

time-honored festival of Apollo, and it is quite likely that Agis's decision here was motivated by sincere religious scruples rather than second thoughts about facing the Argive coalition.[19]

At the invitation of Athens, peace talks were initiated at Mantinea, but when they failed and fighting resumed between Argos and Epidaurus, Agis once again marched out to see what he could do—and once again turned back when the border sacrifices proved inauspicious.[20]

Throughout the winter the Argives and Epidaurians fought one another, and the spring elections at Athens brought an interesting development: Alcibiades was not elected general, but Nicias and several of his friends were. Could this herald the beginning of a new détente between Athens and Sparta?

Looking around the Peloponnesus, however, Agis still felt that action was called for. Not only was Epidaurus endangered, but other cities in the region, sensing Sparta's weakness, were beginning to break away. Starting out from Sparta, he managed to rendezvous at Phlius with an army coming from the north consisting of Boeotian and other troops. Agis sent his combined forces down into the Argive plain by three different paths, surrounding the Argives and their allies. The Spartans and those marching with them blocked their way back to Argos; the Corinthians, Phliasians, and Pelleneans looked down on them from the right; and the huge force of the Boeotians, Sicyonians, and Megarians was approaching from the direction of Nemea. The Argives did not recognize the danger they were in, thinking that their home field advantage would carry the day, even though the Athenians had not yet turned up, and only the Athenians had cavalry to contribute to the allied force. But two of them thought differently: Thrasylus, one of their five generals, and Alciphron, the official representative of Spartan interests at Argos, approached Agis just as battle was about to be joined, offering to submit the Spartans' complaints to arbitration and make peace instead of war. This they did on their own initiative, with no instructions from the Argive assembly. And Agis said that would be fine.[21]

19. On Spartan piety, see M. D. Goodman and A. J. Holladay, "Religious Scruples in Ancient Warfare," *Classical Quarterly* n. s. 36 (1986): 151–71, esp. 151–60.

20. Thucydides 5. 55. 3.

21. Thucydides 5. 59. 5–60. 1.

So without consulting with his troops, and informing only one of the officials who were with him on the campaign, the Spartan king concluded a truce of four months and withdrew. His men followed him, fuming; how could he have backed away, they asked themselves, when they had the enemy completely surrounded? "And indeed," Thucydides wrote, "this had been the finest Greek fighting force ever assembled up to that time."[22] The Argives too (if rather mysteriously) thought they had lost a great opportunity to fight near their city and with many brave allies, and they began to stone Thrasylus.[23] Though Thrasylus escaped with his life by taking refuge at an altar, the state confiscated his property.

At this juncture, the Athenian reinforcements of 1,000 hoplites and 300 cavalry finally arrived, led by Laches and Nicostratus and accompanied by Alcibiades as an ambassador. Incited by Alcibiades to resume the war, the allies attacked and captured Orchomenus (the one in Arcadia in the Peloponnesus, not the one in Boeotia). They also made plans to attack Tegea, where some were preparing to betray the city to them. Back in Sparta the bad news came thick and fast—a disgraceful truce made when the enemy was surrounded; the loss of Orchomenus; disaffection in Tegea. Agis could not have been in worse trouble. The Spartans deliberated about demolishing his house (not an unheard-of punishment in Greece) and fining him the considerable sum of 100,000 drachmas. Though he persuaded them to give him one more chance to distinguish himself on the battlefield, they passed an unprecedented law specifying that he should not conduct warfare without ten advisers, whose approval would be necessary for any future withdrawals from the field of battle.[24] How very humiliating.

22. Thucydides 5. 60. 3.

23. There is an obvious parallel between the action of the Argive Thrasylus here and the Athenian Lycides, who in 479 expressed willingness to entertain Persian peace proposals (Herodotus 9. 5. 1–2). Lycides was in fact stoned to death; V. Rosivach, "Execution by Stoning in Athens," *Classical Antiquity* 6 (1987): 232–48.

24. Thucydides 5. 63. 1–4; on the threat to destroy Agis's house, see W. R. Connor, "The Razing of the House in Greek Society," *Transactions and Proceedings of the American Philological Association* 115 (1985): 79–102.

And so off he marched with his ten advisers to fight at last. This time there would be no inauspicious frontier sacrifices, no last-minute truces.[25] Afraid to show the slightest sign of shying away from battle, Agis had decided not to wait for his northern allies. In the plain of Mantinea Agis and 9,000 or more infantry—Spartans, Tegeates, Sciritae (perioeci from the hills northwest of Sparta), and *neodamodeis* (including those who had fought with Brasidas in Thrace), backed by cavalry, faced an army of close to the same size consisting of at least 3,000 Argives; 1,000 Athenians; 2,000 Mantineans; 1,000 mercenary Arcadians; 1,000 assorted Cleonaeans, Orneans, Aeginetans, and other allied infantry; and 300 cavalry from Athens. The Argive coalition charged in a fury while the Spartans, as was their wont, moved forward in lockstep to the rhythm of the *aulos*.[26] As the two sides advanced toward one another, the drift to the right characteristic of hoplite armies trying to protect their unshielded sides became more severe than usual. Afraid of his left wing being surrounded, just before battle was joined Agis told the Sciritae and the "Brasideans" to move in from their position on the left and ordered the commanders Hipponoidas and Aristocles to fill up the gap thus created by hurling themselves into it with two companies taken from the right wing.

Hipponoidas and Aristocles stayed exactly where they were. Their decision was probably the right one, although the Spartans back home exiled them for cowardice. After a melee in which substantial casualties were sustained by the Argive coalition, Agis's forces finally prevailed, losing only 300 Spartans and a small number of allied forces; the Argive coalition lost more than 1,000 men. Among the Athenian dead were both their generals, Laches and Nicostratus.[27]

At Mantinea—the greatest battle, Thucydides claimed, that the Greeks had fought for a long while—Agis redeemed his reputation and restored the honor Sparta had lost years before at Sphacteria. In this he had help

25. Thucydides 5. 64. 5.

26. Thucydides 5. 70. There is some uncertainty about the numbers and about other matters concerning the battle as well: see J. F. Lazenby, *The Peloponnesian War: A Military Study* (London: Routledge, 2004), 119–26, and Hornblower, *Commentary*, 3, 185–94.

27. Thucydides 5. 74. 3.

from his enemies; Eleian and Athenian reinforcements arrived too late.[28] For the democratic coalition, the defeat was a devastating blow, and in fact during the following winter, pro-Spartans in Argos overthrew the democracy there and broke with Athens; the new government in Argos now allied with Sparta. Soon Mantinea too returned to the Spartan sphere. Though the spirit of democracy was strong in Argos and it was not long before the democrats rose up and retook their city, the coalition had been dealt a major body blow.

NICIAS AND ALCIBIADES

In Athens the rivalry between Alcibiades and Nicias was heating up. Both men were elected to the generalship in 417, and each contrived to gain favor with the demos by playing to his strength. Nicias had always been known for his piety. His devotion often took the form of lavish expenditures. He spared no expense when he consecrated a tract of land he had purchased on the island of Delos to Apollo, or when he sponsored the choral performances at the festival on the island. Whereas the choruses that the other cities sent to the festival arrived haphazardly, Plutarch says, and began singing while they were still putting on their ceremonial garments, Nicias, when he took charge of the choruses from Athens, disembarked the chorus at the nearby island of Rheneia. Then, having brought with him from Athens a carefully fitted bridge of boats magnificently adorned with tapestries, he spanned the narrow channel between the two islands at night so that he could lead the chorus, singing, over to Delos at daybreak.[29] This no doubt made a good impression at the time, but any Athenian who thought the gods would look on Nicias with favor and bless all the enterprises he undertook was in for a nasty surprise.[30]

28. Thucydides 5. 75. 5.

29. Plutarch *Nicias* 3. 4–6.

30. The Athenians did, in fact, consider Nicias favored by the gods, and did indeed suffer mightily for this misperception in 413 when the expedition he led to Sicily failed disastrously after Athens refused his request to be recalled.

Alcibiades, meanwhile, was busy planning a show of his own. In the Olympics of 416 he entered seven chariots—more, he would point out in a speech to the assembly the next year, than any private citizen before him—and three of them came in first, second, and fourth. By so doing, he claimed, he not only demonstrated his own strength and superiority but showed Greeks outside Athens that the city was not devastated by war but rather was greater than in fact it was.[31] Whether all Athenians who heard him speak in this way were impressed that he could do things an ordinary Athenian couldn't is uncertain; as elsewhere in Greece, envy was a powerful force in democratic Athens.

MASSACRE ON MELOS

In 416 the Athenians undertook a campaign that has gone down in infamy and served to define their philosophy of international relations, perhaps more than it should. They sent a substantial armed force to bring the island of Melos into the Athenian empire. Some eighty miles off the Peloponnesian coast and a rare Spartan colony, Melos was the only island among the Cyclades that had stood aloof from the Delian League, wishing to remain neutral in the war.[32] Nicias had tried to subdue it in 426 with sixty ships and 2,000 hoplites, but without success; after he invaded the island, the Athenians demanded tribute, but the tribute does not seem to have been paid.[33]

Then the project was evidently forgotten until something prompted the Athenians to take action again—perhaps frustration that their new alliance on the mainland had collapsed, perhaps something else. And so ten years later, in a time of general peace, they gathered a remarkably large fleet—thirty of their own ships, six ships from Chios, and two from Lesbos—as well as 1,600 of their own hoplites, 300 archers, and twenty

31. Thucydides 6. 16. 2.

32. Most scholarly attention to this episode concerns the dialogue presented in Thucydides' text, but on historical questions concerning Melos, see M. Seaman, "The Athenian Expedition to Melos in 416 B. C.," *Historia* 46 (1997): 385–418.

33. Thucydides 3. 91. 1–3.

mounted archers of their own, plus 1,500 allied hoplites. This was quite a force to launch against a state that could at most put 500 men in the field.[34]

Having established themselves on the island with their troops, the Athenian generals Cleomedes and Tisias sent ambassadors to talk with the Melians. Melos was evidently an oligarchy at this time, for the Melian leadership was not willing to bring the ambassadors before the popular assembly, fearing that the populace would give in to their fear and go over to them at once. Instead, they asked the ambassadors to discuss their mission with the magistrates and "the few." The ambassadors agreed to this, proposing a back and forth conversation rather than long speeches, and excluding from the discussion any consideration of justice—a convenient proviso, since what they had to say was so patently unjust, indeed repugnant. How much of the dialogue that appears in Thucydides' *History* reflects what was really said on Melos and how much represents the historian's own meditation on power and the corruption it works, we cannot be sure. Of all the words reported in Thucydides' work, those spoken at Melos probably merit the least credibility. But some Melians and many Athenians were available as sources, so we should not exclude the possibility that the core of the conversation took place as Thucydides reports it.[35]

Be realistic, the Athenians are portrayed as saying: in the real world, the strong hold all the cards, and the weak must make compromises. The Melians for their part put forward three reasons for refusing to submit to the Athenians: hope, Spartan aid, and divine assistance. (More imminently, all the Melians could rely on was their 500 soldiers, and that was not enough.) The trio of hope, Spartans, and gods is the Thucydidean equivalent of fairy dust. In the end, neither the Melians' hope, nor their founding city Sparta, nor the gods they worship could save them.

34. Thucydides 5. 84. 1.

35. There is much excellent literature on the Melian dialogue; in addition to the long discussion in A. W. Gomme, A. Andrewes, and K. J. Dover, *A Historical Commentary on Thucydides*, 5 vols. (Oxford: Oxford University Press, 1945–81): 4, 155–92, see in particular C. W. Macleod, "Form and Meaning in the Melian Dialogue," *Historia* 23 (1974): 385–400, and A. B. Bosworth, "The Humanitarian Aspect of the Melian Dialogue," *Journal of Hellenic Studies* 113 (1993): 30–44.

The bullying, contemptuous Athenians mocked the Melians for their stubbornness and their optimism. Hope, they said, is "a comfort that can hurt you" unless you can back it up with resources, which you plainly don't have.[36]

As for the Spartans, the Athenians said, you claim that they will not want to betray you because you are their colonists and they would look bad if they abandoned you. But coming to your aid would be a very risky business, because we control the sea; they don't. Have you ever known them to be big risk takers? We certainly haven't.[37]

Most shocking to a Greek audience, the Athenians dismissed the Melians' claim that their piety would save them—that the gods would not stand by and let the righteous be destroyed.[38] It is now that Thucydides reveals the corrosion of the Athenian character in its full distasteful smarminess. "Well," the ambassadors reply,

> when it comes to divine goodwill, we don't think we'll be left out. We're not claiming anything or doing anything outside man's thinking about the gods or about the way the gods themselves behave. Given what we believe about the gods and know about people, we think that both are always forced by the law of nature to dominate everyone they can. We didn't lay down this law, it was there—and we weren't the first to make use of it.[39]

We see here why so many Greeks feared the sophists with their fine words that could make the worse cause appear the better. The Athenians are now unmasked not only as unabashed imperialists, but as people lacking in humility toward the gods—as guilty of hubris. The snide Athenian ambassadors are making no real attempt to persuade the Melians to surrender and avoid a siege that will end in their deaths. In fact, they seem to be gloating over the Melians' helplessness. The outcome of the debate was predictable. The Melian oligarchs felt compelled by their honor to refuse

36. "A comfort that can hurt you": Thucydides 5. 103. 1.
37. Thucydides 5. 107–8.
38. Thucydides 5. 104.
39. Thucydides 5. 105. 1–2.

the Athenian offer. The Athenians laid siege to the city. The Melians put up stiff resistance, even staging a breakout at one point, and in fact the Athenians needed to send reinforcements to bring the siege to a conclusion; this was not the walkover they had anticipated, though they were right that the Spartans were too afraid of the imperial navy to come to their ally's aid. But after ten months, treason worked its way from within the walls, and when the city was handed over to the Athenians they killed all the males of fighting age they could get their hands on and enslaved all the women and children. Typically, Thucydides does not tell us how the men of Melos were killed but rather reports the simple fact. The Athenians then settled 500 of their own people on the island, but we know from Xenophon and Plutarch that after his victory at the Battle of Aegospotami in 405, the Spartan admiral Lysander restored the Melians who had escaped the slaughter to their home.[40] Probably the Spartans, though they did not come to the Melians' rescue in their hour of need, had at least found shelter for the few survivors of the massacre in the intervening decade.

The Athenians' words at Melos evoke their tough speech at Sparta in Book 1: "It is an eternal law," Thucydides reports them as having said there, "that the strong should rule the weak."[41] Their words, combined with their murderous actions at Melos and elsewhere, have led Thucydides to be branded as the founder of realism, and a spate of scholarship beginning in the twentieth century and continuing into the twenty-first has explored just what kind of realist he was.[42] But there is no reason to believe that his countrymen spoke for Thucydides.

The historian's tragic narrative of the fall of Athens from its Periclean heights is full of blood and gore, discord and deceit, hopes raised and disappointed, but the sorrow and the pathos of it all are never far from the surface.

40. Xenophon *Hellenica* 2. 2. 9; Plutarch *Lysander* 14. 3.

41. Thucydides 1. 76. 2.

42. For perspectives on Thucydides' realism, see R. Gilpin, "The Theory of Hegemonic War," *Journal of Interdisciplinary History* 18 (1988): 591–613; D. Garst, "Thucydides and Neorealism," *International Studies Quarterly* 33 (1989): 3–27; M. Doyle, "Thucydidean Realism," *Review of International Studies* 16 (1990): 223–37; P. Ahrensdorf, "Thucydides' Realistic Critique of Realism," *Polity* 30 (1997): 231–65; and W. J. Korab-Karpowicz, "How International Relations Theorists Can Benefit by Reading Thucydides," *The Monist* 89 (2006): 232–44.

OSTRACISM IN ATHENS

Exactly who in Athens had instigated the attack on Melos is uncertain, though Alcibiades is a possible culprit.[43] At some point, moreover, it seems that Alcibiades' lavish lifestyle and ostentatious participation in the raising and racing of horses contributed to his undoing. Boasting about his Olympic victories did not, in fact, endear him to the Athenian people, at least not all of them. Already, Thucydides says, the demos had pegged Alcibiades as an aspirant to tyranny, and historically Olympic victors had actually sought to establish themselves as tyrants in Athens, as Cylon had done in the seventh century.[44] It was probably suspicion of Alcibiades' ambitions that accounted for the ostracism the Athenians decided to hold around this time (416?). The impetus for the ostracism may have come from Hyperbolus, who hoped to become the leader of the demos once either Nicias or Alcibiades was out of the way, but if so, his plan backfired, since when the votes were counted, Hyperbolus was found to be the winner and sent off into exile. Both Thucydides and Plutarch suggest that Hyperbolus was a base nonentity.[45] Quite possibly the slurs against Hyperbolus arose out of sheer class prejudice, since Hyperbolus was the first man ostracized who did not belong to the landed aristocracy; his money came from selling lamps made in his slave workshop.

The five years after the signing of the Peace of Nicias had seen an extraordinary amount of bloodshed—at Scione, at Mantinea, on Melos (so much for peace). And now the Athenians would undertake

43. The evidence for Alcibiades is collected in "Alcibiades and Melos: Thuc 5. 84-116," in M. Vickers, *Sophocles and Alcibiades: Athenian Politics in Ancient Greek Literature* (Ithaca, NY: Cornell University Press, 2008).

44. Thucydides 6. 15. 4; Herodotus 5. 71.

45. Thucydides 8. 73. 3 says he was ostracized not because of the Athenians' fear of him but because he was a disgrace to the city. Plutarch *Nicias* 11. 4 claims that he thought himself in no danger of ostracism since he was a more likely candidate for the stocks. Hyperbolus was the frequent butt of jokes in comedy; see W. R. Connor, *The New Politicians of Fifth Century Athens* (Princeton, NJ: Princeton University Press, 1971), 79–84 and *passim*; D. Rosenbloom, "*Ponêroi* vs. *Chrêstoi*: The Ostracism of Hyperbolos and the Struggle for Hegemony in Athens after the Death of Perikles, Part I," *Transactions and Proceedings of the American Philological Association* 134 (2004): 55–105; and S. Forsdyke, *Exile, Ostracism, and Democracy: The Politics of Expulsion in Ancient Greece* (Princeton, NJ: Princeton University Press, 2005), 170–5.

an enterprise that would entail the spilling of a great deal more blood, much of it their own. Though Alcibiades' role in the Melian expedition is uncertain, there is no doubt about his responsibility for the much larger expedition to Sicily that set sail the following year—a foray in which, ironically, hope and trust in the gods in fact did play a role as events took their course. In the meantime, war was the subject of the trilogy that Euripides presented at the Dionysia in the spring of 415. Three plays about the Trojan War formed his subject matter, but only one has survived, *The Trojan Women*.

REQUIEM FOR A CITY

In 405, when both Aeschylus and Euripides were dead, Aristophanes in his wildly funny *Frogs* would portray the god Dionysus traveling to Hades in search of a good tragic poet to bring back to Athens. After a debate between Aeschylus and Euripides (Sophocles was also dead but may have died too recently to have been worked into the script) Dionysus decides to resurrect Aeschylus rather than Euripides on the grounds that Aeschylus was truly wise whereas Euripides was merely clever. The god could not have been more wrong. Euripides took his role as the instructor and corrector of the Athenians every bit as seriously as his older predecessors—and as Aristophanes himself. Certainly his *Trojan Women*, produced not long after the events on Melos, was as serious a play as had ever been written in Greece, depicting as it did the women of fallen Troy awaiting—and then hearing—word of the various fates the Greeks had lined up for them. Was it indeed fate that had caused their suffering, they wonder, or simply the Greeks? Did their misery lie at the door of necessity, or fortune, or chance, or the gods—Zeus, perhaps, or Ares, the god of war; or, of course, at that of Helen herself, who had triggered this long and awful war? All these possibilities are put forward as the waiting, wailing women try to make sense of their situation and contemplate their future while they anticipate being shipped off to serve Greek masters, some in their beds, some as slaves to their wives.

As the play opens, it is Hecuba, queen of fallen Troy, who would seem to have lost the most. She has seen her husband the king killed in front of her eyes, her sons have died fighting, her city is gone, she will be a slave instead of a queen, and her daughters will now breed sons for Greeks. Her desolation only increases. Where, she wants to know, is her daughter Polyxena? The Greek herald Talthybius is evasive, hemming and hawing about how well she's doing as an attendant at Achilles' tomb. Hector's widow Andromache later speaks to her more candidly: Polyxena was sacrificed as a tomb offering for the Greek "hero." As the play progresses, Andromache is the victim of a more direct response from Talthybius in the only dramatic moment in this rather static play, as he enters once again, accompanied by attendants and plainly bearing bad news. The Greek audience knows, as Andromache does not, just what this chilling news is.

TALTHYBIUS: Oh wife of Hector, the best of Trojans in days now gone,
Do not hate me. It is against my will
That I bring these tidings. . . .
ANDROMACHE: I do not like the sound of this. Your words seem to presage evil.
TALTHYBIUS: It has been decreed . . . your child . . . how can I say?
ANDROMACHE: . . . will have a different master from me? No!
TALTHYBIUS: No Greek will ever rule over your son.
ANDROMACHE: Then will you leave him here, a sad remnant of Troy?
TALTHYBIUS: I do not know an easy way to tell you this.
ANDROMACHE: I applaud your hesitation—unless your news is good.
TALTHYBIUS: The news I bring . . . they are going to kill your son. That's it.[46]

It is a mark of his craftsmanship that Euripides has thought to spark much sympathy in the audience for Talthybius as well as for the devastated Andromache in this scene of pathos, as he cautions her not to

46. *Trojan Women* ll. 709–19.

"make a scene" lest the Greeks deprive her of the right even to bury her son's body. We suspect that one reason he does not want her to make a scene is that he simply cannot bear the sight of her pain.

Having been dragged away into captivity, Andromache has persuaded the Greeks to leave behind Hector's shield in which to bury Astyanax. His burial by Hecuba forms a second climax of sorts to the play (following the earlier climax of Talthybius's grim announcement), as the Trojan queen once more comes to the forefront, lamenting the death of both her grandson and her city, which is being put to the torch. The only bright spot remaining is that its enduring fame gives the lie to the chorus's despairing claim that the name of Troy will be forgotten forever. But of course the desolate women cannot know this.

It would be all too easy to see in this play Euripides' response to the slaughter on Melos and the attendant enslavement of the women and children there by the Athenians, but the time sequence is not right; the playwright would have needed to request a chorus well in advance of the Dionysia, and it takes time to write a Greek tragedy, which was composed in verse according to a fairly strict formula. Tragedies, moreover, were performed in groups of three along with a lighter play called a "satyr drama," so the dramatist had a great deal of work to do before he could request his chorus. Still, the audience watching this ghostly tableau—and the chorus rehearsing the play—were well aware of what their fellow citizens had just done. And not only that: the Dionysia was a broad-ranging festival consisting not merely of dramatic and other performances. Prior to these events came rituals of various kinds, and one of them was the parading of Athenian war orphans across the stage.[47] What, we wonder, did the Athenians, who had made so many war orphans over the past fifteen years, make of this? They had exterminated the male population not only of Melos but also of Scione and Torone. And children without fathers were officially considered orphans, even though their mothers might live.

One aside: to be sure, it took a while to compose a tragedy, and choruses rehearsed sedulously over a long period of time. Yet a few lines

47. Aeschines 3. 154.

here or there might be changed at the last minute. What are we to make of the passage in which the chorus of hapless women, wondering where they will end up, express a preference for, of all places, Athens—"the renowned and blessed land of Theseus," Athens' ancient hero-king?[48] Patriotism or irony? Athens was certainly not a safe haven for women fearing slavery and the extinction of their city.

Greek tragedies served as triggers for discussion, and no doubt this one did. Surely it turned some people against the constant warring in Greece and the attendant extermination of whole cities, and throughout the twentieth and twenty-first centuries it has served as a vehicle for antiwar sentiments. Jean-Paul Sartre's 1965 French rendition, largely faithful to Euripides' Greek text, contained veiled references to European imperialism in Asia. In 1984, the Israeli playwright Hanoch Levin adapted the play into Hebrew, incorporating additional disturbing scenes, and it was performed in Tel Aviv during the war with Lebanon. In 2003–4 director Brad Mays opened his multimedia rendition of the play with a simulated CNN broadcast purporting to bring news of the ongoing war in Iraq. Playwright Charles Mee's adaptation *The Trojan Women 2.0*, incorporated interviews with actual Holocaust and Hiroshima survivors. Despite the clearly political nature of the play's afterlife, however, Greek tragedians rarely wrote simple "message plays." And when the Athenians were offered the opportunity to gain great wealth, not to mention power, by becoming involved in Sicily, a majority jumped at the chance, believing that the possible rewards outweighed the risks. Thoughts that the orphans they would create might be their own were far from their minds as they set sail that summer for the faraway island.

48. *Trojan Women*, ll. 207–8.

11

AN INVITATION AND TWO SCANDALS

THE GREAT WAR BETWEEN Sparta and Athens and their various allies had begun when a crisis in the northwestern outpost of Epidamnus brought ambassadors from Corcyra and Corinth before the Athenian assembly. Twenty years later, a second crisis even farther west, in two little towns in Sicily, brought envoys from the Athenians' Sicilian allies Egesta and Leontini before the assembly to seek help; Egesta was at war with its neighbor Selinus, and the democrats of Leontini had been under attack for several years by Selinus's protector, the powerful Dorian city of Syracuse (see Map 8, Chapter 8). Both Egesta and Leontini had been allied to Athens for some years.[1] After two debates, a majority decided that Athens' interests did indeed lie in becoming involved in Sicilian affairs, and a large armament was committed to the enterprise. Despite the intervention of two religious scandals that rocked Athens to its foundations, the fleet sailed for Sicily in the summer of 415, and, as Thucydides wrote, "very few of those who left ever returned to their homelands again."[2]

INVESTIGATION AND DEBATE

Some Athenians, at least, had been interested in Sicily for a long time. The assembly had voted to send generals there to defend Leontini against

1. For the possible dates of these alliances, see D. Kagan, *The Peace of Nicias and the Sicilian Expedition* (Ithaca, NY: Cornell University Press, 1981), 159–60.

2. Thucydides 7. 87. 5.

Syracuse as early as 427, and in 424 impeachment had befallen the three generals who had acceded to the Gela accords—"Sicily for the Sicilians, and no fighting among the cities of Sicily"—proposed by the Syracusan Hermocrates. In 422, Phaeax sailed with two others as an ambassador to try to rouse the Sicilians against the encroachments of Syracuse, which was once again interfering in the affairs of Leontini, but he returned to Athens having met with little success.[3] Now, in 416/15, the appearance of the envoys from Egesta and Leontini was followed by a visit to Egesta to investigate the Egestaeans' claim that plenty of money was available for an expedition in their aid. The Athenian visitors could expect a pleasant stay in Sicily with a viewing of the splendid Doric temple the Egestaeans were building in their city (figure 9).

Not only did the Athenian investigators return with the promised 60 talents of silver to finance sixty ships for a month, but the sailors reported having been entertained lavishly in private homes where they drank out of goblets of gold and silver. In actuality, they had been served from one set of goblets gathered up both from Egesta and from neighboring towns and surreptitiously passed from house to house.[4] Well soused, the Athenian guests had failed to recognize the dinnerware as familiar. Even before the assembly met to deliberate on the matter at hand, Plutarch reports, both young and old gathered in clusters to draw maps of Sicily and the surrounding seas, paying particular attention to the harbors that faced North Africa and speculating about the possibility of a contest with Carthage down the road.[5] Convinced there would be funds available for the mission and encouraged by the ever-ebullient Alcibiades, the assembly voted its approval for it, agreeing to send sixty ships to Sicily. Both Nicias and Alcibiades would go; the prudence of the older man, they hoped, would serve as a counterweight to the rashness of the younger. And a third general would go as well, the seasoned commander Lamachus. Lamachus would bring to the expedition his many years of military experience and could also mediate between Nicias and

3. Thucydides 5. 4–5.

4. Thucydides 6. 8. 1; 46. 3.

5. Plutarch *Nicias* 12. 1–2.

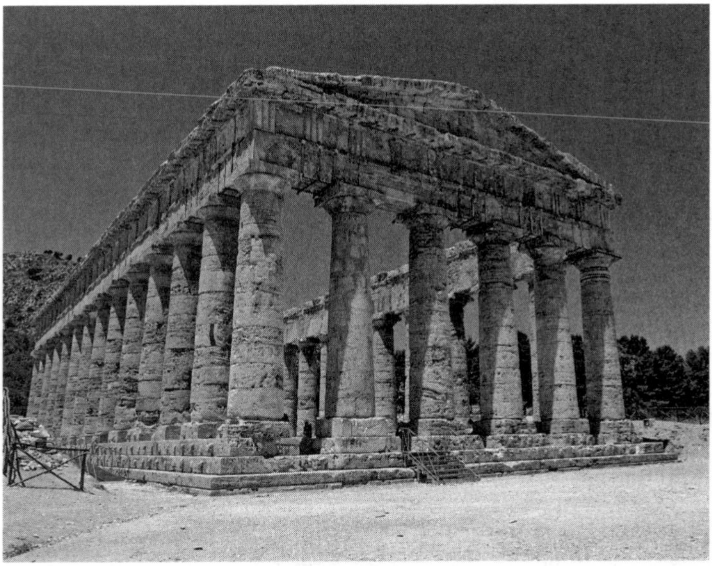

FIGURE 9
Temple of Apollo at Egesta.
Credit: Egesta Temple, courtesy of Shutterstock, Inc. Used by permission.

Alcibiades. Several days later, the assembly met again to fine-tune the arrangements for the expedition.[6] On this occasion, Nicias did something most striking. He suggested that the Athenians reconsider their original decision and scrap plans for the undertaking altogether.

Such a turnabout was highly unusual, and in fact probably illegal, since the Council had not sanctioned a reconsideration of the invasion. It may be that in the days since the first vote the three commanders had met and Nicias had come to realize the extent of Alcibiades' ambitions: according to Thucydides, Alcibiades was interested not only in helping Athens' Sicilian allies but in going on to conquer Carthage as well.[7] In Nicias's eyes, an attack on Sicily while so much tension still existed in mainland Greece was madness. Despite all the bloodshed at Mantinea and elsewhere, Athens

6. On Nicias, Alcibiades, the discussion in the assembly and the course of the invasion, see E. Bloedow, "'Not the Son of Achilles but Achilles Himself': Alcibiades' Entry on the Political Stage at Athens II," *Historia* 39 (1990): 1–19, and B. Jordan, "The Sicilian Expedition Was a Potemkin Fleet," *Classical Quarterly* 50 (2000): 63–79.

7. Thucydides 6. 15. 2.

and Sparta were still technically at peace, and he did not want to see anything happen to change that. Heartsick at the prospect of the peace he had worked so hard to negotiate evaporating before his eyes, Nicias put forward many compelling arguments in favor of staying out of Sicily. The truce between Athens and Sparta, he pointed out, was a peace in name only. After all, it was forced on the Spartans because of the capture of their men on Sphacteria. Besides, some of the most important states in Greece had held aloof from the treaty. A division of Athens' forces would open the door to disaster. And how, he asks, could we rule a place as far away and as large as Sicily even if we were to conquer it? We have only recently had the opportunity to enjoy some respite from war and the great pestilence and to replenish our finances and our population. Let us spend this capital on our own behalf and not on that of men who have done nothing for us.[8]

If Thucydides is correct, Nicias then initiated an ad hominem attack on Alcibiades, a development that turned the debate away from the issues. "Now if a certain person," he said,

> glad to be elected to a command, advises you to set sail, when he is only looking out for his own interests—especially if he is still too young for a generalship and really hopes to benefit from the perquisites of office while being admired for his fine stable of horses—don't put it in the power of such a man to endanger the city just so that he can show off. Bear in mind that such men violate the public trust and squander their private fortunes. This matter is too important for one so young to both plan and then hastily carry out.[9]

In truth, the object of Nicias's concern was about thirty-five years old, and the average age of death for Athenian males was around forty-five. In any case, Alcibiades promptly came forward to tout his qualifications before the assembly with no apology for his youthful ambition or his equestrian opulence. Dismissing Nicias's attack on him with a wave of the hand, Alcibiades listed several reasons for invading Sicily. Their

8. Thucydides 6. 9. 1–12. 1.
9. Thucydides 6. 12. 2.

cities, he conceded, are populous, but they are a multiethnic rabble, and they "easily accept comings and goings into the citizen body": a clear contrast with the Athenians, who proudly identified themselves as an "autochthonous" people, sprung from the very soil of Attica, where they had lived since time immemorial. There would be many "barbarians" there—that is, non-Greek Sicilian natives, who hate the Syracusans and would rise up and join the Athenians in attacking them. (In the event, some did, but some didn't.) Besides, the Athenians had taken oaths of alliance binding them to support Egesta and Leontini; how could they abandon their allies? (This from a man who would in a matter of months defect from his native land and advise the Spartans in their war effort.) Athens, finally, he argued, was by nature an active city, and if an active city falls into inactivity, all its skills decay.[10] Diodorus claims that Nicias pointed out that the Carthaginians, with greater resources than those available to the Athenians, had tried to conquer Sicily but failed.[11]

In a last-ditch effort to stop the expedition, Nicias took the floor once again and sought to deter his countrymen from proceeding by stressing the size of the force that would be necessary. A mere sixty ships would by no means be sufficient. He began by cautioning the Athenians about the strength of the Sicilians, especially in two respects: first, they possessed abundant cavalry, and second, they grew their own grain instead of having to import it, as the Athenians did. Therefore, he says, we must set out not only with a large number of hoplites, but also with many slingers and archers, to oppose the Sicilian cavalry; at sea, the Athenians would need not only warships but merchant ships to bring food from home, and money to pay bakers to make bread from wheat and barley. Pushed to the wall, evidently by the bellicose populist leader Demostratus, he announced that the fleet would have to sail with at least 100 triremes from Athens plus others from the allies, with a minimum of 5,000 Athenian and allied hoplites—more, if possible—and to hire mercenaries as well including archers and slingers.[12]

10. Thucydides 6. 18. 6.

11. Diodorus 12. 83. 6.

12. Plutarch *Nicias*. 12. 4; Thucydides 6. 25–6.

Having heard Nicias speak, the assembly was in no way deterred by the magnitude of the undertaking as he presented it, and they at once voted to approve all the provisions he laid out for the expedition:

The men.
The ships.
And no horses.

What could possibly explain this strange omission from an expedition against an island just reported to be singularly strong in cavalry?

We can imagine why Nicias himself might have omitted cavalry from his list, for he was the official representative of Syracusan interests at Athens, and there is every reason to think that he imagined that, having worked things out between Egesta and Selinus, he could come to an accommodation with Syracuse by diplomatic means. Possibly, he would not even have to make a landing on the island. But this does not explain why the Athenians would have countenanced the omission. To be sure, transporting horses by sea was no easy matter, but it was done regularly; triremes had been converted to horse transports as early as the first year of the war.[13] All in all, it was a very peculiar oversight, and one that would cost Athens many lives.

Supporters and opponents of the undertaking immediately dragged religion into the mix. Plutarch reports that "the priesthood" was opposed to the expedition, though he doesn't say which one. Alcibiades, however, found seers ready to cite ancient prophecies foretelling that the Athenians would bring back great glory from Sicily. Envoys sent to the shrine of Zeus-Ammon in Libya brought back an oracle saying that the Athenians would capture all the Syracusans. They also uncovered less cheerful signs, but the city was so fired up about the expedition that they were afraid to speak of them.[14] But there was one omen nobody could ignore.

13. Thucydides 2. 56; J. R. Hale, *Lords of the Sea: The Epic Story of the Athenian Navy and the Birth of Democracy* (New York: Viking, 2009), 149–50, offers a reconstruction of such a vessel.

14. Plutarch *Nicias* 13. 1–2, 6.

RELIGION INTRUDES

Throughout Athens stood dozens of "herms" (Figure 10), images representing the god Hermes. Each was shaped like a rectangular pillar topped with a stylized bust of the bearded god with a phallus and testicles protruding from the front, sometimes sticking out rather prominently, sometimes carved more delicately in relief.[15]

Herms were an important part of civic life, as indeed were all aspects of religion, for the Greeks knew no separation of church and state. There were herms in the agora; a herm stood at the gateway to the Acropolis. Herms also stood at the entrances of households, standing guard where oikos met polis. They were tutelary images that protected boundaries, and boundaries were important to Greeks, as witness King Agis's refusal to cross the border on the way to Mantinea when the sacrifices were not propitious. Herms were also associated with Athenian patriotism and the Athenian Empire. Following the first battle after the Persian wars in which the Athenians, led by Cimon, won Eion as the first new territory taken from the Persians, the Athenians erected three herms in the agora with inscriptions praising the valor of their leaders and exhorting their future citizens to fight in their country's cause.[16] Of particular significance for the upcoming expedition, Hermes was the protector of travelers, but from his days as a baby stealing Apollo's cattle to his later career purloining sacrifices meant for others, he represented deception—including all the tricks of rhetoric used in the law courts and the assembly. Among other things, then, Hermes was a fine democratic politician.[17] To provoke Hermes was to challenge the democracy itself.

One morning, when plans for the expedition were well under way, the Athenians awoke to the sound of shouting.[18] Those still in bed got up and wandered groggily outdoors to find the cause of the commotion. They

15. See H. Goldman, "The Origin of the Greek Herm," *American Journal of Philology* 46 (1942): 58–68.

16. Plutarch *Cimon* 7–8; Thucydides 1. 98. 1.

17. As pointed out by J. Fredal, "Herm Choppers, the Adonia, and Rhetorical Action in Ancient Greece," *College English* 64 (2002): 590–612.

18. The date was probably early June, perhaps June 7, 415.

FIGURE 10
Herm from Siphnos, c. 520.
Credit© Vanni Archive/ Art Resource, NY.

did not have to wonder very long: most householders noticed immediately that the herm in front of their homes had been defaced. In fact, the herm in front of nearly every house and at every crossroads had been vandalized. Hermes was not what he had been the night before; on most statues, his head—minimally, the nose—had been damaged and in some cases his phallus was no more. Neighbors were screaming and gathering in the streets. Realization must have dawned slowly: first one's own herm, then the herm next door, then the herm across the way; gradually people recognized that this was not the work of a few drunken young men, and in time they came to believe it was part of a plot to overthrow the government.

At the instructions of the assembly, the Council set up a board of inquiry. Astonishingly, one Pythonicus arose and denounced several men—not for mutilating the herms, but in connection with something else entirely: for it was alleged that the rites that were performed annually on the part of initiates in honor of the goddess Demeter and her daughter Persephone had been profaned by being enacted in front of the uninitiated in a private house.[19] And one of the men denounced was none other than Alcibiades himself.

Rivals of Alcibiades, Thucydides says, took up these accusations eagerly, thinking that if they could get rid of him they could take over the leadership of the people, and, linking the profanation of the mysteries with the mutilation of the herms, suggested that Alcibiades must surely have been involved in both, given the generally undemocratic license of his habits.[20] Since everything was ready for the Sicilian campaign—Lamachus's flagship was already in the harbor—Alcibiades demanded an immediate trial, confident of acquittal since he was one of the generals leading the popular expedition. His enemies, however, realizing that his supporters were all still in town, and that the people were grateful to him for inducing the Argives and Mantineans to contribute troops to the mission, thought it better to let him sail with the fleet and then recall him to stand trial while the navy was away.[21]

The fleet sailed with much fanfare around July 1. The magnificence of the sight was spine-tingling—the port was crowded with eager onlookers, citizens and aliens alike—but once the fleet was gone the Athenians resumed their investigation into the mutilation of the herms and the profanation of the mysteries. Some came forward with information, some fled the country, and some did both. A metic by the name of Teucrus testified under immunity that he had taken part in the profanation of the mysteries and named eleven others who had done so; he also named eighteen men as mutilators of the herms, though he was not among them.[22] Somehow nearly all managed to make it out of the country before they could be seized. But most astonishing of all was the story that a certain Diocleides had to tell. Needing to go down to Laurium in southern Attica, where the silver mines were, he had planned to set out

19. Andocides 1. 11–13.
20. Thucydides 6. 28.
21. Thucydides 6. 29.
22. Andocides 1. 14, 15, 34, 35.

early in the morning, but by accident he awoke during the night, and as the moon was full he could see a large group of about 300 men gathering at the theater of Dionysus. Hiding in the shadows, he was able to identify a good number of them. When he returned to Athens and discovered what had been done to the herms, he realized that those men must have been the culprits. Although the government was offering a reward for information, he decided that he could make more money by blackmailing some of the men he had seen. At first his victims were willing to come to an accommodation, but when they backed out, he denounced them and many others to the Council, forty-two in total. In exchange for his cooperation, the Athenians crowned him with a wreath as the savior of the city, and he enjoyed great glory—for the rest of his short life.[23]

But short it was, for the orator Andocides, who had been imprisoned on Diocleides' information, soon told a very different tale: under immunity, he acknowledged that the mutilation was the work of his own *hetairia*, or drinking club. He himself, he claimed, was unable to participate because he had broken his collarbone falling off his horse.[24] These *hetairiai* were groups of young men, normally of aristocratic, even oligarchic inclinations, who gathered periodically for wine and conversation and offered mutual aid in lawsuits. Because they often sought to influence the outcome of elections, supporting candidates of less than pure democratic credentials, they were somewhat suspect in the eyes of the ordinary Athenian. But since they met in private homes, the size of the group was limited to about twenty-five, and one *hetairia*, consequently, could not have carried out the mutilation of so many herms. Regardless of the truth of the matter, Diocleides' story did not stand up to scrutiny: the night in question, people began to remember, was moonless, and so Diocleides could not have seen the faces of the alleged perpetrators. He immediately confessed that his story was an invention and was taken away to execution.[25] When the whole episode was over, up to a hundred Athenians had either been put to death or forced into exile.

23. Andocides 1. 37–42.
24. Andocides 1. 61.
25. Andocides 1. 66.

Who mutilated the herms, and why? The notion that Alcibiades was responsible is the least probable of all. Taken as a bad omen for the Sicilian expedition in which he was so invested, vandalizing these civic symbols was the last thing in which Alcibiades would want to become involved. Some tried to cast blame on the Corinthians, who had after all founded Syracuse and were fellow Dorians; but even the Athenians, who would have preferred that their own citizens be innocent, did not find this credible. The panic over an impending overthrow of the democratic constitution may seem peculiar, yet a few generations later, a man on his way to be initiated into the mysteries at Eleusis had acted precipitately and sacrificed the ritual piglet prematurely in the waters of the Piraeus, attracting a shark with fatal results, and this seemingly random event was taken to portend the destruction of the state.[26] And while it might at first appear that distracting a frantic populace by mass destruction of these cherished icons would be a good first step toward taking control of the government and overthrowing the democracy, the fact is that nothing of the sort happened; four years later, however, the oligarchically inclined were back, and this time their action would be more directly political in nature.[27]

The mass hysteria the vandalism induced had been intensified by reports of profanation of the Eleusinian mystery religion. The sacred rites at Eleusis had been practiced for centuries and would be celebrated for many more. During the second century AD, the Roman emperors Hadrian and Marcus Aurelius were both initiated into the mysteries. The rites were connected with the ancient myth of Demeter, goddess of grain, and her daughter Persephone, more commonly known simply as Kore, "the maiden." The myth about Demeter and Kore is still familiar in its outlines today: Kore had been abducted by Hades, the god of the underworld, but Demeter, after wandering the earth seeking her and, finally, coming to Eleusis, had managed to obtain her release. For a few months out of each year, however, Kore had to return to Hades. Thus every year

26. Scholiast on *Aeschines* 3. 130; Plutarch *Phocion* 28 may refer to the same occurrence.

27. On the *hetairiai* and their political significance in 415, see J. McGlew, "Politics on the Margins: The Athenian 'Hetaireiai' in 415 B.C.," *Historia* 48 (1999): 1–22.

had in it several months in which nothing grew while Demeter grieved for her absent daughter, but also several months in which the land was fruitful while Demeter rejoiced in her daughter's company. The reenactment of this myth seems to have been part of the ritual celebrated at Eleusis.

Fourteen miles (23 kilometers) or so northwest of Athens, Eleusis was a major cult site of Demeter, and two festivals were celebrated there in her honor and that of her daughter. The so-called Lesser Mysteries were celebrated in winter, the Greater Mysteries in summer; those who had been initiated in the Lesser Mysteries were known as *mystai* and became eligible for initiation into the Greater Mysteries. All Greek-speakers, male or female, slave or free, who could pay the initiation fee—which was neither trivial nor inconsiderable—were free to present themselves. Because participation in both involved solemn secrecy as to what transpired, we know much less than we would like about what the mysteries entailed, but we do know a certain amount about the buildup to the final ceremonies, since they were public, involving sacrificing, feasting, and a procession from the public cemetery at Athens up to Eleusis. In Eleusis itself, the *mystai* fasted for a day to commemorate Demeter's fasting as she roamed the earth searching for her lost child. The *mystai* broke the fast while drinking *kykeon*, a special drink made of barley and pennyroyal.[28] It was on the next days that the secret matters took place inside a great hall called a Telesterion, a huge hall capable of holding up to 10,000 people. There in the Telesterion were, it seems, *dromena* (things done), presumably a reenactment of the myth of Demeter and Kore; *deiknumena*, things shown, the display of sacred objects; and *legomena*, things said (to accompany the things shown?). The penalty for divulging just what these were and how they came together was death—and Alcibiades and his friends knew it.

Those who participated in the mysteries were known as *epoptai*—"those who gazed at something"; the core of the encounter with the divine, the element that inspired awe and transformed the *mystai*, was evidently lodged in the sense of sight. The *mystai* were not taught; they were changed. They returned to Athens feeling like different people. It is

28. On Demeter and *kykeon*, see the *Homeric Hymn to Demeter*, 210.

difficult to say which was most important: the sense of spiritual awakening (something not much on offer in traditional Olympian religion) or the promise held out at Eleusis of a happy afterlife—again, not a building block of conventional Greek religion.

The notion that these mysteries might have been enacted in private homes in front of the uninitiated horrified the Athenians, and they were understandably eager to know who had been involved. Gone unpunished, religious transgressions polluted an entire city. But at least one of the suspected perpetrators had sailed off as a general to Sicily, and speculation about him continued in his absence.

SICILIAN STRATEGY

When the Athenians arrived at Rhegium, on the toe of Italy, they discovered that they had been duped; advance ships returning from Sicily cast serious doubts on the wealth of the Egestaeans.[29] Now the three commanders would have to decide what to do in light of this new information. Nicias was for getting Egesta and Selinus to patch up their quarrel and then sailing along the coast to make a display of Athens' power and willingness to support its allies. After that, unless they could find an easy way of helping Leontini, they should return home and not risk harm to the fleet. Alcibiades was of a very different opinion. Doing so little would be a waste of such a substantial armada and would win no glory. Rather, he suggested, they should try to win over Messina, sitting right on the straits where ships crossed over to Sicily, and to gain as many allies as they could among the cities of Sicily, both Greek cities and cities composed of the Sicels, who along with the Sicans comprised the native non-Greek population of the island. Then, when they had accumulated more allies and knew who was on which side, they would attack Selinus and Syracuse. The plan of Lamachus was the simplest: to go after Syracuse immediately, when it was still unprepared for an attack.[30]

29. Thucydides 6. 46. 2–5.

30. Thucydides 6. 47. 1–49. 4. P. Green offers a superb and detailed account of the Sicilian campaign in *Armada from Athens* (Garden City, NY: Doubleday, 1970).

All three plans had merit, but since the generals could not agree, Lamachus threw his support to Alcibiades' strategy. It soon became clear, though, that Alcibiades had been too optimistic in his expectations. Messina would not ally with the Athenians, although Naxos was willing (Naxos on Sicily's eastern coast, not Naxos the Aegean island). Nearby Catana at first declined to join as well, but the Athenians managed to take it through trickery, and Camarina on the southern coast of the island proclaimed its neutrality. But when things were looking a little better—when Camarina was leaning toward Athens—Alcibiades and the expedition received a sharp setback. After a skirmish in Syracusan territory, the Athenians returned to Catana where they found the *Salaminia*, the state trireme that was the twin of the *Paralus* that had carried Phormio to his stunning victory in the Corinthian Gulf over a decade before. The ship had not come to help with the war effort. Rather it bore orders from home to bring back Alcibiades and some of his friends who were accused of profaning the mysteries and mutilating the herms.[31]

The ship's officers were under orders not to arrest Alcibiades, which the Athenians were afraid would cause a mutiny among the sailors, but rather politely to instruct him to return to Athens. As he had come to Sicily on his own ship, he and his friends sailed on it in the wake of the *Salaminia*. They then disembarked at Thurii in south Italy—and disappeared. Eventually they made their way to Sparta, by which time the Athenians had passed a sentence of death on them.[32] Alcibiades fit in nicely at Sparta. He possessed, as Plutarch pointed out, the nature of a chameleon, ideally suited to adapt to the local customs of any people among whom he found himself. He cheerfully partook of the infamous "black soup" that was the staple of the Spartan diet and took brisk baths in the chilly Eurotas.[33]

The disappearance of the fiery Alcibiades left the Athenian forces in a difficult situation. For all practical purposes, Nicias was now in charge, for though the assembly had granted equal powers to all three generals,

31. Thucydides 6. 53. 1; Plutarch *Alcibiades* 21. 5.

32. Thucydides 6. 61. 4–7; Plutarch *Alcibiades* 22. 4 indicates that his property was confiscated.

33. Plutarch *Alcibiades* 23. 3–4.

by a curious twist one of them was on a different plane socially and economically from the others: Lamachus was poor, and even in egalitarian Athens, snobbery deprived him of the kind of distinction Nicias enjoyed, though he was probably the better general. Despite Nicias' unhappiness about the Sicilian campaign, nonetheless he felt unable to take the fleet home, so he and Lamachus continued operations, following Alcibiades' policy of trying to recruit allies and raise money. Their efforts met with little success. Receiving no assistance from the prosperous city of Himera, they came to Hyccara, a small town at war with the Egestaeans, and made the residents their victims; capturing the city, they raised 120 talents by selling its inhabitants into slavery, not suspecting how many of their own men would soon end their lives in the same misery.[34] They were also able to squeeze 30 more talents out of the Egestaeans. But on the whole the Athenians' efforts were not going well. Clearly they would have to return home or fight with what they had, and Nicias did not think that going home, much as he might have longed to, would play very well with the assembly.

The Athenian generals' next move was a good one. Sending a man from Catana to tell the inhabitants of Syracuse that the Athenian forces were up there, they lured the Syracusans away from their city, leaving a window in which the Athenians could create ideal conditions for fighting. The Athenians positioned their troops where they could begin the fighting at a time of their own choosing and where the Syracusans would have the least opportunity of harassing them since they were flanked on one side by trees, walls, houses, and a marsh, and on the other by cliffs. Cutting down the trees nearby, they also made a palisade by their ships; and with stones and wood found in the vicinity, they quickly built a fort.[35] The battle was fought vigorously, with slingers and archers as well as hoplite troops, and it was accompanied by heavy rain and thunder, which struck panic in some of the soldiers. In the end, the Athenians' careful planning paid off—up to a point. The Syracusans lost some 260 men as compared to some 50 on the Athenian

34. Thucydides 6. 62. 4.
35. Thucydides 6. 64. 2–66. 2.

side, but without cavalry, the Athenians were unable to follow up on their victory.[36] The Athenians responded by sending to Athens requesting that cavalrymen and money be sent by spring. The Syracusans for their part decided to replace their fifteen generals with a board of only three, thinking that a concentration of power in fewer hands would result in greater efficiency of command; one of these was the Athenians' old nemesis Hermocrates.[37]

During the winter, the Syracusans prepared for further attacks, expanding the city to make it harder to be surrounded and building forts and fixing stakes along the beach.[38] They also sent ambassadors to their mother city Corinth and to Sparta. The Corinthians were happy to help and in fact sent ambassadors of their own to rouse Sparta not only to send aid to Syracuse but to prosecute the war against Athens directly in Greece.[39] The Spartan assembly, it seems, was all for sending assistance to Sicily, but the ephors were more guarded, presumably because they hesitated to break two treaties that were still ostensibly in force between Sparta and Athens. What the ephors wanted to do was simply to send a message to the Syracusans discouraging them from coming to terms with the Athenians, but not to send military assistance.[40]

Alcibiades, however, had other ideas. How much of what appears in Thucydides' text corresponds to what Alcibiades said to the Spartans—or to Thucydides—is uncertain; since both men were in exile concurrently, it is quite possible that they met and that Alcibiades himself was Thucydides' source for the speech (though even if so, that does not mean that the Athenian renegade reported his outlandish remarks accurately). According to Thucydides, after a sophistic explanation of his complex relationship with the Athenian democracy, Alcibiades went on to lay out the Athenian game plan for the Spartans: to conquer first Sicily, then Italy, then Carthage. Assuming even partial success in Sicily, the Athenians would then take all the Greek soldiers they had

36. Thucydides 6. 71. 2.
37. Thucydides 6. 72. 4–73. 1.
38. Thucydides 6. 75. 1.
39. Thucydides 6. 88. 7–10.
40. Thucydides 6. 88. 10.

acquired in Sicily and Italy, hire veritable hordes of mercenary barbarians from Spain—those generally accounted the most warlike savages in the world—and bring this huge force to bear on the Peloponnesus, blockading it with a fleet consisting not only of their existing ships but also more built with the boundless timber of Italy. Fortresses would be constructed near Peloponnesian cities, and soon Athens would rule the whole Greek world. The generals still in Sicily, Alcibiades insisted, would carry out this program of conquest even without him. Syracuse could not hold out without help. The Spartans would have to send an armed force to Sicily under the command of a Spartan officer, and bring the war home to the Athenians as well. They needed to build a fort at Decelea in Attica; the Athenians had always feared something like this. That way slaves would desert to the Spartans and the Athenians would be deprived of the revenue from the slave-worked silver mines at Laurium, so it would be harder for them to get what they currently did from their land.[41]

Today Sicily, tomorrow the world. An ambitious program of world conquest led by *Nicias*? Surely not. Such a plan had been dubious even with Alcibiades in the mix, but with him in exile and Nicias at the helm, it seemed that there was little to fear. Knowing Nicias to be a cautious man, and fundamentally a friend to Sparta, the Spartans found Alcibiades' tale fantastic. Underwhelmed, the ephors sent a very small force to Sicily. The man they put in charge of it was Gylippus, the son of Pleistoanax's disgraced adviser Cleandridas, who had been sent into exile and condemned to death for taking bribes in the 440s. Gylippus, moreover, was at first given only four ships, two from Laconia and two from Corinth.[42] As for Decelea, the Spartans declined to enter Attica while they were at peace with the Athenians.

Meanwhile in Sicily, having heard reports of aid coming to the Syracusans by sea, Nicias, this man whom Alcibiades had put forward as future conqueror of the Greek world, did nothing at all to intercept the ships. The Athenians had, however, finally received cavalry that could protect

41. Thucydides 6. 90. 1–91. 7.
42. Thucydides 6. 93. 2–3.

them as they constructed siege walls. It was the plan of Nicias and Lamachus to wall off Syracuse by land, cut the Syracusans off from food and drinking water, and use the fleet to prevent supplies from coming in by sea, yet the naval aspect of this strategy was being sorely neglected.

The Syracusans too made their mistakes. Too late did it occur to them to station guards at Epipolae, the plateau overlooking the city; Nicias had already seized the heights (see Map 9). Sending 600 soldiers up to dislodge the Athenians, the Syracusans lost fully half of their men, including their commander Diomilus.[43] The Athenians then built a fort on Epipolae at Labdalum on the northern cliffs for the storage of supplies, equipment—and money. At a place called Syce, near the edge of the plateau, they constructed the fort known as "the Circle," from which they would conduct operations as they laid siege to Syracuse. From there they began to extend the wall they had begun northward to Trogilus on the shore; the Syracusans in turn began work on a counterwall, which the Athenians destroyed. As the Athenians began work on the portion of their siege wall that would extend down from the Circle to the Great Harbor south of the city, the Syracusans once again started work on another counterwall.[44] Moving their fleet into the Great Harbor, the Athenians descended from Epipolae and took the Syracusans by surprise. In the fighting, when the Athenian right wing was hard-pressed by both infantry and cavalry, Lamachus, though on the left, ran to help them. Cut off by a ditch from most of his men, he fell fighting.[45]

The Syracusans then sent some of their men to attack the Circle. These demolished the wall that ran south from the fort. Illness had kept Nicias behind (whether the kidney disease that came to dog him throughout the expedition or some short-term complaint, we do not know), but he still devised a clever way to save the day on Epipolae: realizing that he had no troops with which to rescue the fort, he ordered his aides to set fire to the scaffolding and wood that had been lying next to the wall.

43. Thucydides 6. 97. 2–4.
44. Thucydides 6. 98. 2–99. 2.
45. Thucydides 6. 101. 6.

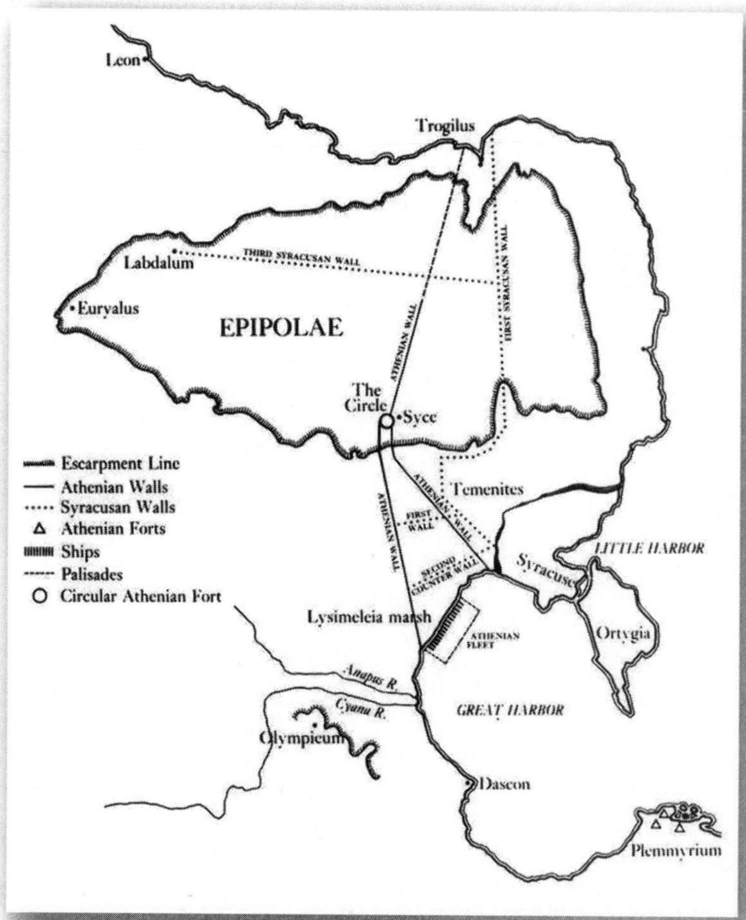

MAP 9
Diagram of Syracuse and Epipolae and fortifications.

The fire stopped the advance of the Syracusans, and the Athenians down below rushed to the relief of the Circle.[46]

Although they had lost two of their three generals, with cavalry to defend them from harassment the Athenians now were in a position to complete their besieging wall. Supplies, moreover, were coming to

46. Thucydides 6. 102. 2–4.

them from throughout Italy, and many Sicel communities that had been waiting to see how events played out now decided to take the Athenian side. Most important, since they had received no help from the Peloponnesians, the Syracusans were talking among themselves—and with Nicias—about coming to terms.[47] Despite some mistakes on Nicias's part, things were looking good for the Athenians and very bad indeed for the Syracusans.

47. Thucydides 6. 103.

12

DELIVERANCE FOR SYRACUSE

THE PICTURE IN SICILY changed radically when help arrived for the Syracusans by way of a Peloponnesian force under the leadership of Gylippus. Despite the Spartans' lukewarm enthusiasm for the project, Gylippus had gathered a number of helots and ex-helot *neodamodeis*, as well as hoplites from Boeotia, Corinth, and elsewhere. The Athenians too received aid in the form of reinforcements led by Demosthenes and Eurymedon, but when Demosthenes' efforts to dislodge the enemy from Epipolae in a daring night raid failed conspicuously, he decided prudently that his long sea voyage had been in vain. So bad did things look for the Athenians, he believed, that he and Nicias would do best to take the entire armament home. Nicias, however, would not hear of it, and so the Athenians stayed and stayed until the situation had degenerated so badly that there was little hope for them or the allies they had dragged with them. In the end, most of the men who had set out from Athens with such fanfare in July of 415 ended their lives horribly, either dying at the hands of their enemies or consigned to the lives of slaves after spending several miserable months imprisoned in quarries, breathing the stench from the decomposing bodies of their dead companions.

ATHENS BREAKS THE PEACE; HELP ARRIVES FOR SYRACUSE

The cooperation of their allies was crucial to the Athenians' war on Syracuse, and key among these allies was Argos, which had sent hundreds of men. In the summer of 414, when the Spartans invaded Argive territory, slashing and burning a great deal of land, the Athenians bowed to the pressure of their ally and sent thirty ships to the Argives' aid, making raids on Laconian territory.[1] This fateful decision would have the gravest consequences for their future. Now it could no longer be denied that once again a state of war existed between Athens and Sparta. The treaty that had been meant to endure for fifty years had lasted only seven—and during that period much blood was shed despite the presumed state of peace.

Meanwhile in Sicily a dramatic turn of events was in the offing. Just as the Syracusans were on the point of holding an assembly to discuss surrendering to Nicias, the Corinthian admiral Gongylus arrived with news that about a dozen Peloponnesian ships were coming to their aid in a rescue mission commanded by Gylippus.[2] The course of Greek history might have been very different had this news arrived later—or if Nicias had acted more decisively. For in fact Nicias had already gotten wind of the approach of Peloponnesian vessels, but, bizarrely, he discounted the ships as a handful of pirate vessels and took no account of them. Only belatedly did he send out a measly four ships in an attempt to intercept them.[3] Heartened by Gongylus's news, the Syracusans immediately abandoned thoughts of surrender.

Gylippus put in at Himera on the north coast and persuaded the Himerans to ally with him, supplying both men of their own and arms for the Peloponnesian soldiers.[4] Gathering other troops from Selinus and Gela as well as perhaps 1,000 from the Sicels, he amassed a force of probably 3,000 infantry and 200 cavalry.[5] With these men he ascended to Epipolae, seizing the Athenian fort at Labdalum and its contents and putting all he found inside to the sword.[6] Soon he began building his own counterwall. Though things no longer seemed promising for the Athenians, Nicias could have taken aggressive action to complete his

1. Thucydides 6. 105.
2. Thucydides 7. 2. 1.
3. Thucydides 6. 104. 3 (pirate ships); Thucydides 7. 1. 2 (four ships).
4. Thucydides 7. 2–3.
5. This calculation of Diodorus (13. 7. 7) is credible.
6. Thucydides 7. 3. 4.

wall and interfere with the construction of the one Gylippus was erecting. Instead, focusing on the naval aspect of the war, he decided to relocate his fleet at Plemmyrium, to the south of the Great Harbor, and built forts there to replace the one that Gylippus had destroyed at Labdalum.[7]

But placing the fleet at Plemmyrium had many disadvantages. For one thing, it divided his forces peculiarly, locating some to the south of the harbor on low ground and others to the north on the high ground of Epipolae. And there was little drinking water and firewood at Plemmyrium, with the result that the Athenians had to go on patrol to obtain these things where the men were easily picked off by Syracusan cavalry.[8] Nicias also had his eye on retreat. Feeling that Gylippus had created a situation in which escape by land to the north would be impossible, he was now thinking of getting away by sea.

Only now did it occur to him to send a serious force to intercept the new fleet of Corinthian, Ambraciot, and Leucadian vessels that was reportedly on its way from Italy to help the Syracusans.[9] But while the energetic Gylippus built walls—making use of some of the very stones the Athenians had previously used themselves—and forced battles on Epipolae, the Athenians proved unable to keep the Peloponnesian fleet out of the harbor at Syracuse.

Scrambling off their ships, the crews provided Gylippus with hundreds of additional construction workers for his wall. To solidify his position, moreover, the Spartan commander traveled around Sicily trying to gain allies and sent to both Sparta and Corinth for reinforcements.[10] Meanwhile the Syracusans busied themselves manning and training a fleet.

NICIAS WRITES HOME

Nicias also sent the Athenians an update on what was going on in Sicily. He had sent dispatches to his countrymen before, but now it was time

7. Thucydides 7. 4.
8. Thucydides 7. 4. 6.
9. Thucydides 7. 4. 7.
10. Thucydides 7. 7. 2–3.

for a comprehensive missive. Comprehensive, yet with a simple subtext: *bring me home.*

By Athenian law, Nicias did not need the home government's permission to order a retreat. He and his fellow generals had been sent out with full powers, and it could certainly be argued that as he was the sole surviving commander, the decision about whether to retreat was his alone. Then again, Athenian law condoned a great deal of harsh treatment of Athenian generals and politicians with whose decisions the populace was displeased. Even the illustrious Miltiades had been impeached after a botched expedition to the island of Paros shortly after his great victory at Marathon.[11] Demosthenes was nervous about returning home after the Aetolian disaster of 426. The three generals who had signed on to the Gela accord in 424 were convicted of taking bribes; the next year Thucydides was impeached after the loss of Amphipolis to Brasidas. Ordering a withdrawal without permission of the assembly, therefore, might well have been asking for trouble. So Nicias sent a letter to the assembly detailing the near-hopelessness of the Athenians' situation, stressing any number of reasons for the unfortunate state of affairs in Sicily: the energy of Gylippus, the desertion of slaves and mercenaries, the deterioration of his waterlogged ships, the loss of men on foraging raids. Nothing, of course, was his fault. The failures to intercept Peloponnesian ships or guard the Euryalus pass are not mentioned. He offered his countrymen two choices: to order the expedition home, or to reinforce it with another equally large body of men and ships, accompanied by a great deal of money. In any case, he said, he needed to be replaced in his command, as his kidney disease had made him unfit to discharge his office.[12] That much certainly was true. It is easy to imagine that Nicias, having learned nothing but too sick to think straight, was trying the same trick that had tripped him up in 415, hoping that the magnitude of the new expedition would discourage the Athenians. Perhaps, but Thucydides says

11. M. Hansen, *Eisangelia: The Sovereignty of the People's Court in Athens in the Fourth Century B. C. and the Impeachment of Generals and Politicians. Odense University Classical Studies* Vol. 6 (Odense, Denmark: Odense University Press), 69; J. Roberts, *Accountability in Athenian Government* (Madison: University of Wisconsin Press, 1982), 78–81.

12. Thucydides 7. 11-15.

specifically that Nicias decided to send this message "now, when he was convinced that they were in desperate straits and that they would be totally lost unless Athens either called them back or sent another very large force immediately."[13] Desperate is the operative word here. Could anything save the Athenians?

GOOD MONEY AFTER BAD?

Just as the temptation to go to Sicily in the first place had proven irresistible, so the Athenians felt compelled to keep moving down the same costly and risky path. The campaign had taken on a life of its own, and the Athenians were now victims of "mission creep." The assembly voted to send a new, larger expedition. So often accused of fickleness—by Thucydides, by Plutarch—the Athenian people had an unshakable and completely unreasonable faith in Nicias, a man considered "lucky" despite the dismal state of the Sicilian campaign.[14] Plutarch reported that out of fear of the wrathful Athenian demos, Nicias "avoided commands that were likely to be arduous, and whenever he did serve as general he made safety his chief goal" and that his string of successes was due in large part to his compulsive avoidance of danger.[15] What a pitiful commentary on a military man.

Yet the Athenians held fast in their belief in this man who had never won a major battle. (Many of them felt the same about Alcibiades, who had never won a battle at all.) Rather, the assembly voted that two men already at Syracuse, Menander and Euthydemus, should assist Nicias as temporary fellow-generals pending the arrival of two regular generals to be sent out: Demosthenes, the hero of Sphacteria, and Eurymedon, the butcher of Corcyra. Eurymedon sailed at once with ten ships and 120 talents of silver, bringing word that Demosthenes was on his way with a much larger force. The war, plainly, was entering a new phase. The question was whether the reinforcements would be able to turn things around

13. Thucydides 7. 8. 1.

14. For accusations of fickleness, e.g., in the impeachment of Pericles, see Thucydides 2. 65. 4, 9; Plutarch *Pericles* 35.4–36.1.

15. Plutarch *Nicias* 6. 2.

for the Athenians or whether at the end of the day these men would just be added to the body count.

A FORT AND A MASSACRE

The next striking developments in the war, however, took place in mainland Greece. Irrespective of any advice tendered by Alcibiades, the Spartans had in fact been toying with building a fort in Attica, but they had no intention of doing so as long as they were at peace with Athens. When the Athenians violated that peace by attacking Laconia, everything changed, and Agis moved to fortify Decelea, a hill about eleven miles (eighteen kilometers) north/northeast of Athens. The consequences for the Athenians' way of life were devastating. Over 20,000 slaves deserted to Decelea, most of them skilled workers, and many sheep and beasts of burden were slaughtered. A number of their horses, moreover, were lamed as the Athenians rode them out to Decelea over rocky ground to protect the countryside or harass the Spartans. Previously, Thucydides says,

> livestock had been quickly brought from Euboea to Oropus and then overland through Decelea. Now, it had to be brought around Sunium by sea, at great cost. Athens had to import everything it needed, and what once had been a city was now a fort. During the day, the men took turns guarding the walls, and everyone except the cavalry guarded it by night, with some men stationed with their arms at various posts, and others up on the wall itself. They suffered winter and summer alike. What caused them more difficulty than anything was the fact that they were fighting two wars at the same time and that they were also oppressed by a need to win so insatiable that it had to be seen to be believed.[16]

As a consequence of the strain on their finances, the Athenians now placed a 5 percent tax on all imports and exports by sea. And not only this: they undertook what seemed like a minor ad hoc measure that had devastating consequences for one small town in Boeotia.

16. Thucydides 7. 28. 1–3.

Among those who had been hired to sail with Demosthenes were some light-armed Thracian mercenaries. Because they arrived too late to accompany the expedition to Sicily, the Athenians declined to pay them and instructed the commander Diitrephes to conduct them home, doing what harm they could to the enemy along the way. Disembarking in Boeotia, he led them against the little town of Mycalessus. They passed the night about two miles from the town by the temple of Hermes, and at daybreak they marched on the undefended city and captured it—easily, since the town was some distance from the sea and was not expecting an attack. Rushing in, the Thracians killed every living thing—women, children, even animals. They even burst into a boys' school just as the pupils had entered and cut them all down. There is no evidence that the Athenians censured Diitrephes for this bloodbath, but he plainly bears much of the responsibility, and in highlighting this episode Thucydides reveals his own horror at the massacre.[17]

DEMOSTHENES SEEKS TO TURN THE TIDE

On their arrival in Sicily, Demosthenes and Eurymedon found the Athenians in low spirits: Gylippus had captured Plemmyrium and its three forts, and the Corinthians had taught the Syracusans how to modify the bows of their ships so as to make them more formidable in battle. Demosthenes saw himself as the savior of the Athenian mission to take Syracuse, and evidently the other generals deferred to his judgment, though he in no way outranked them. The results were catastrophic.

Perhaps because his experience lay in land operations and not in naval warfare, the new arrival set his sights on the counterwall up on Epipolae rather than attempting to retake Plemmyrium or using his substantial fleet to challenge the Syracusans to battle in the Great Harbor.[18] When the conventional daylight attack on the heights failed, he resolved on a more daring

17. Thucydides 7. 29. On Diitrephes as sharing in the responsibility for the massacre, see e.g., L. Kallet, *Money and the Corrosion of Power in Thucydides* (Berkeley: University of California Press, 2001), 140–6.

18. Demosthenes' past experience as a (partial?) explanation of his decision: J. Roisman, *The General Demosthenes and His Use of Military Surprise* (*Historia Einzelschriften* 78) (Stuttgart: Franz Steiner Verlag, 1993), 58.

approach: a nighttime assault, evidently bringing up the entire army of over 10,000 hoplites and an even greater number of light-armed troops.[19] After initial good fortune at the Euryalus pass, the Athenians encountered resistance first from Gylippus and his men; after some successes, they were finally routed by the Boeotians. At that point chaos set in. As each new contingent of Athenians reached the plateau, they did not know which way to go, as Demosthenes had failed to station commanders to transmit orders and direct traffic, and they thought everything in front of them was hostile, even when they were actually looking at retreating friends. In the end the Athenian soldiers were so confused in the darkness that they began fighting with one another. In their attempt to escape, many jumped or fell to their deaths off the cliffs. Those who had come to Sicily with Nicias were sufficiently familiar with the terrain to make their way back to camp, but many of the newcomers who had just arrived with Demosthenes missed the roads and wandered all over until dawn when they were hunted down and killed by the Syracusan cavalry.[20] As Connor has pointed out, Demosthenes' strategy "inadvertently recreated not Pylos, but the Aetolian disaster of 426."[21] The casualties, probably numbering 2,000 to 2,500, were significantly higher than in any other land battle of the war.[22]

Sobered by this disaster, Demosthenes now proposed withdrawal of the remaining force from Sicily and concentrating Athenian efforts on dislodging Agis from Decelea.[23] To his astonishment, however, Nicias was now in favor of remaining! The Syracusans, he claimed, were low on money, and he had it on good authority that a peace faction was on the verge of surrendering. Besides, the assembly would not take it well if the generals brought the troops home.[24] At first, the Athenians lingered

19. Thucydides reports that Demosthenes took "the whole army" (7. 43. 2).

20. Thucydides 43. 2–44. 8.

21. W. R. Connor, *Thucydides* (Princeton, NJ: Princeton University Press, 1984), 193.

22. Plutarch *Nicias* 21. 9; Diodorus 13. 11. 5. Hornblower encapsulates the nocturnal caper brilliantly: "The Epipolai operation is a pocket-edition of the entire Sicilian narrative: daring and confident plan, lavish preparations, initial Athenian success, turn-around of fortune, crushing defeat, poignant aftermath" (S. Hornblower, *A Commentary on Thucydides*, 3 vols. (Oxford: Oxford University Press, 1991–2008), 3, 618).

23. Thucydides 7. 47.

24. Thucydides 7. 48. 2-3.

in indecision, though the sickness brought on by the marshy ground on which they were encamped became steadily worse, but when Nicias saw Gylippus's forces increased not only by significant troops raised in Sicily but also men who had just arrived from the Peloponnesus, having been delayed in Libya by a storm, he withdrew his opposition, and all was made ready for departure. It would be a monumental undertaking, for he had with him not only the Athenians and their tribute-paying allies but the Argives, who came out of their hatred for their ancestral enemies, the Spartans, as well as mercenaries from Arcadia, Aetolia, Crete, Iapygia, and Acarnania; the Acarnanians were also motivated by loyalty to their old friend Demosthenes.[25]

At this point chance intervened: on the night of August 27, 413, there was a total eclipse of the moon.[26] The soothsayers interpreted this as a portent prescribing a delay of "thrice nine days" before moving, and most of Nicias's men were frightened and disposed to wait. Nicias, who Thucydides says was "too inclined to believe in the interpretation of omens and that sort of thing," made no attempt to dissuade them from their fear, although even for superstitious men other ways of construing the eclipse were possible: as Plutarch pointed out, the third-century BC seer and historian Philochorus saw the sign as not at all unfavorable to men who were fleeing, since such a deed required concealment rather than light.[27]

The delaying Athenians were now sitting ducks for the swelled army of Gylippus. Attacked by land and sea, they were defeated on both fronts; and Eurymedon was killed fighting in a hollow of the harbor. The Athenians were now in despair. They had suffered many blows during their time in Sicily, but to be defeated at sea—this was an unspeakable setback. Their disbelief was exceeded only by their regret at having come to Sicily on this fool's errand in the first place: to think that they had attacked the only cities with a character similar to their own, cities also governed by democracies—substantial cities with ships and horses, too.

25. Thucydides 7. 57. 9–11. Other mercenaries from Arcadia had been sent by Corinth to fight for the Syracusans: Thucydides 7. 58. 4.

26. Thucydides 7. 50. 4.

27. Thucydides 7. 50. 4; Plutarch *Nicias* 23. 5.

And now, when everything else had been at a stalemate, they had been defeated *at sea*. It was not only a setback; it was an indignity.[28]

The victorious Syracusans now set about enclosing the Athenian fleet in the Great Harbor by anchoring as many vessels as they could across its mile-wide mouth—triremes, merchant vessels, boats, whatever they could get their hands on.[29] Seeing that the harbor had been sealed, the Athenian commanders gathered to map strategy. They resolved to abandon their upper fortifications and to cut off the approach to their ships by a short cross-wall only as big as would be required to enclose their stores, such as they were, and their sick. They would then board their infantry onto their ships, seaworthy and unseaworthy alike, and fight it out in the harbor. If they won, they would make for Catana; if not, they would retreat in all possible order to friendly territory, whether Greek or non-Greek. In all, they manned about 110 ships. On the decks they placed many archers and javelin-throwers.[30] Nicias did his best to hearten the men for battle, first encouraging the commanders as a group and then turning to each trierarch individually, addressing him by his name, by that of his father, and that of his tribe, reminding them of the fatherland for which they were fighting.[31]

Once the battle in the harbor began, the din was enormous, for shouting came not only from the ships but also from the anxious spectators. Nicias had spread out those of his men who had not gone on the ships as widely as possible on the shore so that they could surround the harbor and cheer on those who were fighting. The crowding of ships in the harbor was immense, with fully 200 vessels jammed into the small space. Ramming attacks were few, and there was little room for the skilled naval maneuvers of the Athenians. The Athenians had prepared grappling hooks with which to board the Syracusan ships, but the Syracusans, having gotten wind of their plans, had covered the prows and much of the upper part of their ships with hides, so the hooks could not gain

28. Thucydides 7. 52. 2 (Eurymedon), 55 (despair).
29. Thucydides 7. 59. 3.
30. Thucydides 7. 60.
31. Thucydides 7. 69.

purchase.[32] The sound of the ships crashing into one another made it next to impossible to hear the calls of the coxswains. Meanwhile on shore the onlookers conducted themselves like spectators at a sporting event, swaying back and forth to see where the action was and crying out in triumph or distress depending on how their side was doing.[33] When it was over, the Syracusans were exulting in their victory over the armada from Athens that had come to enslave their city. The Athenians still had more ships than they did—sixty to the Syracusans' fewer than fifty—and Demosthenes tried to persuade them to try once more in the morning, but his men refused. They had had enough. They wanted to go home.[34]

About 40,000 men, soldiers and civilians, set out on the march from Syracuse, but few of them ever saw home, and certainly not any time soon. For Greeks to depart without burying their dead was unprecedented, and yet they steeled themselves to do it, though each soldier was sickened whenever he caught sight of a familiar friend lying lifeless on the ground. Still worse were the cries of the wounded ringing in their ears, begging to be brought along and not left to die—entreaties they knew they had to refuse if they were to save themselves. As the men who were in shape to march began to move along, the injured clung to them and followed as long as they could stand up, calling on the gods to witness their abandonment.[35]

As so often, Nicias had his own ideas about the gods. Perhaps our troubles will subside, he suggested:

> The enemy has had enough luck, because even if it was one of the gods who begrudged us this expedition, we've been punished enough by now. Men have been the aggressors against others before this and they have been able to endure the punishment for their all-too-human deeds. So now we have reason to hope that whatever god it is will be kinder to us, because right now we are more worthy of pity from the gods than envy.[36]

32. Thucydides 7. 65. 2.
33. Thucydides 7. 71. 1–4.
34. Thucydides 7. 72.
35. Thucydides 7. 75. 3–4.
36. Thucydides 7. 77. 3–4.

But Nicias's expression of hope and wishes for kind gods were as vain as those of the Melians had been not long before.[37] The army set out in the direction of Catana, Nicias in the van and Demosthenes in the rear. When Catana no longer appeared a realistic destination, they made for Gela and Camarina, lighting random fires to throw the Syracusans off the track.[38] After harassing them with cavalry for six days, the Syracusans finally caught up with Demosthenes' army, trapping them in an olive grove and pelting them with missiles from every direction. Finally Demosthenes surrendered his men under the condition that no one should be put to death either by violence or by imprisonment or by deprivation of the bare necessities of life.[39] These men amounted to 6,000, leaving some 1,400 who either escaped to their Sicilian homes—or, more likely, perished at the hands of Syracusan cavalry and javelin men on the march or were taken prisoner en route.

Some distance ahead of Demosthenes, Nicias was encamped with his half of the army. The Syracusans overtook him the next day and subjected his forces to the same pelting as they had those of Demosthenes. The next day the Athenian general tried desperately to lead his thirsty men across the Assinarus River, even as they were being attacked by missiles, hoplites, and cavalry. The Athenians thought, Thucydides says,

> that if they could just get across the river, things would be a little easier for them. They were desperate to stop the pain, to drink some water. When they got to the river, they broke ranks and ran into it, every man struggling to make the brutal crossing first as the enemy bore down. Driven to cross all together, they fell onto one another and trampled each other down. Some were killed immediately by their own spears; others got tangled up in their equipment and with each other and sank into the river. Syracusans positioned on the other bank, which was steep, hurled down spears at the Athenians, most of whom were jumbled together ravenously drinking from the nearly dry riverbed. The Peloponnesians went down

37. The parallel is explored in W. R. Connor, *Thucydides* (Princeton, NJ: Princeton University Press, 1984), 201.

38. Thucydides 7. 80. 1.

39. Thucydides 7. 82. 2-3.

> into the river after them and did most of the killing there; and though it quickly became fouled, the Athenians nonetheless fought among themselves to gulp the muddy water clotted with blood.[40]

Finally Nicias surrendered himself to Gylippus. Only about a thousand of his troops were still alive. The triumphant Syracusans stripped the bodies of the dead; their newfound loot was used to decorate the tallest trees and festoon their horses.[41]

The question now remained what to do with those who had been taken captive. When the day of reckoning came, the promises made to Demosthenes counted for little. Back in Syracuse the assembly voted to enslave the servants of the Athenians and their imperial allies and to put the Athenians themselves and their Sicilian allies in the city's dank stone quarries with rations of only a pint of meal and half a pint of barley a day. The conditions in the quarries were unimaginable, with the stench of excrement and rotting bodies increasing exponentially day by day. After seventy days, all the prisoners who had not died of disease except for the Athenians, Italians, and Greek Sicilians were sold off as slaves, branded on the forehead with the mark of a horse, the symbol of Syracuse. The rest lived (if they lived at all) under these wretched conditions for several months more until they were released to some alternate existence—prison with better rations, perhaps, or teaching (since they were schooled in Greek letters, music, and mathematics). Some, it was said, took advantage of the paucity of books in the Greek-speaking world to advance themselves through their knowledge of the poetry of Euripides, whose works were particularly beloved in Sicily; apparently reciting his poetry gave the prisoners a good shot at freedom or at least a place at a prosperous table. Some were ransomed and did in fact see Athens again. As for Nicias and Demosthenes, both Hermocrates and Gylippus argued in favor of sparing their lives, Hermocrates for reasons of magnanimity and Gylippus because he aspired to win glory by bringing them back to Sparta in chains, but their pleas fell on deaf ears, and

40. Thucydides 7. 84. 2–5.
41. Plutarch *Nicias* 27. 6.

both men were executed. Demosthenes, of course, had done the Spartans great hurt in the Pylos campaign, and as for Nicias, those in Syracuse who had been in correspondence with him about betraying the city were afraid of what he might reveal about them were he to remain alive.

Such was the end of an expedition thought up by an unprincipled young man who had never been tested on the battlefield and led by a sick old man afraid to fight because he might lose and never willing to give up hope that he might win the war by counting on a fifth column that never materialized. It was, Thucydides reported, the largest military undertaking in Greek history down to that time, as well as the most decisive—the most successful for the victors and the most devastating for the vanquished. The explanation for the debacle is overdetermined. The original plan, to aid Egesta against the encroachment of Selinus and even Syracuse, was quite possibly manageable. Once Nicias's rhetorical trick backfired on him and turned the expedition into something much larger—the first stages of mission creep—matters became riskier. Counterfactual history is always risky, but one must ask whether things would have turned out differently had Alcibiades not been recalled. He certainly proved an estimable commander in the years following, though by no means a man of honor. Following Lamachus's strategy and making for Syracuse at once, relying on the element of surprise, might well have worked. And it must be remembered that the Athenians very nearly won: Nicias was very probably correct in his belief that the Syracusans were frequently on the point of surrender.

That said, the Athenians made surprisingly little use of their mighty imperial armada, relying primarily on land operations. And in those operations, it cannot be denied that the failed leadership of Nicias lay at the heart of the problem. To be sure, he made some good decisions (setting the fire at the Circle to head off the Syracusans was certainly inspired, although perhaps someone else suggested it to him), but more bad ones, such as the move to soggy Plemmyrium, and most of all, the failure to focus on completing his fortifications, guarding Epipolae, and preempting the arrival of naval backup for Syracuse. And not all his failures can be put down to his illness: his first mistake was made in Athens when the expedition was being provisioned and he neglected to request cavalry. In the end, not to put too fine a point on it, he proved selfish and cowardly. He had been quite open with Demosthenes about his reason for not bringing his men home: not only was he receiving encouraging messages from his friends in Syracuse about the possibilities of surrender, but he feared that many of the soldiers who were bellyaching about their situation in Sicily would, once they got home, accuse the generals of having withdrawn only because they had been bribed. Given the temper of the Athenians, he said, he would prefer an honorable death on the battlefield to a disgraceful one at the hands of the demos at home after an unjust trial. In light of the punishment meted out to Pythodorus, Sophocles, and Eurymedon himself in 424 on the grounds that they had accepted bribes to withdraw from Sicily, his apprehension for his own welfare was understandable, but only barely; the Athenians had not yet begun to put generals who had displeased them to death, though this would happen later.[42] What is not understandable is his willingness to sacrifice the lives of his men to his own sense of honor. When Demosthenes proposed leading them to safety, it was Nicias's job to join with his colleague in accomplishing that task, not to decline in the interests of his own well-being.

Somewhere in the nexus of Nicias's many faults, the ambition of Alcibiades, and the foolhardiness—and ignorance—of the Athenian assembly lay the disaster that was the failure of the Sicilian expedition. Many who died there were Athenians who had voted for the undertaking, but many were allies conscripted into the project, and many were Syracusans who fought in defense of their city or those loyal to them who fought to drive the invader from their shores. The day the Sicilian envoys came to Athens seeking aid was a dark day for the Greeks, the day Nicias proposed expanding the undertaking into a massive one even darker.

42. Thucydides 7. 48. Pythodorus and Sophocles were exiled for taking bribes after the Gela accords; Eurymedon was fined (Thucydides 4. 65. 3). On the Athenians' subsequent treatment of generals who had given displeasure, see Hansen, *Eisangelia*, Roberts, *Accountability*, and Hamel, *Athenian Generals*, passim.

13

THE EMPIRE STRIKES BACK

THE DRAMATIC NEWS FROM Sicily electrified the Greek world. The Peloponnesians were filled with hope that they might make fast work of a gravely compromised enemy, while the Athenians' imperial subjects, especially the oligarchically inclined, smelled blood and began to plot rebellion from their weakened hegemon. In Athens itself, the mood was grim; indeed, at first the news was so awful that it was not even believed. But as soldiers who had escaped the fighting arrived at the city and confirmed the worst, the dismal truth could no longer be denied. The citizens were enraged at the politicians who had promoted the expedition—as if they had not voted for it themselves, Thucydides points out—and at the soothsayers who had encouraged them to hope for success in Sicily.[1] Nearly every household was overcome with grief, for almost every family had lost a son, a father, a brother, a cousin. Large numbers of women had lost their prospects for marriage and motherhood. Many of Athens' littlest citizens who could barely remember what their fathers looked like had been orphaned. The new moneys that would be needed for the support of fatherless families were in particularly short supply. Already weakened by the loss of Amphipolis and the mines of nearby Mt. Pangaeum that had made it so valuable, now the state had lost a fortune in money as well as men in Sicily. As for the men—from a population already significantly reduced by the plague, the Athenians had lost perhaps 3,000 hoplites. Another 9,000 or so had been lost among the thetes, the lowest census class, who served as rowers in the fleet, and

1. Thucydides 8. 1. 1.

thousands of the metics, the resident aliens, had been lost on the expedition as well, reducing the Athenian fighting force to half what it had been at the outbreak of the war. Many Athenian and allied ships were gone; the fleet now numbered only about 100, and of those, not all were seaworthy. The presence of a Spartan fort and a Spartan king at Decelea was making it difficult to get food from the countryside. And if fear of revolt in the empire was a constant companion, still more immediate was the fear of waking up in the morning to find that a Syracusan fleet had sailed into the Piraeus.[2] In these heady first weeks after the Syracusans' stunning victory, Athens' enemies thought there was nothing they could not do, and Athens feared there was nothing they would not do.

AN ENERGIZED GREECE, AN INTERESTED PERSIA

Despite their terror, the Athenians were as focused on moving ahead as were their foes. They immediately set about forming a ten-man committee of *probouloi*, senior advisers (one from each tribe) chosen to serve unlimited terms.[3] They were to be over forty years of age, and the two names we know suggest that many of them may have been well over that age: Hagnon, the founder of Amphipolis, who was past sixty, and the tragic dramatist Sophocles, now in his eighties. That these men had at one time been associates of Pericles argues against the institution of senior advisers being a step in the direction of oligarchy. Under the guidance of the senior advisers, the assembly also decreed the building of new ships, the construction of a fort at Sunium on the southern tip of Attica, to protect ships sailing by carrying grain, and the abandonment of their fort in Laconia, which was costing money to maintain. All expenses deemed unnecessary were reduced.[4]

The Athenians were not the only ones who saw the need for more ships. Deciding that they would need 100 new triremes, the Lacedaemonians

2. Thucydides 8. 1. 2.

3. Thucydides 8. 1. 3. On the senior advisers, M. Ostwald, *From Popular Sovereignty to the Sovereignty of Law: Law, Society, and Politics in Fifth-Century Athens* (Berkeley: University of California Press, 1986), 338–43.

4. Thucydides 8. 4.

assessed themselves and the Boeotians 25 each and parceled the rest out to various of their allies.[5] Although the full complement of 100 was not realized, the increased navy would stand the Peloponnesians in good stead, for within months the revolts that the Athenians so feared did in fact materialize, and the Spartans received requests for help from Athenian allies poised to rebel if only they could obtain some assistance. Envoys from Euboea and Lesbos came to Agis at Decelea; representatives from Chios and Erythrae went to Sparta, and with them went an ambassador from Tissaphernes, satrap of Sardis. At around the same time Tissaphernes' rival Pharnabazus, satrap of the Hellespontine province, ruling from Dascylium, sent his own envoy to Sparta, seeking aid for the rebellious cities of his territory. Each sought to get credit with the Persian king Darius II for sealing an alliance with the Spartans. (Neither was inclined to negotiate with Athens. After the Sicilian debacle, Sparta looked like the more promising horse to back, and the depredations of the Delian League had left a bitter taste in Persian mouths.)

What a delightful embarrassment of riches had now fallen into the Lacedaemonians' laps. After much debate the Spartans chose first to lend their support to Chios before aiding the other would-be rebels. The reasons for resolving their tough decision in favor of Chios were several. First, Chios had a fleet of about sixty ships that would join the Peloponnesian camp once the rebellion was complete. Second, an eager group there was ready to set the revolt in motion. Finally, Alcibiades, with contacts in Ionia, was pushing very hard for the choice of the Chians as the first rebels to receive aid, betting on Chios as the revolution most likely to succeed. For having fallen foul of Agis—there were rumors that he had not only seduced but impregnated the king's wife—but still enjoying the favor of some Spartans in high places, Alcibiades hoped to make a splash among the Spartan elite; his backup plan, however, was to endear himself to Tissaphernes.[6] And of course, all the while he was plotting a return to his native Athens. Alcibiades' mind was never at rest.

5. Thucydides 8. 3. 2.

6. Alcibiades and Agis's wife Timaea: Plutarch *Alcibiades* 23. 7–9; *Agesilaus* 3. 1–2; *Lysander* 22. 3–4. Rumors of the affair cast doubt on the legitimacy of Timaea's son Leotychidas. This facilitated

In the summer of 412, then, five Spartan ships, along with Alcibiades and the Spartan navarch Chalcideus, sailed to Chios and, acting in concert with local oligarchs, brought about a revolt there. The rebellions of nearby Erythrae and Clazomenae followed immediately afterward. When the Athenians learned what had happened on Chios, they saw themselves as surrounded by a clear and pressing danger: surely the other allies would not remain loyal when they saw that the largest of the subject allies had gone over to the enemy. At once they repealed the penalty of death they had established for so much as proposing the use of the 1,000 talents that had been set aside as an emergency reserve fund at the outset of the war, to be used only in the event of the enemy bearing down on the city with a navy.[7] Now making use of this fund, they built and manned as many ships as possible and sent as many as they could to Ionia. Chios could not be regained, but the Athenians held on to Lesbos (not technically in Ionia, but nearby to the north). Though they retook Clazomenae, Alcibiades also managed to engineer the defection of Miletus.

Tissaphernes now tried to negotiate an alliance between the Lacedaemonians and King Darius—an entirely one-sided document that proclaimed that all territory the king or his ancestors had ever held should belong to Darius and that the Spartans should work with the Persians to prevent Athens from collecting tribute from any of those regions. The Spartans agreed to aid Darius against any rebellions in his territory, and Darius would help them if any ally should try to break away from them. Neither would make a separate peace with Athens. The implications of the alliance were ominous: that not only all the Greek cities of Ionia but much of mainland Greece belonged to the Persian king. The Spartans' war aims were now muddier than ever: did they wish to seize rule over Greece from the Athenians at any price, or hand it over to Persia in exchange for the satisfaction of crushing Athens? In any case this alliance put the nail in the coffin of any notion that the Lacedaemonians still aimed to "free the Greeks."

the subsequent agitation of the ex-navarch Lysander for the succession of Agis's half-brother Agesilaus instead.

7. Penalty laid down at the outset of the war against proposing use of the reserve fund except in the event of the enemy navy attacking the city: Thucydides 2. 24. 1.

A democratic revolution now took place on Samos. (Presumably the democracy the Athenians had imposed after the revolution of 440 had since been replaced by an oligarchy.[8]) There Athenian ships were stationed, able and willing to offer aid in light of the civil unrest festering up and down the coast. The Samian demos put to death about 200 of the most powerful oligarchs and exiled 400 others, redistributing their land and homes among themselves. The Athenians thereupon rewarded the Samians with autonomy for what they considered a display of democratic fidelity, and the Samians repaid them by remaining loyal even after the Athenians' devastating defeat at the Battle of Aegospotami in 405.[9]

A FATEFUL DECISION AT MILETUS

In other respects, things did not go so well for the Athenians. At first it seemed that they could take Miletus back. Attacking with a fleet of forty-eight ships bearing an army of 3,500 hoplites, including 1,500 from Argos, they managed to get the upper hand, though 300 of the Argives, who hastened somewhat rashly into the fray, were killed. But as the Athenians and their allies were making plans to wall off the defeated city, word arrived that a combined fleet of fifty-five Peloponnesian and Sicilian ships (the Sicilian vessels led by Hermocrates himself) was on its way. This put a new slant on things. Among the Athenian generals, most pressed for continuing the fight, but in the end the general Phrynichus persuaded his colleagues that the risk in ships and men was too great. Great was the bitterness of the Argives when they learned that the expedition was being abandoned and that their men had died for nothing.[10]

Whether to fight the enemy fleet at Miletus was a judgment call. A defeat would have been a serious matter, but a victory might well have changed the course of the war in Ionia. The immediate consequence of

8. On Samos, see P. Cartledge, "Sparta and Samos: A Special Relationship?" *Classical Quarterly* 32 (1982): 243–65.

9. Thucydides 8. 21.

10. Thucydides 8. 24–7.

the Athenians' decision not to fight was the loss of their ally, the rebel Amorges, bastard son of the satrap Pissuthnes. Amorges was based on the coast at Iasus, between Miletus and Halicarnassus. The Persians were dead set on getting their hands on him, and now with Peloponnesian aid this would be workable. When the Peloponnesian ships approached Iasus, the inhabitants made no attempt to defend themselves, taking them for the Athenian triremes that had lately been in the neighborhood. The Peloponnesians then helped themselves to the ample booty from the city and enrolled the local mercenaries in their own army. Captives were sold to Tissaphernes for a Daric gold stater each—20 Attic drachmas—and Amorges himself was handed over to the satrap to be sent to the king.[11] The Persians and Peloponnesians were now working happily together, and when Phrynichus proved to be an obstacle to Alcibiades' projected return to Athens, his supporters found the loss of Iasus ready at hand as grounds for impeachment.[12]

Finding that Tissaphernes had also engineered the revolt of Cnidus, the Athenians then made an effort to bring it back into their alliance, but though they very nearly succeeded, in the end Cnidus was lost to them. The first of Tissaphernes' alliances between Sparta and Persia, moreover, was renewed, with stipulations that the king would pay any Spartan troops he, Darius, summoned, although the irate satrap walked out of the conference when one of the eleven Spartans sent to fine-tune the arrangements pointed out that

> it was outrageous for the King to claim that he still ruled over the same territories as his forefathers. That would mean returning to slavery all the islands, as well as Thessaly, Eastern Locris, and everything as far as Boeotia, and instead of freeing Greece, the Spartans would be putting a Persian yoke around its neck.

11. Thucydides 8. 28; on the history of the relationship between Amorges and Athens, H. D. Westlake, "Athens and Amorges," *Phoenix* 31 (1977): 319–29. L. Kallet, *Money and the Corrosion of Power in Thucydides* (Berkeley: University of California Press, 2001), 251–3, stresses Thucydides' interest in the financial aspect of the Iasus campaign and suggests that Tissaphernes was pulling the strings (and that the Spartans did not get good value for their efforts).

12. Thucydides 8. 54. 3–4; J. Roberts, *Accountability in Athenian Government* (Madison: University of Wisconsin Press, 1982), 36–40.

Fuming, Tissaphernes left the conference in a rage, but the agreements between the Spartans and the Persians were undisturbed.[13]

Meanwhile the Lacedaemonians had been receiving requests for aid from the most powerful men in Dorian Rhodes. Arriving there shortly before the Athenians, they brought Rhodes over to their side and came away with 32 talents from the wealthy Rhodians to boot. The winter of 412/11, however, saw a dramatic change in international relations. The Spartan navarch Chalcideus having been killed in action, his successor Astyochus received a letter from home instructing him to have Alcibiades put to death.[14] Now Alcibiades had to put his backup plan into action: just as he had once defected from Athens to Sparta, he now defected from Sparta to Persia—specifically, to Tissaphernes. The good graces of Tissaphernes were only to be a way station in his journey back to Athens; Alcibiades did not plan to remain in Persia forever. And so he advised Tissaphernes to drag out the war as long as possible, wearing the Greeks down by letting neither side win. This was a great money-saver for Tissaphernes, since it enabled him to spend much less on the Spartans, and he had been spending nothing on the Athenians. It also made a fine narrative with which Alcibiades could return to Athens, since it could be reworked as "I dissuaded Tissaphernes from making war on you." His best chance of being recalled, he thought, was if the Athenians were convinced that Tissaphernes was his friend, and could, through him, become theirs. The trap, indeed, had already been sprung: he had sent word to the leading men in the army at Samos asking them to network on his behalf among the most powerful Athenians there and to say that he would return only if Athens were to replace the corrupt democracy that had banished him with an oligarchy.[15] In that event, he said, he could bring Persia into the war on the Athenian side.

A COUP IN ATHENS INTERSECTS WITH WAR ABROAD

At this juncture, the inclinations of many different groups created an even more chaotic situation than had existed before. Some Athenians on

13. Thucydides 8. 43. 3–4.
14. Thucydides 8. 45. 1.
15. Thucydides 8. 45–7.

Samos wished to establish an oligarchy in Athens in order to gain Persian support against Sparta. Among these was the trierarch Thrasybulus, a committed democrat who nonetheless saw no way to defeat the Peloponnesians unless the Athenians recalled Alcibiades, and who saw the establishment of an oligarchy as part of the package. Others who had always opposed democracy—and there were many such among the Athenians—desired to set up an oligarchy for its own sake. Some in the lower ranks of the armed forces opposed an oligarchy but grudgingly went along with it because they were frightened for themselves and their families in view of their increasing impoverishment; only an infusion of money, it seemed, could end the war that was destroying the fabric of their lives. Some were unwilling to have oligarchy in Athens at all. And then there was the question of Alcibiades. Some were persuaded that he was their only hope of winning the war; others did not trust him. The general Phrynichus, once a democrat but now an oligarch, cautioned them that Alcibiades did not give a fig for constitutional change and was interested only in securing his return to Athens, and that there was no reason to think that either Tissaphernes or Darius cared what kind of government the Athenians had. Why would the Persians want to aid their old enemies, the Athenians, whose Delian League had as its express purpose the seizure of land and booty from them? Phrynichus, however, was outvoted, and an embassy headed by Peisander was sent from Samos to Athens to argue for the abolition of the democracy and the restoration of Alcibiades, thus paving the way for friendship with the Persians.[16]

Nervous about the precariousness of his position if his enemy Alcibiades were to be restored to Athens, Phrynichus resorted to the following stratagem: he sent a letter to the Spartan navarch Astyochus telling him of Alcibiades' plans to create an alliance between Tissaphernes and the Athenians. But instead of punishing Alcibiades (who was no longer in his power anyhow) as Phrynichus had hoped, Astyochus told both Tissaphernes and Alcibiades about the contents of the letter. Alcibiades at once wrote to the authorities in Samos informing them of

16. Thucydides 8. 47. 2–49.

what Phrynichus had done. Petrified, Phrynichus, having learned something about the consequences of putting confidential matters in writing, wrote once more to Astyochus complaining about his violation of the secrecy of the first letter and saying that he was prepared to hand over the Athenian armed forces at Samos, which was unfortified, in their entirety, as his greatest enemies had put his life in danger. This he did in full knowledge that he would be betrayed by Astyochus again, and he made sure to let the army on Samos know that they were about to be hit and that they needed to build fortifications. The foreseeable letter from Alcibiades warning the Athenians about the assault and telling them that their general had betrayed them did Phrynichus great credit by suggesting he had excellent intelligence about the attack.[17]

The same divisions that had been found on Samos obtained in Athens itself. Peisander's embassy to the assembly couched its report in euphemistic terms, proposing that in addition to restoring Alcibiades the Athenians should change their government to a "different form of democracy."[18] Predictably, this did not go over well. It had been exactly 100 years since the Athenians had overthrown the tyrants and established their cherished democratic constitution. The two clans who traditionally provided officials for the Eleusinian mysteries, the Eumolpidae and the Ceryces, were appalled at the notion of restoring a man condemned for profaning the sacred cult that they supervised, and they were not alone. The renegade had many enemies when he left Athens, and he had acquired many more now that he had joined with both Sparta and Persia in fomenting revolution in the empire.[19] But at that point, Thucydides says,

> Peisander came forward. In the face of the indignant outcry he called his opponents before him and, reminding them that the Peloponnesians had as many ships ready for action as they, that the Peloponnesians had more allies, and that Tissaphernes and the King were supplying the

17. Thucydides 8. 50–1.
18. Thucydides 8. 53. 1.
19. Eumolpidae and Ceryces: Thucydides 8. 53. 2.

> Peloponnesians with money while Athens was bankrupt, he asked them one by one whether they had the slightest hope that their city could be saved unless they could persuade the King of Persia to come over to their side. Each of them answered "No."[20]

Frightened into believing that Alcibiades and the Persians were their only hope and consoled by Peisander's argument that if they didn't like the oligarchy they could always return to their democracy later (a very peculiar idea, but in the event, correct), the assembly voted to send Peisander and ten others to make arrangements with Tissaphernes and Alcibiades. At the same time, they were persuaded by Peisander to depose Phrynichus and his colleague Scironides from their posts on the grounds that they had betrayed Iasus and Amorges. This accusation, of course, was a shallow pretext. Peisander and those who voted with him wanted Phrynichus out of the way because he was so vocal in his opposition to the recall of Alcibiades.[21] Before leaving Athens, Peisander also made a point of visiting all the *hetairiai*, urging them to set aside their naturally competitive inclinations and instead combine their efforts to overthrow the democracy. Only then did he set out on his mission to the east.[22]

The negotiations among Alcibiades, Tissaphernes, and the Athenian envoys ended in failure. Tissaphernes evidently had less enthusiasm for the Athenian cause than Alcibiades had supposed, and Alcibiades was determined to make it seem that it was the Athenians' fault that an agreement could not be reached. And so, speaking for Tissaphernes, Alcibiades kept piling one demand on another. The Athenians were very agreeable, going so far indeed as to concede all of Ionia and its offshore islands to the Persians. But then Alcibiades demanded that Darius should be allowed to build a fleet and cruise off the coast of his territory with as many ships as he pleased.

20. Thucydides 8. 53. 2.

21. Thucydides 8. 54. 3. It is unclear why Scironides was deposed at the same time as Phrynichus; Thucydides does not indicate that Scironides had supported Phrynichus's argument that the Athenians should abandon the fight for Miletus.

22. Thucydides 8. 54.

Really? How far off the coast? His territory, the Athenians well remembered, went right up to the Hellespont, on which they were dependent for their grain. To agree to these terms would be signing their death warrant.

As Alcibiades had predicted, the Athenians broke off negotiations and returned to their base at Samos in a rage.[23] Tissaphernes now turned back to his original allies, the Spartans, and arranged a third treaty with them, providing for pay for their ships until the arrival of the Persians' promised vessels (the Phoenician fleet). After that the Spartans would have to pay for their own ships—and reimburse the Persians for the moneys they had advanced for the Spartan fleet. As it happened, the Phoenician fleet never materialized, and quite possibly Darius had never authorized its use in the war.[24]

Peisander and his colleagues meanwhile returned to Samos to see what they could do in the way of promoting oligarchic interests there. Then with half the envoys Peisander went back to Athens with the idea of undermining the democracy in the capital; the other half was sent to other subject cities. On their arrival in Athens, Peisander and his colleagues discovered that steps had already been taken. To garner popularity with Alcibiades, some of the young men from the *hetairiai* had assassinated Androcles, who not only was one of the leaders of the demos but also had played a prominent role in Alcibiades' exile. Others had been done away with as well.[25] The *hetairiai* had also circulated the notion that participation in government should be restricted to 5,000 men capable of serving the state without pay. There would no longer be any remuneration for public service such as participation on juries and service on the Council. Men of hoplite status and above, in other words, would continue to have a share in government, but the thetes who rowed in the all-important navy would be cut out.

Although the assembly and the Council continued to meet, they deliberated only on proposals that had been approved by the oligarchic inner circle, and only the oligarchs spoke: anyone who offered an opposing

23. Thucydides 8. 56.
24. Thucydides 8. 58.
25. Thucydides 8. 65.

view "conveniently turned up dead."[26] Peisander and his fellow conspirators soon arranged for a meeting of the citizens not on the Pnyx but in Colonus, a deme outside the city walls, in a precinct sacred to Poseidon, about a mile outside the city. There, having dispensed with the *graphe paranomon* (indictment against illegal proposals), they abolished the existing government and replaced it with a body of Four Hundred to govern with full powers and assemble the Five Thousand whenever they pleased.[27] Not long afterward, the Four Hundred, armed with daggers and backed up by a body of a hundred thugs whom they kept ready to hand for occasions when violence was called for, entered the council chamber with pay for the members of the sitting Council and told the Councilmen to take their pay and go home.

They took their pay and went home.[28] Now ensconced in the council chamber, the Four Hundred ruled Athens with an iron fist, purporting to do so on behalf of the mysterious Five Thousand, whoever they might be. The city was gripped by terror. A few hundred men were plainly enemies of the demos, but what about the others? A scheme that had originated on Samos in a plan to secure Persian support through the recall of Alcibiades had now taken on a life of its own. After a century of comparative harmony within the city following the expulsion of the Peisistratid tyrants, war abroad had given rise to civil discord at home, and to fear of the Peloponnesians was now added fear of one's neighbor.

A CRY FOR HARMONY

In 411, Aristophanes produced his *Lysistrata*, one of the most famous plays of antiquity. In it, the title character, a formidable woman whose name means "disbander of armies," astonishingly brings about peace between the Athenians and the Spartans—at least in fiction. Her strategy is two-pronged: she sends the older Athenian women to seize the Acropolis, thus cutting off the men from the treasury that is funding

26. Thucydides 8. 66. 2.
27. Thucydides 8. 67. 2–3.
28. Thucydides 8. 69. 4.

the war, and she mobilizes the young wives of various Greek states in a panhellenic sex strike. The play is about not only sex but money, and it's hilarious, as the old women douse the fire-bearing elders with water to keep them from getting at their war chest and the young women stick to their guns despite the misery of the husbands who walk around with prosthetic phalluses artificially engorged to stress their discomfort. (Disbelief is suspended as the ready availability of prostitutes and boys as sexual partners is conveniently ignored.) The wives at first agree to do anything the resolute Lysistrata asks if only it will stop the war. I would even climb the highest peak in Laconia, says the Spartan Lampito, if I could catch a glimpse of Peace from there. I would lay down my life, exclaims the Athenian Calonice. Why, says Lysistrata's friend Myrrhine, I would slice myself in two like a flounder and donate half to the cause of peace! But then they learn what Lysistrata has in mind. Okay, then, says Lysistrata: "we must give up . . . the prick."[29]

The wives' faces fall. They start walking away. Tears begin to roll down their cheeks. Let the war drag on, they say. Balefully, Lysistrata chastises the hapless Myrrhine: You too, my little flounder? But by the force of her personality, Lysistrata, backed up by the tough Spartan Lampito, reminds the women of how much the war has made them suffer, and in the end they swear a mighty oath, accompanied, of course, by much wine. (In swigging liberally and swearing to yield to neither husband *nor lover*, the wives are of course confirming the standard male canards about women—drunkenness and nymphomania.) In the climactic comic scene the Athenian Myrrhine, approached by her suffering husband Cinesias, torments him by pretending to yield to his entreaties, only to put one obstacle

29. *Lysistrata* l. 124. Lysistrata's name is suspiciously similar to that of Lysimache, "loosener of battles," a real woman who had served for many years in the high office of priestess of Athena Polias, Athena of the City, and Aristophanes may have intended us to associate the two women. After the temple of Athena Nike was completed in the 420s, moreover, its first priestess was named Myrrhine. Lampito was the name of the mother of that very Agis II who was besieging Athens from Decelea even as the play was being produced. What we are to make of this is uncertain; plainly the Lampito of the play is not Agis's mother, and Lysistrata and Myrrhine seem to be younger than their priestly counterparts, but the Athenian women may derive some authority from their association in the audience's minds with real women in authority (although Myrrhine was a fairly common name in Athens, as was Lampito in Sparta).

after another in the way of his gratification. Wait! she cries. We need a bed. (Returns with cot.) Lie down, I'll undress. Wait! We need a mattress. I'll go get one. Wait! A pillow. Must have one. [Cinesias: I DON'T NEED A PILLOW.] Wait! Some perfume. [Cinesias: WHO NEEDS PERFUME?] Wait! Needless to say, in the end, Myrrhine runs off leaving Cinesias high and dry, more frustrated than ever.[30]

Predictably, one of Athens' ten senior advisers attempts to arrest Lysistrata. The poignant exchange between the two of them underlines the profound seriousness of Aristophanes' message and represents the climax of the play's more somber side. The magistrate's insensitive suggestion that the women have shared none of the war's burdens predictably sets Lysistrata off: *None? None?* On the contrary; we bear more than our share. First, we bear sons whom we must send off to war . . . and then she is interrupted. The adviser cannot bear to be reminded, probably, of the recent catastrophe in Sicily. Then, she continues, when we should be enjoying our lives, we sleep alone because our husbands are away. And it pains me to think of the young unmarried women growing old in their bedchambers. Never one to miss an opportunity to make his situation worse, the adviser observes that men grow old too. This only inflames Lysistrata further, since she points out that a man can always find some young lass to marry upon returning from war no matter how old and gray he may be.

But Aristophanes' point is not that women suffer, although he is clearly moved by their plight. Lysistrata has much more to say than that. She stresses the mess men have made in managing public affairs and the skills women possess that would make them better managers. The oikos, in other words, has become divorced from the polis; the war can only end when the skills women traditionally use in making cloth are brought to bear on managing the polis as well.[31] The war, Aristophanes suggests,

30. *Lysistrata* ll. 915–50, paraphrased.

31. Statecraft is similarly compared to weaving in Plato's *Statesman*, 308d–11c. K. Sidwell identifies the metaphor as Socratic, but it could well have originated with Aristophanes rather than with the philosopher: *Aristophanes the Democrat: The Politics of Satirical Comedy during the Peloponnesian War* (Cambridge: Cambridge University Press, 2009), 263.

has caused a disjunction not only between Athens and its old ally Sparta (both parties being reconciled at the end of the play) but also between oikos and polis.[32] Lysistrata's two-pronged strategy resolves all these disjunctions, and the play ends with song and dance.

But of course the real war does not end, nor was *Lysistrata* a call for Peace Now. Aristophanes' play had a message, but it was a message about the hardships of war and the corruption and bumbling rampant in Athenian politics. The playwright could not have imagined that peace was possible in the winter of 411, for at that time the Spartans would have made peace only on terms of unconditional surrender. It would be months before Athenian victories in the east, at Cynossema and at Cyzicus, would dispose the Spartans to a peace that might possibly be agreeable to the democracy. In *Lysistrata*, Aristophanes sought to point his countrymen in the direction of peace, but he did not see a clear path through—or around—the obstacles that stood in the way.[33] And indeed, few others could either.

32. On oikos and polis in *Lysistrata*, see H. Foley, "The 'Female Intruder' Reconsidered: Women in Aristophanes' *Lysistrata* and *Ecclesiazusae*," *Classical Philology* 77 (1982): 1–21.

33. For a nuanced treatment of Aristophanes' position on a real live peace in Greece in this play, see H. D. Westlake, "The 'Lysistrata' and the War," *Phoenix* 34 (1980): 38–54.

14

DRAMATIC DEVELOPMENTS FOR THE ATHENIANS

IN 411, THE ATHENIANS found themselves in the grip of the Four Hundred. A motley crew with differing goals, this diverse conglomeration hoped somehow to improve their lives and the fortunes of their city by departing from Athens' democratic government and entering into peace negotiations with Sparta. How long they could maintain a government based on the fiction that it was a way station toward a broader oligarchy of Five Thousand was unclear. Much would depend on their success in achieving peace with Sparta. In the end, they did not succeed, and when it became clear to their own members that the leaders of the Four Hundred never intended to establish the Five Thousand, their narrow regime collapsed and was replaced at last by the promised government of the Five Thousand, probably closer to ten thousand. But the years 411 and 410 brought considerable military success to the Athenians, as three dramatic Athenian naval victories in the Hellespont led the disconsolate Spartans to sue for peace—and the Athenians to restore their ancestral democracy.

ATHENS UNDER THE FOUR HUNDRED

The Four Hundred were by no means all cut from the same cloth. Some were die-hard oligarchs who had used the tensions occasioned by the war to stage a coup, while others were moderates who wanted to try an alternative form of government that might have a better chance of securing Persian support in the war with Sparta. The ultimate aim of the first group was an even narrower oligarchy; the second group was probably ignorant of the fact that their colleagues did not ever plan to establish the illusory Five Thousand. In the first group were Peisander, Phrynichus, and the orator Antiphon; in the second group was the moderate Theramenes, son of Pericles' old friend Hagnon. Although the various politicians were divided as to what the peace terms should be, acting as the government of Athens, the Four Hundred now sent heralds to Agis at Decelea indicating that they wanted to end the war.[1] As the condition of peace, the Spartan king insisted on the surrender of Athens' naval empire.[2] Suspecting that there must be strife within the city, as the demos would not give up its liberty so easily, he summoned a large army from the Peloponnesus to meet him near the walls of Athens—whereupon the Athenians sent out cavalry, hoplites, light-armed men, and archers. Agis then retreated to Decelea, and when the next embassy arrived, he directed the envoys to go directly to Sparta, not wanting to take responsibility for negotiations that his home government might find displeasing. He had tasted its displeasure once before, and once was enough.[3]

The oligarchs also turned their attention to Samos, where they feared the reaction of the traditionally democratic sailors in the fleet, sending ten men to reassure them that there were not 400 men governing Athens but really 5,000. The only reason the Five Thousand had not met, they said, was that with all the ongoing foreign expeditions demanding their attention no question had arisen at home important enough to require the deliberation of so many.[4] As it happened, inspired by the propaganda of Peisander, an oligarchy was already in the planning stages on Samos, though democrats loyal to Athens, including Thrasybulus the trierarch and the hoplite Thrasyllus, helped put down the uprising; thirty ringleaders of the coup were executed and three others were exiled.[5] Now it

1. Thucydides 8. 70. 2.
2. Pseudo-Aristotle *Constitution of the Athenians* 32. 3.
3. Thucydides 8. 71.
4. Thucydides 8. 72. 1.
5. Thucydides 8. 73.

was time to send the good news to Athens: because information traveled slowly across the Aegean, the people on Samos knew nothing of the Four Hundred and their doings. When the Samian democrats arrived on the state ship *Paralus* to report their success, the crew was seized and placed under arrest. A certain Chaereas managed to escape, though, and returning to Samos he sought to whip the army into a frenzy, mixing truth with falsehood. He told horrific tales of what was going on in Athens, reporting that everyone was being subjected to lashings, that the wives and children of the soldiers from Samos were being outraged unspeakably, and that the Four Hundred had plans to shut up all the relatives of the men in the army at Samos who were not in sympathy with the government and kill them if the army did not submit.[6]

The first response of the enraged soldiery at Samos was to rise up against the authors of the abortive oligarchy on the island, but Thrasybulus and Thrasyllus managed to calm the waters. The fleet deposed its generals and elected Thrasybulus and Thrasyllus generals in their stead; they agreed to take an oath to be governed democratically, prosecute the war against Sparta vigorously, and be enemies of the Four Hundred.[7] And the men of the fleet at Samos announced themselves to be the true government of the Athenians. It was they who possessed the ancestral democracy of Athens—both the ships and the men.[8] Henceforth, a government in exile would exist on Samos.

Meanwhile, discouraged by their inability to get sufficient pay from Tissaphernes, the Peloponnesians had sent Clearchus to Pharnabazus, the satrap of the Hellespontine region, who was more forthcoming, and they were now able to come to the aid of the Byzantines, helping them to revolt from Athens. Soon the nearby cities of Chalcedon, Cyzicus, and Selymbria all rebelled as well. The alarm this occasioned in the Athenians enabled Thrasybulus to engineer the recall of Alcibiades to Samos. In an assembly there, the former deserter continued to spout the same balderdash he had been feeding his countrymen all along: that he had

6. Thucydides 8. 74. 3.
7. Thucydides 8. 75. 2.
8. Thucydides 8. 76.

Tissaphernes in his pocket; that the Athenians, once they had recalled him, should never want for Tissaphernes' support; and indeed—this was new—that Tissaphernes would sell his very own bed for the Athenians if he had to. Upon hearing this astonishing speech, the Athenians at Samos elected Alcibiades general along with the existing ones and entrusted to him all their affairs.[9]

During the civil strife on Samos, the envoys whom the Four Hundred had sent to pacify the fleet had hidden out on Delos, not sure of their next move. Now they appeared at Samos and tried to address the assembly—not an easy matter. When at last they were permitted to speak, they insisted that their government was not interested in handing the city over to the Spartans, that the Five Thousand would be enrolled in due course, and that the relatives of the soldiers on Samos were all safe and in secure enjoyment of their property in the city. Their irate audience was unimpressed, and there was considerable enthusiasm for sailing on the Piraeus at once. It was Alcibiades who dissuaded them from this course of action that would have left Ionia and the Hellespont unprotected and in the gravest of danger. He also told the envoys that he had no objection to the government of the Five Thousand, but the Four Hundred would have to go.[10] In fact, many of the Four Hundred had developed second thoughts and were actually eager for the Five Thousand to be established, partly out of fear of the government at Samos, partly out of fear of Alcibiades, and partly out of fear that the oligarchy was unstable.[11] The extreme oligarchs, however, were very anxious; Phrynichus was particularly apprehensive because of his bad history with Alcibiades. To be sure, many of the Four Hundred were motivated by ideological considerations. After all, Athens had always been home to a coterie of conservatives devoted to something they considered the true democracy of Athens, a hoplite democracy that limited the franchise to those who could afford hoplite weaponry—the ancestral democracy, they called it: the *patrios politeia* (which of course was not democracy at all). But the Four Hundred also

9. Thucydides 8. 81. 1–82. 1.
10. Thucydides 8. 86. 6.
11. Thucydides 8. 89. 2–4.

had a tiger by the tail: once their regime fell, their lives were no longer secure. And so, much as many of them wanted to see Sparta defeated—and many did—continuing the war was not necessarily a luxury they could afford. It might be that Sparta alone could protect them from the wrath of the Athenian demos. Thucydides outlines their thinking:

> Above all, what the Four Hundred wanted was to keep an oligarchic government and to retain Athens' hegemony over its allies. Failing that, they wanted to hold onto the fleet and the walls and to remain an independent city. Deprived even of that, rather than be the first to be killed by a restored democracy, they would bring the enemy into the city, surrender the ships and the walls, make peace, and keep whatever power they could—all provided they could save their own lives.[12]

The Four Hundred had begun fortifying Eëtionia, a breakwater of the Piraeus, with the idea of admitting a Peloponnesian fleet (though of course they denied that this was their purpose). The breakwater aroused much suspicion and in fact proved the catalyst for a revolution against the oligarchy. Encouraged by Theramenes, many of the men in the Piraeus, including those who had been instructed to build the wall in the first place, began to tear it down, declaring that all who wished the Five Thousand to govern should join in the work.[13] They did not dare claim that they were acting on behalf of the democracy, although they were.

The next day those involved in tearing down the wall marched to the temple of Helen's brothers Castor and Pollux (patrons of sailors), where anxious delegates from the Four Hundred met with them and assured them that the Five Thousand would soon be enrolled. This time they were telling the truth, and a day was appointed for concord to be restored at a meeting in the theater of Dionysus. When the day came, however, alarming news arrived: a Peloponnesian fleet was making its way along the coast of Salamis. The citizens were both frightened by the

12. Thucydides 8. 91. 3.
13. Thucydides 8. 92. 10–11.

appearance of the ships and relieved that enough people had been persuaded by Theramenes to engineer the dismantling of the fortification designed to welcome it. But the forty-two enemy vessels were headed not for the Piraeus but for Euboea, where in addition to capturing twenty-two Athenian ships and killing or capturing their crews, they swiftly accomplished the defection of almost the entire island from Athenian rule, leaving only the city of Histiaea in the north in Athenian hands.[14]

For the men and women of Athens, the loss of Euboea was a major blow. Indeed, they perceived it as a disaster unparalleled even by the debacle in Sicily. Sicily was far away, but Euboea, easily visible across the narrow Euripus straits, had long been virtually an extension of Attica. It was where the Athenians had sent their flocks for safekeeping early in the war, and it was a major source of their provisions now that Agis had established himself at Decelea and cut them off from the farmland of Attica. Agis was nearby and could call up his troops again at any time, the Athenians' ships and army were across the Aegean at Samos in revolt against the home government, there was sedition at home. What if the Spartans, having secured Euboea, should now stage an amphibious attack on Athens itself? Once again the Athenians were gripped by panic.

THE "FIVE THOUSAND" IN ATHENS; WAR IN THE HELLESPONT

Fearing the swift return of the loyal fleet from Samos, the Spartans decided not to chance attacking Athens, and the Athenians breathed a collective sigh of relief. They proceeded with the deposition of the Four Hundred and the institution of the long-promised Five Thousand, a number that proved to be in fact much greater than anticipated, for those men entitled to civic rights according to the new constitution (those who could afford to provide themselves with hoplite equipment or serve in the cavalry) proved to be much more numerous, perhaps as many as 9,000 or even 10,000; still, the thetes were disfranchised, and there was no pay

14. Thucydides 8. 94–5.

for public service. Of the die-hard oligarchs, some like Peisander fled for their lives, taking refuge with Agis at Decelea; others like Antiphon chose to remain in Athens and were executed for treason.[15] Phrynichus, who had been stabbed to death after returning from a peace mission to the Spartans on behalf of the Four Hundred, was even prosecuted posthumously by Alcibiades' friend Critias and convicted of treason; his property was confiscated and his remains removed beyond the borders of Attica.[16]

Under the so-called Five Thousand the Athenians held their own against several aggressive attacks by the Spartan navy. Although they did well, there was no question that they were now on the defensive in every way: their fleet needed to be everywhere at once, and they were running dangerously short of all resources. Time not spent fighting had to be devoted to raising money by whatever means possible, whether by diplomacy or by plunder. Alcibiades, who at last had been recalled by the home government but hesitated to return to the capital until he had accomplished major victories for the city, raised money in Caria in southwest Asia Minor and distributed it to the grateful troops on Samos; Theramenes collected booty from the coasts of Euboea and Boeotia and then sailed north to Macedonia, where he was able to obtain timber for shipbuilding from its new king Archelaus; and Thrasybulus plundered Thasos, which had just recently revolted from the empire.

Meanwhile the satrap Pharnabazus sought to curry favor with Darius by luring the Spartan navarch Mindarus to the Hellespont. There, he hoped, the Athenians would follow, frightened for the security of their grain supply. And indeed the Spartans and the Athenians promptly faced off in a series of naval and amphibious battles. By all rights, victory in the first of these should have gone to the Peloponnesians. In 411 Mindarus with his eighty-six ships outnumbered the Athenians with their seventy-six vessels in the straits between Abydos and Dardanus, and the Spartan commander planned to attack the

15. Withdrawal of Peisander and others to Decelea: Thucydides 8. 98. 1; execution of Antiphon: Thucydides 8. 68. 2.

16. Thucydides 8. 92. 2, [Plutarch] *Lives of the Ten Orators* 833A.

Athenians where the straits were at their very narrowest, right off the promontory of Point Cynossema. There, he expected, he could drive the Athenians onto the shore, where they would face the onslaught of tough Peloponnesian marines. As the Athenian right wing would run to aid the center, Mindarus could station himself between them and the mouth of the Hellespont, cutting off any chance of escape. And this indeed is what should have happened. Attacking the Athenian center, the Peloponnesians drove many Athenian ships ashore, where the Peloponnesian marines followed them. At length, however, overconfident because of their victory, the Peloponnesians began to scatter in pursuit of some Athenian ships still at sea and allowed their fleet to fall into disorder. At this point Thrasybulus, who had been commanding the Athenian right, wheeled around to attack the scattered ships of the Peloponnesians. The Peloponnesians fled to Sestos, and the Syracusans, having been routed by Thrasyllus in command of the Athenian left, were quick to follow their comrades in flight. Victory fell to the Athenians—a great morale booster. Not only did the Athenians capture twenty-one ships at a loss of only fifteen of their own, but, Thucydides says, when the news arrived at Athens,

> coming as it did on top of the recent disaster in Euboea and of their political troubles, their spirits revived, and they thought they still had a chance, that if they got a firm grip on themselves, they could win through to victory in the end.[17]

The fighting off Point Cynossema is the last battle recorded in Thucydides' narrative. Here Thucydides' account of the war stops, whether because Thucydides died before he could write more or because the remainder of his superb narrative is lost.[18] There is no reason to doubt that he intended his work to conclude with the destruction of the Long Walls, where he had put the end of the hostilities at 5. 26. 1, and perhaps it did;

17. Thucydides 8. 106. 5.

18. The common view has been that Thucydides' narrative was never finished, but see now J. Rusten, "Carving Up Thucydides: The Rise and Demise of "Analysis—and Its Legacy," in *A Handbook to the Reception of Thucydides*, ed. C. Lee and N. Morley (Malden, MA: Wiley-Blackwell, 2015).

but Xenophon, who took up the story of the war in his *Hellenica*, did not seem to be aware of any surviving text.

The Battle of Cynossema was followed by further fighting at the Battle of Abydos in late 411, where the tide was turned after a day's intense and evenly matched combat at sea by the arrival toward evening of Alcibiades with eighteen ships; once more the victory went to the Athenians, who not only captured thirty Peloponnesian ships but repossessed the fifteen they had lost at Cynossema.[19] Finally, the Athenians won a decisive victory in an amphibious battle at Cyzicus, retaking the peninsula that Mindarus and Pharnabazus had seized. Our understanding of this battle is somewhat compromised by inconsistencies between the account of Xenophon, who gives the lion's share of the glory to Alcibiades, and that of Diodorus, who stresses the coordination between the several Athenian commanders—not only Alcibiades but Theramenes and Thrasybulus at sea, and Chaereas on land.[20] It is likely that Thrasybulus, architect of the previous victories at Cynossema and Abydos, was also the guiding genius at Cyzicus. There a battle of wits transpired between the Athenians, seeking to deceive the Peloponnesians into thinking they had fewer ships and men than they really did, and the Spartans, commanded by Mindarus. Combining the accounts of Xenophon and Diodorus with those found in Plutarch's *Alcibiades*, it is possible to discern the outlines of the campaign.

In the spring of 410, Mindarus, with eighty ships and the backing of Pharnabazus, had taken Cyzicus by storm. The town was located on a peninsula jutting out into the Propontis from the south in the form of an inverted triangle (see Map 10).

Setting out in three different groups, the combined fleet of Alcibiades, Theramenes, and Thrasybulus—a total of eighty-six ships—made use of the darkness to proceed unnoticed to Proconnesus, an island northwest of the peninsula. They then headed for Cyzicus itself in a rainstorm, hoping the vile weather would conceal the size of their fleet.[21] After putting

19. Xenophon *Hellenica* 1. 1. 5–7.

20. Xenophon *Hellenica* 1. 1. 14–19; Diodorus 13. 49. 2–51. 8; see also Plutarch *Alcibiades* 28.

21. Although on the whole Diodorus's treatment is preferable to that of Xenophon, the foul weather cited by Xenophon (*Hellenica* 1. 1. 16) seems to be an indispensable element of the Athenians' plan, as pointed out by D. Kagan, *The Fall of the Athenian Empire* (Ithaca, NY: Cornell University Press, 1987), 239.

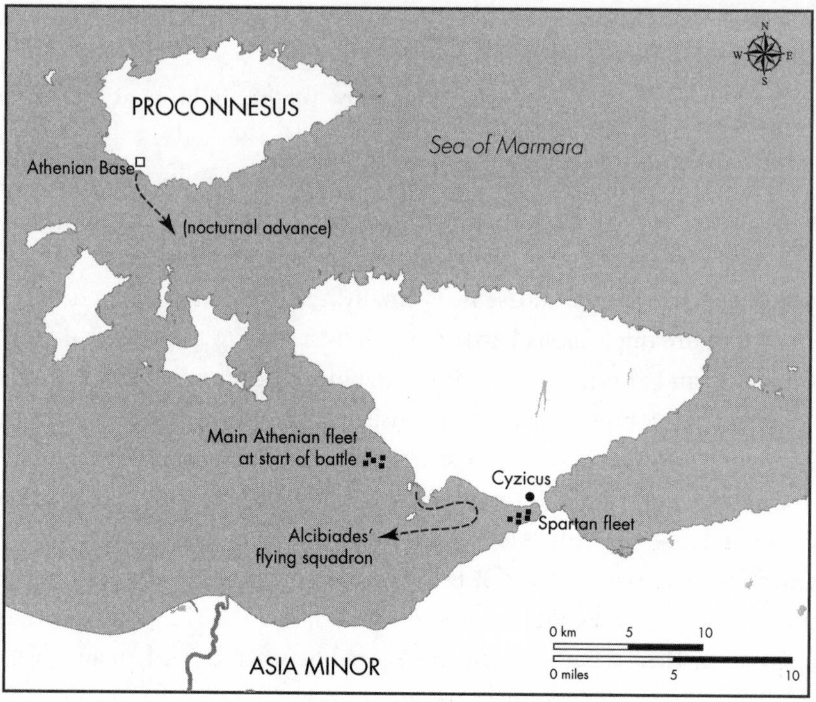

MAP 10
Region of Cyzicus.

Chaereas and his hoplites ashore to march on Cyzicus, they divided the fleet; Theramenes and Thrasybulus would each hide some ships in the small bay to the north, and Alcibiades would move straight at Cyzicus with the remaining forty ships.

Mindarus, with his eighty ships, confidently sailed against Alcibiades, apparently having no idea that he did not in reality outnumber the Athenians two to one. Alcibiades took his fleet in a feigned flight westward but then turned to face Mindarus, who was following him. In the meantime, Theramenes brought his fleet out of concealment to keep the Peloponnesians from reaching the harbor, and Thrasybulus headed out to cut off the escape route from the west. Recognizing the trap that had been sprung, Mindarus astutely headed for the beaches to the south, where Pharnabazus had stationed his forces and indeed came to his rescue, and the Athenians were hard put to drag the Peloponnesian ships off the beaches with the grappling hooks that Alcibiades provided. The battle for the ships was hard fought, as it was difficult for the Athenians to keep their footing in the muddy water even as Chaereas brought up aid.

The bloody game of cat and mouse came to an end only when the Spartan navarch found himself trapped between the troops of Alcibiades and those of Theramenes. Mindarus, Diodorus writes,

> fought nobly around the ships, taking heroic risks before all his men, but though he slew many of the opponents, in the end he was killed by the troops of Alcibiades as he battled bravely for his native land. When they saw that he had fallen, the Peloponnesians and all the allies banded together, struck with terror, and ran for it.[22]

The Athenians captured many prisoners and all the enemy's ships except for those of the Syracusans, who burned them rather than let them fall into enemy hands.[23] Alcibiades remained at Cyzicus for twenty days to collect money, and at Chrysopolis, opposite Byzantium, he set up a fort to be used as a toll station where the Athenians would collect duty on all merchant ships passing through the Bosporus.[24] The Athenians' victory at Cyzicus had been a turning point in the war. Jubilation broke out when a characteristically "laconic" message sent home by Mindarus's second-in-command Hippocrates fell into Athenian hands: "Ships lost. Mindarus dead. Men starving. Don't know what to do."[25] It was beginning to look as if the Athenians might win this war after all. The immediate threat to their food supply had been eliminated, and within just a few months the Spartans had lost some 150 ships.

SPARTA SEEKS PEACE

Predictably, the Athenians' jubilation after their three victories was matched by a corresponding dejection in Sparta. Acting now through

22. Diodorus 13. 51. 6.
23. Xenophon *Hellenica* 1. 1. 18; Diodorus 13. 51. 8.
24. Xenophon *Hellenica* 1. 1. 20–2.
25. Xenophon *Hellenica* 1. 1. 23.

Alcibiades' old family friend Endius, the Spartans sent to Athens seeking peace.[26] Plainly they were quite anxious, since this overture constituted a flagrant violation of their treaty obligations to Persia. The terms offered were simple—indeed, too simple. Each side would keep whatever territory it possessed, with the exception that the Spartans would abandon Decelea and the Athenians would give up Pylos. Prisoners would be exchanged, one Athenian for one Laconian. The problem, from the Athenian standpoint, was that the Spartans held a great deal of key territory—wealthy Rhodes, Chios, a number of places in the Hellespont, and of course nearly all of neighboring Euboea. The Athenians were divided over the proposal. Certainly it would have involved swallowing their pride to admit that they could not, after all, have everything, but they had been so close to losing everything that the proposal did have some merit. In the end they followed the lead of Cleophon, on whom the mantle of Cleon seems to have fallen: he was a brash and popular leader of the demos who, though well off, made his money in trade (in his case, a lyre factory) and was scorned by men of the upper classes. Diodorus accused him of opposing the peace for personal profit; in any case, the assembly was persuaded and voted to reject the Spartans' offer.[27]

THE DEMOCRACY RESTORED AND THE GODS HONORED

Although disinclined to make peace with Sparta, the Athenians at home had come to understand the importance of reaching an accommodation with the sailors who had won the stunning victory at Cyzicus. In or around June of 410 the Five Thousand were deposed at Athens; the government at Samos and the government at Athens were rejoined and the democracy formally restored. Now the thetes who rowed Athens' all-important ships were citizens once again. A board was established to

26. Diodorus 13. 52. 2–8.

27. Diodorus 13. 53. 1–2. Other sources for Cleophon are equally harsh. The fourth-century orator Aeschines (2. 76) claimed that he had gotten himself enrolled as a citizen by fraud but also threatened to cut the throat of any who made mention of peace.

codify and publish the laws of the Athenian democracy, and one particularly memorable one is preserved in Andocides' speech *On the Mysteries*:

> If anyone should overturn the democracy at Athens or hold any public office after it has been overturned, let him be considered a public enemy among the Athenians and someone who can be killed with impunity; his goods may be confiscated and a tithe given to the Goddess. The man who kills such a person or conspires to do so will be considered free of sin or defilement.[28]

Cleophon instituted a poor relief payment of two obols daily to men who needed it, and henceforth the men of Athens would confront the Peloponnesian menace together, not separately.

Now energies could be directed to a project that had lapsed: putting the finishing touches on the temple on the Acropolis known as the Erechtheum (see Figure 11). The Peisistratid building program had included a temple to Athena Polias, Athena of the City, on the Acropolis, but the temple had been destroyed by the Persians. Since the Peace of Nicias, the Athenians had been working in spare hours on a new temple that would stand in its place, but it would not be a temple to Athena alone, who now had both the Parthenon and the temple of Athena Nike (Athena of Victory). No, this temple would reach back to the mythology of the Bronze Age, in some cases probably even earlier, and honor a variety of gods.[29] The pressures of war (lack of money, manpower, and morale) had resulted in constant interruption of the building process, but now work would resume in earnest. The temple proved unusual in appearance not only because of its distinctive caryatid porch, with six carefully sculpted maidens seeming to hold up the roof, but because the rocky, sloping terrain on which it was built resulted in the west and north sides being nearly ten feet lower than the east and south sides.[30]

28. Andocides 1. 96–7.

29. See J. J. Pollitt, *Art and Experience in Classical Greece* (Cambridge: Cambridge University Press, 1972), 131–4, and J. Hurwit, *The Athenian Acropolis: History, Mythology, and Archaeology from the Neolithic Era to the Present* (Cambridge: Cambridge University Press, 1999), 200–209.

30. On the temple and in particular the identity of the caryatids, see A. Rubel, *Fear and Loathing in Ancient Athens: Religion and Politics during the Peloponnesian War*, trans. M. Vickers and A. Piftor (Bristol, CT: Acumen, 2014), 114–20.

FIGURE 11
Erechtheum on the Acropolis of Athens (built 421–406, with interruptions).
Credit: Caryatid porch of Erechtheum, courtesy of Shutterstock, Inc. Used by permission.

Although named for the legendary Athenian king Erechtheus, the temple also functioned as a shrine to other early kings of Athens, Cecrops and Boötes; it was believed to enclose the tombs of all three rulers.

Within the area eventually occupied by the temple were sites associated with a wide variety of ancient cults as well as the miraculous olive tree of Athena and the trident mark and salt spring of Poseidon. Athena and Poseidon were rivals for the guardianship of the city and the role of tutelary divinity of Athens, and the olive tree had sprung from the ground when Athena, defying Poseidon, had struck the rock with her spear. Also encompassed by the temple was the crevice containing the sacred serpent that embodied the child god Erichthonius (sometimes conflated with Erechtheus) and guarded the Acropolis. Cults practiced at the temple were many. Entering from the east, for example, one came to the shrine of the *xoanon*, the wooden effigy of Athena Polias that the Athenians believed had fallen from the sky.

Athena was only one among many gods and heroes the newly restored democracy would be celebrating at the Erechtheum. Finally finished in 406, the idiosyncratic building still stands today, though one of the caryatids has long been in the British Museum in London and the others have been replaced with copies; the originals were moved to the New Acropolis Museum to protect them from the elements. The caryatids caught the imagination of the West and were widely imitated—similar maidens grace the outside walls of Macy's department store at 34th Street in New York City and the porch of St. Pancras New Church on Euston Road in London.

THEATERS OF WAR

No sooner did word reach Agis at Decelea of the regime change at Athens than he decided to make another assault on the city, marching right up to the walls. This was of no consequence except to the families of the few men the alert Athenians killed; Thrasyllus led out a force of Athenians and allies that put the attackers to flight, picking off some of the rearguard.[31] But there were more serious losses on each side. The Spartan colony at Heraclea in Trachis was defeated in battle by its neighbors, losing 700 colonists and its governor Labotas.[32] When the Carthaginians invaded Sicily, moreover, to aid the Egestaeans, whom the Athenians had left helpless when they had been forced to retreat in 413, the Syracusans serving in the Peloponnesian army returned to Sicily to aid the Egestaeans' enemies the Selinuntines, depriving the Spartans of one of their ablest naval allies.[33] The Athenians suffered losses too. Even before the democratic restoration in Athens, a new civil war on Corcyra removed the Corcyraeans from the war, a serious blow to Athenian naval power.[34] An uprising in Megara endangered Athenian control of the port of Nisaea,

31. Xenophon *Hellenica* 1. 1. 33–4.
32. Xenophon *Hellenica* 1. 2. 18.
33. Diodorus 13. 43–4, 54–63.
34. Diodorus 13. 48.

and the Spartans captured the Athenian fort at Pylos, depriving Athens of a prized bargaining chip in any future negotiations.[35] The Athenians did not let either of these strongholds go easily, but their efforts to hang on to them were unsuccessful, and one commander, Anytus, was prosecuted for his failure. When the Athenians learned that the Spartans had besieged Pylos, Diodorus reports, they sent thirty ships to the aid of the Messenians there under Anytus's command. A storm, however, blew up and prevented Anytus from rounding Cape Malea, forcing him to return to Athens. Brought to trial there in 409 and fearing (like Nicias before him) for his life, Anytus was reputed to have been the first Athenian to have bribed a jury.[36] If true, this would have required an enormous outlay of money, as Athenian juries were huge, 501 at a minimum, like the jury in the trial of Socrates in 399. (Ironically, Anytus was one of the accusers of Socrates, who, as it turned out, did have reason to fear for his life.) But Anytus was a wealthy man.

In the same year Sophocles carried off the first prize at the festival of the Dionysia with the trilogy that contained *Philoctetes*. The play was an odd one in some ways, for its characters seem more like people we might meet walking down the street than the austere characters that populate most Greek tragedies. But it is very much a play one would expect during wartime, for the action is contingent on a past decision arising from a wound. En route to Troy, the master archer Philoctetes, to whom the dying Heracles had given his unerring bow, had been bitten by a snake, and the combination of his cries of agony and the foul smell of his pustulent wound prompted his fellow Greeks to abandon him on a deserted island, where he languished in misery for nearly ten years. Only when they learned from a seer that they could not take Troy without Philoctetes and his bow did they return to the island to retrieve him.

35. Diodorus 13. 64. 5–65. 4.

36. Diodorus 13. 64. 6; also Pseudo-Aristotle *Constitution of the Athenians* 27. 5. He had been a lover of the young Alcibiades (Plutarch *Alcibiades* 4. 4–5) and would go on to be one of the three accusers of Socrates at his trial in 399 (Plato *Apology* 18b). On the trial of Anytus, see M. Hansen, *Eisangelia: The Sovereignty of the People's Court in Athens in the Fourth Century B. C. and the Impeachment of Generals and Politicians. Odense University Classical Studies* Vol 6 (Odense, Denmark: Odense University Press, 1975), 84; and D. Hamel, *Athenian Generals: Military Authority in the Classical Period. Mnemosyne Supplementum 182* (Leiden: Brill, 1988), 146.

Inevitably, however, he bore them considerable ill will. How, then, could he be persuaded to help them? This, ostensibly, is the problem the play must confront, and Sophocles deals with it by having the crafty Odysseus put young Neoptolemus, son of Achilles, in charge of getting the bow away from Philoctetes (there is some uncertainty as to whether the Greeks need Philoctetes and the bow or just the bow), persuading the reluctant youth that the end of capturing Troy justifies the means of deceiving the poor man who has already been so ill-used by the Greeks.

The episode turns into a contest for the soul of Neoptolemus. It is the young man's ambivalence and his empathy for the suffering Philoctetes that give the play its poignancy. In the end, he cannot bring himself to deceive Philoctetes. Heracles, however, appears—perhaps as a vision?—and instructs Philoctetes to proceed with the bow to Troy, where he will be healed of his wound by Asklepios and capture the city hand in hand with Neoptolemus.

Philoctetes has been coupled with an earlier Sophoclean play of uncertain date, *Ajax*, in being used in therapeutic settings with modern soldiers and health professionals. Like Philoctetes, Ajax suffered as a consequence of feeling unappreciated by his comrades; when Achilles died and his armor was awarded not to him but to Odysseus, Ajax eventually went mad from actions ensuing from his trauma. Director Bryan Doerries' public health project Theater of War has presented over 300 performances of *Philoctetes* and *Ajax* throughout the United States, Europe, and Japan, giving service members and their families an opportunity to discuss their experiences with different kinds of war wounds.

Certainly Sophocles had known war at first hand, having served as a general at least once, in the bloody Samian campaign with his friend Pericles around 440. He seems to have been a committed democrat and cannot have been happy about the Four Hundred. Athens' military, however, had enjoyed divine favor in the east upon their fall. Whether the Athenians had done right to decline the Spartans' peace offer was uncertain, and one wonders what Sophocles, the former senior adviser and always one for moderation, thought about the grasping mentality that held out for more.

15

ALCIBIADES, CYRUS, AND LYSANDER

THE BATTLES AT CYNOSSEMA, Abydos, and Cyzicus had netted Athens welcome victories, but control of the straits was far from secure. The Spartans still held Sestos, Chalcedon, and Byzantium. Though ultimately the outcome of the war would be decided in the Hellespont, distractions often kept both sides occupied elsewhere; and of course the Athenians were divided about the matter of Alcibiades, whose citizenship had not yet been returned to him even though the "government in exile" at Samos had elected him general. The two coastal satraps, Tissaphernes and Pharnabazus, continued to flex their muscles, enjoying the power they wielded, until their game was brought to an abrupt end by Darius's decision to make his younger son Cyrus satrap of such a wide area as to eclipse Tissaphernes entirely. Once again, as had been the case with Brasidas, the Spartans found a charismatic military commander. At a time when both sides were in desperate need of funds to pay their men, the navarch Lysander not only showed boundless energy but struck up a lucrative friendship with the Persian prince. But even this dangerous alliance need not have presented such a threat to the Athenians' fortunes had it not been for unpredictable developments in Ionian waters.

THE BATTLE FOR THE HELLESPONT

In 409 the Athenians sent Thrasyllus out at the head of a force of fifty triremes, with 5,000 of his men equipped as peltasts and 100 cavalry;

in total, he had 11,000 men.[1] He was to see what he could accomplish in Ionia before moving north to join with Alcibiades in the Hellespont. After some minor successes, however, he was defeated at Ephesus, where he faced not only the Ephesians and their Sicilian allies but also the cavalry of Tissaphernes, who had gotten wind of his impending attack, and when the fighting ended, the Athenians had lost at least 300 men.[2]

Retreating northward after burying their dead, they caught sight of the Syracusan ships retreating from Ephesus and managed to capture four of them. Thrasyllus sent all the crews back to Athens, where—for poetic justice—they were shut up in the stone quarries at the Piraeus. The Athenians were greatly disappointed when the captives managed to dig their way out at night not long afterward.[3] One prisoner, however, was dispatched on the spot. Alcibiades' cousin, also named Alcibiades, of the deme of Phegous, who was already under sentence of death for profaning the mysteries in 415 and had thus shared the exile of his more famous relation, had been fighting along with the Syracusans, and Thrasyllus ordered him stoned to death as a traitor and enemy combatant—an unusual punishment in Athens but not unheard of in cases of treason during wartime.[4]

Thrasyllus and his men then proceeded northward to join Alcibiades' troops at Lampsacus in the narrow Hellespontine straits that divided the Aegean from the Propontis (the modern Sea of Marmara). There the combined forces set about dislodging the Peloponnesians from several key strongholds. In the combat in the Hellespont, both sides would have to exercise determination and vigilance and also think along innovative lines, and there would be no room for error. During this fighting season, it was the Athenians who showed imagination and the Spartans who made a crucial error—more specifically, perhaps, Alcibiades who showed imagination and Clearchus who made the crucial error.

1. I follow here Xenophon *Hellenica* 1. 2. 1 over Diodorus 13. 64. 1 in numbering the ships as fifty, but Diodorus mentions the 100 cavalry.

2. Xenophon *Hellenica* 1. 2. 6–9.

3. Xenophon *Hellenica* 1. 2. 11–14.

4. Xenophon *Hellenica* 1. 2. 13. See V. Rosivach, "Execution by Stoning in Athens," *Classical Antiquity* 6 (1987): 232–48.

The Athenians' siege of Chalcedon opposite Byzantium at first proceeded along traditional lines, as Athenian soldiers enclosed the rebellious city by a wooden wall and Athenian ships blockaded it by sea. When fighting broke out, the wall prevented Pharnabazus's army from joining in, and the Spartan commander Hippocrates was killed. But the Spartan army escaped into the town, creating a stalemate.[5] Because of the proximity of Pharnabazus's considerable forces, the Athenians then did something unprecedented. With Alcibiades absent in search of money wherever he could get it, Xenophon reports,

> the other generals came to an understanding with Pharnabazus that they would spare Chalcedon in exchange for a payment of twenty talents; the satrap would also conduct Athenian ambassadors to the King. Oaths were also exchanged to the effect that Chalcedon would pay the Athenians the same amount as in the past and make up all arrears of payment and that the Athenians would undertake no hostile actions against Chalcedon until the ambassadors had returned from the King.[6]

This innovative arrangement spared everyone the trouble of a siege and scored the Athenians a welcome infusion of cash.

Sitting on the north shore of the Propontis, Selymbria was also in Alcibiades' sights. Fortunately for the Selymbrians, though the determined Athenian commander had raised cash and Thracian troops in Gallipoli, he was hoping to husband his resources for the coming attack on his chief target, Byzantium, and taking their city by storm was not part of his game plan; rather he arranged for a pro-Athenian party in the town to open the gates to him during the night. The Athenians then placed a garrison in the city, collected some money, and doubled back to join Theramenes and Thrasyllus at Byzantium.[7] Founded in the seventh century primarily by colonists from Megara, Byzantium's location at the entrance to the Black Sea led it to prosper as a center of trade, and

5. Xenophon *Hellenica* 1. 3. 2–7.
6. Xenophon *Hellenica* 1. 3. 8–9.
7. Plutarch *Alcibiades* 30. 1–5.

strategically it benefited from its position as a chokepoint for the control of grain from Ukraine. It had entered the Delian League voluntarily in 478/77.

The forces in this key stronghold were about evenly matched when the Athenian generals attacked it in 408, and there seemed to be no way the Athenians could take the city by sheer force. The Peloponnesians were commanded by Clearchus, and he was the only Spartan present; the others, besides the Byzantines themselves, were Megarians (possibly because of the role of Megara in founding the city), Boeotians, perioeci, and *neodamodeis*. But the total number resisting was large, for Byzantium was a substantial city. The Athenians had built siege engines and attacked the city's fortifications both at long range and at close quarters, but to no avail.[8] In their arsenal, however, was a secret weapon: Clearchus's own disposition. Clearchus was a hardy soldier and had given the Athenians a run for their money at Cyzicus, but now at Byzantium his conduct evidently evoked that of an earlier Spartan at Byzantium, the Persian War general Pausanias, who had taken over as regent for Leonidas's underage son Pleistarchus after Leonidas's heroic death at Thermopylae and thoroughly alienated the Greeks by his arrogance.[9] Clearchus seems to have been an unpleasant man, and lacking in judgment as well. Having given all the food in the city to the Spartan and allied soldiers, he let the populace die of hunger, and wanting money to pay his troops and build ships with which to distract the Athenians, he went off in search of funds, leaving the city in the charge of subordinates.

Clearchus plainly did not believe that anyone would betray the key stronghold in the Hellespont to the Athenians, but his confidence was misplaced. A number of prominent Byzantines were so alienated that they conspired with Alcibiades to do just this. Circulating a story that the Athenians were leaving for Ionia, Alcibiades led his forces just far enough away from Byzantium to make the tale credible, but he remained

8. Xenophon *Hellenica* 1. 3. 14–15.

9. Clearchus at Cyzicus, Diodorus 13. 51. 1–4; his disposition, Diodorus 13. 66. 6; Pausanias after the Persian Wars, Thucydides 1. 95. 1–3.

close enough to return at night to attack the Peloponnesian ships in the harbor. When fighting broke out between those loyal to Athens and those persevering in their fidelity to Sparta, Alcibiades issued a proclamation guaranteeing the safety of the Byzantines if they would lay down their arms. They did so—not before killing a good number of the Peloponnesian army—and were then returned to their status as an Athenian ally; no Byzantine was killed or exiled, and the city was not garrisoned. Plainly the Athenians were practicing a gentler policy with the idea of paving the way for peace.[10]

Their request at Chalcedon for a parley with Darius had reflected those hopes for peace. The Spartans, after all, had violated their treaty with the Persians by offering to make a separate peace with Athens. Would the king perhaps now be receptive to overtures from the other side in the conflict?

Unfortunately, the Athenian ambassadors had nothing to offer him, for unlike the Spartans, they possessed territory in Ionia that paid them tribute, and they were not about to give it up. What could have come of a conference with Darius, one cannot imagine. Perhaps the Athenians simply wished to call the king's attention to the Spartans' perfidy in offering them a separate peace and to dissuade him from further subsidizing them. But no such meeting ever took place, for on their journey—which Pharnabazus saw to it was a slow and laborious one—they encountered the Spartan Boeotius and his fellow ambassadors returning from Darius's court, and they brought bad news: the Spartans, they reported, "had gotten everything they wanted from the King."[11] Worse yet, the Spartans were accompanied by their new ally Cyrus, the king's son, who carried with him a letter from his father explaining that the sixteen-year-old youth would henceforth be taking charge of much of the coastal area and helping the Spartans in the war.[12] Thus the Athenians found their substantial military gains offset by a notable diplomatic—and financial—loss.

10. Xenophon *Hellenica* 1. 3. 16–19; Diodorus 13. 66. 6.
11. Xenophon *Hellenica* 1. 4. 2.
12. Xenophon *Hellenica* 1. 4. 3.

THE PRODIGAL SON RETURNS

Despite this setback, the road to Athens now lay open for Alcibiades—or at the very least, he thought it safe to test the waters. He had achieved remarkable military successes since abandoning his foreign allegiances and fighting on the Athenian side. Yet he had lived for years in limbo, accepted first only by the government in exile at Samos and then only by the government of the Five Thousand. Who could be certain that his signal services to the city would guarantee him reinstatement by the democracy that had sentenced him to death, cursed him, and confiscated his property? He proceeded home cautiously, stopping in Caria to raise money (though probably not the full 100 talents claimed by Xenophon), and then went to Gytheum in the southern Peloponnesus, the chief naval base of Laconia, partly to scope out Spartan shipbuilding activities but primarily to wait out the election season in Athens and take the temperature of the demos: were he and his friends in favor?[13] Events proved that they were. He and Thrasybulus, as well as his fellow demesman Adeimantus, who had shared his exile with him, had all been elected to the generalship. Upon hearing this news, he proceeded to Athens. But he was still edgy about the reception that might await him there, and he remained on the deck of his ship until he caught sight of a welcoming coterie of friends and relations. Only then did he disembark and go up to the city, cautiously accompanied by bodyguards.[14] He was plainly a very nervous man.

As he walked, Plutarch says, the old pointed him out to the young, and his presence evoked regret about his exile, sparking the thought that the Sicilian expedition would not have miscarried if he had only been left in charge. For now that he had returned to the Athenian fold, "he had taken the city when it had almost been driven from the sea, when on land it was scarcely able to control its own suburbs, and when discord was rife within its walls, and had raised it up from this wretched plight, not only restoring its rule over the sea, but actually leading it to victory over its enemies everywhere on land."[15] Addressing the Council and the

13. Xenophon *Hellenica* 1. 4. 8, 12.
14. Xenophon *Hellenica* 1. 4. 19.
15. Plutarch *Alcibiades* 32. 5.

assembly, he proclaimed his innocence of all charges brought against him. Diplomatically, he complained of his lot while placing the primary blame for his misfortunes on a certain evil demon of his own rather than individual Athenians. He then wisely turned to the future, exhorting his listeners to high hopes. His calculated rhetoric bore fruit: he was voted crowns of gold and made commander-in-chief, with authority over the other nine generals; the stelae on which the sentence against him was carved were thrown into the sea, the cash value of his confiscated property was restored to him, and the Eleusinian priests (under compulsion) grudgingly withdrew the curses they had placed on him.[16]

As the summer sailing season was at hand, it might have seemed good to Alcibiades to set off at once for eastern waters, but he had unfinished business in Attica. Having lost track of the calendar in his anxiety, he had inadvertently sailed into the Piraeus on the most ill-omened day of the entire Athenian year.[17] For this day, on which the Athenians celebrated the festival of the Plynteria, was considered so inauspicious that all sanctuaries were generally shut, with a barrier of rope placed across the entrances to prevent access. All enterprises undertaken on the day of the Plynteria were held to be ill-fated. The protection of Athena was not available to the city at this time, for the Plynteria was the Festival of Washing, and on this day the ancient wooden statue of Athena Polias (Athena of the City) had its robes and ornaments removed by the women of the family of the Praxiergidae and was taken from the temple for ritual cleansing. The statue was then carried in procession to the nearby port of Phalerum to be purified in the salt sea; the goddess's robe may have been washed by a special laundress as well. The procession returned by the light of torches, after which the statue was dressed again with its robe and jewelry.[18]

This day, when the city was virtually shut down for religious reasons, was the worst possible day for Alcibiades to have returned to his home, and his careless mistake in forgetting about the religious rite may have lent new urgency to a previously conceived plan: he would wipe out the stain of his conviction on charges of religious transgression in 415 by

16. Plutarch *Alcibiades* 33. 2–3; Diodorus 13. 69. 1–3.
17. Xenophon *Hellenica* 1. 4. 12; Plutarch *Alcibiades* 34. 1.
18. H. W. Parke, *Festivals of the Athenians* (Ithaca, NY: Cornell University Press, 1977), 152–5.

conducting a newly energized procession of worshippers overland to Eleusis. Since 413, the presence of a Spartan army at Decelea had forced the Athenians greatly to truncate the celebration of the mysteries, compelling them to make the journey to the shrine of the two goddesses by water instead of by land in order to avoid a Spartan attack; this prevented the Athenians from carrying out many of the cherished rituals that the procession normally performed along the way. Now, however, Alcibiades resurrected the age-old overland procession with all its elaborate pomp, stationing lookouts on the hills and furnishing an armed guard.[19] Those who were not hostile to him even hailed him as High Priest of the parade. As the Spartans made no move to interfere, many Athenians were confirmed in their belief that Alcibiades was surrounded by a force field of sorts that had rendered him a magical charm for the city's success.[20]

Only when this act of piety, Nicias-like in its ostentation, had been completed was Alcibiades voted a force to take east: 100 triremes, 1,500 hoplites, and 150 cavalry.[21] At his first stop, the island of Andros, he managed to secure a fort but failed to take the island, leaving his enemies in Athens glowering. If this small disappointment set people off, far worse was to come.[22] Arriving at the coast of Asia Minor, he found the situation there totally transformed, for the ambitious prince Cyrus, who sought to succeed his father as king, had found an ally in the equally ambitious Lysander, Sparta's new navarch. Lysander was more than twice Cyrus's age, but he and the youngster got on spectacularly, and their rapport spelled serious trouble for the Athenians.

THE RISE OF LYSANDER

Although it was natural for Darius to be pondering a shake-up of the coastal satrapies, as Tissaphernes did not seem to be overseeing them effectively, Cyrus had not been the natural choice for someone to take over

19. Xenophon *Hellenica* 1. 4. 20; Plutarch *Alcibiades* 34. 2–5.
20. Plutarch *Alcibiades* 34. 6.
21. Xenophon *Hellenica* 1. 4. 21.
22. Xenophon *Hellenica* 1. 4. 22; Diodorus 13. 69. 4.–5; Plutarch *Alcibiades* 35. 1.

all Tissaphernes' previous territory; nonetheless Darius had made him lord over Lydia, Greater Phrygia, and Cappadocia, leaving Tissaphernes with only Caria. Among other experienced officials, Darius had an older son, Arsaces. But Darius's half-sister and queen, Parysatis, did not care for her first-born son, nor for his strong-minded wife Statira (whom she eventually murdered), whereas she had great ambitions for Cyrus.[23] The youth had many enemies at court, Statira included, and he needed a friend on the outside if he was to advance himself despite his place in the birth order. His short-term goal was to gain his father's favor by driving the Athenians out of his royal lands, a task at which Tissaphernes had failed so conspicuously; in the long term, he had an eye out for someone who might provide an army if he needed to win the throne by fighting for it. And so he was all too happy to meet with Lysander and his colleagues at Sardis and hear what the Spartan had to say.

Though also a schemer, Lysander was raised in very different circumstances. Unlike Cyrus, he had not been born close to the center of power. To be sure, he was of distinguished lineage, but his aristocratic father had evidently fallen into poverty. From an early age he was focused on getting what he wanted, cultivating men of influence, and putting up with no small amount of condescension in men of authority to gain his ends.[24] One early decision had a profound effect on the rest of his life. It was customary in Greece for boys of twelve or thirteen (perhaps a little older given the later start of puberty) to take older lovers who would function as mentors. Intellectuals whose writings have survived, like Xenophon and Plato, insisted that these friendships were not overtly sexual, but they were not being truthful. These relationships were very often physical, with the men courting the boys with gifts and the boys rewarding them with sexual favors. Although it seems to have been unfashionable for the sexual aspect of the connection to persist after the boy grew a beard, the older man continued to function as a counselor and role model to the youth. This kind of relationship formed an important part of the education of certain elite boys in Athens, where the state provided

23. The murder of Statira: Plutarch *Artaxerxes* 19. 1–5.
24. Plutarch *Lysander* 2. 3.

no public education, and also in Sparta, where it did. The older partner, the "lover," was expected to provide guidance in citizenship to the younger, the "beloved." Involvement in such a relationship in no way precluded relationships with women; all Greek men were expected to marry, although some, like Plato, did not.

The boy whom Lysander chose for his beloved was probably not selected for his charm or beauty but rather for the political advantage he would confer. He was none other than the Eurypontid Agesilaus, half-brother of King Agis. The greatest testament to Lysander's magnetism is that the royal prince, who surely had many suitors, should have accepted his overtures. The sheer nerve of Lysander's courtship of Agesilaus was astounding. One might imagine too that Agis would have taken a dim view of the intrusion of this upstart into his family. Fortunately for Lysander, however, there were no hard feelings. He and Agis saw eye to eye on many things, and they found themselves working together as political allies for years to come.

Lysander, of whom it was said that he made a point of cheating "boys with knucklebones and men with oaths," was a complex package of arrogance and obsequiousness.[25] It was probably a combination of these qualities that he showed to the Persian prince whom he met at Sardis after spending some time building Ephesus into a solid naval base and training his crews. Cyrus for his part reported that his father had instructed him to take an energetic part in the war and that he had brought 500 talents with him; if this did not prove sufficient, he said—echoes of Tissaphernes here—he would break up his own throne of gold and silver and put the money to use for the war. When Lysander asked Cyrus to double the pay of his rowers, however, Cyrus, embarrassed, had to backpedal. He had promised more than his father had authorized him to deliver. This would mean raising their pay from three obols to six, a total of one drachma, and Cyrus did not actually have that much money. But after dinner, when Cyrus asked the navarch what he could do that would please him most, Lysander replied that he would please him most if he would add one obol to the pay of each sailor. This Cyrus dared to do

25. Plutarch *Lysander* 8. 4.

without authorization from his father; he also agreed to pay all arrears and give a month's pay in advance. Now Lysander was in a good position to encourage desertions from the Athenian fleet.[26] Alarmed by news of this conference, the Athenians made a last-ditch effort to meet with Cyrus, but the prince dismissed the possibility out of hand.

AN ACCIDENTAL BATTLE AND THE FALL OF ALCIBIADES

Though the next battle of the war had dramatic consequences, it was not planned by the high command on either side. After his meeting with Cyrus, Lysander returned to his fleet at Ephesus. Alcibiades meanwhile, having sailed down the coast of Asia Minor to raise money, had established himself in a sheltered cove just to the north of Ephesus at Notium. As Lysander showed no signs of wishing to fight, after a month or so Alcibiades headed up to Phocaea, under siege by Thrasybulus. Perhaps if the Athenians could persuade Lysander that Phocaea was under threat, the Spartans would move that way and engage the Athenian fleet. Bringing his land forces on the troop carriers to join Thrasybulus in the siege of Phocaea, Alcibiades left the triremes in the command of his pilot, Antiochus, a personal friend of long standing: Antiochus's claim on his affections dated to the occasion when he caught the quail that had escaped from under Alcibiades' cloak during its unexpected visit to the assembly many years before.[27] This choice of a commander spelled the end of Alcibiades' career.

Alcibiades' decision may have been reasonable, but it was provocative. Although Antiochus may have been a skilled seaman, more skilled even than any of the trierarchs on the spot, some of whom were simply rich men who had the funds to outfit a ship, he had never commanded a fleet before. To be sure, Alcibiades left him with strict instructions under no

26. Xenophon *Hellenica* 1. 5. 2–7.

27. Xenophon *Hellenica* 1. 5. 11; Diodorus 13. 71. 1; Plutarch *Alcibiades* 35. 4. On the quail, Plutarch *Alcibiades* 10. 1.

circumstances to engage with Lysander's ships should they remain at Notium. Still, leaving the fleet in the command of a friend rather than a general or a trierarch looked bad.[28] Could he not have left one of his fellow generals behind in charge? Indeed, Alcibiades should not have left his fleet unattended in the first place. Because of the higher pay the Peloponnesians were offering, the Athenians were hemorrhaging sailors. Though Lysander had ninety ships to Alcibiades' eighty, Thrasybulus had thirty ships at Phocaea, and drawing some down from there should have been a priority since time favored the Spartans. Altogether, Alcibiades chose poorly, and while he was gone, something went seriously wrong.

Hoping to impress his friend with a dazzling fait accompli on his return, Antiochus disobeyed Alcibiades' orders. Just what he did was the object of disagreement among the ancient sources, and it remains so among modern historians.[29] Xenophon and Plutarch report that he led two vessels past the prows of Lysander's ships with taunting words and gestures, whereupon Lysander put out with a few of his own craft to chase him; then when the Athenians came to the aid of their ships Lysander sent out the whole fleet, and captured many ships. Xenophon reports that fifteen ships were taken; Plutarch says that Antiochus was killed.[30]

Other ancient narratives tell a more persuasive story. In their narratives, Antiochus headed for Ephesus at the head of ten ships, instructing the remainder of the fleet to remain at Notium waiting until he and his comrades had drawn the Spartans out some distance from Ephesus. Then presumably the Athenian fleet would have a chance to move in and cut them off from their base. This, however, did not happen. Having learned from deserters that Alcibiades was away and could not be leading the attack, Lysander immediately zeroed in on the lead ship and sank it, killing Antiochus. Seeing the remainder of their ships fleeing, the bulk of

28. Plutarch *Alcibiades* 35. 5.

29. For modern treatments of the Battle of Notium, see D. Kagan, *The Fall of the Athenian Empire* (Ithaca, NY: Cornell University Press, 1987), 310–20; W. Ellis, *Alcibiades* (London: Routledge, 1989), 91–3; J. F. Lazenby, *The Peloponnesian War: A Military Study* (London: Routledge, 2004), 219–21; P. J. Rhodes, *Alcibiades: Athenian Playboy, General and Traitor* (Barnsley: Pen & Sword, 2011), 89–90.

30. Xenophon *Hellenica* 1. 5. 12–14; Plutarch *Alcibiades* 35. 5–6.

the Athenian fleet then set out to the rescue, but in considerable disorder, with the result that Lysander's flotilla proved victorious. Diodorus claims that the Spartans captured twenty-two ships, though most of the vessels were seized sufficiently close to land that the majority of the sailors were able to swim to safety rather than be taken prisoner.[31]

Whatever happened in the waters between Ephesus and Notium on that day, the consequences for the recently reinstated Alcibiades were disastrous. He sought to restore his reputation by bringing Lysander to battle, but the clever navarch knew better than to risk undoing the recent disgrace of his opposite number on the Athenian side. Alcibiades then attacked little Cyme, hoping to accomplish something for Athens, but Cyme seems to have been an allied city (though he accused it of disloyalty), and the Cymaeans not only succeeded in driving him off but promptly complained of him to the Athenians.[32] Now Alcibiades was out of options, and accusations against him accumulated quickly. Those who had always been skeptical about his esoteric brand of patriotism felt vindicated in their doubts. In addition to the Cymaeans, Thrasybulus of Collytus (not to be confused with the great general Thrasybulus of Steiria) set sail from Samos for Athens to denounce him. Alcibiades, he said, had put in charge a man whose only skills lay in drinking and telling sailors' tales, and he had done so that he might be free not only to cruise around collecting money but to engage in his own drunken revelry and sexual excesses with the women who could be had for pay in Abydos and Ionia—and all this with an enemy fleet close by.[33] Others accused him of conspiring with Pharnabazus. Also suspicious was the fact that he had constructed fortresses for himself in Thrace in the event of emergency; people could hardly help wondering just what sort of emergency he foresaw.[34] A motion for his deposition from the generalship was consequently passed in the assembly.[35] With a heavy heart, he elected to withdraw into exile once again, only a few months after he

31. Diodorus 13. 71.
32. Diodorus 13. 73. 3–6.
33. Plutarch *Alcibiades* 36 1–2.
34. Diodorus 13. 73. 6; Plutarch *Alcibiades* 36. 2; Nepos *Alcibiades* 7. 7. 3-4.
35. Plutarch *Lysander* 5.2.

had been welcomed home with such enthusiasm. He could only imagine what public charges and private lawsuits might await him on his return. The priests of Eleusis could not have been happier.

A legend in his own mind, Alcibiades was not a good team player. But he was a better than average commander and an exceptional diplomat, and Athens would feel his loss. Indeed, some seem to have felt it immediately. Just a year after Alcibiades' removal from office, Aristophanes' *Frogs* won first prize at the Lenaean festival. In that play Alcibiades figured prominently in a dialogue set in Hades. As Dionysus presides over a contest for the underworld Chair of Tragedy between Aeschylus and Euripides, now both dead, the god asks the two poets what advice they have to give Athens about Alcibiades. Aeschylus replies:

And what does the city think about him?
DIONYSUS: Well, it longs for him, it hates him, it really wants to have him. Now you two tell me what you think about him.
EURIPIDES: I have no use for the citizen who will prove to be slow to aid his country, quick to do her great harm, resourceful for himself, a bungler for the city.
DIONYSUS: Well said, by Poseidon! Now what's your opinion, Aeschylus?
AESCHYLUS: It's better not to rear a lion cub in the city.
But if you do . . . be prepared to cater to its ways.
DIONYSUS: By Zeus the Savior, I can't make up my mind. One of you spoke wisely, and the other clearly.[36]

The conversation then turns to other solutions for Athens' pressing wartime difficulties. Plainly Alcibiades was still a hot topic in Athens after his departure, but despite his talents, he had done too much harm to be invited back; talk about him was just that—talk.

36. Aristophanes *Frogs*, ll. 1424–34.

16

A SEEMING VICTORY

History is full of ironies. The fall of Alcibiades brought with it the temporary eclipse of his colleagues Theramenes and Thrasybulus, who were not returned to the generalship for the following year. This, however, was a good thing for both them and the city: since the *strategia* of 406/5 brought death or exile to most of those who held it, and Theramenes and Thrasybulus went on to play important parts in the history of the democracy, it may be just as well that they were out of office that year. Although the Athenians won a stunning naval victory in 406 off the Arginusae Islands against the idealistic young navarch Callicratidas, the failure of their eight admirals to retrieve the bodies of sailors living and dead from the choppy waters led to the execution of the six who returned to Athens, their deaths arising from an illegal trial, a procedure over which the assembly president, chosen by lot, refused to preside. (He happened to be the philosopher Socrates.) Having lost some 5,000 men—and six generals—in this great "victory," the Athenians had one more battle in them. Caught napping (some of them literally) on the shore at Aegospotami in the Hellespont by Lysander, the Athenians were captured in a battle that was not much of a battle. The fleet was now gone, the grain route to the Black Sea cut off, and thus the war seemingly over. All that remained to be negotiated was the terms of surrender, a process in which Theramenes would take the lead. The turnaround from the remarkable moment of victory after the defeat of Callicratidas at Arginusae could not have been greater. Yet time would show that the Athenians had fight in them yet.

A NEW KIND OF NAVARCH

To Lysander's bitter regret, the navarchy was a one-year term. He did not plan to welcome his successor warmly, and he primed his men not to welcome him either. Before leaving office he had already gathered various prominent individuals to Ephesus and encouraged them to form *hetairiai* in their own cities, assuring them that once the Athenian empire was destroyed, assuming he was in power, they could rid themselves of their democracies and rule in their stead.[1] The man sent out to replace Lysander was Callicratidas—the most just man, Diodorus said, among the Spartans, lacking in guile and straightforward in character.[2] The sailors groused mightily about having to serve under him until he gathered them together, pointed out that he would have been happy to stay home but had been charged by the state with commanding them, and inquired whether they preferred that he stay or that he sail back to Sparta and report on the insubordination he had found in the ranks.

Not surprisingly, none of the sailors suggested that he return to Sparta with tales of the demoralization rife among them.[3] But Callicratidas's problems went way beyond a lack of loyalty in his men. There was also the question of money. Lysander had not only instructed the men to give weak allegiance to his successor; instead of handing over to Callicratidas the money he had received from Cyrus, in an act that smacks of not only arrogance but out and out treason, he simply returned it to Cyrus. Callicratidas, then, was forced to go begging to the Persian prince for funds with which to pay his men. When Cyrus put him off and told him to wait two days, he was livid. It was a dark day, he said, when Greeks had to grovel before foreigners for the sake of money, adding that if he got home unscathed, he would do his best to bring about peace between Athens and Sparta. Then, having sent home to Sparta for funds, he sailed to Miletus, where he knew there was opposition to his leadership, and

1. Plutarch *Lysander* 5. 3–4.
2. Diodorus 13. 76. 2.
3. Xenophon *Hellenica* 1. 6. 5–6.

delivered such a rousing speech that his erstwhile opponents went out of their way to give him cash out of their own pockets.[4]

Callicratidas's protestations of devotion to the cause of panhellenic peace were sincere. He lacked a distinguished pedigree and had not risen to the position of navarch without royal support. Lysander had won the friendship of Agis by his relationship with young Agesilaus and entrance into the inner circle of the Eurypontid dynasty, which strongly advocated war with Athens and would later advocate war with Persia (though Agis's father Archidamus had not desired an Athenian war). But Sparta, of course, had two royal families, and the Agiad family to which Pleistoanax and his son Pausanias belonged took a very different position with respect to Sparta's foreign policy. Pleistoanax had spent much of his life in exile as a punishment for making peace with Pericles in 446/5. When he returned in the mid-420s, he worked steadily for the agreement that eventually turned into the Peace of Nicias, and after his death in 409, his son and successor Pausanias not only inherited his father's inclination to peace with Athens but developed a marked hostility to Lysander. Time would soon show that neither the arrogant navarch's personal ambitions within Sparta—there was some evidence that he wanted to change the constitution so as to throw the kingship open to election, and Pausanias could well imagine whom he had in mind for the job—nor his foreign policy, which involved an overseas foreign empire, were congenial to the new Agiad king. If Agis had chosen Lysander to prosecute the war, there is every reason to think that Pausanias had chosen Callicratidas to see what he could do to bring about peace.

This, however, could happen only after a settlement had been reached on the seas. Even at war, Callicratidas was hesitant to sell non-Athenian captives into slavery: when he captured Methymna on Lesbos, he resisted pressure from his allies and sold only the prisoners who had been slaves before. To the new Athenian commander-in-chief Conon, however, he sent the following bold message: "I am going to put a stop to your fornication with the sea. She belongs to me."[5] And with his 170 ships

4. Xenophon *Hellenica* 1. 6. 6–12.
5. Xenophon *Hellenica* 1. 6. 14–15.

the inexperienced young navarch blockaded the seasoned admiral at nearby Mytilene in short order, taking thirty of his ships and leaving him with forty.

Conon was in a state of great alarm. His food supplies would soon run out, and if the Peloponnesians were to take his fleet, the war would essentially be over. It was vital to get word of his plight to Athens, but how?

Choosing two of his fastest ships and manning them with his most skillful rowers, he sent them out at midday when the Spartans were least vigilant, some of them even asleep. One he directed to make for the Hellespont, another for the open sea. The unfortunate crewmen of the decoy ship heading for the sea were indeed captured, but the vessel speeding to the Hellespont soon executed a sharp turn when the time came and made for Athens, arriving safely with the news of the danger to Conon's position.[6]

The panicked Athenians immediately recognized their peril and acted accordingly. Now was the time for all good men to come to the aid of their country—indeed, women as well, for it was they who diligently wove the long bolts of linen cloth that others would stitch together into sails in the massive new shipbuilding program. Within thirty days the fleet of some thirty ships had swelled to more than 100.[7] Money too had to be found with which to pay the crews. The gold on the statue of Nike—Victory—on the Acropolis was melted down and coined for the occasion.[8] Reaching both up and down, the Athenians besought their highest-status citizens who would ordinarily serve as hoplites and cavalrymen to swallow their pride and serve in the fleet; they offered citizenship to any slave who would row as well, somehow finding a way to compensate their masters for their lost "property."[9] (Hoplites had sailed on the mission to put down the Mytilene revolt, but not the cavalry class.) This was certainly not the first time slaves had been actively involved in the war, of course—they had plainly fought for many states

6. Xenophon *Hellenica* 1. 6. 19–22.

7. Xenophon *Hellenica* 1. 6. 24.

8. Aristophanes *Frogs* l. 720 with scholion.

9. Xenophon *Hellenica* 1. 6. 24; Aristophanes *Frogs* ll. 33, 693–4 with scholia.

both on land and in the navy—but for the Athenians to offer citizenship was a major concession, for it violated the principle of narrowly held citizenship literally "grounded" in the myth that Athenians were descended from men originally sprung from the very soil of Attica.[10] For the higher born, service in the navy was a dreadful prospect. Life as a rower was strenuous enough for the thetes who were used to it but far more so for those completely unaccustomed to the seawater pouring in through the oarholes, the callused hands and blistered buttocks, the bodily excrescences pouring down from the rowers above them. And rowing entailed far more than the delivery of soldiers to battle; rowers would be themselves battling in the sea fight to come, ramming enemy ships in the maneuver known as the *diekplous* and suffering ramming themselves as the bronze prows of Peloponnesian vessels slammed through their ships—or their bodies. Then there was the question of pay. Would it really be there at the end of their service? It was well known that sailors had sometimes turned up to ask for it and found it lacking. For the slaves, though, the prospect of rowing for freedom was a glorious deliverance well worth the suffering—or so it seemed at first.

SAILING INTO HADES

It was this untrained fleet—amateur sailors, steersmen, captains—hastily thrown together that sailed for the Athenian naval base at Samos and from there, having picked up additional ships, faced the Peloponnesian flotilla commanded by young Callicratidas off the Arginusae islands near Lesbos. Scanning the horizon, Callicratidas's pilot, the Megarian Hermon, saw trouble. There were plainly far more Athenian triremes than expected; the Peloponnesians were badly outnumbered.

10. Slaves and freed slaves had been fighting in the war on both sides for some time—consider all those helots and *neodamodeis*—but this was the first massive use of slaves on the Athenian side. See P. Hunt, *Slaves, Warfare, and Ideology in the Greek Historians* (Cambridge: Cambridge University Press, 1998). For the Athenians' attachment to the notion that they were literally sprung from the earth, see V. Rosivach, "Autochthony and the Athenians," *Classical Quarterly* n. s. 37 (1987): 294–306.

Though Hermon could not take a precise count, the truth was that the Athenians had 155 ships to the Peloponnesians' 120, a dramatic discrepancy. Hermon advised Callicratidas to sail away and fight at another time and place of his own choosing. But Callicratidas would hear none of it. Sparta, he said, would be none the worse for his death, but to flee would be shameful.[11]

Fully eight of Athens' ten generals were present at the battle, and they had given much thought to their strategy. Their numerical superiority was the only thing that might save the Athenians. What Hermon and Callicratidas saw before them was a long line of ships, thirty-five in the center and sixty on each wing—but the wings were arranged in a double line with a doubly wide gap between them, so that if a Peloponnesian ship should attempt to slip between two ships in the front line and turn to ram one in the *diekplous*, a vessel from the rear line could move up and prevent it. Similarly, the doubled gap between the ships prevented another common maneuver, the *periplous*, or encirclement: it extended the Athenian line well beyond that of the Peloponnesians.

Not surprisingly, Callicratidas commanded the Spartan right wing. The Athenian generals were spread out throughout their formation. The fighting began early in the morning and went on for hours. Finally, Diodorus reports, having disabled a number of enemy ships, Callicratidas was killed when his ship rammed a trireme commanded by Pericles the Younger, son of Aspasia and the famous Pericles. The famous statesman's son, finding the two ships stuck tightly together, responded quickly to his danger by casting an iron grappling hook onto Callicratidas' ship, enabling his men to board it, killing the Peloponnesian crew. Callicratidas fought nobly but was eventually killed.[12] The fighting continued for some time after that, but eventually the Peloponnesian vessels dispersed. Giddy with their success, the Athenians saw an opportunity to turn their victory into a knockout blow against the Spartans by diminishing their navy as much as possible. This project proved tragic in its consequences. For in their determination to pursue and capture—or disable—as many

11. Xenophon *Hellenica* 1. 6. 32.
12. Diodorus 13. 99. 4-6.

Peloponnesian ships as they could, the Athenians spread their own vessels over a much wider space than the already large area of the original sea fight. This meant that when the time came to retrieve their own sailors, living and dead, from the water, the men were spread over some two square miles of ocean. The generals conferred about how best to handle the situation—another Spartan fleet, after all, was nearby, blockading Conon on Lesbos—and decided to divide the Athenian fleet in two, some ships heading out to encounter the fleet that was bottling Conon up in Mytilene and others setting out to retrieve the men from the water. (The generals were well aware, Diodorus points out, that the Athenians did not take well to letting the dead go unburied, though of course some were still alive.)[13] At that point a strong wind arose. The men in charge of the rescue operations, Theramenes and Thrasybulus—respected trierarchs who had plenty of experience serving as generals in the past—could not persuade the fearful and exhausted crews to brave the high waves.[14]

The Spartans had lost seventy-seven ships, a staggering percentage of the fleet they had brought to the battle, but the Athenians had lost twenty-five, and on those ships there were thousands of men. When the victory was first announced in Athens, there was great jubilation, but discovery that the men who had won it still lay rotting in the water brought a reaction of a very different kind. The relatives of the lost wanted to know how this could possibly have happened, and the generals were deposed and summoned home to give an accounting of themselves. Two, Protomachus and Aristogenes, wisely turned their prows in the opposite direction and sailed away, choosing not to deal with the wrath of the Athenian demos. The other six returned to Athens.[15] There accusations and blame erupted furiously; though the generals were sometimes able to keep the focus on the storm, at other times anger shifted between the generals and the trierarchs, who the generals were convinced had first planted suspicion about their responsibility for the disaster. It was decided that the generals would be tried by the assembly, not an unusual procedure in the event

13. Diodorus 13. 100. 1.
14. Diodorus 13. 100. 2.
15. Xenophon *Hellenica* 1. 7. 1–2.

of a very serious case. There they alternately blamed the trierarchs and the storm.[16]

The assembly met outdoors, of course, on the Pnyx, making it difficult to count votes in darkness. Thus as the hour grew late the matter was adjourned for the day, and the Council was instructed to draw up a motion prescribing just how the generals should be tried. Before this could happen, however, the festival of the Apaturia intervened. This was a traditional yearly festival rich in sentiment in which family ties were stressed, and inevitably it heightened the Athenians' sense of bereavement. At the next meeting of the assembly, a member of the Council named Callixeinus proposed that the generals' guilt or innocence be determined by a single vote and that if they were convicted they should be executed.[17] Euryptolemus, a relative of Pericles the Younger, was among several who pointed out that Callixeinus's proposal was illegal, violating as it did the "decree of Cannonus," a recognized Athenian usage that specified a regular defense and, presumably, a separate trial for each defendant.[18] Euryptolemus made a rousing speech, and the vote that was then taken supported his position, but when one Menecles lodged an objection on some unknown technicality, the motion of Callixeinus passed instead. Although the assembly had been leaning toward the view that the generals were simply victims of the bad weather, the commanders were now tried *en bloc* and found guilty, and the six who had made the mistake of returning to Athens were executed at once.[19] In vain had the member of the Council who was chosen by lot to preside that day refused to put such an illegal motion to a vote. He was the philosopher Socrates, in the first and last public office he ever held. But somehow the motion was rammed through.[20]

16. Xenophon *Hellenica* 1. 7. 3–6.

17. Xenophon *Hellenica* 1. 7. 8–10. It may be that this Callixeinus was a tool of oligarchs and/or Spartans who did not wish the democracy well and sought to eliminate six of their most gifted generals in one fell swoop.

18. Xenophon *Hellenica* 1. 7. 12; 20–2.

19. Xenophon *Hellenica* 1. 7. 34.

20. On the battle and the ensuing trial of the generals, see A. Andrewes, "The Arginousai Trial," *Phoenix* 28 (1974): 112–22, and D. Hamel, *The Battle of Arginusae: Victory at Sea and Its Tragic Aftermath in the Final Years of the Peloponnesian War* (Baltimore: Johns Hopkins University Press, 2015). It is unclear how Socrates' objections were circumvented—by waiting for the next day or by simply ignoring them.

So died the son of Athens' foremost statesman; Thrasyllus and Diomedon, who had served the democracy again and again; and three other loyal public servants. Some Athenian generals may have been sentenced to death for failure in battle before, but if so, they had managed to escape into exile, including Thucydides himself.[21] These men were the first actually to be executed; they would not be the last. Though what the Athenian assembly did was horrendous, it must be understood in context. In part, it can be explained in terms of the strains of a long war. In part, too, the reason lies in the Greeks' piety with respect to assuring proper burial rites for the dead. It is not only in fifth-century tragedy that we see the importance of these rites to the Greeks. Both Homeric poems offer conspicuous examples. In a dramatic scene in the *Iliad*, Priam, wanting to bury his son Hector, appears most unexpectedly in the tent of Achilles to beg for Hector's body, which the great-hearted Achilles, now restored to himself, grants to him.[22] In his round-trip journey to the underworld in the *Odyssey*, Odysseus finds himself startled to encounter his old comrade Elpenor and learn that he had died in a fall on the island of the witch Circe. At Elpenor's request, Odysseus dutifully returns to the island, locates and burns his body and armor, and builds him a tomb.[23] Real-life examples were not lacking either: when, after a victorious battle near the village of Solygeia, the pious Nicias discovered that he had inadvertently left two of his men unburied, he requested permission of the enemy to collect their bodies, even though he knew that this was tantamount to an acknowledgment of defeat.[24] In fact, one reason Greeks dreaded death by drowning was precisely that they feared the fate of their "shades" in Hades, wandering endlessly, if they lacked burial rites.[25]

21. See the catalogue in D. Hamel, *Athenian Generals: Military Authority in the Classical Period. Mnemosyne Supplementum 182* (Leiden: Brill, 1998). Hamel counts Aristarchus as a general executed at some point in the years prior to Arginusae (Lycurgus 1. 115), but that was in the course of civil strife, not for failure in battle.

22. *Iliad* XXIV 471–620.

23. *Odyssey* 11. 71–78; 12. 10–14.

24. Thucydides 4. 44. 5-6; Plutarch *Nicias* 6. 5–6.

25. For a discussion of the religious aspects of the Arginusae trial, see Rubel, *Fear and Loathing in Ancient Athens: Religion and Politics during the Peloponnesian War*, trans. M. Vickers and A. Piftor (Durham: Acumen, 2000, 2014), 131–45.

Xenophon reports that the Athenians soon repented of their decision and arrested Callixeinus, and that he died of starvation, universally detested, but the generals remained dead just the same.[26] Even with their experienced generals gone, the Athenians were in a good position, for the Spartans soon sued for peace, and the terms they offered were not at all bad. They were willing to evacuate Decelea and otherwise let each side keep whatever it had—this despite the fact that the Athenians had regained control of the Bosporus and access to the Black Sea while all the Spartans had was Abydos, Chios, and the cities of Cyme, Phocaea, and Ephesus on the mainland. Sparta also had ongoing access to Persian money—something that posed a serious threat to Athens if the war were to continue. The offer was not perfect, but it had a great deal to recommend it. Time would soon show that the Athenians should have accepted it, but they did not, in part because they were optimistic about dealing the Spartans a second blow at sea and ending the war on their own terms, in part because they mistrusted them after the way their Peloponnesian allies had failed to cooperate following the Peace of Nicias.[27] The war, then, would go on.

THE ATHENIANS CAUGHT OFF GUARD

Whoever in Sparta was behind the peace initiative, it certainly was not Lysander. Although there was a rule that no man could serve twice as navarch, it was circumvented by the appointment of Aracus as navarch with Lysander his second in command, and nobody doubted who was really in charge.[28] Lysander's first order of business was a meeting with Cyrus to push for more funding, which he got. Next, after some minor expeditions, he headed to Miletus to spark an anti-democratic coup there, arranging for his partisans to kill 340 democrats and expel more

26. Xenophon *Hellenica* 1. 7. 35.

27. Pseudo-Aristotle *Constitution of the Athenians* 34. 1 attributes the Athenians' rejection of the Spartan peace offer to the demagoguery of Cleophon's drunken appearance in the assembly, but no one man could have this much influence.

28. Xenophon *Hellenica* 2. 1. 7; Diodorus 13. 100. 8; Plutarch *Lysander* 7. 2.

than 1,000 others even after the two parties had become reconciled. Here he engaged in the most callous machinations, reassuring the members of the popular party that they were safe in the city and discouraging them from flight when he knew full well they were on the verge of being slaughtered.[29] In Athens, meanwhile, the assembly passed a motion proposed by the general Philocles that any prisoners of war should have their thumbs—or possibly whole hands (our sources disagree)—cut off to prevent them from fighting effectively in the future, a ruthless measure designed to discourage further desertions to the enemy; this was the same Philocles who had thrown overboard the crews of two enemy ships the Athenians had captured.[30]

To get to Miletus, Lysander had to pass the Athenian fleet at its base in Samos. Incomprehensibly, the Athenians let him go by unhindered, a mistake for which they would soon pay dearly. Another peculiar lapse was their failure to block the entrance to the Hellespont. Lysander could not be everywhere at once, but they could certainly expect him there. From Miletus, Lysander moved to Iasus in Caria, where he killed the men of military age—fully 800 of them—and sold the women and children.[31] Attacking Cedreae, a mixed city of Greeks and non-Greeks, he enslaved Greek and non-Greek alike.[32]

The message was clear: the days of Callicratidas were over. Lysander's ultimate target, of course, was the Hellespont, where he knew the real action would lie, but he cleverly made a mad dash west, ravaging Salamis and Aegina and even making landfall briefly in Attica, forcing the Athenian fleet to follow him.[33] Then, heading east again, he took the Athenian stronghold of Lampsacus on the southern shore of the straits by an amphibious assault.[34] There after looting the city—and there was much loot to be had—he set up camp, rightly anticipating that the Athenians

29. Diodorus 13. 104. 5–6; Plutarch *Lysander* 8.

30. Plutarch says thumbs at *Lysander* 9.5; this is more probable than Xenophon's claim of hands (*Hellenica* 2. 1. 32). Xenophon mentions the throwing overboard of the crews (*Hellenica* 2. 1. 32).

31. Diodorus 13. 104. 7.

32. Xenophon *Hellenica* 2. 1. 15.

33. Diodorus 13. 104. 8; Plutarch *Lysander* 9. 2-3.

34. Xenophon *Hellenica* 2. 1. 18–19; Plutarch *Lysander* 9. 4.

would soon materialize to challenge him for their turf. Conon, Philocles, and the rest of the fleet, a full 180-ships strong, were not far behind. After stopping to take on provisions at Sestos, they established themselves on the other side of the straits at Aegospotami, "Goat's Rivers." It was now 405.[35]

No modern town corresponds to this name, and its location is uncertain. All our ancient sources put it directly opposite Lampsacus (now Lapseki), but recently this location has been called into question by naval historian John Hale, who has argued that such close proximity to Lampsacus makes no sense in light of what Xenophon and Plutarch both have written of Lysander's strategy. Each author alleges that every day, after the Athenians had rowed up to Lampsacus and challenged him to battle—a challenge that was routinely refused—and then returned to Aegospotami, Lysander sent spy ships to check on what the Athenians were doing on the opposite shore. Hale points out that the short distance across the straits from the traditional location of Aegospotami would have obviated any need for such ships, since the Athenians' actions would have been plain to the naked eye. Farther north and around a bend, however (see Map 11), each camp would lie out of the other's line of vision. And not only that: After this had gone on for four days, the Athenians were startled by the sound of hoofbeats. A local warlord had ridden down from his mountain fastness to offer his counsel and aid: he was none other than Alcibiades, who had reinvented himself once again and was offering land forces led by nearby chieftains he had befriended—in exchange for a share of the command. The Athenians, he warned them, had gotten themselves into great danger, cut off as they were from food supplies, and he advised them in any case to move to Sestos, where there was access to provisions. But Alcibiades could not easily have seen a camp opposite Lampsacus; he could, however, have seen one farther north, facing Byzantium.[36]

35. Xenophon *Hellenica* 2. 1. 20-21; Diodorus 13. 105. 2; Plutarch *Lysander* 9.5.

36. J. R. Hale, *Lords of the Sea: The Epic Story of the Athenian Navy and the Birth of Democracy* (New York: Viking, 2009), 356–9; Diodorus 13. 105. 3; Plutarch *Alcibiades* 36. 5; Plutarch *Lysander* 10. 4–5.

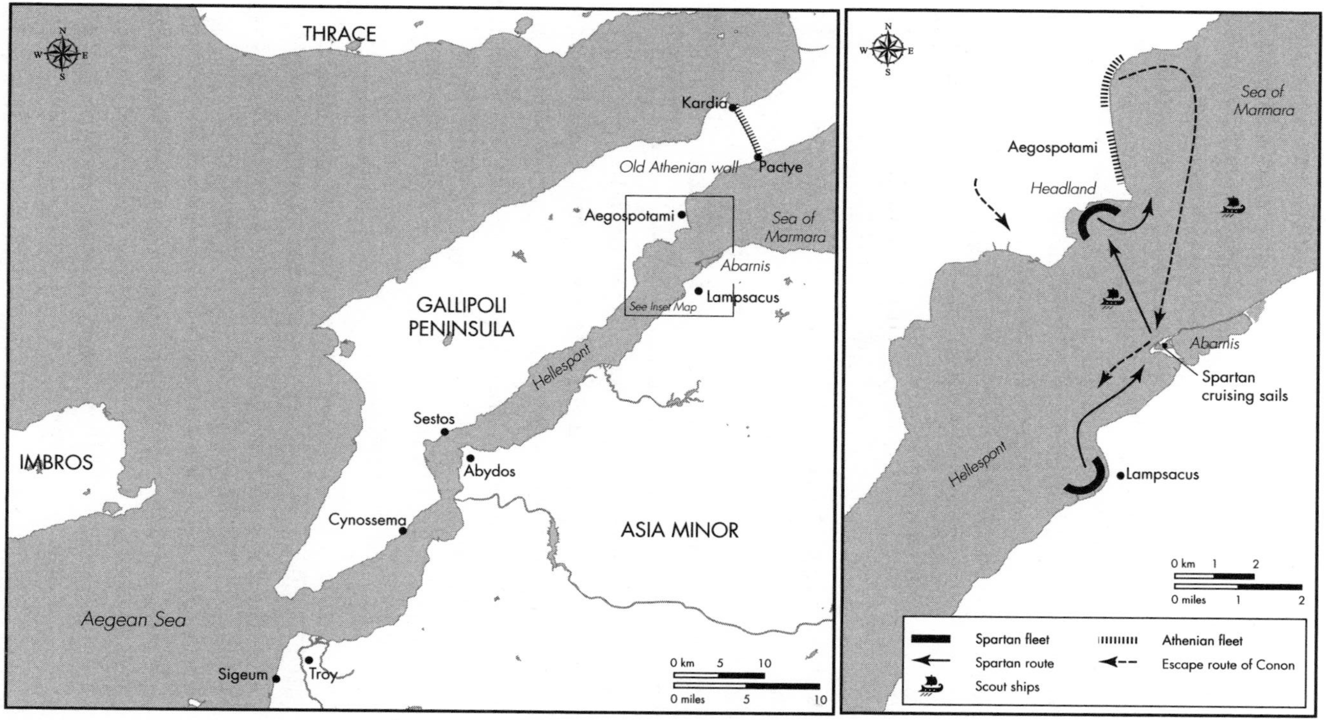

MAP 11
The Hellespont and Aegospotami.

The Athenian generals sent him away, pointing out that they were in command now, and not he. This may have been a terrible mistake—they could certainly have used backup from land forces—but after the trial of the Arginusae generals, they were understandably afraid of what would happen to them if they allowed Alcibiades back into the people's good graces with no authority from home and the campaign then turned sour (whereas if things went well, he would get all the credit). And so Alcibiades mounted his horse and rode away, never again to have anything to do with his native land.[37]

The weakness of the so-called "Athenian" position derived not only from the lack of provisions or proximity to a city or harbor. The men were also by no means all Athenians; many were subject allies with no affection at all for the empire and keenly aware that the man across the straits held the bigger purse. The newly enfranchised slaves and the aristocrats eyed one another warily. The slaves were not enjoying their newfound citizenship very much so far from home in very uncertain circumstances, and the rich found it uncomfortable and undignified to tramp through the underbrush in search of food which was unlikely to be particularly palatable once they found it. Many of the new trierarchs were probably men from the cavalry class who had no experience in naval warfare. The Peloponnesian camp at Lampsacus held a mixed bag as well, of course, but they were ruled with an iron hand by a single master. In Aegospotami, the command alternated among six generals who had been traumatized by the Arginusae trial and had no idea how to handle the situation in the straits, a situation that never should have been allowed to arise in the first place. This was not a state of affairs that inspired confidence. While the demoralization of the men was understandable, the commanders' failure to instill discipline was inexcusable. It is no wonder that the final denouement inspired rumors of treason.

Every day, after unsuccessfully challenging Lysander to battle, the Athenians had rowed back north to Aegospotami and scattered in search

37. Xenophon, *Hellenica* 2. 1. 25–6; Diodorus 13. 105. 4.

of food, and every day they had to go farther afield to find it. Every day Lysander's spy ships reported to the Spartan commander on the Athenians' doings. On the fifth day something changed. According to the Athenian Xenophon (who, after all, was a contemporary), Lysander instructed his spy ships, once they had confirmed that the Athenians were off foraging and inattentive to their stations as usual, to sail back toward Lampsacus with all possible speed and when they were halfway there to signal with a brazen shield; then the Peloponnesians headed for the camp at Aegospotami to catch the Athenians unawares.[38] Diodorus adds a crucial detail oddly lacking in Xenophon's account: in his version, the general Philocles, whose turn it was to command on that day, tiring of the stalemate and concerned about the lack of food in the camp, ordered the other trierarchs to man their ships and dashed ahead himself with thirty triremes—but found that the trierarchs did not attend to the ships as instructed.[39]

It is hard to imagine where Diodorus would have gotten this story if it were not true, yet equally difficult to understand why Philocles would have gone ahead, leaving the other ships in a state of such unpreparedness. Perhaps Philocles' impassioned dash never happened. It is maddening to have such inconsistent and incomplete accounts of such a major battle. Drawing Lysander out by feigning a withdrawal to Sestos might have made sense if the Athenian fleet had been battle-ready, but such was far from the case. All our sources agree that the Athenian ships were not fully manned. They were in fact drawn up on the shore, some with only two banks of oars manned, some only one, and some not manned at all.[40] The men were scattered, some still foraging, some

38. Xenophon *Hellenica* 2. 1. 24, 27, followed by Plutarch *Lysander* 11. 1–2.

39. Diodorus 13. 106. 1–2. The inconsistency is very troubling. J. F. Lazenby, *The Peloponnesian War: A Military Study* (London: Routledge, 2004), 242, points out the extreme difficulty in making any sense of Diodorus's account; Diodorus's story is accepted by C. Ehrhardt, "Xenophon and Diodorus on Aegospotami," *Phoenix* 24 (1970): 225–8 and D. Kagan, *The Fall of the Athenian Empire* (Ithaca, NY: Cornell University Press, 1987), 391–3. Inevitably, there were suggestions at the time that only treachery could have explained the debacle, and the treachery theory is defended in G. Wylie, "What Really Happened at Aegospotami," *L'Antiquité Classique* 55 (1986): 125–41.

40. Xenophon *Hellenica* 2. 1. 28, Diodorus 13. 106. 3.

eating, some actually sleeping. Lysander quickly landed men to seize the headland. On the prows of his ships he had stationed iron grappling hooks, and with these his men dragged the helpless Athenian triremes out to sea. Some of the trierarchs managed to launch their ships with only one or two banks of oars manned, but these were no match for the Peloponnesians and were quickly captured. Lysander's men soon jumped down from the ships and joined the marines who had been stationed on the land, swarming over the Athenian encampment, killing and capturing as many as they could. Only a few ships got away. Conon, who was the first to see Lysander's impending attack, shouted vain instructions to the Athenians to get their house in order and then quickly manned his own division. With the *Paralus* and eight other ships he managed to escape from the melee. Remembering what had happened to the victors of Arginusae, he could only imagine the fate of the losers of Aegospotami, and taking service with his friend Evagoras, the ruler of Salamis on Cyprus (not the Salamis off the coast of Attica), he stayed away from Athens until he had scored a signal victory for the city at Cnidus a decade later, in 394.[41]

The Athenian prisoners numbered between 3,000 and 4,000, allied prisoners many more, considering the size of the fleet: nearly the whole 180 ships.[42] If soldiers wanted to flee into the countryside, it was not worth following them. What Lysander wanted was ships, not men, and he had the ships. In a couple of hours, he had captured the Athenian fleet and thus won the war for Sparta—or so it certainly appeared at the time. He would be dead before it became clear that the events at Aegospotami were not as decisive as they seemed. To be sure, the Spartan victory at sea exacted, within a few months, surrender from the hapless Athenians at home, who had lost their daunting imperial navy. Yet the Athenians recovered from this blow with remarkable rapidity, and it was not long before they gave the Spartans a run for their money in the east—at sea, again.

41. Diodorus 13. 106. 4–6; Plutarch *Lysander* 11. 5–6.

42. The figure of 3,000 comes from Plutarch (*Alcibiades* 37. 3); Pausanias the geographer says 4,000 (9. 32. 9).

THE FATE OF THE VANQUISHED

At the enthusiastic urging of the allies, the Athenian prisoners were executed to a man, perhaps by drowning, perhaps by the blade.[43] Lysander then set about starving out the Athenians back home by swelling the population as much as he could, giving all Athenian garrisons safe conduct back to Athens, smug in the knowledge that the more people he could cram into the city, the sooner it would surrender.

It was nighttime when the *Paralus* pulled into the Piraeus with the dreadful news, and word of the disaster passed quickly up to the city proper. That night, Xenophon says, nobody slept, as they mourned for those who had died, but more still for what they thought lay in store for them, expecting that they would now be dealt with as they had dealt with cities like Melos and Scione and many other states. The Spartans soon had Athens surrounded; Agis moved down from Decelea, Pausanias moved up from the Peloponnesus, and Lysander anchored at Piraeus with 150 ships. Meanwhile in the Aegean all their allies except Samos were defecting furiously to Lysander.[44] The determined Spartan also overthrew existing governments and established instead boards of ten, so-called decarchies—ten men friendly to him personally—to govern the various cities of the Greek world.[45]

The Athenians blocked up most of their harbors and prepared for the siege to come. Some probably were simply in denial, unaware that they had no cards to play. Others more knowledgeable, however, may have been waiting for cracks to develop between the various factions in Sparta, for Pausanias's attitude toward Athens was not the same as that of his co-king or Lysander, and a rift between them might open up as time passed. Darius, moreover, was not a well man, and his death would almost certainly put an end to Cyrus's games in Asia Minor. Sending various peace offers to the Spartans—first to Agis, and then when he turned them away, to the ephors—they threw one of their citizens, Archestratus, into prison

43. Xenophon *Hellenica* 2. 1. 31–2.
44. Xenophon *Hellenica* 2. 2. 3–9.
45. Plutarch *Lysander* 13. 3–4.

when he proposed accepting the Spartan terms that included destroying much of the Long Walls; they actually imagined they would be able to keep them.[46] As more and more Athenians died of hunger and had to be buried, they still clung to the hope of a negotiated peace. Theramenes was charged with going to Lysander personally, but Lysander, after holding him for three months, sent him back to the ephors. The Spartans seemed determined to keep the Athenians dangling as long as possible to maximize their desperation. Finally an assembly of the allies gathered in the Peloponnesus to listen to what the latest Athenian delegation had to say. The Corinthians and Thebans argued that Athens should be destroyed, plain and simple; one Theban, in fact, Erianthus, proposed that the city be left as a pasture for sheep.[47]

The Spartans would not do it. Putting forward all manner of high-minded rhetoric about Athens' service to Greece during the Persian Wars and the like, they came up with peace terms that were eminently mild considering that the Athenians had nothing to bargain with.[48]

Nobility of spirit probably had nothing to do with it. It is more likely that the Spartans were motivated by their fear of a power vacuum into which Corinth and Thebes would rush. After all, both the Corinthians and the Boeotians had been bad citizens of the Peloponnesian League after the Peace of Nicias. There was also the matter of the wealth that would pour into Sparta from a destroyed Athens, no small cause for concern. Even as it was, the booty from Lampsacus and other sacked cities was upsetting the traditional Spartan way of life.[49]

In the end the terms of the peace dictated by Sparta were these: The walls of the Piraeus and the Long Walls would have to come down. The Athenians could keep the territory of Attica but would have to give up the empire. Exiles would have to be recalled. (These, of course, would be largely of oligarchic sympathies.) All but twelve ships would have to be

46. Xenophon *Hellenica* 2. 2. 15.

47. Plutarch *Lysander* 15. 2.

48. Xenophon *Hellenica* 2. 2. 20.

49. See A. Powell, "Why Did Sparta not Destroy Athens in 404, or in 403 BC?" in *Sparta & War*, ed. S. Hodkinson and A. Powell (Swansea: University Press of Wales, 2006), 287–303.

surrendered. The Athenians would have to have the "same friends and enemies" as Sparta, that is, to join the Peloponnesian League.[50] Not all Athenians voted in favor of accepting the peace, but a strong majority saw that no better terms could realistically be expected. The walls were pulled down, Xenophon says, amid great enthusiasm to the music of young women playing the *aulos*.[51]

Considering what the Athenians had done to cities they had captured during the war, they could count themselves lucky that circumstances conspired to net them such gentle handling. Of course, the extermination of Athens would have been logistically formidable. There would be far, far more corpses to dispose of in Athens than at Aegospotami. Still, a good case could have been made that they got what they deserved, and as Xenophon claimed, it was precisely what they anticipated in light of their conduct toward those they had vanquished in the course of the long war. On balance, the Athenians fared remarkably well. Had history turned out differently and the Peloponnesians found themselves on the losing side, it is not at all clear what their fate would have been.

THE THIRTY TYRANTS

When the walls came down, Xenophon reported, people believed that they were witnessing the beginning of freedom for Greece.[52] It would soon become apparent that nothing could be farther from the truth. For one thing, the fighting was not over; bloody clashes would soon break out in Athens itself, and not that long afterward war would consume the Greek poleis once again. It is puzzling that Thucydides should have considered the war over when the walls came down and did not deem the events that followed immediately to be part of it. But the capture of the magnificent imperial fleet, the starvation of the city, and the demolition of the Long Walls evidently blinded the two historians to an alternative

50. Xenophon *Hellenica* 2. 2. 20.
51. Xenophon *Hellenica* 2. 20. 23.
52. Xenophon *Hellenica* 2. 20. 23.

interpretation. The Spartans, however, would not use their newfound power graciously, and the Athenians would not take the Spartans' misconduct toward them lying down.

Lysander bore Athens particular ill will, and the Athenians would soon find themselves under the thumb of a singularly brutal oligarchy. The pro-Spartan decarchies that Lysander had set up across the Aegean were all very well for smaller states, but clearly keeping Athens in check called for something on a larger scale. In August of 404 the democratically elected generals were deposed and a temporary board of five "ephors" was put in place to serve as an interim government.[53] The Spartan terminology seemed ominous, and equally disturbing, one of the ephors was Critias, a longtime admirer of the Spartan constitution and friend of Alcibiades who had been banished briefly by the democracy, presumably for his pro-Spartan leanings. In September Lysander arrived and, claiming that the Athenians had not carried out the terms of the surrender, proceeded to impose on them a board of thirty Athenians who favored an oligarchic government. There would also be a council of 500, but it would serve only to ratify the acts of the Thirty. The Board of Ten in charge of the Piraeus was also chosen from oligarchs, as were the Eleven in charge of executions.[54] Order was maintained by 300 whip-bearing mercenaries.

Not surprisingly, the Thirty promptly put an end to the popular courts. They also reconfigured the hill of the Pnyx, the base of political power for what it considered the "naval mob," so that the podium no longer faced the sea. Now it faced inland—and accommodated fewer people.[55] Realizing they were making themselves unpopular, the

53. It is not clear whose idea this was and who chose the men; Lysias says it was the *hetairiai* (Lysias 12. 43), but it might have been the assembly itself. The principal extant sources for the rule, and fall, of the Thirty are Lysias 12. 69–78; Xenophon *Hellenica* 2. 3. 2–4. 43; Pseudo-Aristotle *Constitution of the Athenians* 34. 2–39. 6; Diodorus 14. 3–6; and Plutarch *Lysander* 15. There are some inconsistencies in the sources; this is my best reconstruction of events. Among modern historians, see in addition to P. Krentz, *The Thirty at Athens* (Ithaca, NY: Cornell University Press, 1982) R. Stern, "The Thirty at Athens in the Summer of 404," *Phoenix* 57 (2003): 18–34, with bibliography.

54. Pseudo-Aristotle *Constitution of the Athenians* 35. 1.

55. Plutarch *Themistocles* 19. 4.

oligarchs soon sent for a Spartan garrison, offering to pay for it themselves.[56] Meanwhile, on Lysander's orders, exiles were pouring in from all over the Aegean. As these men were demanding the restoration of their confiscated property—or, rather, of its cash value, since it had long since been sold off—now the Thirty needed money to reimburse the exiles and pay the Spartan garrison. At first they had used their power to get rid of blackmailers and informers, but now they moved on to executing others as well. Not all victims were citizens who could possibly have been perceived as political enemies; a large number were wealthy metics whose money they coveted. Before long they had killed no fewer than 1,500 men.[57]

Perhaps the least oligarchic of the Thirty was Theramenes. Although he did have a habit of turning up when oligarchy was afoot, just as predictably he developed qualms at its actions. He had taken a leading role in overturning the Four Hundred, to which he had belonged. Now Theramenes suggested to Critias that it would be a good idea to expand their government to include a reasonable number of other citizens, as the populace was becoming dangerously restive, and Critias agreed to enroll 3,000 of those he considered fitting men.[58] (Among these was the philosopher Socrates.) For both Theramenes and the Thirty, this was the beginning of the end. When Theramenes offered an eloquent argument against the notion that there were precisely 3,000 good men in the city and the Council was plainly moved by his words, Critias struck his name off the list of the 3,000, thus depriving him of the right to a trial.[59] Condemned to death and forced to drink hemlock, Theramenes went out in style and not without irony, toasting Critias's health with the last drops.

Now Athens had come to resemble Sparta in a manner most Athenians found chilling. The Thirty—who have gone down in history as the Thirty Tyrants—seemed parallel to the Spartan *gerousia*, the Council of Elders (28 men, plus the 2 kings); the 300 mercenary whip-bearers paralleled the

56. Xenophon *Hellenica* 2. 3. 13–14.
57. Pseudo-Aristotle *Constitution of the Athenians* 35. 3–4.
58. Xenophon *Hellenica* 2. 3. 16–18.
59. Xenophon *Hellenica* 2. 3. 51.

kings' bodyguard of 300; and the 3,000 men with citizen rights seemed about the same number as that of the *homoioi* (Peers) who were left of the original purported 9,000 or so in Sparta. Who was the originator of this peculiar project? Plainly it was Socrates' pupil Critias. A relative of Plato (who distrusted the demos as well), he was a dabbler in all things intellectual and had long been known for his pro-Spartan views. This was not unusual at Athens, where many of the elite admired the order evident in the Spartan system and the discipline it produced in Sparta's citizens, but Critias's adulation for Sparta went to rather peculiar extremes. Some of his writings on Sparta survive, and they include praise of Sparta's drinking cups, household furniture, and dance steps.[60]

Predictably, resistance against the tyranny soon gathered strength. When they forbade those not on the list of the Three Thousand to enter Athens and confiscated many of their farms, the Thirty created a dangerous body of bitter exiles. Though Sparta had forbidden neighboring states to receive refugees from Athens, the bloody conduct of the oligarchy there had sparked sympathy for the beleaguered state, and neither Thebes nor Megara nor Corinth was disposed to turn away Athenians fleeing the brutal Spartan-backed regime. The refugees received a particularly warm welcome from the Thebans, whose policy was guided at that time by the anti-Spartan Ismenias: under Ismenias's leadership the Thebans voted to fine anyone who, witnessing an exile being led off, did not give him aid, and the fine was to consist of the considerable sum of a talent. They also voted that no one take notice of anyone bearing arms against the Thirty.[61] It was in Thebes that the Athenian exiles mounted their campaign to retake their city. It was one thing to exhort the Spartans to destroy Athens root and branch but quite another to see them virtually annex it. Under the leadership of the stalwart democratic general Thrasybulus, some seventy men gathered at the fortress at Phyle on the border of Attica and Boeotia. From it, on a clear day, the homesick democrats could even glimpse the Parthenon. Soon their number had swelled to 700, and they had good armor. In part this was due to the support of the metic orator

60. On Critias and Sparta, see Krentz, *The Thirty*, 45.

61. Diodorus 14. 6. 1–3; Plutarch *Lysander* 27. 2–4; Plutarch *Pelopidas* 6. 4.

Lysias, whose family had come to Athens from Syracuse and who had become wealthy through his arms factory. Motivated by his loyalty to the democracy and his bitterness over the Thirty's execution of his brother Polemarchus (not to mention his own narrow escape from death at the hands of the oligarchs), Lysias seems to have provided hundreds of mercenaries and shields for the enterprise.[62] In their first encounter with the forces of the Thirty, Thrasybulus and his men were victorious. Afraid for their security even with the pricy Spartan garrison to protect them (probably *neodamodeis,* but still not cheap), the Thirty established a secondary power base in Eleusis, in no way deterred by the fact that this project required the murder of many of the inhabitants.[63] Thrasybulus meanwhile advanced on the Piraeus and seized the hill of Munychia overlooking the port. With him was another committed democratic leader, our old friend Anytus, suspected briber of jurors.

Attacking uphill, the forces of the Thirty were at a serious disadvantage, and those who were killed included Critias himself.[64] While the bodies of the dead were being returned under a truce, Cleocritus, the herald of those initiated into the mysteries at Eleusis, who had a particularly fine voice, called for silence and exhorted those who had supported the Thirty to withdraw their loyalty; and in fact the Thirty, who were feeling demoralized from their recent defeat anyhow, were deposed and replaced with a board of Ten, one from each tribe.[65] The remains of the Thirty retired to Eleusis, but conflict continuing, they joined with the 3,000 in sending to Sparta for help.[66]

The power dynamic in Sparta and the Peloponnesian League at this time was highly problematic. Lysander, of course, immediately responded joyfully to the request and sent his brother Libys with the navy to blockade Piraeus on behalf of the oligarchs; meanwhile he would command a land force. Pausanias, however, having gained the support of three out of the

62. On the role of Lysias in aiding the democrats, see Krentz, *The Thirty*, 73, n. 11.

63. Xenophon *Hellenica* 2. 4. 8.

64. Xenophon *Hellenica* 2. 4. 19.

65. Xenophon *Hellenica* 2. 4. 20–3; Pseudo-Aristotle *Constitution of the Athenians* 38. 1; Diodorus 14. 33. 5.

66. Xenophon *Hellenica* 2. 4. 28.

five ephors, decided that he himself would go out to command the expedition. He was sick of being upstaged by Lysander, and he was afraid, too, that Lysander wished to make Athens his personal fiefdom.[67] He called on the allies to march with him, but, in a sign of further developments to come, the Corinthians and Boeotians declined, arguing that the Athenians had done nothing to violate the peace. Their real concern, Xenophon said, was that Sparta was planning to take Athens and keep it as its own territory.[68] Plainly the Corinthians and Boeotians bore the Spartans ill will just as they had after the Peace of Nicias—just as they had never stopped doing, indeed, and would continue to do.

Although Pausanias first fought the democrats as expected, killing a number of men and losing some of his own in the process, when he began to realize that the ferocity of the democrats and the lack of enthusiasm from his own allies did not bode well for a successful outcome, he did an about-face and turned his energies toward effecting a reconciliation between the two parties. Each side then laid down its arms, and a general amnesty was declared. It was agreed that all confiscated property was to be returned. No one was to be prosecuted for crimes committed before 403 with the exception of grievous acts such as murder. Those who had held high office under the Thirty would have to undergo a scrutiny of their conduct in office. Anyone who wished could leave Athens and join the oligarchs already in Eleusis, as long as he left quickly. In September of 403 Thrasybulus led his men unopposed to the Acropolis, where they sacrificed to Athena in gratitude for the salvation of the city and their own safe return.[69] And Critias? He lay buried in a tomb on which was depicted a personification of Oligarchy setting fire to Democracy. On it were inscribed the words: "This is a memorial to good men who for a short time restrained the hubris of the damned democracy of the Athenians."[70]

67. Xenophon *Hellenica* 2. 4. 29; Plutarch *Lysander* 21. 3.

68. Xenophon *Hellenica* 2. 4. 30.

69. Xenophon *Hellenica* 2. 4. 39.

70. Scholiast on Aeschines 1. 39. This was not entirely the happy ending it seems. In 401, on the pretext that some of the oligarchs in Eleusis were hiring mercenaries for the project of retaking Athens, the democrats attacked the oligarchic community there and reunited Eleusis with Athens, not without bloodshed.

This bloody episode in Greek history served as an inoculation against future discord, and Athens remained singularly free of civil war throughout the decades that followed—decades during which there was substantial civil unrest in other poleis. Rather, the fault lines would lie within the Peloponnesian League and within Sparta itself as disagreements persisted concerning how to deal with Athens—and between Lysander, waiting in the wings to return to power, and members of the royal family.

ATHENS AFTER THE THIRTY

The years of fighting had taken a tremendous toll in lives, in spirit, and in material goods. Tens of thousands had died throughout the Greek world, certainly over 100,000. In Athens with its heavy investment in naval warfare, casualties were particularly high, and of course, many had died of the plague. It seems likely that the number of fighting men in the city was an alarmingly low 40 percent of what it had been at the outset of the war.[71] Many men had been murdered by the Thirty. Even countless metics had died fighting, and malnutrition may have affected the fertility of the women at home.[72] Already at the outset of the Ionian war, Aristophanes' Lysistrata had complained of the dearth of husbands; the situation had grown exponentially worse over the years that followed.

After the expulsion of the Thirty, Athens found itself distinctly poorer for the lack of imperial tribute—varying depending on circumstances, but probably about 1,000 talents a year on average. Public building projects and the salaries that went with them ground to a halt. The city's defenses were derelict. Gone were all the jobs connected with the fleet: the transportation of timber from its distant sources in the north, the construction

71. Victor Hanson has estimated that a recent parallel would be if the United States had lost about 44 million killed in combat dead during World War II: *A War Like No Other: How the Athenians and Spartans Fought the Peloponnesian War* (New York: Random House, 2005), 296.

72. On Athenian population decline during the war, see B. Strauss, *Athens after the Peloponnesian War: Class, Faction, and Policy 403–386 B. C.* (Ithaca, NY: Cornell University Press, 1986) 71, 81 plus appendix, 179–82.

and maintenance of the ships, the buzzing labor in the dockyards, and of course the rowers' pay. No longer did imperial subjects flood the city with their business as in the past, when they had appeared perforce to plead their cases before Athenian courts, spending their money on food, housing, transportation, and often female company. (Prostitution, it should be remembered, was a remunerative business not only for its practitioners and their owners, since many of them were slaves, but for the state, as it was taxed.) Native Athenians suffered from the loss of their overseas property.[73]

Although Athens was conspicuous for its involvement in commerce, most Athenians owned land and derived their income, small or large, from it. This was true after Aegospotami as it had been before it. Agriculture had been gravely harmed during the decades of fighting, first by Peloponnesian ravaging during the Archidamian War and then again after the fortification of Decelea and the attendant defection of some 20,000 slaves. (It may be, though, that the Spartans dug in at Decelea cultivated some of the land nearby for their own benefit.) A slave cost about 150 drachmas to replace. Animals had been slaughtered and buying new ones would be costly. The beasts that had been sent to Euboea for safekeeping were lost with the Euboean revolt from the empire in 411. The destruction of the olive trees was somewhat less serious; these regenerate fairly quickly.[74] But vines, which are rather small plants, are another matter: a good stomping will destroy them, and that is precisely what they had gotten.

On the bright side, the availability of all the demes of Attica after the Spartan withdrawal was a welcome relief, though some Athenians who had grown accustomed to city life and had picked up craft skills chose to remain in town. The damage done to agriculture by the ravaging of the land had not proven permanent. Since the drop in population meant fewer mouths to feed, moreover, the absence of tribute did not make it impossible to pay jurors. Indeed, after an influx of Persian

73. Barry Strauss has painted a detailed picture of Athens at this time in *Athens after the Peloponnesian War*, 42–86.

74. V. D. Hanson, *Warfare and Agriculture in Classical Greece* (Berkeley: University of California Press, 1998), 159–71.

money in 394/3, pay for attendance at the assembly was soon introduced, probably to facilitate attendance by the poor, and then it was raised. Athens, moreover, remained a remarkably stable state throughout the fourth century at a time when other poleis were experiencing considerable discord among the citizens. This may in part have been because the coup of the Four Hundred and the tyranny of the Thirty had driven home to the Athenians the perils of civil strife; perhaps too it had something to do with the great number of casualties among the poor rowers in the war: discord tended to be most common in cities with the largest number of poor. In the cities that had once belonged to the Athenian empire, however, suffering continued as the populace found itself under the thumb of garrisons imposed by Lysander, put in place to uphold oligarchies that had replaced democracies.

17

ATHENS AFTER THE AMNESTY

ATHENS REBOUNDED SURPRISINGLY QUICKLY from the double blow of its military defeat at Aegospotami and the depredations of the Thirty, but this recovery could not possibly have been predicted in 403, nor could the ultimate collapse of Spartan power. In the years immediately following the amnesty, life was very difficult for the Athenians. Tempers were short. At the same time, a lively intellectual dialogue that had begun centuries earlier had continued throughout the war and culminated in the work of the men who would lay the cornerstone of the Western philosophical tradition: Socrates and his pupil Plato. Not long afterward, Plato's pupil Aristotle would make his own contributions to both philosophy and political theory. The bulk of the fourth century would be marked by bloody warfare on the one hand and far-reaching intellectual speculation on the other.

GREEK PHILOSOPHY BEFORE SOCRATES

For Socrates (Figure 12), as for Plato and Aristotle after him, the goal of philosophy was to determine the ends of life. Those who came before him—the thinkers who, in tribute to Socrates, are known as the Presocratics—focused rather on the beginnings. Of what was the world made? How did change come about, or was change, perhaps, an illusion? And what implications did this questioning have for traditional thinking about the Olympian gods? What was the best kind of state? Some of these issues also interested the more intellectual among the sophists. Socrates and Plato were heirs to this

FIGURE 12
Bust of Socrates.

speculation, and Socrates engaged with some of these schools of thought in the dialogues Plato wrote with Socrates as a central character.

A major characteristic of the Presocratics was the replacement of mythological, god-centered explanations of the natural world with scientific ones—or, we would be inclined to say, proto-scientific ones, since these early thinkers lacked the ability to conduct experiments. Some, like Thales (624–546), claimed that everything arose from water or moisture; others, air. Or did two extremes alternate, wet and dry, as was suggested by Xenophanes (c. 570–c. 470)? Perhaps earth, water, air, and fire combined in various proportions? Pericles' friend Anaxagoras (c. 500–428) from Clazomenae believed that material objects were composed of infinitely divisible particles. The shadowy Leucippus believed that these particles were not, in fact, infinitely divisible, and called them atoms, a word meaning literally "uncuttable."

Heracleitus (535–475) of Ephesus in Ionia maintained that conflict was inevitable. Indeed, it made the world go around. War was the father of all and king of all; everything was in flux. He is still famous for his saying that one cannot, therefore, step in the same river twice. The search for stability, he argued, was futile. Parmenides (510–440), however, who came from Elea in southern Italy, denied the very possibility of change. How, he asked, could anything change, since for something to change would mean that it became what it was not, and that would be impossible? Parmenides was concerned that people drew their conclusions about the nature of the world from their senses rather than from abstract thought; and it is here that he played a key role in the development of Greek thought. For in reliance on abstract thought—in departing from the previous tendency to speculate about the natural world based on mere conjecture—he set the stage for the kind of conceptual approach that would mark the thought of Plato and later philosophers in the Western tradition. Although Socrates was more interested in matters of truth and justice and definition than in the workings of the universe, the character we know as "Socrates" certainly is depicted as discussing the theories of Heracleitus and Parmenides in dialogues like Plato's *Theaetetus*.[1]

Perhaps the most significant of these thinkers was Pythagoras (c. 570–c. 495), who construed the world in the context of harmony and mathematics. He gave his name to the Pythagorean theorem, which he was credited (though incorrectly) with proving, namely, that the square of the hypotenuse of a right triangle is equal to the sum of the squares of the other two sides. His interest in harmony and mathematics made a profound impression on Plato: there is a strong echo of Pythagoras in Plato's emphasis on mathematics as a cornerstone of abstract thought and a basis for philosophy. Certainly Aristotle, who studied with Plato for many years, believed that Plato's philosophy was strongly influenced by the thinking of Pythagoras.[2] Pythagoras was born in Samos but relocated in Croton in southern Greece around 530 and established a community of followers there. The Pythagoreans believed in the immortality

1. Plato *Theaetetus* 179e–187a
2. Aristotle *Metaphysics* 1. 987a.

of the soul and its progress through various incarnations not only in human form but in the bodies of animals as well, hence their conviction that all life is kin and the universe as a whole a living creature. Pythagoras himself was said to recollect all his previous incarnations (in one of which he had been a courtesan!)

The speculation of the Presocratics certainly raised questions about the role of the Olympian gods in ordering the universe, but as Socrates would soon complain, none of their theories was demonstrable; what was more, their conjectures about the composition and operation of the universe failed to provide a guide to a useful life or a path to virtue. This is not to say that these men had no important observations to make about how people should live or think. Xenophanes came down hard on his fellow Greeks for their exaltation of athletic prowess over the kind of wisdom he possessed as what we might call an intellectual, for, he said, no boxer or wrestler could bring good government to the city. In his poetry, he also criticized the Greeks' anthropomorphizing of their gods: if cattle and horses and lions had hands to paint with as people do, he claimed, the cattle would depict gods in the shape of cattle, the horses in the shape of horses, and the lions in the shape of lions.[3] With the exception of Pythagoras, however, none of the early Greek cosmologists offered a clear manifesto for living one's life, as humanity got short shrift in their speculations. Nor did the education offered in the *poleis* of Greece encourage students to explore the meaning of life; rather, they were expected to focus on such things as memorizing poetry.

THE BEGINNINGS OF POLITICAL THEORY

Throughout the fifth century, men (and no doubt women too, but they have not left us records of their reflections) devoted considerable thought to the best life in the best state. Political thinking, and politics itself, was one of the great products of ancient Greece. Many democratic thinkers

3. H. Diels, *Die Fragmente der Vorsokratiker* (Berlin, 1903; 6e, rev. by Walther Kranz, Berlin: Weidmann, 1952), Xenophanes frag. 15.

put their ideas into action, most conspicuously in Athens—Solon and Cleisthenes already in the sixth century, and Ephialtes and Pericles later on. Solon also left verses describing his political ideas.[4] Snatches from various Attic dramas show a lively and ongoing dialogue about what was best for the polis, although words placed in the mouths of individual characters and even a chorus must be interpreted with care.[5] One of the most memorable prose passages about government appears in Herodotus's *Histories* in the form of a dialogue in Persia around 522. Some find it hard to believe, the historian says, but nonetheless this conversation did indeed take place. After killing the previous illegitimate rulers of Persia, three of the assassins debated what the best government would be with which to replace it. Otanes argued against the arrogance of one-man rule, claiming that an unaccountable autocrat would disrupt the customs of the past, rape women, and execute people without trial. Instead he advocated something that sounds very much like Athenian democracy (so much so that many have indeed suspected that these words could not have been spoken in 522 Persia). Majority rule, he says,

> is called by the fairest of terms: Equality before the Law. Next, it requires something the tyrant never allows: people hold office by lot, they are accountable for the actions of their administrations, and their deliberations are held in public. I propose, therefore, that we abolish the monarchy and increase the power of the people, for in the many we are one.

Indeed accountability was one of the distinctive marks of Athenian government, in which officials were regularly audited at the end of their terms and frequently impeached for financial and other malfeasance.[6]

4. Solon's poetry is available in Greek and English in *Greek Elegiac Poetry from the Seventh to the Fifth Centuries B. C.* (Loeb Classical Library No. 258), trans. D. Gerber (Cambridge, MA: Harvard University Press, 1999).

5. A number of these appear in M. Gagarin and P. Woodruff, *Early Greek Political Thought from Homer to the Sophists*, an excellent collection of primary sources (Cambridge: Cambridge University Press, 1995).

6. See J. Roberts, *Accountability in Athenian Government*, passim (Madison: University of Wisconsin Press, 1982).

Aeschylus in his *Persians* portrays Xerxes' mother describing her son as "unaccountable" for his actions; we can well imagine an Athenian audience nodding knowingly at the playwright's pointed contrast of Persian autocracy with Athenian democracy.

Megabyzus disagreed sharply with Otanes, claiming that there was "nothing stupider or more arrogant than an idle mob." The common people know nothing and "mindlessly rush through the business of government like a raging torrent." Rather he proposed that he and the others select a group of the "best men" (among whom they will be included), for the best men will naturally produce the best counsel.

Darius for his part argued in favor of monarchy, maintaining that no one could govern better than the best man (a belief espoused by Plato in his late dialogue the *Statesman*). Divisions, he says, arise in both oligarchies and democracies. In the end the counsel of Darius prevailed, and it was under the rule of Darius, and then Xerxes, that the Persians attacked Greece.[7] But there were other ways of living in freedom and under the rule of law besides democracy, and Herodotus spoke highly of Sparta as well. The fact that the Spartan king-in-exile Demaratus had withdrawn to Xerxes' court and accompanied him on his invasion of Greece gives the historian an opportunity to offer a dialogue illustrating the difference between the Persian, absolutist point of view and the rule of *nomos*. Tell me, Herodotus shows the king asking the Spartan, will the Greeks really resist me, outnumbered as they are? Let me focus my response on the Spartans alone, Demaratus replies. When they fight one at a time, they're as good as any, but when they fight as a group, they're the best in the whole world:

> Because though they're free, they aren't totally free. Custom (or perhaps law) (*nomos*) is the despot who stands over them, and they secretly fear it more than your people fear you. They do whatever it commands, and its command is always the same: not to run away from any force, however large, but to stay in formation and either prevail or die.[8]

7. Herodotus 3. 80.1–83.1.
8. Herodotus 7. 104. 4–5.

Some time after Herodotus seems to have composed the bulk of his work, at some point during the Peloponnesian War, an ironic pamphlet about Athenian democracy appeared, written by a man whose identity is unknown but who was once thought, wrongly, to be Xenophon and is now nicknamed "the Old Oligarch" (although that attribution may be equally incorrect). In it the author outlined the nefarious but highly efficient manner in which the Athenians went about running their democratic government. In discussing the constitution of the Athenians, he says, he cannot praise it, since in choosing it they preferred for the base masses to do better than the respectable citizens. Given, however, that they have made this choice, he will show how well they preserve their constitution. It might be objected, he argues, that not all men should be permitted to speak in the assembly and serve in the Council but only the best; but by allowing the mob a voice here, the Athenians are acting in their own best interests, for if only the respectable were permitted to speak, benefit would accrue to that class alone and the masses would be harmed; as it is, any wretch who so desires rises and speaks, and as a member of the mob he learns what is to the advantage of his kind. Practices like these do not produce the best city, but they are the best way of preserving democracy, for the common people do not wish to live as slaves in an admirably governed city, but to be free and to rule the city; they are not disturbed by inferior laws, for what you would consider bad government is the very basis of the common people's strength and freedom.[9]

The dichotomy here between the base and self-serving demos on the one hand and the prudent elite on the other is a common theme in Greek thought. It contrasts strikingly with Otanes' representation of the functioning of democracy in the constitutional debate set in Persia, where Otanes dubs majority rule as "equality before the law" (*isonomia*, a watchword for Athenian democracy) and "the fairest of terms." Otanes' claim that "in the many, we are one" represented a view diametrically opposed to the "Old Oligarch"'s construction of democracy.

9. Pseudo-Xenophon *Constitution of the Athenians* 1. 6-8.

A contemporary of the Old Oligarch, Thucydides also had passionate feelings about Athenian democracy. The Old Oligarch may or may not have been an Athenian; Thucydides certainly was, yet he became alienated from the democracy with the passing of time as its leadership passed from the hands of Pericles, whom he greatly admired and whose idealized picture of Athens is conveyed in the Funeral Oration of 431, into those of men he considered inferior. Each of these men competed with one another, he wrote, surrendering the framing of policy to the whims of the demos to gain popularity; he particularly censured the way in which the ambitions of the leading politicians at home undermined the efforts of the fighting force in Sicily and introduced civil strife at home. The post-Periclean democracy, moreover, impeached Thucydides himself for his failure at Amphipolis in 424. The Athenians impeached numerous others before and after Thucydides, and Thucydides was only the first of many to excoriate them for this practice; when Pericles was returned to office after his impeachment, Thucydides observed that the Athenian *homilos*—the mob—re-elected him after one of those changes of heart to which they were prone.[10] No friend to democracy uses this word, a common slur on the demos.

To some degree Thucydides' disillusionment with democracy after his exile and the Athenians' mismanagement of the war paralleled Plato's after the execution of Socrates and the Athenians' many military setbacks. Yet it was hardly the case that Thucydides' admiration was limited to men of the upper classes; though he had the highest admiration for the oligarch Antiphon, whom he called second to none among Athenians of his generation, he was fully aware of Nicias's fatal weaknesses, and he reserves special praise for Themistocles, who was entirely lacking in aristocratic pedigree.[11] Themistocles, he wrote, "was a man who consistently showed the strengths of his nature. . . . . He had an innate intelligence that needed neither coaching nor hindsight."[12] The democracy, in other words, stood or fell in large part on the quality of the men in charge.

10. Thucydides 2. 65. 4.

11. On Antiphon, see Thucydides 8. 68. 1.

12. Thucydides 1. 138. 3.

In terms of a constitution, he singles out the moderate oligarchy of the Five Thousand for praise, writing that in this constitution the balance of oligarchic and democratic elements made the government run smoothly for the first time in his lifetime. In the end, however, what he sought after in government was wise men at the top, and this was precisely what Plato would aim at in his writings. Like Thucydides, Plato lacked faith in the ability of the masses to govern; but his particular fascination lay not, like Thucydides', in international relations, but rather in how philosophy might educate the individual to become a wise ruler. Thucydides had been drawn to innately astute men like Themistocles and Pericles; Plato's goal was developing a form of education that would nurture the intellect.

This gap was at first filled by the sophists. To be sure, some of them simply taught young men how to get ahead in life—in the assembly, in the law courts—by developing skills in rhetoric. They were, as had often been observed, the "consultants" of the Greek world; indeed more than one modern consulting firm has chosen the name "Sophist." Others, however, thought deeply about the kinds of questions that went on to perplex modern philosophers. The observations of Protagoras and Gorgias, for example, had bearing on the nature of ontology (the study of the nature of being) and epistemology (the exploration of how to distinguish knowledge from mere conviction). Both of these, of course, remain key areas of philosophy. Plato portrayed both men talking with Socrates, and each has a dialogue named after him. In *Protagoras*, the sophist is accorded a long speech, part of which is devoted to a myth explaining the principles that undergird Athenian democracy. There is every reason to believe that the speech reflected Protagoras's true beliefs, for it is both charming and persuasive, and it certainly does not replicate Plato's own views of democracy.

The gods, Protagoras says, assigned Epimetheus the task of doling out to each species the tools for survival; he fitted them out with such assets as fur, hides, hooves, and claws, but he was a bad planner, for when he was through, he had nothing left to give mankind. Fortunately for humanity, Epimetheus's twin Prometheus, seeing the hash his brother had made of things, stole fire from Hephaestus and technical skills from Athena and gave them to mankind to compensate for Epimetheus's lapse. But as they lived separately, without cities, mortals had no defense against wild animals, and so they founded cities. Since they lacked civic wisdom, however—*politike techne*—they were so quarrelsome that they constantly wronged one another and the cities disintegrated. Zeus, fearing the extinction of the race, sent Hermes down to bring to men *aidos* (reverence) and *dike* (right), to make civic life possible. How, Hermes asked his father, am I to distribute these? Shall I hand them out the same way as I dealt out the crafts—different crafts to different people, such that one man who possessed medical skill was able to treat many ordinary men, and similarly with the other crafts? Do I give reverence and right only to a few, or to all?

> "To all," replied Zeus. "I want everyone to have a share, for cities cannot exist if only a few share in these as in the other arts. And furthermore make a law of my ordaining, that he who cannot partake of reverence and right shall die the death of a public pest."[13]

It was for this reason, Protagoras concluded, that when questions concerning good craftsmanship in some practical skill arose in Athens, only a few were considered competent to advise, but when it was a political decision that needed to be taken, advice was accepted from everyone, since it is believed that states cannot exist unless everyone partakes of justice and good sense.[14]

Although Protagoras is handled with respect in the dialogue that bears his name, it was not only in regard to political theory that he differed with Socrates and Plato. Protagoras's famous dictum that each individual person was the measure of all things, for example, denied the existence of an absolute reality. Nothing, his claim implied, was intrinsically hot or cold; what any individual perceived as hot for him or her was indeed hot for that person, even if another person perceived it as cold, in which case it would indeed be cold to that individual. This foreshadowed the "perspectivism" of Friedrich Nietzsche (AD 1844–1900), who began his life as a classicist but then became a prominent philosopher famous for his

13. Plato *Protagoras* 322d.
14. Plato *Protagoras* 323a.

rejection of conventional values. Gorgias's spellbinding piece *On Non-Being*—and Gorgias did believe that fine words cast spells—also raised interesting questions about objective reality, for it included the observation that ultimately people are unable to convey what they perceive to others: how, for example, could a sound or a color be described in words, since everyone hears sound and sees color differently?

Issues of *nomos* and *physis*, as we have seen, had exercised many of the finest minds of the fifth century. Was *nomos* a positive force in the world, shoring up civilized society, or did it constrain people from the self-actualization they could attain by acting according to the dictates of *physis*? *Nomos* (custom/law) and its plural *nomoi* (the laws of the state) are opposed to *physis* in the discussion of the civil war on Corcyra interpolated by an unknown author into the text of Thucydides; the later author, who plainly had some understanding of Greek thinking about *nomos* and *physis*, came down firmly on the side of *nomos* as the bulwark of the polis and of civilization, painting the participants in the bloody outbreak in the darkest of colors, writing

> human nature (*physis*), came to predominate over the laws (*nomon*); human nature, which habitually breaks laws anyway, showed itself in its purest form as eager to be above the law, as the enemy of all authority. . . . If it were not, if people were not insane with malice, they would not have placed revenge above piety, and self-interest above justice. In taking their revenge on others, people annul the common laws of mankind, which are the hope of everyone who falters and would find safety, leaving none behind for the time when they are themselves in danger and have need of them.[15]

A contemporary of the real Thucydides who had very different ideas about *nomos* and *physis* probably appears in Thucydides' narrative: it is likely that Antiphon the oligarch, put to death by the restored Athenian democracy in 410, was the same person as Antiphon the sophist, of whose speculations about justice and the polis fragments survive.

15. [Thucydides] 3. 84. 2–3.

Antiphon encouraged people to flout social norms when he suggested that laws and customs—*nomoi*—were in conflict with nature and were thrust upon people as a constraint on their natural pursuit of pleasure and power: Justice, he said,

> consists in not transgressing whatever is the law of the city of which one is a citizen. A person can therefore best conduct himself in accord with justice if he obeys the laws (*nomoi*) when observed by witnesses but in accord with nature (*physis*) when alone without witnesses. For the edicts of the laws are artificial, but those of nature are necessary. Consequently the person who violates the laws can avoid disgrace and punishment if he is not detected by those who have agreed on the legal code; but if someone should try to violate one of the inherent requirements of nature—which is impossible—he would suffer the same degree of harm if he is seen by nobody, for he is harmed not in reputation but in reality.[16]

The speculations of these men formed a large part of the intellectual heritage of Socrates (469–399) and his pupil Plato (c. 428/7–348/7), though of course the drama and historiography of the fifth century played their role as well. For Socrates and Plato, however, the fact that some of the sophists had raised interesting questions did not make them philosophers. Several obstacles stood in the way: the fact that the sophists took money for their services; the emphasis so many of them placed on words rather than truth; the way in which they sold their students a knowledge they claimed to have as a finished "product" rather than leading them on a journey in a joint quest for wisdom; and their moral relativism. The philosopher, Plato said, was in love with truth rather than the changing world of sensation. We know from Plato's dialogues how much of Socrates' time was spent in the back and forth of dialogue rather than speechifying. We know too that Socrates claimed that he knew nothing except that he knew nothing (although we are free to doubt the sincerity of this claim). But Socrates had made a lot of people angry by his question-and-answer method, for just as he purported to know nothing

16. Diels, *Fragmente*, Antiphon frag. 44, 7b.

himself, he sought to demonstrate in his interactions with others that they too were without understanding, a pattern of behavior that was distinctly provocative. Events during the last decades of the fifth century had also disposed his countrymen to bear him substantial ill will.

THE TRIAL OF SOCRATES

In 399, three Athenians, Anytus, Lycon, and Meletus—all men of democratic sympathies—took Socrates to court.[17] (It was customary in Athens for cases to be brought by private prosecutors rather than by the state.) Because of the amnesty of 403, they could not accuse him of collusion with the traitors Alcibiades and Critias, both of them men with whom he consorted regularly, so instead they accused him of not believing in the gods of the state, of introducing new gods, and of corrupting the young. Though the charges brought against Socrates were certainly unusual at Athens, precedents were not lacking. In addition to Protagoras, Pericles had counted among his friends Anaxagoras of Clazomenae, who maintained that the sun was not a divinity, as other Greeks believed, but rather a very hot stone a little bigger than the Peloponnesus. In the 430s when Pericles' political enemies sought to undermine him by attacking his associates he had needed to spirit Anaxagoras out of town to avoid his being tried for impiety. What the accusations against Anaxagoras and Socrates had in common was that there was a large political element in the charge: the defendants were believed to associate with the wrong people. Similarly the charge of impiety that prompted Aristotle's flight after the death of

17. The classic source for the trial of Socrates is Plato's *Apology of Socrates*; Xenophon has an *Apology* also. Neither is completely credible—why would the Athenians have convicted the speaker of Xenophon's piece?—but they are all we have that was written close to the time of the trial, although other authors tried their hands at defense speeches (see Waterfield, below). The secondary literature on the trial of Socrates is immense and continues to grow. Particularly recommended are T. Brickhouse and N. Smith, *Socrates on Trial* (Princeton, NJ: Princeton University Press, 1989); M. Hansen, "The Trial of Sokrates—from an Athenian Point of View," in *Démocratie athénienne et culture*, ed. M. Sakellariou (Athens: Academy of Athens, 1996), 137–70; T. Brickhouse and N. Smith, eds., *The Trial and Execution of Socrates: Sources and Controversies* (New York: Oxford University Press, 2002); and R. Waterfield, *Why Socrates Died: Dispelling the Myths* (New York: W. W. Norton, 2009).

Alexander in 323 arose from his pro-Macedonian sympathies: in an overt reference to the trial of Socrates, Aristotle observed upon his departure that he would not allow Athens to sin twice against philosophy.[18]

A majority of the jurors voted to convict Socrates, and he was sentenced to death. It is not hard to understand why an Athenian jury would have found the accusations credible and important. The tyranny of the Thirty and the bloody civil war that followed were just the last in a series of cataclysms that had rocked Athens since the fighting had begun in 431. It is impossible fully to grasp the effect of the war years on the Athenians or to disentangle the impact of the war from that of domestic affairs. Some of this had entailed religious violations, and in the scandals of 415, two key suspects were pupils of Socrates—Alcibiades in the matter of the Eleusinian mysteries, and Critias in the matter of the herm-chopping (although Critias was acquitted on the evidence of Andocides—curiously, another man brought to trial for impiety in 399, though he was acquitted); more important, Critias was a key member of the bloody Thirty. In 423, a fanciful version of a character called Socrates had been depicted in Aristophanes' *Clouds*.[19] There the philosopher had been portrayed not only as a crooked sophist who runs an airborne Thinkery in the sky in which aspiring pupils encounter Unjust Argument as well as Just Argument; he also explains the universe scientifically as the product of *Dinos*, "Whirl," denying that the meteorological phenomena customarily ascribed to Zeus are in fact the product of divine action since, he argues, the traditional gods do not exist (although the Clouds, of course, are goddesses in Socrates' new religion). Surrounded by a chorus of these divinities, he offers education in both science and sophistic argument to paying pupils. None of this was calculated to endear Socrates to the audience—or to the jurors some years later at his trial: in fact, Plato's *Apology of Socrates*, the defense speech Plato depicts Socrates offering

18. Aelian *Miscellany* 3. 36.

19. The play came in only third. Miffed and hoping to do better with a second version, Aristophanes decided to revise it for subsequent production, but he seems to have abandoned the revision at some point between 419 and 416. Though the later production never took place, the revised manuscript was circulated and is in fact the only one to have survived. The revision is only partial, since the play still contains references to Cleon as if he were still alive.

there, makes reference to the play as a source of the prejudice that has arisen against him.[20] Further explanation as to what his enemies might mean by "introducing new gods" seems to lie in the divine voice that Socrates said had spoken to him from time to time since childhood and had not warned him against coming into court and making his defense speech. It may well have been perceived as a god, and an anti-democratic god at that, since it did not speak to the people at large.[21] To be sure, new gods were introduced frequently at Athens—Bendis, for example, who had come from Thrace just after the outbreak of the Peloponnesian War, and Asklepios, who had been brought to the city after the Peace of Nicias. But Socrates' particular "divine voice" was his own god, not a god of the city, and it is easy to see how this could give offense.

In times of stress, people frequently look for scapegoats, and they often find them in those who stand out as different. Socrates certainly did that. He did not fit easily into Athenian society. He was an Athenian citizen, not an itinerant sophist, but he did not take part in politics. Worst of all, he gathered around him young men who preferred to learn from him rather than from their fathers as they were expected to do. That was a recipe for disaster.

Since Socrates, like Jesus, never wrote anything, we are dependent for our knowledge of his thought on words put in his mouth by his pupils and admirers Plato and Xenophon. A few things we can be confident of. He seems to have spent his time with young men, engaging them in conversation about weighty matters such as the definitions of X or Y or Z—courage or virtue or piety. Plato may have exaggerated in insisting that Socrates had nothing in common with the sophists. To be sure, Socrates differed from the sophists in that he did not take money for teaching. But it may not be true that he was not, like them, a teacher. Xenophon certainly showed him teaching. And it is by no means clear that the sophists were such terrible people. They filled a yawning gap in Greek education. Although Plato and Socrates were shocked by their moral relativism, their instruction in fine speaking was of enormous value in an

20. Plato *Apology* 19c.
21. Plato *Apology* 31c–d.

age in which speech in the assembly and the law courts was a crucial skill for a citizen. One could hardly get up in the assembly and recite key passages from Homer—a basic building block of conventional Greek education—to make one's point. The ability to make a cogent argument, moreover, was not so different from the skill in reasoning that Socrates had to offer (or the skills taught in required composition courses in universities today). Most conspicuously, Socrates resembled the sophists in encouraging the youth of Athens to challenge received wisdom rather than to learn the art of good citizenship by simply emulating their elders. Whom, Socrates asks Meletus in Xenophon's rendition of his defense speech, do I corrupt? "By God," Meletus replies, "I know some—those you've persuaded to obey you rather than their parents."[22]

Nobody could forget that Socrates had been the teacher of Critias and others who had done great harm to the city, and his long and intimate association with the traitor Alcibiades was all too well known: in the youthful Alcibiades, Socrates had seen, wrongly, the makings of a statesman who might save Athens from itself. Now, at the time of Socrates' trial, that was in the past. No longer a young firebrand, Alcibiades had been murdered in Asia Minor, possibly as the result of a plot hatched by Lysander and the Thirty, perhaps with some assistance from Pharnabazus—or perhaps by the brothers of a young woman he had seduced. But his baneful spirit lived on in the minds of those who remembered his treacherous relations first with the Spartans and then with Tissaphernes.

While Socrates' most intimate relationship was with Alcibiades, however, he did consort with other youths, and this was a time when a visible generation gap was opening up in Athens. This generation gap had been front and center in Aristophanes' *Clouds*, produced at the City Dionysia in 423 and, evidently, a major building block in the suspicions that gathered around Socrates: in that play the elderly farmer Strepsiades sends his son to Socrates' Thinkery in the sky and is horrified when the young man returns home filled with arguments that justify beating his father. He even threatens to beat his mother as well. It is hard to know what most bothered the Athenians about Socrates—the charge of not believing in

22. Xenophon *Apology* 20.

the gods of the state, the charge of introducing new gods, or the charge of corrupting the young. It is certainly not hard to see how someone could have thought that he corrupted the young—only some of them, but those few included important men who had betrayed the democracy.

Like other trials in Athenian courts, Socrates' trial lasted one day and took place before a large jury; 501 men decided his fate, the odd number being designed to avoid a tie. Plato and Xenophon both provide versions of what Socrates said, each called the *Apology of Socrates*, the Greek word *apologia* meaning not apology in the modern sense but rather a refutation. Neither can accurately reflect what actually took place at the trial—both violate the rules of Athenian courtroom procedure—but Plato's has lived on as a memorable testament to the power of philosophy and contains the famous dictum that the unexamined life is not worth living for a human being.[23] An Athenian trial really entailed the scrutiny of a man's whole life. There were no narrow rules of evidence or lawyers at hand ready to jump up and protest that their clients' rights were being violated. Juries were not compelled to limit themselves to weighing the charges at hand; thus they were free to take into consideration any evidence of anti-democratic behavior on Socrates' part, such as his decision to remain in the city under the Thirty—routinely viewed as evidence of oligarchic involvement—or his refusal to put the motion against the victors of Arginusae to a vote. Ultimately juries could do whatever they wanted. They could act as capriciously as they wished—there was no appeal from their verdicts—but they might also act in accordance with what they thought was best for the city. Nearly half of the jurors voted to acquit Socrates. Most, however, voted for conviction. The prosecutors had asked for the death penalty. Socrates was given the opportunity to propose an alternative penalty, and surely his accusers expected him to suggest exile. He did not. Instead he recommended that the Athenians provide him with free meals for the rest of his life as a benefactor of the state, just as they did for Olympic victors. But perhaps under pressure from his friends, he backed down from this provocative stance and proposed instead a smallish fine of 100 drachmas and then, under still further pressure (and offers of money, which

23. Plato *Apology* 38a.

he himself did not have, coming from Plato and other devotees), a more substantial fine of 3,000 drachmas. The damage, however, was done. The jury returned a verdict of death (some of those who had originally voted for acquittal having evidently been outraged by Socrates' suggestion that he be rewarded instead of punished), and Socrates was executed by being forced to drink hemlock.

The jurors who sentenced Socrates to death showed a mixture of wisdom and ignorance. Greeks believed that the favor of their gods was essential for their *polis* to flourish; in their terms, consequently, Athenians had every reason to be concerned that every citizen worship the traditional Olympian gods. They were also justified in being suspicious of an eccentric oddball who had been the teacher of traitors. Yet they failed to heed the warning that (at least in Plato's fantasy) Socrates issued at his trial. I am making my defense, Socrates says, not for his own sake but for that of the Athenians, so that they may not by condemning him blunder in their treatment in the gift bestowed on them by the god. For

> if you put me to death, it will not be easy for you to find anyone else who, to make use of a rather incongruous image, attaches himself to the *polis* like a gadfly to a horse, which, though large and of good breeding, is sluggish on account of his size and needs to be aroused by stinging. It seems to me that the god fastened me upon the city in just such a role, and I never cease to arouse and urge and scold each one of you, alighting on you everywhere all day long. Another like this is not likely to turn up in your midst, gentlemen, but if you listen to me, you will spare me; perhaps, on the other hand, you might be angry, like those who are awakened from a nap, and might, under the influence of Anytus, slap me and easily kill me. Then you would spend the rest of your lives asleep unless the god, out of his concern for you, should send someone else to sting you.[24]

But the short view won out in the end, and Socrates did become a scapegoat for the ills of a city that had suffered war, economic collapse, demographic devastation, and civil strife.

24. Plato *Apology* 30e–31a.

Few of the jurors in Socrates' case had any understanding of his philosophy or knew that tearing down people's erroneous beliefs was meant to be preliminary to entering on a meaningful discussion that would lead to true knowledge. Ask someone what happiness is and he or she is likely to respond, in the words of Charles M. Schulz, "happiness is a warm puppy"; but Socrates points out that this is only an example and disassembles his interlocutors' beliefs about happiness until they are ready to undertake a serious search for a definition. Eventually they must be open to searching for definitions of truth, beauty, justice. Socrates passed this focus on to Plato and we read about it in Plato's many dialogues, in nearly all of which Socrates appears as a literary character. Socrates seems to have had no impulse to write things down; it is interesting to wonder what would have become of his ideas had he not had a pupil who was not only so very bright but as interested in writing as Socrates was uninterested.

Socrates and Plato were born into different ages and had different temperaments. Socrates' youth was spent in the heyday of the Athenian empire as tribute poured in to adorn the Acropolis—and, ironically, to fund the very kind of jury that would send him to his death. He engaged enthusiastically with a wide variety of men—with sophists like Protagoras and Gorgias (though he talked rings around them) as well as with poets and shoemakers. Though his appearance was quirky—he evidently had a snub nose and potbelly, and he did not hesitate to wear the same cloak and sandals all day and evening—in most respects he was fully integrated into Athenian society. He served in the military, he married, he produced a family; he held public office as a member of the Council for the year 406/5. Plato, on the other hand, was born into a world of woe. He knew nothing but grisly war for nearly all his life. Despite his aristocratic background, he dwelled on the fringes of Athenian society in several key respects; he is not known ever to have performed military service; he never married or had children or held public office. If he had ever had hopes for the Athenian democracy (and it is not likely that he had), they were destroyed by the democracy's conduct of the war: the brutal massacres in Mytilene, Scione, and Melos, the catastrophic Sicilian expedition, and the execution of the victors of Arginusae. The Thirty, among whom he had friends and relations, had disappointed his hopes for an oligarchic answer to the city's ills. The last nail in the coffin, of course, was the execution of his beloved mentor. Socrates had been interested in learning how to define and attain virtue, but with the death of Socrates, Plato seems to have turned at least some of his thought to developing the virtuous state, for there seemed to be no hope for the one in which he lived—hence his most famous dialogue, the utopian *Republic*, and with it a great step forward for political theory.

CHANGE AND CONTINUITY

To moderns, the condemnation of Socrates by a jury that knew no narrow rules of evidence and from whose verdict there was no appeal may seem like an event that would have encouraged the Athenians to make some changes in their system of administering justice, but they saw no problem with the kind of jury that had sent Socrates to his death. Although Athenian democracy did undergo minor structural changes after 403, the power of the demos was undiminished.

After the overthrow of the Four Hundred and then the Five Thousand, the first steps had been taken in tidying up the laws. A distinction was now made between *nomoi*, laws, and the more ad hoc *psephismata*, decrees, and the passing of laws became a more cumbersome process with the creation of a board of 500 legislators, men of thirty years or older who belonged to the *heliaea* (the jury pool established by Solon) and had taken the jurors' oath. Proposers had to examine the law code and repeal any law that conflicted with the law they wished to have enacted; the proposal had to be read out at three meetings of the assembly; and the legislators would have final authority to pronounce on it. The fourth-century democracy differed from that of the fifth in other ways as well. In the fifth century, minor matters concerning public building projects were decided in full assembly; in the fourth, the state had permanent architects in its employ, and plans would be approved by the council or a law court.[25]

25. On these changes, see P. J. Rhodes, "Athenian Democracy after 403 B. C.," *Classical Journal* 75 (1980): 305–23, and M. H. Hansen, *The Athenian Democracy in the Age of Demosthenes* (Oxford: Blackwell, 1991), 300–20.

More important still, in time, was the rise of important individuals as financial commissioners of one sort or another. By the 350s Eubulus came to be in charge of the Theoric Fund, which provided free seats at public spectacles. Getting a law passed that all surplus moneys should be assigned to this fund, he used it not only for this purpose but on work projects such as the repair of roads and fortifications. The fact that the Theoric Fund was forbidden to finance military expeditions stood in the way of the assembly's authorizing ill-considered military campaigns, which deprived the poor of the pay they normally received as rowers in the fleet, but the Theoric Fund with its various distributions and work programs compensated to a considerable degree for the absence of these wages. Gradually taking control of the state's finances, Eubulus brought Athens to a condition of considerable prosperity. Afterward Lycurgus, first a student of Plato and then of Isocrates, similarly solidified the city's fiscal situation in the 330s. None of these developments, however, in any way limited the authority of the demos or altered the fact that Athens fell into the category of the radical democracy so roundly condemned by Aristotle in his *Politics*.[26] Pay was introduced, and then increased, for attendance at the assembly. The legislators were chosen by lot in the demes from rich and poor alike.

As in the fifth century, there was no property qualification for citizenship; offices were short term and many officials were selected by lot; and more power was in the hands of the many poor than in those of the rich few. Officials were held to strict account for what the demos considered proper performance of their duties, and accountability trials like those of Anytus in 409 and of the Arginusae generals in 406 continued with the impeachment of Andocides and three other ambassadors after a failed peace embassy in 392/91, the impeachment of the general Ergocles in 389 for treason and embezzlement, the impeachment of the general Dionysius in 387/86 for treason, and many others.[27] That the frequency of these trials

26. Aristotle *Politics* 1317b.

27. M. Hansen, *Eisangelia: The Sovereignty of the People's Court in Athens in the Fourth Century B. C. and the Impeachment of Generals and Politicians. Odense University Classical Studies* Vol. 6 (Odense, Denmark: Odense University Press), 87–9; J. Roberts, "The Athenian Conservatives and the Impeachment Trials of the Corinthian War," *Hermes* 108 (1980), 100–114; B. Strauss, "The Cultural Significance of Bribery and Embezzlement in Athenian Politics: The Evidence of the Period of 403–383 B. C.," *Ancient World* 11 (1985): 70–1.

increased after 403 seems to have been a consequence not so much of the war as of the freeing up of energy after a letup in the fighting. A spate of private lawsuits followed, for the fourth century was the age of forensic speaking par excellence; the passion for oratory that had begun in the fifth century with speakers like Antiphon, Andocides, and Lysias continued into the fourth, as Andocides and Lysias continued their careers and were joined by the many students of Gorgias's pupil Isocrates, who did not, except at the beginning of his career, speak himself but taught many other speakers, including Isaeus, who in turn taught the most famous of Greek orators, the anti-Macedonian crusader Demosthenes.

In drama, the temporary end of the fighting after Aegospotami—it certainly resumed soon enough—seemed to mark a watershed, but of course it was not the war that killed Sophocles and Euripides. The deaths of the two tragedians in 406 were certainly a turning point in drama, which was never the same afterward, and much more responsible for a decline in tragedy than any effects of the years of fighting. But Attic tragedy had never been confined to the works of Aeschylus, Sophocles, and Euripides. Aeschylus's son Euphorion defeated both Sophocles and Euripides at the Dionysia in 431, and it was in honor of Agathon's first victory at the Lenaea in 416 that the banquet featured in Plato's dialogue the *Symposium* was held. The writing of tragedy underwent a hiatus of a generation or so after the deaths of the famous tragedians, whether because the Athenians had lost their best or because they had been demoralized by the war. Then the writing of tragedy resumed, but those plays do not survive. Aeschylus's great-grandson Astydamas gained his first victory in 372, Theodectes in 368. Although tragedy may never have reached the heights of the fifth century, it was certainly not dead. Aristotle discussed Theodectes' *Lynceus* at length in his *Poetics*.[28] Many traditions persisted. The rise of virtuoso "star" actors like Nicostratus and Theodorus began in the fifth century and continued into the fourth. In the fourth century as in the fifth, Attic tragedy was performed extensively outside of Athens—quite possibly more so. Aeschylus had visited Sicily and had his work performed there. Euripides and Agathon both moved to Macedon

28. Aristotle *Poetics* 1455b20.

toward the end of their lives and produced plays there; in the fourth century tragedies were performed widely throughout the Greek world, in Eretria and Corinth, for example. A new feature in performance also appeared: the prevalence of traveling actors, who set up stages in Italy and Sicily.[29] In 386 revivals of Aeschylus, Sophocles, and Euripides were introduced as a non-competitive element in Athens' City Dionysia.

To be sure, the genre known as Old Comedy died with Aristophanes, whose *Wealth*, written in 408, was produced again with minor changes around 388, two years before the poet's death, and whose *Ecclesiazusae* (*Assemblywomen*) appeared in 392; these (in particular *Wealth*) are sometimes counted in the lighter genre of Middle Comedy. The comedy of the fourth century (Middle Comedy and then New Comedy) did not pack quite the same punch as the obscene and highly political Old Comedy of the fifth century. There had, however, been other successful practitioners of Old Comedy, prize-winners whose work survives only in fragments. Of these, Cratinus died during the war and not because of it, but we are not so certain about Eupolis: there are several traditions about his death, and one makes him indeed a casualty of the war in the Hellespont. Perhaps Old Comedy would have lived on had he survived.[30]

But it would not be in drama that the legacy of fourth-century Greece would lie. Rather, the fourth-century would provide the cornerstones for Western philosophy in the dialogues of Plato and the treatises of Aristotle (though Aristotle lies rather outside the scope of this book). In this regard, for all the ongoing warfare that consumed the major states of Greece and many of the minor ones, the fourth century represented one of the pinnacles of Greek civilization.

29. On Greek tragedy in the late fifth and early fourth century, see E. Hall, "Greek Tragedy, 430–380 B. C.," in *Debating the Athenian Cultural Revolution: Art, Literature, Philosophy, and Politics 430–380 BC*, ed. R. Osborne (Cambridge: Cambridge University Press, 2007), 264–87.

30. On the various traditions concerning Eupolis's death, see I. C. Storey, *Eupolis: Poet of Old Comedy* (Oxford: Oxford University Press, 2003), 56–7.

18

THE GREEK STATES IN A CHANGING WORLD

THE VICTORS OF AEGOSPOTAMI were not immune to problems of their own. After Lysander's stunning success in the Hellespont, fate called on the Spartans to decide how to exercise the power that had fallen to them. If we are to believe Thucydides, Alcibiades had suggested to them that when they proved victorious over Athens they would enjoy a hegemony over Greece grounded not in force but in goodwill.[1] But events proved that the Spartans, taking a page from the playbook of Cleon—and of Machiavelli—preferred to be feared than loved. This fatal preference dictated their policy throughout the fourth century and would contribute in large part to their downfall. In short order they made enemies of their former allies and, losing track of the importance of Persian support in international affairs, even elected to make war on the mighty Persian Empire. All this would come back to bite them when a coalition formed against them in mainland Greece and the Athenian Conon gained command of a combined Persian-Phoenician fleet in the east.

GREECE IN THE FOURTH CENTURY

It was not only the years after 403 that showed internal strains within the Greek states (Sparta included). Problems had begun well before that, but

1. Thucydides 6. 92. 5.

some of them became more acute—or more visible—during the brief lull in the fighting between Athens and Sparta that extended from 403 to 395. The civil strife that Thucydides had identified as endemic to the Greek states turned out not to be as rooted in the war, when each side could count on the support of one of the superpowers, as he had imagined. Xenophon in his *Hellenica,* which deals with the period from 411 to 362, cites more than thirty instances of such strife. In 392 Corinthian democrats murdered oligarchs, some of them in temples where they had taken refuge. In 370/69 Argive democrats murdered 1,200 members of the elite and then turned on their own leaders, killing them as well.[2] Economic inequality had been apparent in Athens during the last decade of the fifth century when Aristophanes wrote his *Wealth*, in which the personified god comes among mortals and finds them in great anguish about the unfair distribution of riches, the unworthy having much and the worthy having little; his *Assemblywomen*, produced in the late 390s, takes as its premise the need of women to take over the assembly in order to institute a communistic government so that everyone will have enough—and this in a relatively prosperous state like Athens. Civil strife was worst where there was a large number of poor people, and poverty was widespread, especially in the Peloponnesus.

Many Greeks had returned from the fighting to find their farms in disarray. Not only had the farmers themselves left to serve their countries; they had often taken slave helpers to carry their baggage. While the very young, the very old, and the women had picked up a great deal of the slack and worked the land the best they could, still things were not the way they had been before. Now the veterans also discovered that the metics and artisans in the cities had skills with which they could not compete. Since their expertise now lay in fighting, service as a mercenary seemed to many like the best—perhaps the only—route to survival. The effect on family structure of these long years of fighting had been devastating, and now the continuing lure of mercenary service would prolong the disruption. When Cyrus decided to challenge his brother Artaxerxes for the Persian throne, he managed to gather around 13,000 mercenaries, largely (though not entirely) Greek, to march with him into the heart of

2. Diodorus 15. 57. 3–58. 4.

the Persian Empire—men who to their horror promptly had to march out again when the prince's attempt failed. The terrain was rough, many of the locals hostile, and the weather vile as they fled the murderous wrath of Tissaphernes. Xenophon, who marched with them, wrote up this remarkable tale some years later in his *Anabasis* (*March Upcountry*).

Their unique social system and unusual inheritance laws brought the Spartans particular problems, so that despite their victory over Athens, the Spartans also found themselves under stress. One reason they had hesitated to raze Athens was the fear that money from an annihilated Athens would pour into Sparta, destroying their ancestral way of life. After his victory at Aegospotami, Lysander had sent Gylippus, the victor of Syracuse, back to Sparta with huge amounts of public money, along with the gifts and crowns he himself had received. Gylippus, however, not realizing he was also carrying tallies of all the riches, skimmed a goodly amount of the silver for himself and hid it under the tiles of his roof. The discovery of a huge discrepancy between the amount on the tally and the amount delivered drove home to the Spartans the corrupting effects of money, and one of them approached the ephors, imploring them to purify the city of all silver and gold as "imported curses." Plutarch reports that it was finally decided to permit silver and gold to be held by the city for public use but to punish any private person with the death penalty if he was caught possessing them.[3] If this is so, the rule was widely disobeyed and soon fell into abeyance.

Although the imperial city had been saved from destruction, booty from the war and tribute imposed on its former possessions—even if not the full 1,000-plus talents reported by Diodorus—did make its way into Sparta and destabilized the former agricultural monolith, further exacerbating the distinctions between rich and poor that had existed since well before the war. Sparta had already suffered a drop in manpower as a consequence of the earthquake of 464, and in the half century since the Battle of Mantinea in 418, the Spartiate population experienced yet another decrease of more than 50 percent as wartime losses continued and the partition of land among heirs male and female deprived many of the ability to make the required contribution to the *syssition*; in

3. Plutarch *Lysander* 16–17.

Sparta—unlike, say, in Athens—daughters probably inherited half the portion allotted to sons. Men affected by these inheritance laws often fell out of the ranks of the *homoioi*.[4] In Athens a poor man just became a thete, but in Sparta he ceased to be a citizen. Increasingly Sparta began to fill up with *hypomeiones*—"inferiors" who had lost their status as *homoioi*. Among the *homoioi* still around, some were much wealthier than others, and they were no longer so timid about showing it.

A mysterious crisis in 400 or very shortly afterward revealed the cracks that were opening up in Spartan society. One Cinadon, who had evidently fallen from the Spartiate class into the ranks of the "inferiors" and was smarting from his loss of status, thought to fan the flames of revolution. By all rights he should have succeeded. Adding up the *neodamodeis*, the inferiors, and the helots, the disaffected vastly outnumbered the shrunken Spartiate class, and Cinadon thought he could count on the perioeci as well. Two obstacles, however, stood in his way. The first was rather curious: not all those he expected to be ripe for revolt were in fact all that discontented. The perioeci had been fighting loyally beside the Spartans for generations; Spartans had been gradually absorbing helots and then *neodamodeis* into the army; and while there were no grants of citizenship under consideration, Cinadon's claim that everyone outside the inner circle would jump at the opportunity to eat a Spartiate even raw was not true. The second was of a more immediate nature: he shared his plot with the wrong person, who promptly reported it to the ephors. The rebellion, consequently, came to nothing. But it speaks to the breadth of disaffection in Greece that it should have made itself felt even in Sparta, which had been stable for more than half a century.[5]

SPARTA ON THE WARPATH

Feeling that they had sufficiently humbled the Athenian enemy and no longer having their hands full with the war, the Spartans at once

4. I accept here as probable the interpretation of G. L. Cawkwell, "The Decline of Sparta," *Classical Quarterly*, n. s. 33 (1983), 385–400, esp. 390.

5. Xenophon *Hellenica* 3. 3. 4–11.

busied themselves attending to lingering grudges and alienating their allies. In 420 they had gotten into a dispute with Elis that had resulted in the Eleians, who controlled access to Olympia, banning them from the Olympic games. This interdiction had probably remained in force for the balance of the war; and the Eleians had subsequently forbidden Agis to enter Olympia to perform a sacrifice on the grounds that an established usage precluded Greeks from consulting the oracle regarding a war fought against fellow Greeks. In addition, in the diplomatic chaos that had followed the Peace of Nicias, Elis had allied with Mantinea, Argos, and Athens against Sparta. Now in 401 Agis took the occasion to pounce. Life was always made easier for the Spartans if they could garner a majority vote in the Peloponnesian League to back their actions, and the chances of this were enhanced by the existence of many small members whom they could pressure into voting in favor of the policies they preferred. Seeing that Elis had grown more powerful by incorporating several small states into itself, Sparta demanded that it allow these states their freedom, and when the Eleians refused, the Spartans declared war. Conspicuously, the Thebans and the Corinthians did not send the contingents their hegemon requested, although the cowed Athenians did. In the end the Eleians were forced to grant eight states independence.[6]

The Eleian war sent a clear message that the Spartans intended to use their newfound power to meddle in the affairs of other states. Shortly after the events at Elis, an important change took place at Sparta: in 400, Agis died. Under normal circumstances, he would have been succeeded by his son Leotychidas. These, however, were not normal circumstances, for Lysander, the erstwhile lover of Agis's half-brother Agesilaus, was standing by ready to foment trouble, using the long-standing rumor that Leotychidas had in fact been fathered by Athens' wayward son Alcibiades during his sojourn in Sparta.[7] Having failed in his efforts to get the kingship thrown open to Spartans outside the two royal families—no oracle anywhere would give him the necessary go-ahead—he decided to content himself with putting Agesilaus on the throne and controlling him as

6. Xenophon *Hellenica* 3. 2. 21–31; Diodorus 14. 17. 4–12; 34. 1.

7. Plutarch *Alcibiades* 23. 7–9; *Agesilaus* 3. 1–2; *Lysander* 22. 3–4.

he ruled. (As it turned out, Agesilaus proved quite resistant to any such influence by the kingmaker.) The former navarch was dogged in his determination and even prevailed against the esteemed oracle interpreter Diopeithes, who pointed out an existing prophecy warning the Spartans of a danger posed to them by a "lame kingship"—for Agesilaus was lame in one leg. The lameness to which the oracle referred, Lysander insisted, was that of the bastard kingship that would result from the accession of a man not descended from the line of Heracles like other Spartan kings. Not coincidentally, Lysander himself belonged to a Heraclid family. Amazingly, he prevailed and Agesilaus became king of Sparta.[8]

At Lysander's urging, the new king soon set out for Asia. But to what end? The Spartans had entered the war promising to liberate the Greeks from Athenian domination only to sell the Greek cities of Asia Minor to the Persians in exchange for money with which to defeat Athens at sea. What now would be the relationship between Sparta and Persia? When Cyrus had challenged his brother for the Persian throne, he received not only the unofficial backing of thousands of Greek and non-Greek mercenaries but the official backing of Sparta. In a sense, the Spartan decision to side with Cyrus in the contest for the Persian throne had brought them good luck: when the states of Ionia, hard-pressed by an irate Artaxerxes via his henchman Tissaphernes, sought assistance from the Greek homeland, the Spartans in coming to their aid could now reactivate their slogan of "freeing the Greeks." Already in 400 a large Spartan force had been sent to Asia, led first by Thibron and then by the more effective Dercyllidas, swollen by the soldiers who had fought to put Cyrus on the throne. Now in 396, having heard rumors of major Persian naval preparations, Agesilaus appointed himself leader of the crusade.[9] The beginnings of the undertaking, however, were not auspicious. Agesilaus had with him 2,000 *neodamodeis*, 6,000 allies, and 30 Spartiate advisers. Added to the men already in Asia, his force would be enormous, even though the Corinthians and Thebans refused to go. (The Athenians had already contributed some of the cavalrymen who had served under the

8. Xenophon *Hellenica* 3. 3. 1–4; Plutarch *Lysander* 22. 5–6; Plutarch *Agesilaus* 3.
9. Plutarch *Agesilaus* 6. 1.

Thirty to the army of Thibron, wanting to get them out from underfoot and hoping indeed that they would never return alive.)[10] Agesilaus had thought to make sacrifice at Aulis in Boeotia before sailing for Asia, as Agamemnon had done before setting out for Troy. Before he could complete the sacrifice, however, the cavalry of the Boeotian League, presumably at the instigation of the anti-Spartan democrat Ismenias and his partisans, rushed up and ordered him to desist. Not only was Agesilaus's imitation of Agamemnon unsettling in its hubris, but the vast size of the expedition was worrisome, and the anti-Spartans in Thebes were anxious. Just how powerful a force did this king expect to become in Asia? Calling upon the gods to witness this affront to his dignity, Agesilaus departed, but he never forgot the insult, and he lived a long time.[11]

Once in Asia, Agesilaus moved with great speed up and down the coast. His efforts paid off: in the summer of 395, his troops defeated those of Tissaphernes resoundingly at the Battle of Sardis, and Artaxerxes responded by ordering the unsuccessful satrap's execution.[12] Visions of an empire even greater than the one Athens had enjoyed now danced dizzily in Spartan heads. Persian suzerainty might even be confined as far east as the Halys River.[13] Agesilaus's victory energized the eastern Greeks, and at his instigation they soon had constructed and manned no fewer than 120 ships—a good plan, since the Persians had been building up their own navy. Since 398/7, indeed, the vice-admiral of that navy was none other than the Athenian Conon, whose good fortune and presence of mind had facilitated his escape from the debacle at Aegospotami.[14] His motivation to strike a blow against Sparta knew no bounds. He more than anyone recalled the terror of Aegospotami and the tsunami unleashed on the Athenians by Lysander's men, and of course, remembering the fate of the victors of Arginusae, he could not safely return home without scoring a signal victory for Athens.

10. Xenophon *Hellenica* 3. 1. 4.

11. Xenophon *Hellenica* 3. 4. 3–4; Plutarch *Agesilaus* 6. 4-6.

12. Xenophon *Hellenica* 3. 4. 25; Plutarch *Agesilaus* 10. 3–4.

13. As pointed out by S. Ruzicka, "The Eastern Greek World," in L. A. Tritle, ed., *The Greek World in the Fourth Century* (London: Routledge, 1997), 112.

14. Xenophon *Hellenica* 3. 4. 28.

Now too, however, hearing about Conon's leadership of a mighty fleet, mainland Greeks who had been cowed by Agesilaus's successes began to think differently about Sparta (though some were still skittish and hesitated to send aid to Conon). Perhaps this was an enemy that could be beaten and Aegospotami had not been the end of the line after all. Many Thebans and other Boeotians, moreover, found the Spartans' behavior troubling. The northern outpost of Heraclea Trachinia, once wrested from Spartan control by the Boeotians during the Peloponnesian War, was now back in Spartan hands, governed by the bloody harmost Herippidas (the position of harmost being an invention of Lysander, technically meaning just the head of a garrison in a recently conquered city or region; but often harmosts were tasked with putting down democracies, and the word developed bad associations).[15]

The Spartans also seem to have expanded into Thessaly, installing a garrison at Pharsalus, the southernmost of the four major Thessalian cities. This development may well have taken place around the same time as the retaking of Heraclea.[16] Lysander was plainly gathering allies in the north. Spartan meddling in the internal politics of Thebes was also becoming intolerable, and some Thebans were giving serious thought to a war of revanche, for opposed to the party of Ismenias was that of Leontiades, whose father was probably the Eurymachus who had died in the Theban assault at Plataea, and the Spartans had supported this faction. This, the Oxyrhynchus Historian reports, was why the party of Ismenias "strove to involve the nation in war against the Spartans, wanting to overthrow their power so as not to be destroyed by the Lacedaemonians through the agency of pro-Spartan Boeotians" such as Leontiades.[17] At first, the proposition had seemed hopeless, but now things were beginning to change. It was probably in 396 that a man named Timocrates arrived from Rhodes, sent by a Persian official and bearing a substantial sum of money to distribute among Greek states ready for war against Sparta: the

15. Diodorus 14. 38. 4.

16. Diodorus 14. 82. 6. The date is conjectured by P. Cartledge in *Agesilaos and the Crisis of Sparta* (London: Duckworth, 1987), 289.

17. *Hellenica Oxyrhynchia* 13. 1.

king, plainly, was hoping to draw Agesilaus away from his territory by stirring up trouble in the Greek homeland.[18]

The Thebans were now optimistic that Corinth and Sparta's old enemy Argos would join them in a war against Sparta. Athens, which had made a substantial economic recovery since Aegospotami, surely would as well. And there was encouraging news from an Athenian abroad as well. Conon had engineered Rhodes' defection from Sparta, and in 395 a democratic revolution took place there. The supplies that the Peloponnesians had expected to be sent there from the Egyptian king Nephereus (could it really have been the 100 triremes and 500,000 measures of grain Diodorus reports?) then fell into Conon's welcoming hands.[19]

Still, some Greeks were edgy about war with the once mighty Spartans. Some impressive maneuvering would be called for if Ismenias and his partisans were going to be able to convince their fellow Greeks—first Boeotians, then others—to go to war. The spark was provided by a long-standing conflict between the Phocians and their neighbors to the east, the Opuntian Locrians, over some sheep-grazing land near Mount Parnassus. Encouraged by Ismenias and like-minded Thebans, the Phocians invaded Locris and ravaged the land. In response, the Locrians appealed to Boeotia for assistance.[20] Again encouraged by the faction of Ismenias, the Boeotians voted to grant it, feeling obliged by their treaty obligations to the Locrians. Learning of the Boeotians' decision, the Phocians sent to the Spartans asking them to enjoin Boeotia from attacking them. Predictably, the Boeotians found the Spartans' conduct high-handed, and the Thebans now voted to invade Phocis.[21] For all practical purposes, the Corinthian War (395–86) was on.

18. *Hellenica Oxyrhynchia* 2. 2; Xenophon *Hellenica* 3 5. 1–2; Polyaenus 1. 48. 3; Pausanias 3. 9. 8. The chronology of this period is much debated, particularly the relationship between Timocrates' arrival in Greece and the other events leading up to the decision to go to war with Sparta.

19. Diodorus 14. 79. 4–7.

20. *Hellenica Oxyrhynchia* 13. 2–5; *Xenophon Hellenica* 3. 5. 3–4; Pausanias 3. 9. 9–11.

21. *Hellenica Oxyrhynchia* 13. 4.

THE CORINTHIAN WAR

Predictably, the Spartans determined to attack Boeotia in full force. Lysander was instructed to invade from the north via Phocis, and Pausanias would advance from the south. Their forces would meet on a predetermined day at the town of Haliartus in western Boeotia. When the Thebans learned what was happening, they sent to the Athenians for aid, suggesting that the time had come for them to set about regaining their earlier power. Probably on the motion of Thrasybulus, the Athenians voted to ally with the Boeotian Confederacy.[22]

Xenophon reports that the vote was unanimous, but this is not credible, for since their defeat at Aegospotami, the Athenians had been divided into several factions.[23] Loosely speaking, there were affluent men who wished to maintain the status quo, some of them people who had supported the Thirty; radicals who wanted to resume the war with Sparta as soon as possible; and moderates, democrats who certainly had thoughts of resuming the war but had no intention of doing anything until the time was propitious. Thrasybulus probably led this last faction, but it is questionable whether he could have carried the entire assembly with him even now that the time did indeed seem right. (One man who could not vote on the matter was Conon, who was off in the east leading the Persian fleet in preparation for an attack on Sparta. His own feelings were clear, and he had a good deal of support in Athens.)

The coordination between the Spartans Lysander and Pausanias in Boeotia in 395 was no more successful than that of the Athenians Demosthenes and Hippocrates had been in Boeotia in 424. The plan was for the two commanders to meet at Haliartus. Lysander arrived on schedule; Pausanias did not. Restless for action, Lysander engaged the enemy without waiting for the king. One can imagine Pausanias's astonishment when he learned on his arrival at Haliartus that Lysander, son of Aristocleitus, the world-famous victor of Aegospotami, lay dead under the city walls.[24]

22. P. J. Rhodes and R. Osborne, *Greek Historical Inscriptions 404-323 B. C.* (Oxford: Oxford University Press, 2003), No. 6.

23. Xenophon *Hellenica* 3. 5. 16.

24. Xenophon *Hellenica* 3. 5. 17–19.

Astonished, but not necessarily distressed, Pausanias cannot have shed many tears over Lysander's demise. The navarch had long been a thorn in his side. Even so, the king was to suffer mightily for the debacle at Haliartus. Many of Sparta's allies had fled in the night, and right after Pausanias's arrival the Boeotians' Athenian reinforcements materialized. Pausanias found himself badly outnumbered in cavalry. Recovering the bodies of Lysander and those who had died with him seemed a better choice than fighting against dubious odds. When the Thebans allowed him to collect his dead only on condition that the Spartans withdraw from Boeotia, he and his advisers agreed, but upon his arrival home, he was brought to trial, ostensibly for his conduct of the campaign. Wisely, he fled to Tegea, correctly foreseeing a verdict of death.[25] It was in Tegea that he lived out the rest of his years, which were not inconsiderable; he was still alive when his son Agesipolis died in 380, fifteen years later. The Spartans' rough handling of their king was most unfair and had much to do with his lenience toward the Athenians nearly a decade earlier: it was Lysander, who had rushed into battle prematurely, who needed to be taken to be task for the failure of coordination at Haliartus, but of course Lysander was dead, and Pausanias, with whom the Spartans were angry already, made a convenient scapegoat.

Within a decade of Lysander's stunning victory at Aegospotami, Sparta's ambitious imperialism in Asia had combined with its graceless diplomacy in the Greek homeland to forge a coalition between its old allies and its ancestral enemies. The Spartans now faced a determined quadruple alliance of Boeotia, Corinth, Argos, and Athens, backed by forces from Acarnania, Leucas, Euboea, and the Chalcidian League. The Corinthian War had begun, the detritus of the Peloponnesian War and Sparta's relentless conduct afterward—its installation of the Thirty, its battering of its allies.[26] Despite his victories in Asia, plainly Agesilaus would have to be recalled to attend to affairs on the mainland. He was not a happy man.

25. Xenophon *Hellenica* 3. 5. 22–5; Plutarch *Lysander* 30. 1.

26. On the outbreak of the Corinthian War, see I. A. F. Bruce, "Internal Politics and the Outbreak of the Corinthian War," *Emerita* 28 (1960), 75–86; D. Kagan, "The Economic Origins of the Corinthian War," *La Parola del Passato* 16 (1961), 321–41; S. Perlman, "The Causes and Outbreak of the Corinthian War," *Classical Quarterly* n. s. 14 (1964) 64–81; C. Hamilton, *Sparta's Bitter Victories*,: Politics and Diplomacy in the Corinthian War (Ithaca: Cornell University Press, 1979), 182–207; and B. Strauss, *Athens after the Peloponnesian War*, 89–125.

The forces of the two sides first collided near the dry bed of the Nemea River in Corinthian territory; Agesilaus was not present, as he was still on the march. The Spartan force numbered some 20,000 hoplites, 600 cavalry, 300 paid Cretan archers, and some light-armed troops. The troops of the allies totaled 24,000 hoplites plus 1,500 cavalry and somewhat more light-armed men. Spartan casualties were about 1,100, but the allies lost around 2,800; the unusual formation of the Boeotians—they were drawn up over sixteen-men deep—was an interesting innovation, but in the end it did not help them. Still, the allies had achieved their goal of keeping the Spartans' forces from entering central Greece via the isthmus.[27]

Now they would face an army under the command of Agesilaus himself, who had regretfully left 4,000 men in Asia to garrison the Greek cities there before crossing the Hellespont to deal with matters at home. The quadruple alliance met him on his southward march at Coronea in Boeotia, and once again they were defeated.[28]

The Spartans, however, could not dislodge their enemies from their position on the isthmus. Xenophon took the occasion of the encounter to offer a vivid account of the hoplite battle and its aftermath. "Crashing their shields together," he wrote, "they shoved, they fought, they killed, and were killed."[29] Further details appear in his life of Agesilaus, who was wounded on that day. There was no shouting, he says, but neither was there silence, just the peculiar noise that rage and battle together will produce. And when the fighting ended,

> an eerie spectacle met the eye—the earth red with blood, friend and foe lying dead side by side, shields smashed to bits, spears broken in two, the naked blades of daggers removed from their sheaths, some on the ground, some stuck in bodies, some still grasped in hands[30] (Figure 13).

One Athenian who died in this war was the cavalryman Dexileus, who was heroized in a beautiful memorial in Athens' national cemetery

27. Xenophon *Hellenica* 4. 2. 9–23; Diodorus 14. 83. 1–2.
28. Xenophon *Hellenica* 4. 3. 10–21.
29. Xenophon *Hellenica* 4. 3. 19.
30. Xenophon *Agesilaus* 2. 12–14.

FIGURE 13
Monument of the cavalryman Dexileus. 394. Athens, Ceramicus. Oberlaender Museum.
Photo: Marie Mauzy/Art Resource, NY.

that depicted him on his horse bearing down on an enemy. The glorious image on his tombstone sanitizes his dismal death.

But operations at sea were far kinder to the allies than their land operations: in 394 Pharnabazus and Conon (now promoted to high admiral of the combined fleet) led a flotilla of Phoenician and Persian ships—along with a large force of Greek mercenary sailors—to victory over the Peloponnesians off Cnidus, capturing or sinking fifty of their eighty-five ships. The inexperienced navarch Peisander, chosen for the job only because he was brother-in-law to Agesilaus, died fighting on his flagship.[31] The Athenian and the Persian then sailed along the islands and coastal cities of Asia Minor, expelling the Spartan harmosts who remained and, at Conon's insistence, granting autonomy wherever they

31. Xenophon *Hellenica* 4. 3. 10–12; Diodorus 14. 83. 4–7.

landed (though they failed to dislodge the Spartan Dercyllidas, tenacious in his hold on Sestos and Abydos).

The consequences of the Battle of Cnidus were momentous and went a long way toward muting Lysander's stunning success at Aegospotami. The Spartan naval empire had lasted only a decade; at least Lysander had not lived to witness its demise. In building up the fleet to counter the Spartans' naval efforts in Asia Minor, moreover, Artaxerxes had funneled an enormous amount of money to Conon, with which the Greek émigré hired large numbers of sailors from home, thus building up the Athenian fleet for the future. In the following year Conon and Pharnabazus crossed the Aegean, raiding the coast of Laconia and striking great fear in the Spartans by garrisoning the island of Cythera off the Peloponnesus. They then proceeded to the isthmus, where Pharnabazus encouraged the envoys of the quadruple alliance with both words and money. In Athens, already experiencing economic recovery, the first steps in rebuilding the fortifications of the Piraeus and the Long Walls had been taken before Conon's great victory. Now Conon sailed into the Piraeus with eighty triremes, and with the help of his crews and money from Pharnabazus the work of restoration took a giant leap forward.[32] Persian gold, which once enabled Lysander to order the Long Walls destroyed, now aided in their reconstruction (Figure 14).

Gaining in confidence, the Athenians retook some of their old island possessions—Scyros, Imbros, and Lemnos—and established there the distinctive Athenian settlements known as "cleruchies": not colonies, which were politically autonomous, but outposts whose inhabitants retained their Athenian citizenship. Back in the Greek homeland, the Spartans had been made nervous by a novel arrangement between Corinth and Argos: an "isopolity" whereby the two states had reciprocal rights in each other's polis, though Argos was inevitably the stronger partner by virtue of its greater size.[33]

Money supplied by Pharnabazus enabled the Corinthians to build ships and challenge the Spartans for control of the Corinthian Gulf. In addition, the Spartans had taken a tremendous hit financially with

32. Xenophon *Hellenica* 4. 8. 1–2, 7–9.

33. G. T. Griffith, "The Union of Corinth and Argos (392–386 B. C.)," *Historia* 1 (1950), 236–56.

FIGURE 14
Remains of walls at Piraeus, rebuilt by Conon and Athenians after Battle of Cnidus in 394.
Photo: Lawrence Tritle.

the forced recall of Agesilaus and Conon's naval victory at Cnidus. Returning to Greece, Agesilaus had paid a 100-talent tithe of his eastern booty at Delphi, indicating that he would be losing 1,000 talents of booty, a sum that could have been repeated again and again had events not forced him to return, and the defeat of his brother-in-law's fleet off Cnidus had meant the end of the annual tribute of 1,000 talents coming in from Lysander's settlement of 404.[34] Athenian control of Cythera too was profoundly disquieting, and the Athenian Iphicrates maintained an ominous presence at Corinth. His innovations in the gear of the light-armed fighters signaled an important expansion of Greek warfare: converting the dagger into a short sword suited to hand-to-hand combat and fitting men out with a longer javelin, he also designed boots (named after him) that were cheaper, lighter, and more easily put on and taken off. In light of these developments, in 392 Sparta sent Antalcidas as an ambassador to Tiribazus, the satrap of Sardis (and later of Lydia), with the goal

34. Xenophon *Agesilaus* 1. 34.

of attaining peace between Sparta and Persia and, if possible, diverting Persian support from Athens to Sparta. Hearing of these negotiations, the members of the quadruple alliance sent envoys as well. But negotiations fell through, the fighting continued, and in the midst of the war Conon died, much mourned throughout the Greek world, where many statues of him were erected; in Samos and Ephesus the people tore down statues of Lysander in order to memorialize Conon with statues instead.

The Athenians' imperialist ambitions had been reawakened and would not be subdued. Though it seems that the propertied classes favored peace, the majority hoped to regain the overseas assets that had been lost in the long Peloponnesian War. Around 390, Thrasybulus was sent out with forty ships. He obtained the alliance of Thasos, settled a quarrel between the two Thracian kings Amadocus and Seuthes and secured the friendship of both, and of course already had control of the route toward the Hellespont through the Athenian cleruchies in Lembros, Imbros, and Scyros. Byzantium having been betrayed to him by its democratic faction, he also moved into Chalcedon. Working his way south in need of funds, he did not scruple to collect money by raiding, and this was a mistake. In Aspendus, by the Eurymedon River—where around 467 his countryman Cimon had defeated the Persians so soundly that some Greeks questioned whether there was still any need for an alliance against their old enemy—the outraged locals burst into his tent and killed him.[35] So died Thrasybulus of Steiria, the great hero of the Athenian democracy, who had commanded the city's forces in many battles and, most of all, had led the exiles who retook the city from the Thirty Tyrants in 403. But like many Athenians, he was not only a democrat but an imperialist, and it was as an imperialist that he died.

THE KING'S PEACE (387/6)

Not long afterward Tiribazus persuaded Artaxerxes to switch his loyalty to the Spartans. In addition to the gains they had made in Asia Minor under Thrasybulus, the Athenians had become involved in the revolt of

35. Xenophon *Hellenica* 4. 8. 30; Diodorus 14. 99. 4.

Evagoras of Cyprus from the Persian Empire— Evagoras, who had received honorary Athenian citizenship and who had offered a home to Conon upon his flight from Aegospotami. With the help of Tiribazus and Dionysius, tyrant of Syracuse, the Spartan Antalcidas managed to assemble a fleet of more than eighty vessels and with it to stop the grain ships that were sailing from the Black Sea for Athens. Another fleet, operating from Aegina, blockaded Athens itself.[36] The echoes of Aegospotami were unmistakable. The Athenians caved, and as the other allies were unwilling to fight on without them, peace was made. But in a disturbing replication of the years leading up to Aegospotami, the dramatic developments of these years—Conon's victory at Cnidus, the Peace of 387/6—all seemed to hinge on Persian intervention.

The peace was conceived in the most humiliating terms possible, constructed as it was in a rescript from the king himself beginning "I, King Artaxerxes, consider it just. . . ." The king went on to specify that the cities in Asia plus the islands of Clazomenae and Cyprus should belong to him, but all other Greek cities should be autonomous, though Athens could keep Lemnos, Imbros, and Scyros. On any who did not accept the peace, the king would make war along with any who would help him "by land and by sea, with ships and with money."[37] There may well have been other specifications not mentioned by Xenophon.[38] The Spartans would serve as the guarantors of the peace. So ended the years of squabbling—bloody squabbling—among the Greek states: with a Persian victory but certainly a nod to Sparta as well. The first of several agreements reached in the fourth century that might qualify as the sort of "Common Peace" many Greeks desired grounded in a principle of autonomy, this one in fact excluded a huge swath of Greece, selling out as it did the cities of the East to the Persian king.[39]

36. Xenophon *Hellenica* 5. 1. 25–9.

37. Xenophon *Hellenica* 5. 1. 31.

38. On this and the other peace treaties of the first half of the fourth century, see G. Cawkwell, "The King's Peace," *Classical Quarterly* n. s. 31 (1981), 69–83. Cawkwell takes a dim view of Xenophon as a source.

39. There would be more stabs at "Common Peace" down the road. On the topic, T. T. B. Ryder, *Koine Eirene: General Peace and Local Independence in Ancient Greece* (London: Oxford University Press, 1965).

Autonomy was one of the most cherished concepts in Greek hearts—and least understood. Agesilaus made the enforcement of the autonomy clause his personal crusade. With great relish he mobilized his army and headed north when the Theban envoys claimed the right to swear on behalf of the entire Boeotian federation. Thebes backed down. The isopolity between Corinth and Argos was also sacrificed on the altar of autonomy and Corinth forced to rejoin the Peloponnesian League.[40] As after their victory at Aegospotami in 405, it remained to be seen what else the Spartans—and Agesilaus—would do with the newfound power that circumstances had dropped in their laps as the de facto enforcers of the autonomy clause of the new "peace" (although the real victor in this war was plainly Artaxerxes). The Peloponnesian War and its immediate aftermath had led to a bitterness against Sparta the consequences of which were ruinous.

Having seemingly won the war at Aegospotami, the Spartans went on to be defeated at Cnidus in Asia Minor and to lose the peace in mainland Greece. Yet despite Conon's great naval victory, the war sparked by Spartan aggression and meddling in mainland Greece led to a resurgent Athenian imperialism that finally prompted, as during the previous war, Persian intervention, putting Sparta in a favorable position once again and leaving the Greeks to wonder whether they would ever be free to settle their own affairs. There seemed to be no end to the fighting. The rhetorician and educator Isocrates exhorted the Greeks to unite against Persia once and for all, but that union was not in their nature. It would never come until it was forced on them by an autocrat from the north: Philip of Macedon.

40. Thebes, the isopolity: Xenophon *Hellenica* 5. 1. 33–4.

19

CONTINUING WARFARE AND THE END FOR SPARTA

As the guarantor of the King's Peace, the Spartans were now once more in a strong position in the Greek world and, as after their success at Aegospotami, their foreign policy in the years after the Peace was marked by aggression and meddling. History was repeating itself. This time, however, their victory was over Athens in a technical sense only, for they were no longer particularly interested in the Athenians, and this time, too, it took somewhat longer for them to pay the price for their imprudence. But by 371 their reckless belligerence and heavy-handed diplomacy had resulted in a stunning battlefield defeat and the resounding loss of their status in Greece. It did not come at the hands of the Athenians, with whom they had been fighting for so many years, but rather from the new enemy they had worked so hard to make—the Thebans. The Athenians, meanwhile, took a different path. In their more forward-thinking polis, oratory and philosophy flourished, and a new naval league was created, founded on far more equitable principles than those that had characterized the Delian League. While the Spartans, mired in old habits of thought and action, were pushing their allies away, the Athenians were drawing new allies in.

GREECE AFTER THE KING'S PEACE

Agesilaus hated democracy almost as much as he hated Thebes. This explains some, though not all, of his conduct during the years following the peace. In 385, democratic Mantinea was ordered to raze its walls on the grounds that it had not offered appropriate support during the Corinthian War. When the Mantineans refused, the Lacedaemonians diverted a river so as to wash away part of the mud-brick walls, forcing the Mantineans to surrender. The defeated Mantineans were compelled to dissolve themselves into the five villages out of which they had originally been composed many years before. The villages were to be governed oligarchically, each with the obligation to furnish military assistance to Sparta when requested.[1] Next to receive the Spartans' attention was Phlius, where civil war had broken out between oligarchs and democrats. After a siege of twenty months the city surrendered and was placed under the government of an extreme oligarchy.[2]

In 383/2 the Spartans became aware of disquieting developments in the north. A league of Chalcidic cities had been in existence for some decades; citizens shared rights of intermarriage with those of other cities and could acquire property in any town in the league, and there was a shared coinage. The capital of the league was at Olynthus. The league had allied with the enemies of Sparta in the Corinthian War, but there is no evidence that it actually participated in the fighting. But now it was expanding and pressuring unwilling cities to join, and in 382 envoys came to Sparta from Acanthus and Apollonia, cities in the Chalcidic region, reporting on the danger posed by the league both to their cities and to Greece as a whole. The Olynthians, they said, had swept up into the league not only a number of cities in Chalcidice but many in Macedon as well, nearly driving its ruler Amyntas III from his kingdom. They were even negotiating with the Thracians. Should those negotiations bear fruit, the road to the gold mines of Mt. Pangaeum would lie open. This news was most alarming to the Spartans, who had not given up their dreams of hegemony over all Greece, and of course the Olynthians' violation of the principle of autonomy could provide a rationale for interfering. Sparta promptly persuaded its allies to mobilize for war.[3]

1. Xenophon *Hellenica* 5. 2. 1–7; Diodorus 15. 5. 3–5; 12.
2. Xenophon *Hellenica* 5. 2. 8-10, 5. 3. 10–17, 25.
3. Xenophon *Hellenica* 5. 2. 11–24.

The campaign against Olynthus was hard-fought but ultimately successful, though it cost the young Agiad king Agesipolis his life, as he died of a fever while besieging the city. In 379 the league was forced to disband.[4] Amyntas's kingdom was fully restored to him. In championing the principle of autonomy, the Spartans were taking advantage not only of the autonomy clause of the King's Peace but of the sentimental attachment the Greek cities had always felt toward their independence; but in fact the Chalcidic League would have been a valuable counterweight to the ambitions of Amyntas's son and successor Philip II, who gobbled up the states of Greece and bequeathed them to his son Alexander as the cornerstone of an empire that would reach as far as India.

It was while Spartan forces were en route to Olynthus that an enticing opportunity presented itself in Thebes. There the city had for some time been divided between the partisans of Ismenias, who favored democracy, and those of Leontiades, who favored oligarchy—and Sparta. In 382 while the Spartan commander Phoebidas was encamped near Thebes on his way north, Leontiades approached him offering to betray to him the Theban citadel, the Cadmea. Phoebidas was delighted, and up the hill they went, Leontiades carrying the keys. The timing was singularly propitious, as the city was celebrating the women-only festival of the Thesmophoria and the citadel was free of males. They then arrested Ismenias, 300 of whose followers—including the future liberator Pelopidas—prudently fled to Athens. At Sparta, Agesilaus approved Phoebidas's action on the grounds of expedience, and the commander was merely fined. The unfortunate Ismenias was tried before a court of the Spartan Alliance on a charge of collusion with Persia and condemned to death—a profound irony in light of the Spartans' willingness to cooperate with Persia to improve their own position in Greece on any and all occasions that presented themselves. Even Xenophon, who was well disposed to the Spartans in general and to his friend Agesilaus in particular, was shocked by the Spartans' irreligious conduct on this occasion.[5]

4. Xenophon *Hellenica* 5. 3. 26.

5. Xenophon *Hellenica* 5. 2. 25–36; Plutarch *Pelopidas* 5; Plutarch *Agesilaus* 24. Xenophon's condemnation of Spartan seizure of Cadmea as impious: *Hellenica* 5. 4. 1.

The Spartans did not long luxuriate in their occupation of the Cadmea and the attendant domination of Boeotia. The combination of Theban and Athenian resentment soon reached the point of combustion, and the Theban patriot Pelopidas harnessed this resentment to retake his country. In 379, Theban exiles under his leadership returned from their asylum in Athens and contrived to enter a party where the polemarchs were celebrating the end of their term of office and wine was flowing freely. Dressed as women who had been promised as companions for the evening, the exiles shortly drew their swords, threw off their disguises, and dispatched the revelers. Then three of the plotters proceeded to the house of Leontiades and killed him as well. Soon scores of other exiles had returned in arms from Athens, and two Athenian generals were on the scene with troops.[6]

Besieged on the Cadmea, the Spartan harmost, who had only a small force with him, agreed to evacuate the citadel under a safe conduct; for this he was executed at home. Though they accepted—reluctantly—that they had lost control of Thebes, the Spartans were not prepared to let go of Boeotia entirely, and in 378 the Agiad king Cleombrotus marched out in a show of force. On his return march, he stationed a force of allies near Thebes in Thespiae under the harmost Sphodrias. If his intention was to frighten the Athenians, he was successful: they promptly dissociated themselves from the Theban coup by condemning to death the two generals who had supported it, executing the one who made the mistake of turning up for his trial. Presumably these generals had acted on their own initiative, albeit with a lot of unofficial support from many sympathetic Athenians.[7] Not long afterward Sphodrias decided to strike a blow for Sparta—and for himself—by seizing, of all things, the Piraeus, via a determined night march. His daring plan failed dismally, for sunrise found him and his men in the Thriasian plain west of the city, many miles from their goal. Spartan envoys who happened to find themselves in

6. Xenophon *Hellenica* 5. 4. 1–12; Diodorus 15. 25–27; Plutarch *Pelopidas* 7–13.

7. Or perhaps not; see Diodorus 15. 25–7 and Dinarchus 1. 38–9. The possibility that the generals were dispatched by an official vote of the assembly and then simply scapegoated is discussed (but dismissed) in my *Accountability*, 81–3 with notes.

Athens swore that he had acted on his own initiative and would be dealt with, but the trial that followed at Sparta gave no satisfaction. Agesilaus's son Archidamus was in love with Sphodrias's son Cleonymus. His co-king Cleombrotus, moreover, had only recently come to the throne, and Cleombrotus and Sphodrias shared many friends. Thinking it a bad start for his relationship with Cleombrotus to come down hard on Sphodrias, after much agonizing the king threw in his lot with Sphodrias and secured his acquittal.[8]

The Athenians were enraged. Incensed that they had condemned to death the generals who had gone to aid the Thebans and had let the Spartan envoys leave town, they immediately set about allying with Thebes, and over the next three years they supported the Thebans against Spartan attacks. Agesilaus now utilized a new organization of the Peloponnesian armed forces (possibly already operational during the Olynthus campaign), dividing them into ten parts; each section could, if it preferred, provide money instead of men—money with which the Spartans could hire mercenaries. Late in 378 Agesilaus invaded Boeotia with more than 18,000 hoplites as well as 1,500 cavalry, but he soon returned home, intimidated by the combined forces of the Athenians and the Thebans. Cleombrotus had no better luck when he sought to attack two years later. In the meantime the Thebans had overcome the Spartan garrison at Thespiae, killing the commander there—none other than their old nemesis Phoebidas.[9] In 375 two Spartan brigades were overtaken at Tegyra by the Sacred Band under the command of Pelopidas. Recently established by Pelopidas along with Gorgidas and probably so called because it originally guarded the shrines on the Cadmea, this body consisted of 150 pairs of lovers who, it was expected, would fight all the more bravely so as not to disgrace themselves in the eyes of their partners in love.[10] Engaging Pelopidas, both Spartan polemarchs were killed, and the triumph of the Thebans became instantly famous, for it was the first time that a Spartan

8. Xenophon *Hellenica* 5. 4. 32. I follow here the interpretation of Cartledge in *Agesilaos and the Crisis of Sparta*, 137–8, 157–8.

9. Xenophon *Hellenica* 5. 4. 34–45; Diodorus 15. 33. 6; Plutarch *Pelopidas* 15.

10. Plutarch *Pelopidas* 18.

force had been defeated by a smaller number.[11] The Spartans did not consider this to be a good sign, and they were right to be nervous.

The rivalries of the Greek poleis seemed to know no solution. In particular, the triangulation of Athens, Sparta, and Thebes continued throughout much of the fourth century with no end in sight. Periodic peace treaties were short-lived. Around the same time as the abortive raid of Sphodrias, the Athenians set about establishing a naval alliance for the express purpose of protection against Sparta; whether their first steps in this direction provoked Sphodrias's action or were taken in response to it is a matter of some uncertainty. The league began in 378 with alliances between Athens and Chios, Byzantium, Mytilene, and Rhodes. Methynma on Lesbos and Thebes joined shortly afterward. The decree (Figure 15) establishing the alliance survives on a stele, reassembled from twenty fragments, in the Epigraphical Museum at Athens.[12] Its preamble shows that it was proposed by the Athenian Aristoteles. It stated that the assembly was taking this action "so that the Spartans may allow the Greeks to live in peace."

They would exact no tribute, the Athenians promised, nor would any Athenians acquire property in allied territory, neither land nor houses; any that they did possess, they would relinquish. There would be no interference with local government. Anyone who proposed a measure contrary to the wording of the decree was to be punished by death or exile after a trial before the Athenians and the allies. Two bodies of equal weight determined league policy, the Athenian assembly and the assembly of the allies, which would sit in permanent session in Athens. Because each state sent only one delegate to the assembly of the allies, however, the Athenians could intimidate the smallest states, and they also controlled military operations. To be sure, after a while there was some backsliding from all these fine-sounding promises, and of course it would be impossible to run

11. Plutarch *Pelopidas* 17.

12. The text of the decree (*IG* 2^2 43 = Rhodes and Osborne, *Greek Historical Inscriptions*, 22) appears with English translation on pp. 16–27 of J. Cargill, *The Second Athenian League: Empire or Free Alliance?* (Berkeley: University of California Press, 1981). On the League, see in addition to Cargill above; S. Accame, *La Lege Ateniese del Sec. IV A. C.* (Rome: Signorelli, 1941) and G. Cawkwell, "The Foundation of the Second Athenian Confederacy," *Classical Quarterly* 67 (1973), 47–60.

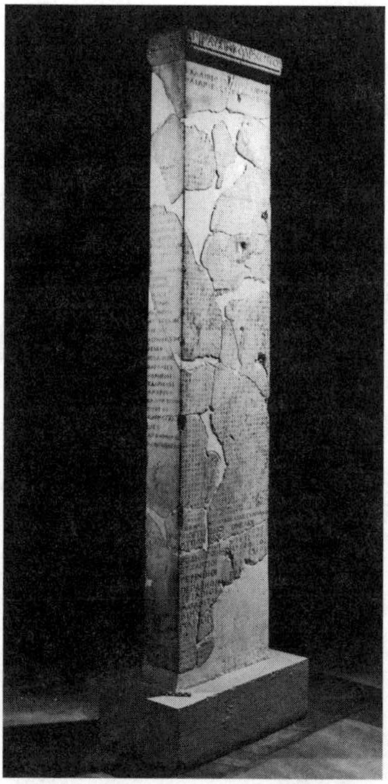

FIGURE 15
Decree of Aristoteles showing members of Second Athenian Confederacy, 377. Athens, Epigraphical Museum.
Credit: The Epigraphical Museum, Greece.

such an organization without money; in time members were called on to pay "contributions." But it says something about the quality of Athenian imperialism that about half the organization's seventy-odd members were erstwhile members of the fifth-century Delian League.

Led by their prominent admiral Chabrias, the new confederacy soon won an important naval victory over the Peloponnesians off Naxos. Ironically, Chabrias might well have annihilated the entire Spartan fleet had he not focused his energy after the battle on rescuing his men from their disabled ships, remembering the fate of the generals in command at the Battle of Arginusae. Thus did the Athenians reap the rewards of that sordid episode in their history.[13] In the west, Conon's son Timotheus brought several new

13. Diodorus 15. 34. 3–35. 2.

states into the organization. But even with contributions from allies, these operations were expensive, and in 375 the Athenians were as tired of fighting as were the Spartans and Thebans. The drive toward a Common Peace in Greece received a boost from Artaxerxes who, as usual, had his own reasons for wanting to put a stop to the fighting: busily preparing an expedition against Egypt, he calculated that a Greece at peace would be a better source of mercenaries than a Greece at war. He sent envoys to turn wish into fact, and a Common Peace on the principle of autonomy was agreed on, although it is not clear how many states beyond Sparta, Thebes, and the new Athenian League signed on to it.[14]

THE SCHOOLS OF GREECE

Not everyone in Greece was actively engaged in warfare, of course. Some—even those intensely interested in politics—led quieter lives. Pericles, in the funeral oration delivered at the end of the first year of the Peloponnesian war, had labeled Athens "the school of Greece," stressing his city's unique role as a model of democratic civility and versatile ingenuity. Now in the fourth century, two Athenians established schools that offered a concrete education to both Athenians and others, something more cohesive than what they could get from itinerant sophists. The heads of these schools were two admirers of Socrates, Isocrates and Plato. Of these, Isocrates participated in Greek politics vicariously through the many pamphlets and speeches that he wrote (though the speeches were delivered by others); Plato's relationship to political life was much more oblique. Both men had pupils who were active in public life, though the pupils of Plato did not play a large role in Athenian politics. In time, moreover, Plato's student Aristotle would found his own school, the Lyceum. Much of what concerned Greek intellectuals had nothing to do with political life, but much did, and as they looked around at the poleis of their day, they were troubled. They were right to

14. Xenophon *Hellenica* 6. 2. 1; G. Cawkwell, "Notes on the Peace of 375/4," *Historia* 12 (1963): 84–95.

be, for the unremitting warfare among the Greek states did not bode well for the survival of the independent polis.

Having studied the arts of persuasion under Gorgias, Isocrates, in need of funds since his family had lost its money during the Peloponnesian War, began his career as a "logographer," writing speeches for others to deliver in law courts. This was not an unusual profession in Athens where there were no lawyers. Around 392 he opened a school and took in paying pupils. For many decades he also continued to write speeches and political pamphlets, and the contents of his written work give some idea of what he taught at his school: fine speaking grounded in civic virtue. His concept of civic virtue seems not to have been married to any particular constitution, since he was willing to attach himself to monarchs as well as democrats. He wrote glowingly of Nicocles, the philhellenic Cypriot king of Salamis in Cyprus, addressing two speeches to him and making him the subject of a third. He was convinced that nobody who chose to speak or write words deserving of praise could possibly support unjust causes rather than honorable ones devoted to the common good. A man who wishes to persuade people, moreover, would strive to be an honorable man.[15]

Both Isocrates and Plato viewed the world around them as morally bankrupt, but they construed this lamentable situation differently and responded to it in different ways. To Isocrates it seemed that his native city had experienced a decline from earlier times when it had been guided by men like Solon, Cleisthenes, and other statesmen. He billed these leaders specifically as practitioners of oratory—"the most distinguished orators who brought the city most of its blessings."[16] Solon, Cleisthenes, and Themistocles all come in for considerable praise, but Pericles most of all,

> because he was a good leader of the people and an excellent orator who so adorned the city with temples and monuments and all other manner of beautiful things that even today all who visit the city consider her worthy of ruling not only the Greeks but the whole world. And on top of this, he stored away in the Acropolis no less than ten thousand talents. And of all

15. Isocrates *Antidosis* 276, 278.
16. Isocrates *Antidosis* 231.

> these men who accomplished these great things, not a one neglected the study of rhetoric, and indeed they applied their minds to rhetoric more than to anything else.[17]

In his own day, however, he believed it was an uphill battle to maintain the moral fiber that was the necessary foundation for oratory, and it was this fiber that he sought to inculcate in his pupils. How far he succeeded is difficult to tell, but he certainly made quite a bit of money trying. His students included not only the general Timotheus, Conon's son, but other important men in Athenian public life, such as the anti-Macedonian activist Hypereides, the financial manager Lycurgus, and Plato's nephew Speusippus, who succeeded Plato as the head of his school, the Academy. The historians Ephorus (on whose work much of Diodorus Siculus's history was based) and Theopompus were also among his pupils, as were the tragedians Astydamas, Theodectes, and Aphareus; the orator Isaeus studied with him and in turn taught the famous anti-Macedonian crusader Demosthenes (not, of course, the fifth-century general of the same name). Honor was paid to him by Timotheus at Eleusis, where the general set up a statue to his teacher as a token of his affection and admiration.[18]

Isocrates was passionately concerned about the welfare of Greece, and increasingly toward the end of his long life (he lived to the age of ninety-eight) he dreamed of a panhellenic union against the Persians. In 380 he published his *Panegyricus* calling for just such a coalition. A weak voice and nervous temperament held him back from public speaking, but through his pamphlets and his pupils he sought to bring about a unity in Greece that was destined never to be realized until the Macedonian conquest—something he thought would be rather a good idea, bringing as it did the prospect of a war of revanche against Persia at last.

Around the same time that the ignominious terms of the King's Peace of 386 were handed down, Plato, a very different sort of individual, founded his Academy in a gracious shaded suburb of Athens near the national cemetery where Pericles had delivered his funeral oration. There

17. Isocrates *Antidosis* 234-5.
18. [Plutarch] *Lives of the Ten Orators* 838D.

curious intellectuals gathered to attack problems in various spheres—mathematics (geometry in particular), astronomy, logic, perhaps some biology, and more. The development of definitions (something that also plays a large part in Plato's dialogues) seems to have occupied a great deal of the residents' time and energy. How interested Plato was in shaping Athenian politics vicariously through his students is unclear. Though many of them became intensely involved in the government of other states, few seem to have engaged with the politics of Athens itself, from which Plato had become alienated after the failure of the Thirty, for whom he had once had hopes, and a fortiori after the execution of Socrates. Although his interest in thought experiments and his failure to speak in his own voice in his dialogues makes it impossible to be absolutely certain of his political opinions, his aversion to democracy seems clear. Plato surely gave lectures at his school, but so, it seems, did others. Many brilliant minds were drawn to the Academy, some of whom were famous in their own right—the mathematician Theaetetus, and Eudoxus of Cnidus, renowned for his expertise in both mathematics and astronomy; and of course Aristotle, who had come from Stagira in Chalcidice at the age of seventeen. Plato was evidently happy to have others teach in their specialties, and so the mathematicians worked on mathematical problems and the astronomers on astronomy. Not all members of the Academy were rich men. A few were poor men who took on work outside the school to meet their living expenses (Plato does not seem to have charged fees, but one had to eat), and two were women, Lasthenia of Mantinea and Axiothea of Philesia. Axiothea was said to have come to the Academy after reading Plato's dialogue the *Republic* and being captivated by its notion of a ruling class in which women and men, having received the same education, governed side by side.[19]

Presumably many of the ideas tossed around at the Academy were those we find touched on in Plato's many dialogues, all of which seem to have survived, such as the *Symposium*, on love; *Euthyphro*, on piety;

19. Oddly, we are very ill informed as to what actually went on at the Academy. M. Baltes reconstructs the activities there with great confidence in "Plato's School, the Academy," *Hermathena* 155 (1993): 5–26, but he may go beyond the evidence.

Laches, on courage; *Phaedo*, on the immortality of the soul; and the *Republic*, a much longer dialogue in which Plato sets forth a blueprint for an ideal state. Plato's *Gorgias* gives the famous sophist an opportunity to showcase his wares, though he does not come off too well. The subject of the dialogue is rhetoric, which Socrates construes as a mode of pleasing people by telling them what they want to hear rather than what is good for them, and it is in the context of this discussion that Socrates casts Athens' most famous politicians in a very different light than did Isocrates. Claiming to have heard that "Pericles has made the Athenians idle, cowardly, loquacious and greedy" by initiating the system of state payment for state service, he maintains that Pericles' success as a trainer of men is belied by the Athenians' impeachment of him toward the end of his career. Would a herdsman in charge of donkeys or horses or oxen be considered a good trainer if the creatures under his jurisdiction became more ungovernable rather than less so? Yet Pericles, Cimon, Themistocles, and Miltiades all met similar fates at the hands of the demos they had been charged with improving. Initially, Plato depicts Socrates as saying,

> Pericles was popular and the Athenians passed no shameful sentence on him so long as they were "worse"; but as soon as they had been made good and true men by him, at the end of his life they convicted him of embezzlement and came this close to sentencing him to death, on the grounds that he was a villain.

As for Cimon, Socrates goes on,

> Did not the people whom he was looking after ostracize him so that they would be spared from hearing his voice for ten years? And didn't they do the same to Themistocles, and exile him as well? And Miltiades the hero of Marathon—didn't they vote to put him to death?[20]

So much for the illustrious politicians praised so highly by Isocrates.

20. Plato *Gorgias* 515d–516e.

In many of his dialogues Plato portrays Socrates and his interlocutors pursuing a definition of something, and in the *Republic*, that "something" is justice. This work is one of the foundational documents of "political theory"—literally, "contemplating the polis," for it was in looking at the city-states of Greece in his time, during the Peloponnesian War and after, that Plato developed his ideas. It is in the course of seeking to define justice that "Socrates," that is, the literary character Socrates, outlines Plato's utopia. In that state, people would be divided into three classes. Only the top class, known as Guardians, would participate in governing. They would be characterized by rationality, inculcated by years of proper education. Below them would be the Auxiliaries, marked by a spirited temperament that suited them for the military. (Plato accepted the inevitability of warfare in human life, but he made clear that it should ideally be undertaken only against non-Greeks and expresses a great deal of distress about the kind of Greek-on-Greek warfare that has characterized his lifetime.) Below the Auxiliaries would be found everyone else, who would do all the other jobs required by the state. Each caste would reproduce biologically. On the rare occasions when a child appeared to have been born into the wrong class, he or she would be transferred—downward, one imagines: it's not clear how a particularly gifted farmer or artisan would be identified and marked for promotion.

Plato outlines in great detail the education of the guardian class, and not surprisingly it focuses on mathematics. For Plato believed that the study of mathematics was the best route to understanding his theory of Forms. In Plato's view, what was most "real" in the world was not the concrete things we know through the senses but rather ideal forms of things. An orange or a tennis ball might seem to be a sphere, but of course it is not a perfect sphere; the only perfect sphere is the set of all points equidistant from a given point. That is not something one can touch—but it can be found easily in the realm of mathematics. For Plato only concepts are real. Tangible objects are debased copies.

Plato's guardian class spent many years being educated, and it differed from other elites in many respects. One important difference between Plato's Guardians and the ruling class in other states was that the guardians were of both sexes, for, Plato argued, though of course the average man was smarter than the average woman, there were many women just as intelligent as men. Thus women could certainly be expected to manage the Guardians' rigorous education. Did the education Plato outlines in the *Republic* correspond at all to what went on in the Academy? We have no idea. And did Plato expect his blueprint for an ideal state to be put into practice anywhere in Greece? Certainly the ideal state of the *Republic* was so radically different from the real states of Greece that it is difficult to imagine Plato's contemporaries sitting down and making it a reality. Plato himself did make some effort to establish an ideal state in Syracuse by turning its ruler Dionysius II toward philosophy and by seeking land and settlers for his own community. His efforts failed, however, and he was forced to return to Athens.

Plainly the premium Plato's ideal state placed on the intellectual education of the elite would be unacceptable to the Spartans, and the split between farmers and the decision-making class was a marked departure from Athens—but not from Sparta, where the citizens did not raise their own food. In the *Republic*, the debate over the best kind of government appears again in Greek literature but takes a distinctly vitriolic turn in what Plato's "Socrates" has to say about democracy. As could be expected from what Socrates was portrayed as saying in *Gorgias* about Athens' most revered politicians, Plato carries forward the anti-democratic tradition in that debate. In the "cycle of constitutions" that appears in Book 8, Socrates compares democracy to a multicolored cloak such as would appeal to boys and women. In a city like this, he says, you need not submit to the laws unless you please, or make war or peace according to the laws of the city. In fact, he says, even people condemned to death or exile remain in the city and wander the streets as if they were invisible—what more bizarre statement could Plato put in the mouth of Socrates of all people?[21] This sort of constitution will degenerate (as if it could get worse) into anarchy when liberty and equality run riot to the point that slaves are as free as their masters, traditional sex roles break down, and horses and donkeys stride down the street with the greatest of entitlement, bumping into anyone who does not have the presence of mind to

21. Plato *Republic* 557a–558a.

step aside.[22] This was quite a collection of complaints, particularly given that it was only in Aristophanes' *Acharnians* that any Athenian made a private peace; that the Guardian class of the *Republic* itself made no distinction between male and female roles; and that Plato's claim that this anarchy will lead to tyranny has little basis in the history of his native Athens. Throughout Greece in the fifth and fourth centuries, governments tended to oscillate between democracy and oligarchy.

In the *Laws*, his longest dialogue, Plato seeks to establish a constitution midway between monarchy and democracy for an imaginary city, "Magnesia," that is supposedly being founded on Crete, taking as his premise that an unnamed "Athenian stranger" is conversing about this new foundation with a Spartan and a Cretan. When the Athenian discovers that the city will be located not far from the shore, with excellent harbors, he expresses great concern. Magnesia, he says, will need not the constitution he is proposing but rather "a mighty savior and divine lawgivers" to spare it from a wealth of depraved habits.[23] He proceeds to discuss Athens directly in lamenting its conversion to a naval power when the cowardice of sailors, always ready to retreat to their ships to escape danger, is so well known (compare the reliability of "steadfast hoplites").[24] Having thus put itself in a position where power has to be granted to the less respectable sort of people, the Athenians were bound to accept an inferior sort of government. The argument is clear: some classes of people are superior to others, and the Athenians' use of the lot to allocate offices, while it wards off unrest on the part of the masses, fails to serve the ends of justice. It works instead in the interest of a specious and superficial sort of equality; but the truest and best equality "is the judgment of Zeus . . . which produces all good things; for it grants more to the greater and less to the lesser, doling out due measure to each in accord with nature."[25]

22. Plato *Republic* 563b–c.
23. Plato *Laws* 704d.
24. Plato *Laws* 706b–c.
25. Plato *Laws* 757b–c.

Unlike the quirky portrayal of democracy in the *Republic*, what Plato has to say in the *Laws*, then, is an attack both on the principles of democracy and on the democracy of his native city itself.

AN ERA OF TREATISES—AND INNOVATION

An era of reflection, the fourth century was an age of treatises (rarely as long as the *Laws*) as well as dialogues. In addition to the *Hellenica*, the *Anabasis*, and a number of dialogues in which Socrates appears, Xenophon produced short works on such topics as horsemanship and hunting. It is no coincidence that much of what Xenophon wrote concerns warfare in one way or another, and one of the most important treatises that survives from the fourth century is the lively and imaginative *How to Survive under Siege*, the work of an author we know as Aeneas the Tactician, probably Aeneas of Stymphalus, who was General of the Arcadian League in the 360s.[26] Rife with examples from the Peloponnesian War and the first half of the fourth century, it still makes wonderful reading today. Aeneas covers a wide range of topics: scouting, sawing through a bar (and preventing bars from being sawn through), watchwords, patrols, controlling panics, setting and extinguishing fires (vinegar and birdlime are useful for the latter), and sending secret messages in code. He cites numerous military innovations of the fourth century, such as the lighter boots devised by Iphicrates. As Iphicrates' creativity attests, however, plainly thinking about military affairs was not confined to the study. Archaeological evidence shows an expansion of fortifications far beyond anything known in the fifth century. The Peloponnesian War and the decades that followed, for example, taught the importance of protection, and during the fourth century walls around several Greek cities would come to enclose far larger areas than in the fifth and resemble medieval castles with turrets, battlements, and moats.

When it came to treatises, no fourth-century writer could touch Plato's pupil Aristotle (384–22). Whereas his teacher Plato had written

26. Xenophon *Hellenica* 7. 3. 1.

up his ideas in dialogue form, Aristotle produced treatise after treatise. His *Rhetoric* and *Poetics* fill important gaps in our knowledge of Greek drama of the fifth and fourth centuries beyond Aeschylus, Sophocles, and Euripides. His vast output dealt with numerous aspects of philosophy and natural science and has gripped the minds of scholars well into the modern world. We are indebted to Aristotle for much of our understanding of the Greek polis. At his school the Lyceum he assigned students to gather information on the constitutions of 158 Greek city-states (nearly all lost, alas). The Aristotelian *Constitution of Athens* (evidently not written by Aristotle himself but rather the work of one of his students) is the fruit of one of these projects. Aristotle's amazing and comprehensive *Politics* remains a handbook for the principles of civic life. It is there that we find his statement that man is a political animal. The polis, he says,

> is a natural growth, and man by nature a political animal. A man who by his nature rather than by chance does not live in a polis is either an inadequate kind of being or a superior one, like the man censured by Homer as "clanless, lawless, hearthless," insofar as he is unsociable—and will inevitably become a lover of war.[27]

This definition of man as a "political animal"—a creature whose nature it is to live as a citizen in a state—was to become one of the most famous premises in all of Western thought.

THE END FOR SPARTA

A good case could be made that though the Spartans had a well-defined concept of their polis and had thought hard about what it was all about, they had ceased to be effective political animals: they had neglected to bulk up their citizen body, and under Agesilaus had pursued a self-destructively aggressive foreign policy. Sparta's days as a major power in Greece were numbered. The Common Peace of 375 never really took

27. *Politics* 1.1253a.

hold. Fighting between Athens and Sparta was taking an economic toll on both states, and the Thebans angered Athens by destroying Plataea and absorbing nearby Thespiae. The Spartans and Athenians became tired of warring with nothing to show for it, and the Athenians were alarmed at the increasing aggressiveness of the Thebans, who were also failing to make their required contributions to league finances. Now in 371 another peace conference was held at Sparta, attended by delegates from not only Thebes, Athens, and Sparta and their various allies but numerous other Greek states—and Persia to boot. As usual, there was much blather about autonomy, and it was agreed that all armies and garrisons were to be recalled. When it came time to swear to the peace, the Spartans swore on behalf of themselves and their allies; no objections were posed. The Athenians swore for themselves, but their allies swore separately, city by city. As for the Thebans, they at first signed for themselves, but the next day the Theban leader Epaminondas returned and, fearing that the Boeotian League would be held to violate the principle of autonomy, demanded that the wording be changed so as to read "the Boeotians."[28] Not suspecting the ominous chain of events he was setting in motion, Agesilaus then erased the Thebans' name from the list of signatories entirely, leaving the Thebans isolated in the world of Greek diplomacy.[29] Everyone believed he was doing a good thing. This line of thinking, however, was mistaken. The Thebans would prove dangerous enemies, and in alienating them, Agesilaus had borrowed serious trouble for his polis.

The Athenians and Spartans dutifully recalled all their armies and garrisons—with one exception. King Cleombrotus was already in the field, en route to Phocis. Instead of ordering him home, the Spartans bade him march at once against the Thebans unless they granted autonomy to the cities of Boeotia. Predictably, the Thebans refused.[30] Cleombrotus then marched by a circuitous and sometimes arduous route until he reached

28. Xenophon *Hellenica* 6. 3. 19.

29. On the peace conference, see G. L. Cawkwell, "Epaminondas and Thebes," *Classical Quarterly* 66 (1972): 254–78, and J. Buckler, *The Theban Hegemony 371–362 BC* (Cambridge, MA: Harvard University Press, 1980), 48–54.

30. Xenophon *Hellenica* 6. 4. 1–3; Diodorus 15. 51. 3–4.

the hills just south of the plain of Leuctra in the territory of Thespiae.[31] With him he had some 5,000 Spartan hoplites plus 300 men in the royal guard, in addition to another 5,000 allied hoplites and a total of 1,000 cavalry.[32] When the Boeotians found him there and camped on the hills north of the plain, they seem to have had about 6,000 hoplites led by six of the Boeotarchs and Pelopidas in charge of the Sacred Band; the seventh Boeotarch, Bacchylidas, joined them, presumably with an additional 1,000 infantry.[33] They may also have had as many as 700 cavalry. Some of their forces were Theban, the rest from elsewhere in Boeotia, but none seem to have come from outside Boeotia; they fought without allies.

Epaminondas, two of his fellow Boeotarchs, and Pelopidas were determined to fight. At first, the other Boeotarchs were unwilling, given the greater size of the Spartan forces, but when Bacchylidas, who had been away, returned, he broke the deadlock, and battle was engaged. Cleombrotus planned to send out his cavalry ahead to stir up dust on the flat plain in order to conceal the Spartans' movements from their enemies. But it was not clear exactly what more Cleombrotus' strategy involved. He may simply have relied on the greater length of his line, which of course extended far beyond that of the Thebans. Epaminondas, however, had given a great deal of thought to how to win this crucial battle, and he was not without hope. Although overall the Boeotians were outnumbered, the Thebans and Laconians were about evenly matched, and of the Laconians only about 700 were Spartans. It was between these men that the real contest would be; how much enthusiasm any of the others had for the fight was uncertain.

In previous encounters, the Thebans and the Spartans had faced one another on the right ends of their own lines. Thus in 394 each side was victorious on its right wing, but on each occasion the Spartans won the battle when the victorious wings engaged with one another. This time Epaminondas had a different plan: Theban and Spartan forces would

31. For the route of Cleombrotus, I follow Buckler, *The Theban Hegemony*, 56–9.

32. On the Spartan numbers, see Lazenby, *The Spartan Army* (Warminster, UK: Stackpole Books, 1985, 2012), 178–9. Overall Lazenby offers a sound exploration of the alternate interpretations of this key battle.

33. Diodorus 15. 52. 2–3.

go head to head straight off. Cleombrotus had stationed himself and his royal guard among the Spartan infantry on the right wing just behind the cavalry. The allies, along with some mercenaries, were on the left. Epaminondas in response placed the Thebans on the left behind his own cavalry, including the Sacred Band led by Pelopidas, and the remainder of the Boeotians on the right, but with a difference. While the Spartans were arrayed in their usual depth of twelve, the Thebans, who were not unaccustomed to unusual formations (they had massed twenty-five deep at Delium and at least sixteen deep at Nemea) made their phalanx fully *fifty men deep*. This, of course, involved enormous risk, as it narrowed the width of their line substantially, but in the event, the risk paid off. First the cavalry, then the highly trained Sacred Band, then the heavy wedge—it just might work, and in the end it did.[34]

The fighting began around the middle of the day, after the Spartans had lunched and were a little high on the wine they had drunk.[35] (Perhaps not all of them; there might only have been wine enough for the royal guard.) Reconstructing the battle is not easy, but evidently in the cavalry skirmish the Spartans got the worst of it. According to Xenophon this was predictable, as the Theban cavalry had been regularly tested in battle for years whereas in Sparta the horses were owned by the rich and bore riders provided at the last minute for the occasion.[36] Now, it seems, Pelopidas charged with the Sacred Band.[37] The deep wedge pressed in behind them, pushing them forward into the Spartans, who were thus driven back and

34. There has been much ink spilled on the battle; this is my best reconstruction. See especially Buckler, *The Theban Hegemony*, 61–5; M. Munn, "Thebes and Central Greece," in *The Greek World in the Fourth Century*, ed. L. A. Tritle (London: Routledge, 1997), 81–6; J. Lazenby, *The Spartan Army*, 176–88; V. Hanson, "Epameinondas, the Battle of Leuktra (371 B. C.), and the 'Revolution' in Greek Battle Tactics," *Classical Antiquity* 7 (1988), 190–207; and S. Rusch, *Sparta at War: Strategy, Tactics, and Campaigns 550–362* (London: Frontline Books, 2011), 194–9. A. Devine has argued ingeniously that Epaminondas drew up his men not in columns but rather in an *embolon*, a wedge formation resembling the Greek capital letter lambda, a two-sided triangle open at the bottom, i.e., a solid front with two wings behind it ("EMBOLON: A Study in Tactical Terminology," *Phoenix* 37 [1983]: 201–17), but I think his arguments have been successfully refuted by J. Buckler in "Epameinondas and the 'Embolon,'" *Phoenix* 39 (1985): 134–43.

35. Xenophon *Hellenica* 6. 4. 8.

36. Xenophon *Hellenica* 6. 4. 11.

37. Plutarch *Pelopidas* 23. 2.

cut off from their allies as Epaminondas had hoped. Although there was some confusion in the melee between cavalry and infantry, the brave Spartans were at first able to hold their own. Cleombrotus, however, was soon killed along with the polemarch, Deinon, and many of those around them, including Sphodrias and his son Cleonymus.[38] The Spartans may have tried to roll their longer line around the deep line of Epaminondas, but if they did, they did not succeed.

Much uncertainty remains about this battle. In his *Stratagems in War*, the second-century AD man of letters Polyaenus famously reported that Epaminondas, when the fortunes of the battle hung in the balance, called out to his men to "give him one step more" and he would give them the victory.[39] His comment is often cited to show the efficacy of the hoplite "shove" in pitched battle. But is it credible that the battle's outcome hung in the balance? If Epaminondas really saw the two sides as evenly matched and the outcome uncertain, the Spartans must have been doing remarkably well against the crushing weight of the Theban column. But Polyaenus may have gotten it wrong. The Spartans, however, were not doing well enough. This was the first time a Spartan king had fallen in battle since Leonidas had died trying to hold the Thermopylae pass in 480. Cleombrotus was carried off the battlefield still breathing, and in the rush to save him the entire royal guard seems to have been massacred, along with some hundred others nearby. In total the Spartans lost a thousand men.[40] The Boeotians had lost perhaps 300.[41] In the daze of battle, it took the Spartans some time fully to absorb the magnitude of the disaster that had befallen them. The number of full-blooded Spartiates, some 8,000 at the Battle of Plataea in 479, had now dropped to a tenth of that. Some wished to regroup and resume the contest, but the high command—what was left of it—could not be persuaded, for they saw that the allies had no heart for the fighting. Instead they sought a truce and

38. Xenophon *Hellenica* 6. 4. 14.

39. Polyaenus 2. 3. 2.

40. Xenophon *Hellenica* 6. 4. 15.

41. Diodorus 15. 56. 4. Diodorus offers casualty figures of 300 Boeotians and 4,000 Spartans. The first figure is credible, the second not. Pausanias reports 47 Theban and other Boeotian dead (Pausanias 9. 13. 13).

went about the dismal business of recovering the hundreds of bodies that lay dead on the field.[42]

Cleombrotus had been outgeneraled by the genius of Epaminondas. Though the Spartans might recover their dead, their reputation was lost forever. Compared to Leuctra, Sphacteria had been a temporary setback. When the news of the disaster reached Sparta, the ephors informed the next of kin of their bereavement but cautioned the females not to cry out but to endure their suffering in silence.[43] Perhaps Spartan women were not as tough as legend would have it; the echoes of Pericles' cautions in his funeral oration are unmistakable. But on the next day, Xenophon says, one could see the relatives of those who had been killed in the battle going around with bright and happy faces, while most of the survivors' relatives kept to themselves, and the few of those who were seen in public looked very gloomy indeed.[44] When the Spartans' weakness became apparent to their allies, democratic revolutions broke out throughout the Peloponnesus. Mantinea once again became a single state, under a democratic government.[45] Tegea too became democratic, and a league was formed consisting of Mantinea, Tegea, and the communities of central and southern Arcadia. The new league quickly received the support of Thebes. When Epaminondas marched into the Peloponnesus, he was accompanied by an army of more than 40,000 men. Though they were unable to take the city of Sparta, they ravaged the land of Laconia, and, more important, liberated the territory of Messenia and the helots who dwelled there, helping in the foundation of Messene as a center for Messenia in 369 and in the establishment of a new capital for the Arcadian League, Megalopolis (Great City) in 368. Within just a few years Thebes under Epaminondas and Pelopidas had succeeded where generations of Athenians had failed. Sparta was finished as a major player on the international scene, any hopes of its revival dashed by the loss of most of the massive underclass that had for so long undergirded its economy.[46]

42. Xenophon *Hellenica* 6. 4. 15.

43. The gruesome women portrayed in Plutarch's "Sayings of Spartan Women" would have been positively ecstatic to learn that their sons had died for Sparta.

44. Xenophon *Hellenica* 6. 4. 16.

45. Xenophon *Hellenica* 6. 5. 3–9.

46. Diodorus 15. 66. 1; 72. 4; Plutarch *Agesilaus* 34. 1–5, *Pelopidas* 24; Pausanias 4. 27. 1-9.

The underlying cause was a pig-headed foreign policy on the part of the Spartan elite themselves. Led first by the bloody Lysander and then by the compulsively bellicose Agesilaus—placed on the throne by Lysander himself—the Spartans had made one mistake after another, turning their friends into enemies, and now their time was over. Ironically, it was the rising power of Thebes that proved their undoing and not their old enemies in Attica. The Athenians in fact were somewhat alarmed when a herald arrived from Thebes bedecked with the customary garland to report the great victory at Leuctra. They did not even offer him the customary meal of hospitality, let alone proffer aid to the victors, who had been such half-hearted members of their confederacy.[47] Indeed, it was not long before they agreed to aid the Spartans against Thebes, dispatching Iphicrates at the head of an army in 369.[48]

Clearly a sea change had taken place in the system of alliances in Greece. The Peloponnesian War seemed, at last, to have ended, yet there was victory for neither side. In the end, there was no victory for Thebes either. Pelopidas was killed fighting in 364, and though the Thebans successfully (though barely) defeated a coalition of Athens, Sparta, and a number of other Greek states at Mantinea in 362 that challenged their claim to hegemony, their victory counted for little since Epaminondas was killed in the fighting. As he had neglected to build a structure that would outlive him, with his last breath he advised his countrymen to make peace. From 368 to 365, however, Philip, the young son of the Macedonian king Amyntas III, had lived as a hostage in Thebes, where he was close to both Epaminondas and Pelopidas. Returning to Macedon well schooled in military and diplomatic affairs, he acceded to the throne in 359, only three years after Epaminondas's death. From that moment, the freedom of the squabbling Greek city-states was in peril.

47. Xenophon *Hellenica* 6. 4. 20.
48. Xenophon *Hellenica* 6. 5. 49.

20

EPILOGUE

WAR WITHOUT VICTORY

WRITING SOME YEARS AFTER the Spartan collapse at Leuctra, Plato in his last dialogue the *Laws* portrays the Cretan Cleinias observing that peace is only a word; in truth, Cleinias says, "it is a law of nature that every polis is engaged perpetually in an undeclared war with every other polis."[1] It was not quite as bad as all that. There were times in the history of the Greek city-states when they were not engaged in constant warfare. But Plato's perspective was inevitably shaped by the period that had begun with his birth, when the Peloponnesian war had just broken out, and the fighting that had begun then had still not ceased except for short intervals.

Neither the course nor the conclusion of the war was in any way foreseeable at its outset. The plague in Athens could not have been predicted. It was made worse by the crowding in the city, of course, but the Athenians could hardly have been expected to reject the "island strategy" on the grounds that it would make the populace vulnerable to an epidemic—one that not only killed a staggering quarter to a third of those alive at the time but substantially reduced the size of the next generation of fighting men. It also killed Pericles, who might well have devised creative strategies for the Athenians when it became clear that the island strategy was not working. All this was a truly terrible stroke of bad luck for the Athenians.

1. Plato *Laws* 626a.

Much else in the course of this war can be put down to luck as well. Two weather events played key roles: the storm that blew the Athenians' ships into Pylos and laid the groundwork for the fortification of the promontory, and the wind that came up after the Battle of Arginusae that prevented the Athenians from recovering the bodies of their men, dead and alive, from the choppy waters. In each case, of course, human agency responded to the contingency with free will: the Spartans made the mistake of landing soldiers on Sphacteria Island, and the Athenians condemned their generals to death for failing to retrieve the sailors from the sea. The tragedy at the Arginusae trial was the product of mob psychology and the strains of the long war, but its outcome was also dependent on several contingencies and was a close-run thing. The generals got themselves into trouble by changing their story: after first blaming the storm in letters home for not having picked up the men in the water, they then began blaming the trierarchs, conjecturing that the trierarchs had begun to undermine them at Athens. Even so, had darkness not prevented the counting of votes on the first day, the generals almost certainly would have been let off; and on the second day of the trial, the assembly, moved by the speech of Euryptolemus, was leaning toward acquittal when Menecles interposed the technical objection that sealed the generals' fate.

The Battle of Amphipolis in 422 was a stunning victory for Sparta, and well planned on Brasidas's part. Yet here too chance intervened. The Athenians lost some 600 men, the Spartans only seven. But one of those seven was Brasidas. And on the Athenian side, Cleon died—not necessarily by the coward's death that his enemy Thucydides attributes to him, but nonetheless, the battle took the lives of both men who were most conspicuously keeping the war alive. It might well have turned out otherwise.

Both sides made mistakes. The Athenians never fomented a serious helot rebellion, despite their connections with the Messenians, or extended their attacks on the Peloponnesus beyond intermittent raiding, and they failed to guard Chalcidice and Amphipolis adequately against Brasidas. The Spartans neglected to take the wishes of their allies adequately into consideration in either the Peace of Nicias or the treaty of

404. The Spartans and Athenians entered into a fifty-year alliance with one another that blatantly advertised their indifference to the concerns of other poleis—developments that do not fall into the category of mischance but rather mismanagement.

As to the Sicilian expedition, it was probably a mistake, short on grain though the Athenians may have been. Once in Sicily, the ailing Nicias certainly showed a lack of vigor in prosecuting the campaign, but he was the official liaison between Athens and Syracuse, and he was correct that a peace party in Syracuse was prepared to negotiate and that there was some profit in waiting out this opportunity. Indeed the Corinthian general Gongylus arrived with news of the impending arrival of Peloponnesian ships just as the Syracusans were on the brink of holding an assembly to discuss surrendering. Had Gongylus been delayed—say, by adverse winds—he might well have found Syracuse in Athenian hands. Meanwhile in mainland Greece the Athenians, by giving in to pressure from Argos to attack Laconia, officially broke the Peace of Nicias, an act that resulted in Peloponnesian aid to Syracuse and the fortification of Decelea.

In hindsight, the Athenians should have accepted the offer of peace tendered by the Spartans after Arginusae, setting aside suspicions of bad faith grounded in memories of the Peace of Nicias. But like a heady gambler on a winning streak, they chose to hold out for more and wound up losing what they had.

In the alliance of Lysander and Cyrus, chance played only a small part. While the chemistry between the two men—the man and the boy, really—was not foreseeable, Lysander's careful calculation made success a high probability before they ever set eyes on one another (not that Cyrus's own ambitions played a negligible role in the combustion). The meeting of the highly focused navarch and the eager prince was fateful for the Athenians. It did not, to be sure, seal their doom. Had the storm not come up off the Arginusae islands, had the generals and trierarchs not cast blame on one another, and had the demos not lost six of its most experienced generals as a result, Athens might have been spared the demoralization that allowed its navy to be trapped by Lysander in the straits. Still, the diplomatic seduction of Cyrus by Lysander was an ominous development, and once the Athenians had put to death six of their generals and forced two others into exile, there were no "almosts," no "if onlys." It was sheer incompetence that led them to find themselves bottled up and captured in the Hellespont by Lysander. The Spartans' success at Aegospotami seemed to leave them holding all the cards; the question remained what they would do with their victory. In the event, divisions among them stood in the way of strategic planning for the future. First of all, as in 421, a gulf opened between them and their allies as the Thebans, Corinthians, and Megarians pushed for the annihilation of the tyrant city only to have their wishes thwarted by their hegemon, which feared the various sorts of disruption that would ensue—Thebes spilling over into Attica, Athenian owls flooding Sparta. Some Spartans feared this more than others: Lysander, with his imperialist dreams, would need money to realize them, but others were concerned about the possible corrupting effects of great wealth. A growing gap also opened within Sparta between Lysander and Pausanias. It was Pausanias who assisted the Athenians in expelling the oligarchy of the Thirty Tyrants, puppets of Lysander, so detested that even Athens' former enemies, most conspicuously the Thebans, aided the Athenian patriots in their war of liberation.

Pausanias did well to participate in the expulsion of the Thirty. Athens as a powder keg of democratic revolution would do no good to anyone. But the years that followed showed Spartan foreign policy characterized by extreme myopia oblivious to long-term interests, as one Spartan leader after another—most conspicuously Agesilaus—pursued a relentlessly aggressive policy, alienating former allies with disastrous consequences. Though Agis, who began this program of aggression, might well have continued it had he lived longer, it was Agesilaus who carried it out. Thoroughly devoted to Sparta, Agesilaus had tunnel vision about where his polis's interests lay. His conviction that war was the solution to any problem, real or imaginary, served Sparta ill. What Sparta required in the fourth century but did not get was a radical "redistricting" along the lines of the reforms instituted late in the third century by Cleomenes III, who, having crippled the ephorate and other bodies that might get in his way, pooled the land, redistributed it in equal lots to the citizens, canceled debts, and incorporated worthy perioeci (at last) and even some foreigners into the citizen body, bringing the citizenry up to the robust size of 4,000.[2] But such measures, though badly needed, were beyond Agesilaus's imagining. The results of the war that seemed to have ended in 404, grave as they were, did not account for the woes of fourth-century Greece and the ultimate conquest of the Greek city-states by Philip of Macedon. Rather, the explanation lies in the subsequent conduct of the Spartans. Combined with the interference of Persia and the Greeks' susceptibility to seduction by the nebulous principle of autonomy, it was Spartan aggression against its own allies following Aegospotami that was responsible for the weakening of Greece.

One of Agesilaus's first mistakes was to make an enemy of Persia. Though the Spartans, through Tiribazus, would in time bring Artaxerxes into world affairs on their side, it would take some work to undo the harm done by the king's campaigning. It was not long after the Spartan victory at Aegospotami that storm clouds began to threaten Sparta from the east. For Conon, who had taken refuge with Evagoras in Cyprus, had wormed his way into the graces of Artaxerxes. The Persian king had had quite enough of Agesilaus's campaigning in royal lands. Named admiral of the Persian-Phoenician fleet, along with Pharnabazus, Conon defeated the Spartans at Cnidus in 394, whereupon the victorious Athenian sailed into Piraeus bringing Persian money with which to build up the walls of Athens and Piraeus.

Conon also had with him Athenian sailors whom he had paid to row in the fleet; these would now serve in the resurgent Athenian navy. Only now did the Peloponnesian War truly come to an end—and it was no longer so clear that the Spartans had won. Not only had they lost fifty ships at Cnidus. In the Corinthian War that had just broken out in the Greek homeland they faced a formidable coalition of former friends and old enemies.

Greece was still at war but with a shifting combination of allies. No wonder Plato was inclined to think that war was endemic to the Greek states. In this new war, the Corinthian War, the real victor would prove to

2. Plutarch *Cleomenes* 6–11.

be—was it Sparta, or was it Persia? As in the Peloponnesian War, Sparta's enemies fought well, but the Spartans did too, and the vacillating Persian king eventually decided to grant them his favor. The King's Peace of 387/6 in which it culminated was a Persian victory in that it specified that all the Greek cities in Asia Minor should belong to Artaxerxes. Though it also set Sparta up as its guarantor and established as its guiding principle that of autonomy, the Spartans had no particular interest in making life hard for the Athenians. Agesilaus had other fish to fry. Gleefully he went about enforcing the autonomy principle in accord with Spartan interests and even countenanced Phoebidas's seizure of the citadel of Thebes, an act that plainly had nothing at all to do with autonomy. Would there be no end to Spartan interference in the affairs of other states? Together Thebes and Athens fought the Spartans on and off throughout the 370s until finally the Thebans dealt their former Peloponnesian hegemon a death blow on the field of Leuctra in 371. In the absence of any far-sighted land reforms, the diminishing population of Spartiates now dropped to below 1,000 as some 400 Spartiates died fighting, and no effort to save Spartan prestige could rescue the Lacedaemonians' faltering fortunes.

The Spartans had been fortunate to come out of the Peloponnesian War as well as they did, given that both sides were evenly matched and they had delayed in building a navy. Though they had captured the Athenians' fleet in 405 and destroyed their empire, the escape of Conon left them vulnerable to a future attack at sea in the east, and a shortsighted foreign policy fixated on settling petty grudges led to a new war within less than a decade. They did well in that war too, but they gained whatever power they had won in it by their continuing pattern of aggression in mainland Greece. Just as the Cold War grew out of World War II, the wars of the fourth century grew out of the Peloponnesian War—with the difference that there was no threat of nuclear holocaust to direct hostilities into proxy wars and away from direct combat among the principals. And there was one other key difference: While the United States and Soviet Russia, leaders of opposing coalitions during the Cold War, had been allies during World War II, Athens and Sparta found themselves ranged against one another from the outbreak of the Peloponnesian War well into the decades that followed, despite brief periods of détente such as the fifty-year alliance just after the Peace of Nicias or the years when Athens was forced to join the Peloponnesian League after the peace of 404. Yet when Sparta was finally dealt a death blow in 371, it was not by Athens but rather by the rising power of Thebes. Only then did the Peloponnesian War really end, but there were no winners, only losers.

CAST OF CHARACTERS

All dates are BC unless specified otherwise.

Agesilaus II Eurypontid king of Sparta, ruled 400–360. Extremely bellicose, he always saw war as the answer to Sparta's problems.

Agesipolis I Agiad king of Sparta, ruled 395–380. Came to power after the banishment of his father Pausanias.

Agis II Eurypontid king of Sparta, ruled 427–400.

Alcibiades 450–c. 404. Rakish Athenian aristocrat who defected to Sparta during the Peloponnesian War and after that to Persia, finally returning to Athens in 407, after which he shortly found himself in exile again.

Archidamus II Eurypontid king of Sparta, ruled 467–427. Although he opposed the war with Athens, he dutifully led the Peloponnesian troops into Attica more than once.

Aristophanes c. 445–386. Athenian dramatist in the genre of Old Comedy. The fact that so much of Aristophanes' work focused on politics and politicians as well as on intellectuals and daily life in Athens makes it a valuable addition to the writings of historians in understanding conditions in Athens during the Peloponnesian War.

Artaxerxes II king of Persia, ruled 404–358.

Aspasia c. 465–? Highly cultivated courtesan from Miletus who relocated in Athens and became Pericles' common-law wife, c. 445.

Brasidas c. 460–422. Daring and innovative Spartan general whose capture of Amphipolis in 424 resulted in the exile of Thucydides.

Callicratidas d. 406. Spartan navarch. He hoped to bring about concord in Greece after defeating Athens at sea but was killed at the Battle of Arginusae.

Cleombrotus I Agiad king of Sparta, ruled c. 380–371. Killed at the Battle of Leuctra.

Cleon c. 462–422. Brash populist politician in Athens, pilloried by Thucydides and Aristophanes alike.

Conon c. 444–389. Athenian admiral who managed to escape from Aegospotami to take refuge in Cyprus and in 394 to defeat the Spartan fleet at the Battle of Cnidus.

Critias c. 460–403. Athenian aristocrat, most prominent member of the Thirty Tyrants.

Cyrus the Younger c. 424–401. The younger son of King Darius II of Persia, Cyrus provided the Spartans with crucial funding for their navy.

Darius II king of Persia, ruled 423–404.

Demosthenes c. 457–413. A distinguished Athenian general who nonetheless failed in his attempt to rescue the Athenians' faltering campaign in Sicily and was executed by the Syracusans.

Diodorus Siculus fl. c. 60–30. Author of a *Library of History* grounded in numerous earlier sources; for the period of the Peloponnesian War he relied particularly on Isocrates' pupil Ephorus (c. 400–330). His work contains the occasional detail absent from Thucydides' narrative and often conflicts with Xenophon's *Hellenica*.

Epaminondas c. 410–362. The brilliant Theban general and statesman who broke the power of Sparta, engineering King Cleombrotus's defeat at Leuctra in 371 and then leading several successful expeditions into the Peloponnesus over the next decade, prompting helot revolts. He was killed at the Battle of Mantinea in 362.

Euripides c. 485–406. A prolific playwright, Euripides composed tragedies that evoked intense emotions. His *Trojan Women* of 415 illustrated the pathos of war's murderous destruction at a time when the Athenians had themselves been wiping out cities, enslaving the captured women and children.

Gorgias c. 485–380. Renowned sophist and rhetorician from Leontini in Sicily who went on tour in mainland Greece to demonstrate his skills.

Gylippus disappeared c. 405. His arrival in Sicily in 414 with a relief force of Peloponnesians turned the tide of war in Sicily in favor of the Syracusans.

Isocrates 436–338. Athenian teacher and rhetorician.

Lamachus d. 414. Experienced Athenian general chosen by the assembly to accompany Nicias and Alcibiades to Sicily in 415.

Lysander d. 395. Brilliant Spartan admiral and diplomat who won over the Persian prince Cyrus and gained from him funding with which to build up his fleet and ultimately defeat Athens at Aegospotami in 405. After starving Athens into submission, he installed the bloody Thirty Tyrants there.

Mindarus d. 410. Spartan commander in the East in the Ionian War. He died fighting bravely at Cyzicus.

Nicias c. 470–413. Prominent Athenian politician and general, a rival first of Cleon and then of Alcibiades. Inclined toward peace with Sparta, he was the lead Athenian negotiator on the Peace of Nicias of 421 that bore his name. He did not handle the Sicilian campaign well, and he was executed by the Syracusans in 413.

Pagondas c. 487–after 424. By his military genius he engineered a spectacular victory for the Boeotian forces over Athens at Delium in 425.

Pausanias Agiad king of Sparta, c. 460–380 or later. He played a key role in the overthrow of the Thirty Tyrants at Athens, making him unpopular in Sparta; he was subsequently exiled in 395.

Pelopidas d. 364. It was Pelopidas who along with Gorgidas established the corps of 150 pairs of lovers known as the Sacred Band, which in 375 routed a much larger force of Spartans at Tegyra and played a key role at the Battle of Leuctra in 371. It was annihilated by the troops of Philip II of Macedon at the Battle of Chaeronea in 338.

Pericles c. 495–429. A uniquely prominent statesman in fifth-century Athens. Pericles was instrumental in building the Athenian empire and furthering the democracy by establishing state pay for state service. Pericles framed the Athenian policies that led to the Peloponnesian War, and he also devised the creative but ultimately unsuccessful "island strategy" for winning the war within three years.

Pharnabazus d. 370. Satrap of Hellespontine Phrygia, with its capital at Dascylium.

Pleistoanax Agiad king of Sparta, ruled 458–409, although he spent about two decades of his reign in exile, evidently accused of accepting a bribe from Pericles.

Plutarch c. 50–120 AD. A biographer and essayist from Chaeronea in Boeotia who lived when Greece had been incorporated into the Roman empire. Plutarch was the author of numerous biographies of ancient Greeks and Romans. A collection of miscellanea called *Moral Essays* also survives (containing such useful items as *Sayings of the Lacedaemonians*).

Socrates c. 469–399. Brilliant philosopher who gained immortality as a result of his condemnation by an Athenian jury and the many Platonic dialogues in which he appears as a character.

Sophocles c. 496–406. One of the most famous playwrights of antiquity and author of *Oedipus Rex* (Oedipus the King), Sophocles also held several high offices in the government of Athens, including that of general and senior adviser.

Theramenes d. 404. A puzzling figure who sometimes seems to be a moderate and sometimes just a time-server. Originally a member of the Four Hundred in 411, he soon broke with them; initially a member of the Thirty, he broke with them too, a rupture that cost him his life.

Thrasybulus of Steiria c. 440–388. A committed democrat, after the Thirty had been installed by Lysander he led those who had fled Athens in retaking the city and expelling the oligarchs.

Thucydides c. 460–? An affluent Athenian aristocrat and general and the brilliant author of *The Peloponnesian War.*

Tissaphernes 445–395. Satrap of Lydia, based in the capital at Sardis.

Xenophon c. 428–354. An associate of Socrates, a soldier and a man of letters whose varied writings shed a great deal of light on his times (see A Note on Sources).

GLOSSARY

assembly The body of adult male citizens who gathered to vote on important measures. In Athens the assembly, which met outdoors on the hill called the Pnyx, deliberated, sometimes vociferously, as well as voting; in Sparta the assembly only voted, by shouting, after listening to speakers.

council The Council of 500 at Athens, consisting of 500 men chosen by lot. It prepared business for the assembly, was the city's chief administrative body, and also tried some court cases itself.

decarchies Narrow oligarchies of ten Spartan sympathizers established by Lysander in a number of cities of the former Athenian Empire in the late fifth century.

Delian League The confederacy organized under Athenian leadership in 477 BC after the defeat of Persia. As Athens began to force unwilling states to join and to prevent restive states from withdrawing, the League was converted into an Athenian Empire.

ephors Five officials elected annually for one-year terms in Sparta from candidates over the age of thirty. The ephors oversaw the kings on behalf of the people and were empowered to depose them when they saw fit. They also dealt with foreign embassies, and one ephor gave his name to the year.

general Beginning in 487, the ten generals (and, from 477, the ten treasurers of the Delian League) were the only high officials chosen by election at Athens, the others being selected by lot; thus they eclipsed all others in prestige. They also had the privilege of speaking first in the assembly and were often respected for their political aptitude as well as their military skills.

gerousia The Council of Elders at Sparta, consisting of the two kings plus twenty-eight elected men older than sixty who served for life.

hegemon A state that headed an organization of states.

helots The state serfs of Laconia and Messenia on whom the Spartans' way of life depended.

hetairia An upper-class, often oligarchically minded drinking club. They were prominent in Athens and sometimes suspected of subversive, anti-democratic political activity.

homoioi The "peers" or "equals" who formed the Spartiate male citizen class in Sparta. This was based largely on birth, but *homoioi* were expected to make a minimum contribution to their military mess (see "*syssition*"), and if they could not, they found themselves demoted to the class of "inferiors."

hoplite The heavily armed infantryman, so named from his shield (*hoplon*), who formed the hoplite phalanx of the Greek army beginning in the seventh century. A complete set of hoplite armor would be costly and heavy, so hoplites who were less well off would go into war with less substantial weapons when the panoply was not provided by the state. (Truly poor men would serve as light-armed soldiers or rowers in the fleet.)

King's Peace The settlement handed down by King Artaxerxes II of Persia that ended the Corinthian War in 387/6 BC.

money Frequently mentioned units of Athenian currency were the obol, the drachma, the mina, and the talent. Six obols added up to a drachma; a hundred drachmas made a mina; and sixty minas made a talent. Anyone who had a talent or more was wealthy. Sparta did not coin money until after the classical period but relied on either uncoined silver and gold (despite their lawgivers' purported disapproval of it) or the coins of other states.

peltasts Lightly armed soldiers who functioned as skirmishers.

perioeci "Dwellers round about," peoples who lived in Laconia and Messenia who enjoyed local autonomy and, though having no civic rights in Sparta, were obligated to fight for the Spartan state.

phalanx The tactical formation of a hoplite army.

polis The self-aware Greek city-state consisting of a principal city or town and its surrounding countryside.

satrap The title accorded to the governor of a Persian province.

Second Athenian Confederacy A voluntary organization instituted in 378 by Athens to which dozens of Greek states signed on, many of them former members of the Delian League.

sophists Itinerant rhetoricians and teachers in classical Greece, intellectuals mocked by Aristophanes and criticized by Plato.

syssitia Eating clubs to which all Spartiate males belonged. Each member was expected to attend regularly and make a contribution; members who were more well off might contribute more, such as meat from the hunt. Those who failed to make the minimum required contribution would be expelled and thus lose their status as *homoioi*.

trireme The standard Greek warship in the Classical era. Propelled by 170 oarsmen in three banks of oars, the trireme disabled enemy ships with its bronze ram.

tyranny The extra-legal seizure of power in a polis by an individual strongman. Tyrannies erupted in several city-states during the seventh and sixth centuries and frequently served as a transition from a narrow oligarchy to a more democratic form of government.

BIBLIOGRAPHY

Accame, S. 1941. *La Lega Ateniese del Sec. IV A. C.* Rome: Signorelli.

Adcock, F. 1957. *The Greek and Macedonian Art of War.* Berkeley: University of California Press.

Adcock, F. and D. J. Mosley. 1975. *Diplomacy in Ancient Greece.* London: Thames and Hudson.

Ahrensdorf, P. 1997. "Thucydides' Realistic Critique of Realism." *Polity* 30, 231–65.

Allen, D. *Why Plato Wrote.* 2010. Malden, MA: Wiley-Blackwell.

Anderson, J. K. 1965. "Cleon's Orders at Amphipolis. "*Journal of Hellenic Studies* 85, 1–4.

Anderson, J. K. 1970. *Military Theory and Practice in the Age of Xenophon.* Berkeley: University of California Press.

Anderson, J. K. 1974. *Xenophon.* New York: Scribner.

Andrewes, A. 1953. "The Generals in the Hellespont. 410–407 B. C." *Journal of Hellenic Studies* 73, 2–9.

Andrewes, A. 1962. "The Mytilene Debate: Thucydides 3. 36–49." *Phoenix* 16, 64–85.

Andrewes, A. 1974. "The Arginousai Trial." *Phoenix* 28, 112–22.

Andrewes, A. 1982. "Notion and Kyzikos: The Sources Compared." *Journal of Hellenic Studies* 102, 15–25.

Azoulay, V. 2014. *Pericles of Athens.* Princeton, NJ: Princeton University Press.

Badian, E. 1993. *From Plataea to Potidaea. Studies in the History and Historiography of the Pentecontaetia.* Baltimore: Johns Hopkins University Press.

Bagnall, N. 2004. *The Peloponnesian War: Athens, Sparta, and the Struggle for Greece.* London: Pimlico.

Baltes, M. 1993. "Plato's School, the Academy." *Hermathena* 155, 5–26.

Blanco, W., trans. and J. T. Roberts, ed. 2013. *Herodotus: The Histories*, 2e. New York: W. W. Norton.

Blanco, W., trans. and J. T. Roberts, ed. and Thucydides. 1998. *The Peloponnesian War.* New York: W. W. Norton.

Bloedow, E. 1973. *Alcibiades Reexamined.* Wiesbaden: F. Steiner.

Bloedow, E. 1987. "Pericles' Powers in the Counter-Strategy of 431." *Historia* 36, 9–27.

Bloedow, E. 1990. "Not the Son of Achilles but Achilles Himself: Alcibiades' Entry on the Political Stage at Athens II." *Historia* 39, 1–19.

Bommelaer, J.-F. 1981. *Lysandre de Sparte: histoire et traditions.* Paris: Diffusion de Boccard.

Bosworth, A. B. 1993. "The Humanitarian Aspect of the Melian Dialogue." *Journal of Hellenic Studies* 113, 30–44.

Bosworth, A. B. 2000. "The Historical Context of Thucydides' Funeral Oration." *Journal of Hellenic Studies* 120, 1–16.

Bradeen, D. 1960. "The Popularity of the Athenian Empire." *Historia* 9, 257–69.

Bradeen, D. 1969. "The Athenian Casualty Lists." *Classical Quarterly* 63, 145–59.

Briant, P., trans. P. J. Daniels. 2002. *From Cyrus to Alexander. A History of the Persian Empire.* Winona Lake, IN: Eisenbrauns.

Brice, L. L. and J. T. Roberts, eds. 2011. *Recent Directions in the Military History of the Ancient World, Publications of the Association of Ancient Historians* 10. Claremont, CA: Regina Books.

Brickhouse, T. and N. Smith. 1989. *Socrates on Trial.* Princeton, NJ: Princeton University Press.

Brickhouse, T. and N. Smith, eds. 2002. *The Trial and Execution of Socrates: Sources and Controversies.* New York: Oxford University Press.

Bruce, I. A. F. 1960. "Internal Politics and the Outbreak of the Corinthian War." *Emerita* 28, 75–86.

Bruce, I. A. F. 1966. "Athenian Embassies in the Early Fourth Century." *Historia* 15, 272–81.

Bruce, I. A. F. 1967. *An Historical Commentary on the* Hellenica Oxyrhynchia. London: Cambridge University Press.

Brunt, P. A. 1965. "Spartan Policy and Strategy in the Archidamian War." *Phoenix* 19, 255–280.

Buckler, J. 1980. *The Theban Hegemony 371–362* BC. Cambridge, MA: Harvard University Press.

Buckler, J. 1985. "Epameinondas and the 'Embolon.'" *Phoenix* 39, 134–43.

Burkert, W. 1983. *Homo Necans: The Anthropology of Ancient Greek Sacrificial Ritual and Myth.* Berkeley: University of California Press.

Cairns, D. L. and R. A. Knox, eds. 2004. *Law, Rhetoric, and Comedy in Classical Athens. Essays in Honour of Douglas M. MacDowell.* Swansea: Classical Press of Wales.

Calhoun, G. 1970. *Athenian Clubs in Politics and Litigation.* Reprint: New York: B. Franklin.

Camp, J. M. 2001. *The Archaeology of Athens.* New Haven, CT: Yale University Press.

Campbell, B. and L. A. Tritle, eds. 2013. *The Oxford Handbook of Warfare in the Classical World.* New York: Oxford University Press.

Campbell, R. 1951. "How a Democracy Died." *Life* 30, 88–98.

Carcopino, J. 1935. *L'ostracisme athénien*, 2e. Paris: F. Alcan.

Cargill, J. 1981. *The Second Athenian League: Empire or Free Alliance?* Berkeley: University of California Press.

Cartledge, P. 1977. "Hoplites and Heroes: Sparta's Contribution to the Technique of Ancient Warfare." *Journal of Hellenic Studies* 97, 11–23.

Cartledge, P. 1982. "Sparta and Samos: A Special Relationship?" *Classical Quarterly* 32, 243–65.

Cartledge, P. 1987. *Agesilaos and the Crisis of Sparta.* London: Duckworth.

Cartledge, P. 1995. *Aristophanes and His Theatre of the Absurd.* London: Bristol Classical Press.

Cartledge, P. 2001. *Spartan Reflections.* Berkeley: University of California Press.

Cartledge, P. 2002. *Sparta and Lakonia: A Regional History 1300 to 362* BC, 2e. London and New York: Routledge.

Cartledge, P. 2006. *Thermopylae: The Battle that Changed the World.* New York: Overlook.

Cartledge, P. 2009. *Ancient Greek Political Thought in Practice (Key Themes in Ancient History).* Cambridge: Cambridge University Press.

Cartledge, P. 2016. *Democracy: A Life.* New York: Oxford University Press.

Casson, L. 1971. *Ships and Seamanship in the Ancient World.* Princeton, NJ: Princeton University Press.

Casson, L. 1991. *The Ancient Mariners: Seafarers and Sea Fighters of the Mediterranean in Ancient Times*, 2e. Princeton, NJ: Princeton University Press.

Cawkwell, G. L. 1963. "Notes on the Peace of 375/4." *Historia* 12, 84–95.

Cawkwell, G. L. 1972. "Epaminondas and Thebes." *Classical Quarterly* n. s. 22, 254–78.

Cawkwell, G. L. 1973. "The Foundation of the Second Athenian Confederacy." *Classical Quarterly* n. s. 23, 47–60.

Cawkwell, G. L. 1981. "The King's Peace." *Classical Quarterly* n. s. 31, 69–83.

Cawkwell, G. 1997. *Thucydides and the Peloponnesian War*. London: Routledge.

Christ, M. 2001. "Conscription of Hoplites in Classical Athens." *Classical Quarterly* n. s. 2, 398–422.

Christ, M. 2004. "Draft Evasion Onstage and Offstage in Classical Athens." *Classical Quarterly* n. s. 54, 33–54.

Chroust, A.-H. 1967. "Plato's Academy: The First Organized School of Political Science in Antiquity." *Review of Politics* 29, 25–40.

Cloché, P. 1919. "L'affaire des Arginuses (406 avant J. C.)." *Revue historique* 130, 5–68.

Cohen, E. 1992. *Athenian Economy and Society: A Banking Perspective*. Princeton, NJ: Princeton University Press.

Connor, W. R. 1971. *The New Politicians of Fifth Century Athens*. Princeton, NJ: Princeton University Press.

Connor, W. R. 1977. "A Post-Modernist Thucydides?" *Classical Quarterly* 72, 289–98.

Connor, W. R. 1984. *Thucydides*. Princeton, NJ: Princeton University Press.

Connor, W. R. 1985. "The Razing of the House in Greek Society." *Transactions and Proceedings of the American Philological Association* 115, 79–102.

Crane, G. 1996. *The Blinded Eye: Thucydides and the New Written Word*. Lanham, MD: Rowman & Littlefield.

Crowley, J. 2012. *The Psychology of the Athenian Hoplite: The Culture of Combat in Classical Athens*. Cambridge: Cambridge University Press.

David, E. 1985. "The Trial of Spartan Kings." *Revue internationale des droits de l'Antiquité* 32, 131–40.

Davies, J. K. 1971. *Athenian Propertied Families 600–300 B.C.* Oxford: Clarendon Press.

Desmond, W. 2006. "Lessons of Fear: A Reading of Thucydides." *Classical Philology* 101, 359–379.

Develin, R. 1989. *Athenian Officials, 684–321 B. C.* Cambridge: Cambridge University Press.

Devine, A. 1983. "EMBOLON: A Study in Tactical Terminology." *Phoenix* 37, 201–17.

DeVoto, J. 1986. "Agesilaus, Antalcidas, and the Failed Peace of 392/91 B. C." *Classical Philology* 81, 191–202.

Dewald, C. 2005. *Thucydides' War Narrative: A Structural Study*. Berkeley: University of California Press.

Diels, H. and W. Kranz. 1952. *Die Fragmente der Vorsokratiker*, 6e. Berlin.

Dillery, J. 1995. *Xenophon and the History of His Times*. New York: Routledge.

Donlan, W. and J. Thompson. 1976. "The Charge at Marathon: Herodotus 6. 112." *Classical Journal* 71, 339–43.

Donlan, W. 1979. "The Charge at Marathon Again." *Classical World* 72, 419–20.

Dover, K. J. 1972. *Aristophanic Comedy*. Berkeley: University of California Press.

Doyle, M. 1990. "Thucydidean Realism." *Review of International Studies* 16, 223–37.

Ducat, J., trans. E. Stafford, P. J. Shaw, and A. Powell. 2006. *Spartan Education: Youth and Society in the Classical Period*. Swansea: Classical Press of Wales.

Edmunds, L. 2004. "The Practical Irony of the Historical Socrates." *Phoenix* 58, 193–207.

Ehrenreich, B. 1997. *Blood Rites: Origins and History of the Passions of War*. New York: Holt.

Ehrhardt, C. 1970. "Xenophon and Diodorus on Aegospotami." *Phoenix* 24, 225–28.

Ellis, W. 1989. *Alcibiades*. London: Routledge.

Farrar, C. 1989. *The Origins of Democratic Thinking: The Invention of Politics in Classical Athens*. Cambridge: Cambridge University Press.

Fine, J. V. A. 1983. *The Ancient Greeks: A Critical History*. Cambridge, MA: Bellknap Press of Harvard University Press.

Finley, M. I. 1981. *Economy and Society in Ancient Greece*, ed. B. Shaw and R. Saller. London: Chatto & Windus.
Flory, S. 1988. "Thucydides' Hypotheses about the Peloponnesian War." *Transactions and Proceedings of the American Philological Association* 118, 43–56.
Foley, H. 1982. "The 'Female Intruder' Reconsidered: Women in Aristophanes' *Lysistrata* and *Ecclesiazusae*." *Classical Philology* 77, 1–21.
Fornara, C. 1971. *The Athenian Board of Generals from 501 to 404*. Wiesbaden: F. Steiner.
Fornara, C. 1975. "Plutarch and the Megarian Decree." *Yale Classical Studies* 24, 213–23.
Fornari, F. 1975. *The Psychoanalysis of War*. Bloomington: Indiana University Press.
Forrest, W. G. 1968. *A History of Sparta, 950–192 B. C.* London: Hutchinson.
Forsdyke, S. 2005. *Exile, Ostracism, and Democracy: The Politics of Expulsion in Ancient Greece*. Princeton, NJ: Princeton University Press.
Foster, E. and D. Lateiner, eds. 2012. *Thucydides and Herodotus*. Oxford: Oxford University Press.
Foxhall, L. and A. D. E. Lewis, eds. 1996. *Greek Law in Its Political Setting: Justifications not Justice*. Oxford: Clarendon Press, 1996.
Fredal, J. 2002. "Herm Choppers, the Adonia, and Rhetorical Action in Ancient Greece." *College English* 64, 590–612.
Freeman, E. A. 1891–1894. *A History of Sicily*. 4 vols. Oxford: Clarendon Press.
Frost, F. J. 1964. "Pericles and Dracontides." *Journal of Hellenic Studies* 84, 69–72.
Furley, W. 1996. *Andokides and the Herms: A Study of Crisis in Fifth-Century Athenian Religion*. London: Institute of Classical Studies.
Gagarin, M. and P. Woodruff. 1995. *Early Greek Political Thought from Homer to the Sophists*. Cambridge, UK: Cambridge University Press.
Garland, R. 1985. *The Greek Way of Death*. Ithaca, NY: Cornell University Press.
Garst, D. 1989. "Thucydides and Neorealism." *International Studies Quarterly* 33, 3–27.
Gilpin, R. 1988. "The Theory of Hegemonic War." 1988. *Journal of Interdisciplinary History* 18, 591–613.
Girard, R. 2005. *Violence and the Sacred*. London: Continuum.
Goldhill, S. 1990. "The Great Dionysia and Civic Ideology." In J. Winkler and F. Zeitlin, eds., *Nothing to Do with Dionysos? Athenian Drama in Its Social Context*. Princeton, NJ: Princeton University Press.
Goldman, H. 1942. "The Origin of the Greek Herm." *American Journal of Philology* 46, 58–68.
Goldstein, R. N. 2014. *Plato at the Googleplex: Why Philosophy Won't Go Away*. New York: Vintage.
Gomme, A. W., A. Andrewes, and K. J. Dover. 1945–81. *A Historical Commentary on Thucydides*. 5 vols. Oxford: Oxford University Press.
Goodman, M. D. and A. J. Holladay. 1986. "Religious Scruples in Ancient Warfare." *Classical Quarterly* 36, 151–71.
Gray, V. 1980. "The Years 375 to 371 BC: A Case Study in the Reliability of Diodorus Siculus and Xenophon." *Classical Quarterly* n. s. 30, 306–26.
Gray, V. 1987. "The Value of Diodorus for the Years 411–386 BC." *Hermes* 115, 72–89.
Gray, V. 1989. *The Character of Xenophon's* Hellenica. Baltimore: Johns Hopkins University Press.
Green, P. 1970. *Armada from Athens*. Garden City, NY: Doubleday.
Grethlein, J. 2005. "Gefahren des *logos*: Thukydides' 'Historien' und die Grabrede des Perikles." *Klio* 87, 41–71.
Gribble, D. 1999. *Alcibiades and Athens: A Study in Literary Presentation*. Oxford: Clarendon Press.
Griffith, G. T. 1950. "The Union of Corinth and Argos (392–386 B. C.)" *Historia* 1, 236–56.
Grote, G. 1845–56. *A History of Greece*. 12 vols. New York.

Grundy, G. B. 1948. *Thucydides and the History of His Age.* 2 vols. Oxford: Blackwell.

Guthrie, W. K. C. 1971. *The Sophists.* London: Cambridge University Press.

Hack, H. 1978. "Thebes and the Spartan Hegemony, 386–382 B. C." *American Journal of Philology* 99, 210–27.

Haid, S. 2008. "Why President Obama Should Read Thucydides." *DIAS Analysis* 34, 1–10.

Hale, J. R. 2009. *Lords of the Sea: The Epic Story of the Athenian Navy and the Birth of Democracy.* New York: Viking.

Hall, J. M. 2013. *A History of the Archaic Greek World,* ca. *1200–479* BCE. 2e Malden, MA: Wiley-Blackwell.

Hamel, D. 1998. *Athenian Generals: Military Authority in the Classical Period. Mnemosyne Supplementum 182.* Leiden: Brill.

Hamel, D. 2015. *The Battle of Arginusae: Victory at Sea and Its Tragic Aftermath in the Final Years of the Peloponnesian War.* Baltimore: Johns Hopkins University Press, 2015.

Hamilton, C. 1979. *Sparta's Bitter Victories: Politics and Diplomacy in the Corinthian War.* Ithaca, NY: Cornell University Press.

Hamilton, C. 1991. *Agesilaus and the Failure of Spartan Hegemony.* Ithaca, NY: Cornell University Press.

Hammond, N. G. L. 1986. *A History of Greece to 322 B. C.*, 3e. Oxford: Oxford University Press.

Hansen, M. 1975. *Eisangelia: The Sovereignty of the People's Court in Athens in the Fourth Century B. C. and the Impeachment of Generals and Politicians. Odense University Classical Studies*, vol, 6. Odense, Denmark: Odense University Press.

Hansen, M. 1991. *The Athenian Democracy in the Age of Demosthenes.* Oxford: Blackwell.

Hansen, M. 1996. "The Trial of Socrates—From an Athenian Point of View." In M. Sakellariou, ed., *Démocratie athénienne et culture.* Athens: Academy of Athens. 137–70.

Hanson, V. 1988. "Epameinondas, the Battle of Leuctra (371 B.C.), and the 'Revolution' in Greek Battle Tactics." *Classical Antiquity* 7, 190–207.

Hanson, V., ed. 1991. *Hoplites: The Classical Greek Battle Experience.* London: Routledge.

Hanson, V. 1998. *Warfare and Agriculture in Classical Greece.* Berkeley: University of California Press.

Hanson, V. 2005. *A War Like No Other: How the Athenians and Spartans Fought the Peloponnesian War.* New York: Random House.

Hanson, V., with an introduction by J. Keegan. 2009. *The Western Way of War: Infantry Battle in Classical Greece*, 2e. Berkeley: University of California Press.

Harding, P. 1974. "The Theramenes Myth." *Phoenix* 28, 101–11.

Harloe, K. and N. Morley, eds. 2012. *Thucydides and the Modern World: Reception, Reinterpretation and Influence from the Renaissance to the Present.* Cambridge: Cambridge University Press.

Harrison, A. R. W. 1968–71. *The Law of Athens.* 2 vols. Oxford: Clarendon Press.

Harvey, F. D. 1985. "Dona ferentes: Some Aspects of Bribery in Greek Politics." In P. A. Cartledge and F. D. Harvey, eds., *Crux, Essays Presented to G. E. M. de Sainte Croix on his 75th Birthday.* London: Duckworth, 1985.

Haskins, E. V. 2004. *Logos and Power in Isocrates and Aristotle.* Columbia: University of South Carolina Press.

Hatzfeld, J. 1940. *Alcibiade: Etude sur l'histoire d'Athènes à la fin du Ve siècle.* Paris: Presses Universitaires de France (2e. 1951).

Henderson, B. W. 1927. *The Great War between Athens and Sparta: A Companion to the Military History of Thucydides.* London: Macmillan.

Henry, Madeleine. 1995. *Prisoner of History: Aspasia of Miletus and Her Biographical Tradition.* New York: Oxford University Press.

Herbst, L. 1855. *Die Schlacht bei den Arginusen.* Hamburg: Meissner, 1855.

Higgins, W. E. 1977. *Xenophon the Athenian: The Problem of the Individual and the Society of the Polis.* Albany: State University of New York Press.

Hignett, C. 1952. *A History of the Athenian Constitution.* Oxford: Oxford University Press.

Hodkinson, S. 2000. *Property and Wealth in Classical Sparta.* London: Duckworth, and Swansea: Classical Press of Wales.

Hodkinson, S., ed. 2009. *Sparta: Comparative Approaches.* Swansea: Classical Press of Wales.

Hodkinson, S. and A. Powell, eds. 1999. *Sparta: New Perspectives.* London: Duckworth, and Swansea: Classical Press of Wales.

Hodkinson, S. and A. Powell, eds. 2006. *Sparta & War.* Swansea: University Press of Wales.

Holladay, A. J. 1978. "Athenian Strategy in the Archidamian War." *Historia* 27, 399–427.

Holladay, A. J. and J. F. C. Poole. 1979. "Thucydides and the Plague of Athens." *Classical Quarterly* n. s. 29, 282–300.

Holland, T., with critical apparatus by P. Cartledge. 2015. *The Histories: Herodotus.* New York: Penguin.

Hoppin, M. 1981. "What Happens in Sophocles' Philoctetes?" *Traditio* 37, 1–30.

Hornblower, S. 2011. *The Greek World 479–323 BC*, 4e. London: Methuen.

Hornblower, S. 1987. *Thucydides.* Baltimore: Johns Hopkins University Press.

Hornblower, S. 1991–2008. *A Commentary on Thucydides.* 3 vols. Oxford: Oxford University Press.

Hornblower, S., A. Spawforth, and E. Eidinow. 2012. Oxford Classical Dictionary, 4e. Oxford: Oxford University Press.

Hunt, P. 1998. *Slaves, Warfare, and Ideology in the Greek Historians.* Cambridge: Cambridge University Press.

Hunter, J. H. 2005. "Pericles' Cavalry Strategy." *Quaderni Urbinati di Cultura Classica* n. s. 81, 101–8.

Hunter, V. 1973. *Thucydides: The Artful Reporter.* Toronto: Hakkert.

Hurwit, J. M. 1999. *The Athenian Acropolis. History, Mythology, and Archaeology from the Neolithic Era to the Present.* Cambridge: Cambridge University Press.

Hutchinson, G. 2006. *Attrition. Aspects of Command in the Peloponnesian War.* Stonehouse: Spellmount.

Hutchinson, G. *Sparta: Unfit for Empire.* 2014. Barnsley: Frontline Books.

Jacoby, F. 1923–40. *Die Fragmente der griechischen Historiker.* 3 vols. I–II, Berlin, 1923–30; vol. III, Leiden, 1940.

Jameson, M. 1971. "Sophocles and the Four Hundred." *Historia* 20, 541–68.

Jones, N. 1977. "The Topography and Strategy of the Battle of Amphipolis in 422 BC." *Classical Antiquity* 10, 71–104.

Jordan, B. 1975. *The Athenian Navy in the Classical Period.* Berkeley: University of California Press.

Jordan, B. 1986. "Religion in Thucydides." *Transactions and Proceedings of the American Philological Association* 116, 119–47.

Jordan, B. 2000. "The Sicilian Expedition Was a Potemkin Fleet." *Classical Quarterly* 50, 63–79.

Kagan, D. 1961. "The Economic Origins of the Corinthian War." *La Parola del Passato* 16, 321–41.

Kagan, D. 1965. *The Great Dialogue. History of Greek Political Thought from Homer to Polybius.* New York: Free Press; London: Collier Macmillan.

Kagan, D. 1969. *The Outbreak of the Peloponnesian War.* Ithaca, NY: Cornell University Press.

Kagan, D. 1974. *The Archidamian War.* Ithaca, NY: Cornell University Press.

Kagan, D. 1981. *The Peace of Nicias and the Sicilian Expedition*. Ithaca, NY: Cornell University Press.

Kagan, D. 1987. *The Fall of the Athenian Empire*. Ithaca, NY: Cornell University Press.

Kagan, D. 1991. *Pericles of Athens and the Birth of Democracy*. New York: Free Press; Toronto: Collier Macmillan Canada.

Kagan, D. 2003. *The Peloponnesian War*. New York: Viking.

Kagan, D. 2009. *Thucydides: The Reinvention of History*. New York: Viking Penguin.

Kagan, D. and G. Viggiano, eds. 2013. *Men of Bronze: Hoplite Warfare in Ancient Greece*. Princeton, NY: Princeton University Press.

Kallet, L. 2001. *Money and the Corrosion of Power in Thucydides*. Berkeley: University of California Press.

Kaplan, R. 2002. *Warrior Politics: Why Leadership Demands a Pagan Ethos*. New York: Random House.

Karavites, P. 1985. "Enduring Problems of the Samian Revolt." *Rheinisches Museum* 128, 40–56.

Kebric, R. 1977. *In the Shadow of Macedon: Duris of Samos*. Wiesbaden: Steiner.

Kelly, T. 1982. "Thucydides and Spartan Strategy in the Archidamian War." *American Historical Review* 87, 25–54.

Kennell, N. 1995. *The Gymnasium of Virtue: Education & Culture in Ancient Sparta*. Chapel Hill: University of North Carolina Press.

Kennell, N. 2010. *Spartans: A New History*. Malden, MA: Wiley-Blackwell.

Kerferd, G. B. 1981. *The Sophistic Movement*. London: Cambridge University Press.

Knight, D. W. 1970. "Thucydides and the War Strategy of Perikles." *Mnemosyne* 4th series 23, 150–61.

Korab-Karpowicz, W. J. 2006. "How International Relations Theorists Can Benefit by Reading Thucydides." *The Monist* 89, 232–44.

Krentz, P. 1982. *The Thirty at Athens*. Ithaca, NY: Cornell University Press.

Krentz, P. 1982. "Fighting by the Rules: The Invention of the Hoplite Agôn." *Hesperia* 71, 23–39.

Krentz, P. 1985. "The Nature of Hoplite Battle." *Classical Antiquity* 4, 50–61.

Krentz, P. 1985. "Casualties in Hoplite Battles." *Greek, Roman, and Byzantine Studies* 26, 13–20.

Krentz, P. 1989. "Athenian Politics and Strategy after Kyzikos." *Classical Journal* 84, 206–15.

Krentz, P. 1989. *Xenophon: Hellenika I–II. 3. 10*. Warminster: Aris & Phillips.

Krentz, P. 1995. *Xenophon: Hellenika II. 3. 11–IV. 2. 8*. Warminster: Aris & Phillips.

Krentz, P. 2010. *The Battle of Marathon (Yale Library of Military History)*. New Haven, CT: Yale University Press.

Kurtz, D. and J. Boardman. 1971. *Greek Burial Customs*. London: Thames and Hudson.

Lang, M. 1990. "Illegal Execution in Ancient Athens." *Proceedings of the American Philosophical Society* 134, 24–9.

Lanni, A. 2008. "The Laws of War in Ancient Greece." *Law and History Review* 26, 469–89.

Lateiner, D. 1976. "Tissaphernes and the Phoenician Fleet (Thucydides 8. 87)." *Transactions and Proceedings of the American Philological Association* 106, 267–90.

Lateiner, D. 1985. "Nicias' Inadequate Encouragement (Thucydides 7. 69. 2)." *Classical Philology* 80, 201–13.

Lazenby, J. F. 1985, 2012. *The Spartan Army*. Warminster, UK: Stackpole Books.

Lazenby, J. F. 2004. *The Peloponnesian War: A Military Study*. London: Routledge.

Legon, R. P. 1968. "Megara and Mytilene." *Phoenix* 22, 220–25.

Legon, R. P. 1969. "The Peace of Nicias." *Journal of Peace Research* 6, 323–34.

Legon, R. P. 1981. *Megara: The Political History of a Greek City-State to 336 B. C.* Ithaca, NY: Cornell University Press.

Lendon, J. E. 2010. *Song of Wrath: The Peloponnesian War Begins*. New York: Basic Books.

LeShan, L. 1992. *The Psychology of War. Comprehending Its Mystique and Its Madness*. Chicago: Noble Press.

Lewis, D. 1977. *Sparta and Persia*. Leiden: Brill.

Lewis, D., J. Boardman, S. Hornblower, and M. Ostwald, eds. 1994. *The Cambridge Ancient History*, 2e., vol. 6, *The Fourth Century BC*. London: Cambridge University Press.

Liebeschuetz, W. 1968. "Thucydides and the Sicilian Expedition." *Historia* 17, 289–306.

Liebeschuetz, W. 1968. "The Structure and Function of the Melian Dialogue." *Journal of Hellenic Studies* 88, 73–7.

Littman, R. 1968. "The Strategy of the Battle of Cyzicus." *Transactions and Proceedings of the American Philological Association* 99, 275–2.

Littman, R. 2009. "The Plague of Athens: Epidemiology and Palaeopathology." *Mount Sinai Journal of Medicine* 76, 456–67.

Loraux, N., 1986. *The Invention of Athens: The Funeral Oration in the Classical City*, trans. A. Sheridan. Cambridge, MA: Harvard University Press.

Low, P. 2005. "Looking for the Language of Athenian Imperialism." *Journal of Hellenic Studies* 125, 93–111.

Low, P., ed. 2007. *Interstate Relations in Classical Greece: Morality and Power*. Cambridge: Cambridge University Press.

Low, P, ed. 2008. *The Athenian Empire*. Edinburgh: Edinburgh University Press.

Luginbill, R. 1994. "*Othismos*: The Importance of the Mass-Shove in Hoplite Warfare." *Phoenix* 48, 51–61.

Luraghi, N. and S. Alcock, eds. 2003. *Helots and Their Masters in Laconia: Histories, Ideologies, Structures*. Cambridge, MA: Harvard University Press.

Ma, J., N. Papazarkadas, and R. Parker, eds. 2009. *Interpreting the Athenian Empire*. London: Duckworth.

MacDonald, B. 1983. "The Megarian Decree." *Historia* 32, 385–410.

MacDowell, D. 1962. *Andocides on the Mysteries*. Oxford: Clarendon Press.

MacDowell, D. 1978. *The Law in Classical Athens*. Ithaca, NY: Cornell University Press.

MacDowell, D. 1995. *Aristophanes and Athens: An Introduction to the Plays*. Oxford: Oxford University Press.

Macleod, C. W. 1974. "Form and Meaning in the Melian Dialogue." *Historia* 23, 385–400.

McCann, D. S. and B. S. Strauss, eds. 2001. *War and Democracy: A Comparative Study of the Korean War and the Peloponnesian War*. Armonk, NY: M. E. Sharpe.

McCoy, J. 1977. "Thrasyllus." *American Journal of Philology* 98, 264–89.

McGlew, J. 1999. "Politics on the Margins: The Athenians 'Hetaireiai' in 415 B. C." *Historia* 48, 1–22.

McGregor, M. 1956. "The Politics of the Historian Thucydides." *Phoenix* 10, 93–102.

McGregor, M. 1963. "The Genius of Alcibiades." *Phoenix* 19, 27–46.

McKechnie, P. R. *Hellenica Oxyrhynchia* (Classical Texts). 1988. Warminster: Aris & Phillips.

Marianetti, M. 1992. *Religion and Politics in Aristophanes' Clouds*. New York: Olms-Weidmann.

Marincola, J. 1997. *Authority and Tradition in Ancient Historiography*. Cambridge: Cambridge University Press.

Marr, J. 1998. "What Did the Athenians Demand in 432 B.C.?" *Phoenix* 52, 120–4.

Marvin, C. and D. W. Ingle. *Blood Sacrifice and the Nation: Totem Rituals and the American Flag*. Cambridge: Cambridge University Press, 1998.

Matthew, C. and M. Trundel, eds. 2013. *Beyond the Gates of Fire: New Perspectives on the Battle of Thermopylae*. Barnsley: Pen and Sword.

Mattingly, H. 1996. *The Athenian Empire Restored*. Ann Arbor: University of Michigan Press.

Meiggs, R. 1972. *The Athenian Empire*. Oxford: Oxford University Press.

Meiggs, R. and D. Lewis, eds. 1969. *A Selection of Greek Historical Inscriptions to the End of the Fifth Century B. C.* Oxford: Clarendon Press.

Meritt, B., H. Wade-Gery, and M. McGregor. 1939–53. *The Athenian Tribute Lists*. 4 vols. Vol. 1, Cambridge, MA: Harvard University Press, 1939. Vols. 2–4, Princeton, NJ: Princeton University Press, 1949–53.

Michell, H. 1964. *Sparta*. Cambridge: Cambridge University Press.

Mitchell, B. M. 1991. "Cleon's Amphipolitan Campaign: Aims and Results." *Historia* 40, 170–92.

Morrison, J. S., J. F. Coates, and I. Rankov. 2000. *The Athenian Trireme: The History and Reconstruction of an Ancient Greek Warship*. Cambridge: Cambridge University Press.

Mosley, D. J. 1971. "Diplomacy and Disunion in Ancient Greece." *Phoenix* 25, 319–30.

Munn, M. 2000. *The School of History. Athens in the Age of Socrates*. Berkeley: University of California Press.

Nussbaum, M. 1980. "Aristophanes and Socrates on Learning Practical Wisdom." *Yale Classical Studies* 26, 43–97.

Ober, J. 1985. *Fortress Attica: Defense of the Athenian Land Frontier, 404–322 BC*. Leiden: Brill.

Ober, J. 2015. *The Rise and Fall of Classical Greece (The Princeton History of the Ancient World)*. Princeton, NJ: Princeton University Press.

Oliva, P. 1971. *Sparta and Her Social Problems*, trans. I. Urwin-Lewitová. Amsterdam: Hakkert.

Osborne, R., ed. 2007. *Debating the Athenian Cultural Revolution: Art, Literature, Philosophy and Politics 430–380 BC*. Cambridge: Cambridge University Press.

Ostwald, M. 1986. *From Popular Sovereignty to the Sovereignty of Law: Law, Society, and Politics in Fifth-Century Athens*. Berkeley: University of California Press.

Palagia, O. 2009. *Art in Athens during the Peloponnesian War*. New York: Cambridge University Press.

Parke, H. W. 1933. *Greek Mercenary Soldiers*. Oxford: Oxford University Press.

Parke, H. W. 1977. *Festivals of the Athenians*. Ithaca, NY: Cornell University Press.

Parker, R. 1996. *Athenian Religion: A History*. Oxford: Oxford University Press.

Parry, A. 1972. "Thucydides' Historical Perspective." *Yale Classical Studies* 22, 47–61.

Pelling, C. 2000. *Literary Texts and the Greek Historian*. London: Routledge.

Perlman, S. 1964. "The Causes and Outbreak of the Corinthian War." *Classical Quarterly* n. s. 14, 64–81.

Podlecki, A. 1998. *Perikles and His Circle*. London: Routledge.

Pollitt, J. J. 1972. *Art and Experience in Classical Greece*. Cambridge: Cambridge University Press.

Pomeroy, S. B. 2002. *Spartan Women*. Oxford: Oxford University Press.

Pomeroy, S. B., S. Burstein, W. Donlan, J. T. Roberts, and D. Tandy. 2011. *Ancient Greece: A Political, Social, and Cultural History*, 3e. New York: Oxford University Press.

Poulakis, T. 1997. *Speaking for the Polis: Isocrates' Rhetorical Education*. Columbia: University of South Carolina Press.

Poulakis, T. and D. Depew, eds. 2009. *Isocrates and Civic Education*. Austin: University of Texas Press.

Powell, C. A. 1979. "Religion and the Sicilian Expedition." *Historia* 28, 15–31.

Pritchard, D. M., ed. 2014. *War and Democracy in Classical Athens*. Cambridge: Cambridge University Press.

Pritchett, W. K. 1971–85. *The Greek State at War*. 5 vols. Berkeley: University of California Press.

Pritchett, W. K. 1965–89. *Studies in Greek Topography*. 7 vols. Berkeley: University of California Press.

Quinn, J. C. 2007. "Herms, Kouroi and the Political Anatomy of Athens." *Greece and Rome* 54, 82–105.

Raaflaub, K. A., ed. 2007. *War and Peace in the Ancient World*. Malden, MA: Blackwell.

Raaflaub, K. A. and N. Rosenstein, eds. 1999. *War and Society in the Ancient and Medieval Worlds, Asia, the Mediterranean, Europe, and Mesoamerica*. Cambridge, MA: Harvard University Press and Center for Hellenic Studies.

Raaflaub, K. A. and H. van Wees, eds. 2009. *A Companion to Archaic Greece*. Malden, MA: Wiley-Blackwell.

Rahe, P. 1980. "The Military Situation in Western Asia on the Eve of Cunaxa." *American Journal of Philology* 101, 79–98.

Rawlings, H. R. III. 1981. *The Structure of Thucydides' History*. Princeton, NJ: Princeton University Press.

Rengakos, A. and A. Tsamakis, eds. 2012. *Brill's Companion to Thucydides*. 2 vols. Leiden: Brill.

Rhodes, P. J. 1972. "The Five Thousand in the Athenian Revolutions of 411 BC." *Journal of Hellenic Studies* 92, 115–27.

Rhodes, P. J. 1980. "Athenian Democracy after 403 B. C." *Classical Journal* 75, 305–22.

Rhodes, P. J. 1992. *A Commentary on the Aristotelian Athenaion Politeia*. Oxford: Clarendon.

Rhodes, P. J. 1987. "Thucydides on the Causes of the Peloponnesian War." *Hermes* 115, 154–65.

Rhodes, P. J. 2011. *Alcibiades: Athenian Playboy, General and Traitor*. Barnsley: Pen & Sword.

Rhodes, P. J. and R. Osborne, eds. 2003. *Greek Historical Inscriptions 404–323 BC*. Oxford: Oxford University Press.

Rider, T. T. B. 1965. *Koine Eirene: General Peace and Local Independence in Ancient* Greece. London: Oxford University Press.

Ridley, R. 1979. "The Hoplite as Citizen: Athenian Military Institutions in Their Social Context." *L'Antiquité Classique* 48, 508–48.

Roberts, J. 1980. "The Athenian Conservatives and the Impeachment Trials of the Corinthian War." *Hermes* 108, 100–114.

Roberts, J. 1982. *Accountability in Athenian Government*. Madison: University of Wisconsin Press.

Roisman, J. 1987. "Alkidas in Thucydides." *Historia* 36, 385–421.

Roisman, J. 1993. *The General Demosthenes and His Use of Military Surprise. Historia Einzelschrift* 78. Stuttgart: F. Steiner.

Rood, T. 1998. *Thucydides: Narrative and Explanation*. Oxford: Clarendon Press.

Rosenbloom, D. 2004. "*Ponêroi* vs. *Chrêstoi*: The Ostracism of Hyperbolos and the Struggle for Hegemony in Athens after the Death of Perikles, Part I." *Transactions and Proceedings of the American Philological Association* 134, 55–105.

Rosivach, V. 1987. "Autochthony and the Athenians." *Classical Quarterly* n. s. 37, 294–306.

Rosivach, V. 1987. "Execution by Stoning in Athens." *Classical Antiquity* 6, 232–48.

Rubel, A. 2000, 2014. *Fear and Loathing in Ancient Athens: Religion and Politics during the Peloponnesian War*, trans. M. Vickers and A. Piftor. Durham, UK: Acumen.

Rubincam, C. 1991. "Casualty Figures in the Battle Descriptions of Thucydides." *Transactions and Proceedings of the American Philological Association* 121, 181–98.

Rusch, S. 2011. *Sparta at War: Strategy, Tactics, and Campaigns 550–362*. London: Frontline Books.

Rusten, J. 2015. "Carving Up Thucydides: The Rise and Demise of Analysis—and Its Legacy." In N. Morley, ed., *A Handbook to the Reception of Thucydides*. Malden, MA: Wiley-Blackwell.

Ryder, T. T. B. 1965. *Koine Eirene. General Peace and Local Independence in Ancient Greece*. London: Oxford University Press.

Ste. Croix, G. E. M. de. 1956. "The Constitution of the Five Thousand," *Historia* 5, 3–23.

Ste. Croix, G. E. M. de. 1972. *The Origins of the Peloponnesian War*. Ithaca, NY: Cornell University Press.

Salmon, J. B. 1984. *Wealthy Corinth: A History of the City to 338 B. C.* Oxford: Clarendon; New York: Oxford University Press.

Schwartz, A. 2009. *Reinstating the Hoplite: Arms, Armour and Phalanx Fighting in Archaic and Classical Greece.* Stuttgart: F. Steiner.

Sallares, R. 1991. *The Ecology of the Ancient Greek World.* Ithaca, NY: Cornell University Press.

Seager, R. 1976. "After the Peace of Nicias: Diplomacy and Policy, 421–416 B. C." *Classical Quarterly* n. s. 70, 249–69.

Sealey, R. 1975. "The Causes of the Peloponnesian War." *Classical Philology* 70, 89–109.

Sealey, R. 1976. *A History of the Greek City-States* ca. *700–338 B.C.* Berkeley: University of California Press.

Seaman, M. 1997. "The Athenian Expedition to Melos in 416 B. C." *Historia* 46, 385–418.

Shapiro, H. A., ed. 2007. *The Cambridge Companion to Archaic Greece.* Cambridge: Cambridge University Press.

Shepherd, W. and P. Dennis. 2013. *Pylos and Sphacteria 425 BC. Sparta's Island of Disaster.* Oxford: Osprey.

Sicking, C. M. J. 1995. "The General Purport of Pericles' Funeral Oration and Last Speech." *Hermes* 123, 404–25.

Sidwell, K. 2009. *Aristophanes the Democrat: The Politics of Satirical Comedy during the Peloponnesian War.* Cambridge: Cambridge University Press.

Snodgrass, A. 1980. *Archaic Greece: The Age of Experiment.* Berkeley: University of California Press.

Solomos, A. 1974. *The Living Aristophanes.* Ann Arbor: University of Michigan Press.

Spence, I. G. 1990. "Perikles and the Defense of Attika during the Peloponnesian War." *Journal of Hellenic Studies* 110, 91–109.

Stadter, P. 1989. *A Commentary on Plutarch's Pericles.* Chapel Hill: University of North Carolina Press.

Stamatopoulou, M. and M. Yeroulanou, eds. 2002. *Excavating Classical Culture. Recent Archaeological Discoveries in Greece. Studies in Classical Archaeology* 1. Oxford: Archaeopress.

Stern, R. 2003. "The Thirty at Athens in the Summer of 404." *Phoenix* 57, 18–34.

Stow, S. 2007. "Pericles at Gettysburg and Ground Zero: Tragedy, Patriotism, and Public Mourning." *American Political Science Review* 101, 195–208.

Strassler, R., ed., Thucydides, and R. Crawley, trans. (revised). *The Landmark Thucydides: A Comprehensive Guide to the Peloponnesian War.* 1996. New York: Free Press (Simon & Schuster).

Strassler, R., ed., Xenophon, and J. Marincola, trans. 2009. *The Landmark Xenophon's Hellenika.* New York: Random House.

Strauss, B. 1983. "Aegospotami Reexamined." *American Journal of Philology* 104, 24–35.

Strauss, B. 1985. "The Cultural Significance of Bribery and Embezzlement in Athenian Politics: The Evidence of the Period of 403–383 B. C." *The Ancient World* 11, 67–74.

Strauss, B. 1986. *Athens after the Peloponnesian War: Class, Faction, and Policy 403–386 B.C.* Ithaca, NY: Cornell University Press.

Strauss, B. 1993. *Fathers and Sons in Athens: Ideology and Society in the Era of the Peloponnesian War.* Princeton, NJ: Princeton University Press.

Strauss, B. 2005. *The Battle of Salamis: The Naval Encounter That Saved Greece—and Western Civilization.* New York: Simon and Schuster.

Talbert, R. J. A., ed. 2000. *Barrington Atlas of the Greek and Roman World.* Princeton, NJ: Princeton University Press.

Tannenbaum, R. 1975. "Who Started the Peloponnesian War?" *Arion* n. s. 2, 533–46.

Taylor, M. 2010. *Thucydides, Pericles, and the Idea of Athens in the Peloponnesian War.* Cambridge: Cambridge University Press.

Thucydides. 1942. *Thucydidis Historiae.* 2 vols. Oxford: Oxford University Press.

Tod, M. 1933–48. *A Selection of Greek Historical Inscriptions.* 2 vols. Oxford: Clarendon Press.

Too, Y. L. 2009. *The Rhetoric of Identity in Isocrates: Text, Power, Pedagogy (Cambridge Classical Studies).* Cambridge: Cambridge University Press.

Tritle, L. A., ed. 1997. *The Greek World in the Fourth Century.* London: Routledge.

Tritle, L. A. 2000. *From Melos to My Lai: Violence, Culture, and Survival.* London: Routledge.

Tritle, L. A. 2010. *A New History of the Peloponnesian War.* Walden, MA: Wiley-Blackwell.

Turner, F. 1981. *The Greek Heritage in Victorian Britain.* New Haven, CT: Yale University Press.

Tuplin, C. 1982. "Fathers and Sons: Ecclesiazusae 644–45." *Greek, Roman and Byzantine Studies* 23, 325–30.

van Wees, H., ed. 2000. *War and Violence in Ancient Greece.* London: Duckworth and the Classical Press of Wales.

van Wees, H. 2004. *Greek Warfare: Myths and Realities.* London: Duckworth.

Vickers, M. 1997. *Pericles on Stage: Political Comedy in Aristophanes' Early Plays.* Austin: University of Texas Press.

Vickers, M. 2008. *Sophocles and Alcibiades: Athenian Politics in Ancient Greek Literature.* Stocksfield: Acumen, 2008.

Vlastos, G. 1983. "The Historical Socrates and Athenian Democracy." *Political Theory* 11, 495–515.

Waterfield, R., trans. with notes by C. Dewald. 1998. *Herodotus: The Histories.* Oxford: Oxford University Press.

Waterfield, R. 2009. *Why Socrates Died: Dispelling the Myths.* New York: W. W. Norton.

Westlake, H. D. 1945. "Seaborne Raids in Periclean Strategy." *Classical Quarterly* 39, 75–84.

Westlake, H. D. 1962. "Thucydides and the Fall of Amphipolis." *Hermes* 90, 276–87.

Westlake, H. D. 1971. "Thucydides and the Uneasy Peace: A Study in Political Incompetence." *Classical Quarterly* n. s. 21, 315–25.

Wills, G. 1992. *Lincoln at Gettysburg: The Words that Remade America.* New York: Simon & Schuster.

Wilson, J. 1981. "Strategy and Tactics in the Mytilene Campaign." *Historia* 30, 144–63.

Wilson, J. 1982. "'The Customary Meanings of Words Were Changed'—Or Were They? A Note on Thucydides 3. 82. 4." *Classical Quarterly* n. s. 32, 18–20.

Wood, E. 1986. "Socrates and Democracy: A Reply to Gregory Vlastos." *Political Theory* 14, 55–82.

Woodhead, A. G. 1970. *Thucydides on the Nature of Power.* Cambridge, MA: Harvard University Press.

Wylie, W. 1962. "Cunaxa and Xenophon." *L'Antiquité Classique* 61, 119–34.

Wylie, G. 1986. "What Really Happened at Aegospotami?" *L'Antiquité Classique* 55, 125–41.

INDEX